# The
# Essential
# Mediterranean

## ALSO BY NANCY HARMON JENKINS

*The Mediterranean Diet Cookbook*

*Flavors of Puglia*

*Flavors of Tuscany*

# The Essential Mediterranean

WITHDRAWN

HOW REGIONAL COOKS TRANSFORM KEY INGREDIENTS

INTO THE WORLD'S FAVORITE CUISINES

Nancy Harmon Jenkins

HarperCollins*Publishers*

HarperCollins books may be purchased for educational, business, or sales promotional use. For information, please write: Special Markets Department, HarperCollins Publishers Inc., 10 East 53rd Street, New York, NY 10022.

FIRST EDITION

*Designed by Ralph L. Fowler*
*Illustrations by Kathleen Edwards*

Printed on acid-free paper

Library of Congress Cataloging-in-Publication Data
Jenkins, Nancy Harmon.
The essential Mediterranean : how regional cooks transform key ingredients into the world's favorite cuisines / Nancy Harmon Jenkins.—1st ed.
p.   cm.
Includes bibliographical references and index.
ISBN 0-06-019651-3 (hardcover)
1. Cookery, Mediterranean.   I. Title
TX725.M35J46   2003
641.59'11822—dc21
2002069054

07   ❖/RRD   10   9   8   7   6   5   4   3   2

*Catherine Brandel*

IN MEMORIAM

# CONTENTS

# ACKNOWLEDGMENTS

I have been helped enormously by a great number of people during the years I've spent researching and writing about the Mediterranean. To list them all would entail another book, but I do want to acknowledge the assistance of three organizations: Oldways Preservation & Exchange Trust in Boston, the International Olive Oil Council in Madrid, and the Culinary Institute of America in California, each of which made possible journeys that I otherwise would not have been able to make.

In addition, I want to express my appreciation to those who have been particularly helpful in putting this book together, among them especially my editor, Susan Friedland, whose immediate enthusiasm was gratifying, to say the least, and Dana Cowin, Tina Ujlaki, and others at *Food & Wine* magazine, who shot down only my most outlandish ideas. And a very special thank-you to Gail Watt, who diligently tested recipes, and retested, and tested again, until each one was right.

Although I take full responsibility for any misstatements of fact or misinterpretations herein, I would also like to thank the following people for their input, advice, and good company: in Italy, Benedetto and Claudia Cavalieri, Carlo and Carla Latini, Leo Bertozzi of the Parmigiana Reggiano Consorzio, Rossella Speranza of Oldways Italia, Matilde Antolini in Tuscany, and Concetta Cantoro in Puglia; in Sicily, Antonia d'Ali-Staita of the Saline Ettore & Infersa, Anna Tasca Lanza of Regaleali, Giuseppe Licitra and Anya Fernald of the Cacciocavallo Ragusano Consorzio, Mary Taylor Simeti, and Gianfranco Becchina; in Spain, Norberto and Carmen Jorge, Clara Maria Amezua, Aktham Habbaba, Jane Walker, and Jose Puig; in France, Dennis Dupeux of Les Salins du Midi, Jean-Benoît and Cathérine Hugues, Daniel Brunier of Vieux Télégraphe, Kermit Lynch, and Mort Rosenblum and Jeannette Hermann; in Tunisia, Abdelmajid Mahjoub and the entire Mahjoub family, and Abderrazak Haouari; in Syria, Dr. Miloudi Nachit of ICARDA, Roland Shelhot of Beit Sissi, Tony Hill, and May Marmabachi; in Lebanon, Youmna Ghorayeb and Kamal Mouzawak; in Turkey, Engin Akin, Ayfer Unsel, Nevin Halici, and Filiz Hosukoglu; in Greece, Dr. Antonia Trichopoulou, Diane Kochilas, Diana Farr Louis, Manolo Psillakis, and Christine Lacroix; last, but certainly far from least, in the United States, Carol Woodbury, Ed Behr, K. Dun Gifford, Karen Mitchell, Charles Perry, Fred Plotkin, William Woys Weaver, Paula Wolfert, and Daphne Zepos. Thanks to you all. And a special thank-you to Dr. Bruce Ames for explaining the intricacies of G6PD deficiency.

# The
# Essential
# Mediterranean

# Introduction

THE HIGH, ROLLING PLATEAU that unfolds around the baroque town of Ragusa in southeastern Sicily is like no other Italian landscape that I know. If I were to show you a favorite black-and-white photograph from the region—a small cluster of unmortared stone farm buildings, a few cows grazing on a barren heath, a hillside denuded of trees and dissected by a complex labyrinth of low dry-stone walls running off to the horizon—if I were to show you this and ask you where it is, you would probably, and understandably, reply, in Scotland.

Nonetheless, this is the Sicilian home of Caciocavallo Ragusano, a fine raw-milk cheese made from the milk of prized Modicano cows using an ancient technique of stretching curd, as in mozzarella making, then hanging the bricks of cheese, which are as big as cement blocks, in an airy warehouse to age for a year and a half or more. It is quite possible that cheese has been made here, more or less in this same fashion, for the last couple of thousand years. Perhaps more. Together cheese and terrain have evolved in a manner that I think of as quintessentially Mediterranean, suggesting an intimate and dynamic relationship between humans and their immediate environment that is expressed in many fashions, but in none more intensely than in food.

Giuseppe Licitra, at the headquarters of the Ragusano cheese consortium of which he is president, showed me another picture, also in black-and-white, emphasizing its antiquity, although it was taken in the 1960s: Down an unpaved cart track, a peasant, vigorous-looking but slightly bowlegged, leads a docile cow and her calf to market. Over a rough stone wall that edges the track hang the branches of a massive old carob tree. "You see," Licitra said, "there is a relationship, animal to man, man to stone walls, stone walls to carob trees, even the baroque cathedral in the market town, all are made by the same culture." Licitra, a burly, bearded Cornell graduate, is steeped in this culture, a necessary corollary, he says, to his role as chief promoter and defender of the venerable cheese that has its own protected denomination of origin, legally recognized by the bureaucrats in far-off Brussels. "And when you eat our cheese or drink our wine or taste our olive oil," Licitra said, "you're not just eating cheese or wine or olive oil—you're eating a piece of our story, a piece of our culture."

I T   I S   J U S T   T H A T   C O N N E C T I O N   B E T W E E N   food and culture that has always intrigued me in the countries surrounding the Mediterranean Sea. And it was in trying to tease out that connection that I came to write this book, which tells the stories of a number of ingredients, speaking very broadly, that I think we need to understand if we want to understand the cuisine—or cuisines—of the Mediterranean. Many of these ingredients (salt and beans, for instance) are characteristic one way or another of most of the world's cuisines, major and minor alike. Others (pork, tomatoes, and peppers), while not universal, are just as important in other great culinary traditions—I think especially of China, of Mexico—as they are in the Mediterranean. Some few (olive oil, wine, pasta, and couscous) are almost exclusive to the Mediterranean kitchen. But each and every one of them has a story to tell that is specific to the Mediterranean, stories that are made up of equal parts history and romance, folklore and myth, religion and philosophy. I've spent the best part of my adult life listening to those stories and collecting them.

The relationship between food and environment, food and history, is not exclusive to the Mediterranean by any means. Everywhere that traditional foodways still exist, in Africa, in India, in Central Asia, and in South America, a similar story can be told of how people have struggled to produce food in its simplest form, and then added imagination and cunning to elaborate it into a cuisine. But the Mediterranean is different, not least because the food from this part of the world is the kind of food we Americans want to eat now. It's delicious, it's simple, it's easy for us to reproduce in our own homes, and it has a kind of immediacy of taste that speaks to us in very strong terms. Moreover, for most of us Americans, the language of Mediterranean food is something we understand without a great deal of study or effort. With very few exceptions, it's based on ingredients we can buy in our markets, with a little thought and a minimum of effort, and carry back to our kitchens to make into appealing dishes for friends and family, for the customers in our restaurants, for the people who come to us to be nourished.

I can tell you exactly when and where I first felt that sense of the Mediterranean and Mediterranean food as a story that I wanted to hear, then tell and retell. It was years ago, just outside Nice, in fact, during a long summer trek through France and Italy with friends from school. We had driven all down the Rhône Valley, traveling on the cheap, although someone's parents had arranged for us to dine in one of the great three-star restaurants in Lyons, Chez La Mère Something-or-Other. It left absolutely no impression on us, focused as we were quite single-mindedly on meeting boys.

So we passed on down the Rhône, on a steady course to the south, the sun, the possibility of Marcello Mastroianni (or someone equally dashing) in the flesh. And then, all of a sudden, at the end of the road there was the sea, a luminous, incandescent aquamarine that danced in the summer sunshine like nothing I had ever seen on the blue-gray Atlantic, and we stopped for a quick lunch in a little-nothing restaurant right at the edge of the Mediterranean, its warm waters lapping on the cobble beach below the restaurant terrace.

*Sandwich au jambon, salade de tomates, et voilà!* Epiphany, pure and simple.

I grew up on tomatoes straight from my father's vegetable gardens, but I had never eaten tomatoes like the ones in the salad that day. (I'm not certain that I've eaten a tomato since that has affected me like those summery tomatoes from Provence.) Lush, succulent, juicy, full of sweetness and tart acidity in perfect balance, with a texture that melted in my mouth even as it gave me something to chew on. Those wedges of tomato, dripping olive oil and vinegar onto the crisp-crusted bread, itself interleaved with fat-rimmed slices of *jambon de pays,* quite literally opened my palate. It was, I thought, like eating the sun.

I confess that I did not immediately rush out to the market crying: "I must know more!" Rather, I thought to myself, this is very, very appealing. This food has flavor. This food has character. A person could get quite seduced by this food. A person could even, for a time, forget the boys and focus on the food.

That was the beginning of a life-long love affair with the food and flavors of the Mediterranean, one that continued while I made my way around the Inner Sea over the next thirty or so years—living, working, studying, raising a family, traveling, and, not incidentally, eating, drinking, marketing, gardening, and, of course, cooking. I've had the extraordinary good fortune to make my home in many different parts of the Mediterranean, from Spain in the west to Lebanon in the east, from great cities like Rome, Madrid, and Beirut to obscure hill-country villages on the north coast of Cyprus, and along the confines between Tuscany and Umbria. Living in these places has given me the opportunity to travel deep into the dunelands of the North African desert, up in the high snows of the Alps and Pyrenees, along the coasts of Turkey and Syria, through the chain of *pueblos blancos*, the white towns of Andalucia, around islands such as Majorca, Sardinia, Sicily, and Crete, and along the great river valleys, the Nile, the Po, the Ebro, and back to the Rhône.

Wherever one goes in the Mediterranean world, there's always something undiscovered, something unfinished, to go back to. It's difficult to develop that jaded "been-there/done-that" feeling that so much of the world evokes these days. A couple of years ago, I went with an American friend to a remote valley in our home turf of Tuscany. Together we counted a combined sixty years of experience in Italy, yet when we came down from the valley, we agreed that we had seen and smelled and tasted things we had never known before. That's the world of the Mediterranean—no matter how many times you've been there, there's almost invariably something very new (or very old) to be experienced for the first time. And most of it has to do, one way or another, with food.

That's because food is present in Mediterranean cultures in a way it's not in our own. I don't want to suggest that it's an obsession—that's the wrong word entirely. But food is a constant presence, and it comes up all the time, in the most casual and natural way imaginable, with men and women, old people and young children alike—the way it's grown and harvested, the way it's prepared, what's in season and out, what we're having for lunch, what we had for dinner last night, how the grapes are ripening, where the wild mushrooms can be found, whether the peaches from the tree in the backyard are as good this year as we remembered them to be, whether the fava bean soup that Aunt Sophie makes is as good as Granny's. Eating is a natural, unassuming, but vital piece of people's lives, and gathering around the table two or three times a day is the chief means of expressing solidarity as well as community for most people in the Mediterranean, even if they don't call it that.

In 2001, ISTAT, the Italian national statistics institute, reported that a full 75 percent of all Italians—men, women, and children—still go home for lunch every day; bustling twenty-first-century cities like Madrid and Beirut, Istanbul and Tunis, experience four traffic jams daily as working people break at midday to go home for a substantial meal, often followed by a brief siesta (a factor that some nutritional scientists have speculated is part of the reason for such a generally good health profile among Mediterranean populations). If I visit my neighbors at mealtime in the Tuscan hill country where I spend part of each year, I invariably find at least three generations seated at the table together. So it's no wonder that, when I think about the places I've been and the things that I've seen, it's almost always in terms of eating and drinking, cooking and sharing food.

I've spent lots of time in recent years trying to convey in words and recipes the full impact of Mediterranean moments like the one I experienced on the beach outside Nice that day, or in countless other places since. But mere words and recipes don't quite cut to the heart of the matter. Which leads me back to the subject of this book—the key ingredients, the foods, the foodways if you will, that I think we have to understand if we want to comprehend why this food is so delicious, so good for us, and, above all, so easy to bring into our own lives.

A recipe, after all, is a formula, and a properly written formula should produce the same results each time it is tested. Cooking, on the other hand, especially as practiced in Mediterranean kitchens, is a strategy, and a strategy adapts itself to a variety of situations, depending on what's available and who's to be fed. Despite attempts to codify it, there is no way the cooking of the Mediterranean can be reduced to formulas. What the cook must do instead is develop a true, immediate, and instinctive sense of flavors and ingredients. What is on hand? What does it taste like? What *should* it taste like? How and with what can it be combined to enhance and not disguise the ingredients available? This sense is not something easily culled from cookbooks or cooking teachers, although their guidance can help, enormously. But direct experience, over and over again, is the key. It's only when you put the salt, the oil, the bitter orange juice right on your own tongue that you begin to understand what it's all about.

That doesn't mean that all of us who love good food have to cash in our life savings and move to the Mediterranean. There's plenty of good food (not to mention good wine) right here in North America. But what is lacking in our American attitude, what the Mediterranean kitchen can help us develop, I think, is that astute Mediterranean sensibility toward food that recognizes that good cooks and good dishes begin with good ingredients. Once you've got good ingredients, the rest is easy. Which is why the best advice is always: Spend your time in the market, not in the kitchen. Seek out the best produce, whether in a farmer's market or a supermarket with a produce manager who cares. Look for the freshest fish, which, again, might well be in your local supermarket, and free-range chickens—they cost more than factory-farmed birds but, as with other meats, the payoff in flavor, not to mention the health benefits, makes such options cost-beneficial.

Apart from meat from free-range animals, the best, the tastiest, the most wholesome ingredients need not be the most expensive. If you shop like Mediterranean cooks, that is, seasonally, you'll find that the best often costs less than second-rate fancy ingredients or out-of-season fruits and vegetables. A good example is polenta. Time and time again, I see shoppers reaching for an expensive box of imported Italian cornmeal polenta, not realizing that that box may have been on the shelf for 6 months and in transit from Italy for 6 months before that. If you can find a good source of locally grown and ground cornmeal, it's going to give your polenta so much more flavor and texture than anything imported—and you'll be supporting local agriculture, too, which is always a plus.

It's great to support local farms and farmers, but the bottom line for most cooks is flavor, and that's where the Mediterranean has so much to teach us all—including that band of professional chefs who consider the addition of foie gras, crème fraîche, or balsamic vinegar to be the true mark of a sophisticated palate. No, the true mark of a sophisticated palate is simply the ability to taste, and to recognize what you're tasting.

I'm reminded of an encounter I once witnessed between that great cooking teacher (and sophisticated palate) Marcella Hazan and an Italian chef who was cooking in America for the first time. "Everything is different," mourned the chef, wringing his hands, "even the salt tastes different here."

"Taste, taste, taste," intoned Dottoressa Hazan in her marvellously gravelly voice. "You must taste, taste, taste—only then will you begin to understand."

More than a collection of delicious and unusual recipes from here-there-and-everywhere, this book, I hope, shows how the food of the Mediterranean, the cooking of the Mediterranean, begins—not in formulaic recipes, but in what Italians call *la materia prima*, the primary ingredients without which the cuisine simply does not and cannot exist. The *materia prima* itself begins with the landscape and the human culture that has evolved in the landscape over centuries—farmers and fishermen, shepherds, cheese and wine producers, market purveyors, as well as the home cooks and restaurant chefs who transform the *materia prima* into a cuisine, or rather many cuisines.

The primary ingredients differ in many parts of the Mediterranean, just as the cuisine differs; one would never expect to find the complex spices of a North African cook on a northern Greek table, or the yogurt-based soups of the Eastern Mediterranean in a Catalan or Provençal kitchen. Yet there is a similarity that unites the differences. Think of the ubiquitous Mediterranean seafood stew. Yes, the ingredients vary from fishing port to fishing port, depending on what the boats have brought in that day. Saffron may go into a bouillabaisse from Marseilles, while cinnamon will flavor a *stifatho* of octopus from Cyprus, and a dollop of harissa gets stirred into a Tunisian *chorba*—and yet the technique is very much the same in all three places.

Another example is olive oil, the preferred frying medium whether for zucchini blossoms in Central Italy or falafel in Beirut; oftentimes cooks are too poor to afford it, but almost always they use it if they can. Bread is another unifying ingredient, whether baked on the hearth as in Umbria, on a griddle as in Turkey, in a free-standing oven as in northern Syria, or in a traditional baker's wood-fired oven in Provence.

More unifying even than ingredients and techniques, though, is the attitude of respect toward food that is a dominating characteristic throughout the region. Much of the Mediterranean may seem rich to us today, and it is, compared to the past. The specter of famine and malnutrition has disappeared for the most part, but in the hill country of Central Italy, my elderly neighbors remember all too vividly the *miseria* of food deprivation between the wars, when families often subsisted on chestnuts, cornmeal, and foraged greens. Waste not, want not: It's a constant in the Mediterranean kitchen, which is why there are so many dishes that call for stale bread, why the pig is such a practical animal—everything but the squeal gets used, they say with evident pride, each time a pig is slaughtered.

That respect for food also manifests itself in an almost universal deference to the seasons. The first oranges start to come north from Sicily, Valencia, and Andalucia in November, in time for Christmas, but you don't look for delicious blood oranges with their tart juice until late in the winter. Fresh fava beans, planted in December, are the first green garden crop of the spring, and in Rome, the streets are lined with discarded pods, scattered by school children eating favas on their way to class. In Beirut, it is not fully spring until May, when the green walnuts and green cherries appear on peddlers' carts, to be consumed with a sprinkling of salt to cut their acerbic flavors. In a Greek village, as in a Sicilian or a Tunisian one, the weeks of early autumn find industrious housewives cutting up tomatoes and salting them to dry and concentrate for making into tomato paste, hanging up golden cobs of maize corn to store for people and animals alike, drying and sorting chickpeas, haricots, and lentils, and giving them an extra bit of drying in a stone or masonry oven after the bread has been taken out. No one would dream of eating strawberries in winter or artichokes in summer or chestnuts in the spring. Even though all these things are available in supermarkets in parts of the Mediterranean where the tentacles of the global village have begun to reach, there's not a lot of interest, and they sell as curiosities to consumers who remain convinced that the seasonal things, the local things, are far superior to anything brought in from far away.

In selecting the *materia prima* for this book, I had inevitably to leave some things out; otherwise the text might have, would have, gone on forever. Some may disagree with my choices. No one, I think, would dispute that salt is obviously the most primary of all ingredients, and that olive oil and bread are fundamental to Mediterranean cooking, as are tomatoes, a more recent arrival in regional kitchens. But why is there no chapter on eggplant, for which Turks claim at least two hundred recipes? Where is the onion family, whose members, chopped, sliced, diced, and sautéed, form the basis of so many soups, stews, and sauces? And where are the cabbages and other greens, wild and domesticated, that have sustained Mediterranean diets from the beginning of time? They are all here, believe me, even if they don't all get a chapter to themselves. The criteria I used to make my choices were, first, that the subject had to be central to the Mediterranean table, like salt and olive oil; secondly, that it had to be interesting in itself, like pork—fresh pork as well as salted hams, bacons, sausages—which is essential to roughly half the population and thoroughly abhorred and detested by the other half; thirdly, that it had to have some historical relevance, telling a story that, like tuna, like tomatoes and peppers, is part of the long enduring story of the Mediterranean.

Readers will find a good deal of Italy in this book. That is in part because it's the place in the Mediterranean that I know best. But it also represents an undeniable fact, that Italy, in terms of both geography and history, is the heart of the Mediterranean, a distinctive cultural tapestry that carries within it the discernable strands and threads and patterns of the entire Inner Sea—Greeks and Romans, Phoenicians and Carthaginians, North Africans and peoples of the Adriatic, Celts and Iberians, not to mention the throngs of newcomers, both immigrants and transients, who populate the fringes of Italian culture today. And that speaks for food as much as—perhaps more than—it does for any other aspect of the culture.

## HEALTH AND THE MEDITERRANEAN DIET

In January 1993, a conference in Cambridge, Massachusetts, jointly sponsored by the Harvard School of Public Health and Oldways Preservation and Exchange Trust (a group of which I was a founder), gathered together scientists, nutritionists, public health specialists, food journalists, and others interested in the relationship between diet and health to look at the scientific reasoning behind claims that the traditional diet of people in the Mediterranean was a principal cause of the generally very good health profile of those same people. Updates of the Mediterranean Diet Conference have been held periodically since.

This is not the time or place to review the evidence, which is sometimes complex—and sometimes, too, still a work in progress. But the conclusion of these and other, similar gatherings, is incontrovertible—a diet like the traditional Mediterranean one, with a high consumption of fresh fruits and vegetables as well as complex carbohydrates, and a low consumption of, especially, red meats, a diet that is not particularly low in fat but in which the principal fat consumed is unrefined olive oil, a monounsaturated fat, is closely related to the low rates of certain chronic diseases, especially coronary heart disease and cancer, among Mediterranean populations.

The diet has been criticized, most often by those who claim that people in the Mediterranean don't actually eat the way proponents of the diet say they do. These critics usually turn out to be anthropological tourists or food writers who have spent brief periods in some Mediterranean region where meat consumption is especially high—either because they are dining primarily in restaurants or because they have been entertained by people for whom a banquet means meat, often lots of it, but whose day-to-day diet is much more meager.

It is true, also, that life in many parts of the Mediterranean is changing and not necessarily for the better. International trade brings food products from all over the globe and government policy reinforces such commodities to the detriment of local production. Women's lives have changed, too, and fewer and fewer younger women are willing or able to spend the time marketing and preparing food that their grandmothers did. And meat consumption is indeed increasing. Recently it was reported that per capita consumption of meat in Greece now exceeds that in that traditional nation of beef eaters, England (which in part represents the extraordinary spread of vegetarianism in England, but that's another story). Nonetheless, when all is said and done, it remains incontrovertible, based on solid anecdotal and scientific evidence, that the traditional Mediterranean diet, and I emphasize *traditional*, is one of the most healthful diets in the world. And the fact that it is one of the tastiest and most interesting of the world's diets is, perhaps not icing on the cake, but certainly the dressing on the salad.

# Salt

AS SEAS GO, THE MEDITERRANEAN is a salty one, more so than the oceans most North Americans are used to, more so than the rest of the classic Seven Seas. Swimmers instantly sense it in the extra buoyancy that makes the water feel so soft, so embracing, and in the salt that leaves a dusty sheen on arms and legs as they dry in the sun.

There's a reason for the saltiness, and, as with many things in and around this Inner Sea, it has to do with geography. For the Mediterranean is a nearly enclosed body of water, with only the narrowest of connections linking it to the North Atlantic at the Straits of Gibraltar, to the Black Sea at the Dardanelles, and to the Red Sea through the Suez Canal. Moreover, very little fresh water enters the Mediterranean, which, apart from the Ebro, the Rhône, the Po, and the Nile, is not blessed with great river systems. The climate—especially the characteristic long, hot, dry summers, with little or no rainfall—means a fairly constant evaporation of moisture and concentration of salt in the water.

The Mediterranean, then, is an ideal place for salt making. The Romans knew that and sited salt pans in broad, flat deltas and lagoon areas all over the Mediterranean. Indeed, historians say, the city of Rome was established where it is because of salt pans already functioning at the mouth of the Tiber near the port town of Ostia. Around 500 B.C.E., water levels in the Mediterranean, which were much lower than today, began rising, to reach a peak nearly a thousand years later in 400 C.E., and over and over during that time, the Ostia salt works were relocated as water levels rose. Finally, the *saline* (salt pans) were abandoned, not to return to production for another five hundred years or so when, like the rest of that part of Italy, they came under the control of the Papal States.

But salt production goes back much further than these upstart Ancient Romans. Salt, it can be argued, is at the beginning of everything, literally of life itself. Like other great oceans, the Mediterranean is what's left of a salty stew that once enveloped the earth. Out of this stew emerged our remotest ancestors, primitive organisms just one or two steps beyond salty protoplasm. They merged with each other, evolved, added complexity and structure, brains and central nervous systems, blood and bone, most of which developments came about because of the osmotic properties of salt. There is salt in our tears and in all our other bodily fluids—blood, sweat, urine, sperm, saliva. Salt regulates blood pressure and maintains stomach acid levels, but above all else, salt is necessary for neurotransmissions, the vital exchange of information between neurons and muscle membranes that allows us to move, breathe, talk, eat, smile, frown, sleep, make love, and make war, at every step of the way from birth to the end.

Thus we need a quantity of salt in our diets each day, the amounts depending on our size and age. But salt does other things, too. It helps turn curdled milk into cheese, fresh meat into hams and sausages, and fish into long-keeping staples, such as salted or brine-pickled anchovies and sardines. Extending the harvest, making protein available year-round, as cheese, cured meat, or salt fish, was probably one of the first forms of "cooking" that humans knew. Sun-drying seeds, legumes, fruits, and nuts was the initial step, but right after that came salt-preserved meat and fish. Throughout Mediterranean history, most people ate salted meat when they ate meat at all, with fresh meat (a barnyard chicken, pigeon, or duck) only an occasional treat that was consumed on the day it was slaughtered.

Try to imagine a world without refrigeration, and you quickly understand why salt is so necessary, and why, for example, in early Rome, the Forum Boarium (the livestock market) and the Salinae (the salt store) were located side by side, probably at the beginning of the via Salaria, the salt road that led from Rome to the

Adriatic. In a climate that was warm for much of the year, it was impossible to keep fresh meat from spoiling, so animals were slaughtered to order in the forum, and any meat not sold was salted to preserve it. "This is one reason why meat was not part of the ordinary diet," historian Joan Frayn says, "and why, when poor people did have any, it was usually ham (*perna*) or salt pork."

Like pork, tuna was also salted to preserve it; it was called the pig of the sea because, like the pig, it was entirely useful from head to tail. The custom of salting tuna to preserve it lasted until the spread of the canning industry in the last century, but it seems to have begun long, long before, perhaps at the time the Phoenicians expanded westward across the Mediterranean from their home base on the coast of Lebanon to found colonies in places such as Carthage on the Tunisian coast, the little islands of Motya off Sicily and San Pietro off Sardinia, and Cádiz on the Atlantic just outside the entrance to the Mediterranean. What drove them this far? Salt, say many historians, and tuna, for their settlements were often sited near both salt flats—broad, shallow, sunny lagoons where salt could be extracted from sea water with relative ease and efficiency—and those offshore areas where tuna congregate during their annual migrations into and around the Mediterranean to spawn.

OFF THE WEST COAST OF SICILY, between the cities of Trapani and Marsala, lies the island of Motya, a low hump like a sleeping tortoise on the near horizon. To get to the island, you take a motor launch from a place called simply "*l'embarcazione per Motia*," a dock next to an area of broad salt flats dominated by an old-fashioned windmill. The island, so small that you can pretty much walk around it leisurely in the space of an hour or so, is a small, tranquil refuge, its silence disturbed only by gulls crying and the lap of water on the shore. You get the feeling that nothing much has happened here since the year 397 B.C.E. when Greek warriors ravaged a centuries-old Carthaginian-Phoenician settlement, enslaved the survivors, and carried them off. Looking westward from Motya, way off in the distance you see other islands, high purple shimmers on the edge of the blue sea. This is the Egadi chain, which borders the Canale di Sicilia, the main conduit for water passing from the western to the eastern Mediterranean. In the deep cold waters of the Canale (which never go above 20°C, even in summer) bluefin tuna, on an annual migration eastward from the Atlantic, congregate each May. Out there on Favignana, there is still a tuna *mattanza*, an organized slaughter of the big fish, a last relic of what was for centuries a vital industry. In the other direction, looking eastward to the western edge of Sicily, you can just make out the erect vanes of the windmill that stands as a sentinel in the midst of the salt pans extending over acres of the flat coastal plain. Now you see why the Phoenicians settled on Motya, between the salt and the tuna, and established the colony whose ruined walls, temples, marketplace, and graveyard are scattered across this lovely little island.

BACK AT THE SALT WORKS ONE DAY, I met up with Dottore Antonio d'Alí-Staita, head of the family that owns the two *saline,* Ettore and Infersa, that extend north and south of the windmill, each of which makes 5,000 to 6,000 tons of salt annually by an artisanal process that has changed very little over the centuries. At 80-plus-years-old—he won't reveal how much plus—Dr. d'Alí is tanned, erect, a gentleman, one senses, with the narrowed eyes of a sage who has spent much of his life focusing on the dazzling glare of salt heaped in the Sicilian sun in high pyramids called *cumuli* (clouds). The *saline* have been in his family only since the early nineteenth century when they were bought, he tells me, by the father of the grandfather of his mother—in other words, his great-great-grandfather.

The Ettore and Infersa *saline* are documented as far back as the sixteenth century, but it is likely that salt has been harvested here since the Phoenicians. And before them? The flat coastal plain extends back many miles, broken only by the sugarloaf peak of Erice just east of Trapani. That holy mountain, the only high point around here, is called San Giuliano today, but it was once devoted to the cult of the self-renewing mother goddess—Astarte, Aphrodite, Isis, in the Mediterranean world she has had many names—and is still dedicated to her modern incarnation, the Blessed Virgin Mother. Millennia ago, perhaps, the mountain was revered and the salt harvested by Paleolithic ancestors of the Siculi, the original inhabitants of Sicily.

The windmill, the vanes of which we saw from Motya, originally was erected to grind the thick salt crystals into finer flakes. It can be made to function but it's mostly decorative these days, the focus of a little museum to salt that Dr. d'Alí has established. A diorama in the museum shows the layout of the salt works, which, simply put, consists of a series of basins through which the sea water moves on its journey from liquid to crystallized salt—the *vasche fredde* (cold basins), the *vasche calde* or *servitrice* (the "hot" or "serving" basins), and the *vasche salante* or *cristallizante* ("salting" or "crystallizing" basins).

Out on the raised dike that separates the sea from the *vasche fredde,* smaller, less visible windmills are positioned to turn the screws that draw in water to feed the salt pans. The water, Dr. d'Alí recites, has a density of 3.5 percent of which 2.7 percent is sodium chloride, 1.5 percent is calcium sulfate, and about 0.3 percent other elements, including copper, gold, silver, mercury, and iron—elements that are present in sea water everywhere, around the globe. These trace elements precipitate first, collecting on the bottom of the *vasche calde,* to be followed by the calcium, which precipitates when the water has evaporated to a density of 24 to 25 percent. At this point, the water, now heavy with salt, is moved to the *vasche salante,* and the thick crystals of salt are the eventual result.

Put more simply, 100 liters (about 25 gallons) of Mediterranean water with around 2,700 grams (just under six pounds) of salt is reduced by the combined action of sun and wind to 11 liters of very salty brine with just a fraction less than six pounds of salt in the whole. It takes sixty days from the time the sea water first enters the *saline* until the salt is harvested, and the harvest takes place three times over the season, in July, August, and September, although the July harvest is the most important.

Dr. d'Alí is a firm believer in the virtues of his salt. Perhaps that's what keeps him so youthful, so healthy. Why is this salt better than all other salts? I ask. "Magnesium," he says, "pure and simple." Because the salt is harvested by hand, it doesn't need washing so it retains more magnesium than salt produced by other methods. Colloidal clay at the base of the salt pans also affects magnesium in the salt. Magnesium, naturally present in sea water, is not absorbed into the clay as the water dehydrates but remains in the brine and thus in the salt. You can't add magnesium to the salt later—it must be combined in the crystals of the salt itself. "Magnesium is good for the bones," says Dr. d'Alí. "Twenty-five grams of magnesium chloride in a liter of water will cure rheumatism."

R HEUMATISM OR NOT, salt has always been recognized, by all people everywhere, as a symbol of purity, of a kind of bottom-line integrity—"salt of the earth," we say to describe someone of unquestionable honesty. There's a feeling of elemental cleanness out here on the salt flats, too—something that comes from the bright sun, the fresh, snapping breeze off the water, the crisp white clarity of the salt that has been piled up in long salt pyramids, covered for protection with overlapping terra-cotta roof tiles. Sprinkle a few big grains of this salt in the palm of your hand and see how the translucent quality changes to light as sunlight refracts off the crystals. Then taste the salt, let the lucid crystals melt on your tongue and flood your palate with the dense brine of the sea. The taste is complex yet fundamental, mineral but not metallic, a taste as old as the sea itself. Most salt used in North American kitchens is produced by industrial evaporators from mined rock salt rather than sea salt. The process makes a very pure sodium chloride that tastes of salt and almost nothing else, although iodine and magnesium carbonate (lime) are added to it. Unprocessed sea salt, on the other hand, naturally dried in the sun, has coarse, irregular grains, with a high moisture content and lots of calcium chloride and magnesium chloride, which lend a complex of flavors, sharpness, bitterness, all of them pleasant.

S ALT WAS LONG CONSIDERED the property of the state, whether Greek, Roman, Byzantine, Ottoman, or Papal; in Italy, it continued to be a government monopoly until 1973. Up until that date, if you wanted salt for your pasta water, you had to go to the tobacconist, where you might also buy cigarettes, playing cards, stamps, and *carta bollata*, the special paper on which government documents were printed. If salt seemed strange in such company, it was explained by the theory that anything from the earth—or from the sea, which in legalistic terms is pretty much the same thing—belongs to the crown, which is to say the state. Its sale, like that of tobacco and playing cards, was controlled by the state, which could charge whatever it wanted for it. Raising the salt tax was a quick and easy way to raise money since everyone needed salt. Unsalted bread, it is said, came about as a way of resisting the government salt tax. In France, the infamous *gabelle* (salt tax) was a source of unrest throughout that country's history until it was finally ended in 1945.

The French are noted for the production of Atlantic sea salt, which is marketed either as *sel gris* (gray salt) or as *fleur de sel* (flower of salt). French salt from the Mediterranean may be less well known but, to my taste at least, it is more appealing, with a distinct clarity of flavor that Atlantic salt lacks. The principal Mediterranean salt works are at Aigues Mortes (the name means "dead waters"), in the vast stretch of lagoons and marshes that make up the Camargue south of Nîmes. Greek colonists may have been the first to harvest salt here, but local tradition claims that the *salins* (salt pans) were founded by one Peccius, otherwise known to history only as "a Roman engineer." Since his time, there have been many owners, including the Church, several feudal lords, the King of France, and once an American industrial salt producer. But the salt works, officially called Les Salins du Midi, are known locally as *les salins de Peccais*, for that possibly mythical Peccius. Here, in an extensive area stretching across the Etang du Roi, the king's lagoon, most of the 1,300,000 tons of French Mediterranean sea salt are produced each year.

That figure doesn't include the small quantity of *fleur de sel*, which is produced only when certain conditions, the sun's heat and especially the wind, coincide. Rather than forming a deposit that settles on the bottom of the salt pan, *fleur de sel* crystallizes on the water's surface. Most of the salt from the Salins du Midi is harvested by machine, but *fleur de sel* is delicate and must be harvested entirely by hand, using a wooden-handled scoop that looks like a snow shovel. Pure, light, and flaky, the salt retains a certain humidity within the crystals that gives it a startling melting quality.

*Fleur de sel* is considered so special, so prized, that each *saunier*, as the salt harvesters are called, produces his own and puts his signature on the product. The small round tin of *fleur de sel* that I bought in a shop set into the medieval walls of Aigues Mortes had been signed by Bernard Pliou, who had harvested it the previous season. It's the salt of salts, *fleur de sel*, the bottom line, "*ce cadeau fugitif de la nature*," this fleeting gift of nature, as the label on the tin read.

Or "the *ne plus ultra*," according to Dominique Dupeux, who has worked twenty-two years for the Salins du Midi and has yet to feel his enthusiasm for salt diminish in the slightest. Dupeux was showing me around the *salins* in the middle of June. Despite the brilliant sunshine, heavy spring rains earlier in the year had Dupeux a little worried about this year's collection of *fleur de sel*, due to start in mid-July. "And if you don't get it?" I asked.

"Oh, we have to get it," he said, "otherwise. . . ." He gave that expressive shrug with which the French contemplate disaster. We had been driving a good ten miles or more, zigzagging along dirt cart tracks that cut between the big rectangular salt basins (*tables salants* or *cristallisoirs*) and the broad irregular reaches of open marsh land (the *partènements*) where the salt begins its journey. The area of the *salins*, 18 kilometers (nearly 11 miles) long and 13 kilometers (nearly 8 miles) wide, covers 11,000 hectares—the equivalent, Dupeux told me with evident pride, of the City of Paris. Salt production begins on the fringes of the *salins* in the *partènements*, naturally irregular ponds or lagoons where the water, let in from the surrounding sea, begins to evaporate and concentrate its salinity. Out at the edge of the *partènements*, sea water was pouring through a single sluice, a wide opening at the distant edge where the marsh meets the sea. The current flowed steadily into the canal and from a bridge overhead small boys were jumping like frogs off a lilypad into the rushing surge, in defiance of a sign that clearly read "No Swimming Allowed."

The wind off the water was brisk but balmy and laden with the crisp, lip-licking flavor of salt that crystallizes in the corners of one's mouth. The mistral, the cold wind from the north that means crotchety tempers elsewhere in the south of France, brings good fortune to the *salins*. It's the mistral blowing down the Rhône Valley that makes the salt, or rather the combination of cold dry north wind and hot summer sun. Here the only enemy is rain, which dilutes the solution and melts the already forming crystals of salt.

The sea water takes three to four months to move through the interlocking series of *partènements*, gradually increasing its concentration of salt until it reaches a saturation of around 250 grams per liter, when it is transferred to the *tables salants* or *cristallisoirs*. At this point it often turns a startling shade of rose, so deep it looks as though dye had been added to it. The color comes from the natural proliferation of microscopic salt-loving algae, *Dunaliella salina*, which in turn colors a tiny shrimp called *Artemia salina* that lives off the algae and is itself eaten by flamingoes, hence passing the pink color up the food chain from algae to shrimp to big birds. It was at one of these basins that Dupeux caught my arm. "There!" he cried. "It's beginning." And it was—hard to discern immediately in the soft efflorescence of the salty water, but then I could see, slowly turning like iridescent diamonds held to the light, the first crystals forming of the precious *fleur du sel*.

All of the salt at the Salins du Midi was harvested by hand until the end of World War II. Back then, a two-man team of skilled workers, one to scoop the salt into piles, the other to transport each pile in a wheelbarrow, could collect between 15 and 20 cubic meters daily (a cubic meter of salt weighs a ton). That task is now accomplished by *récolteurs*, big machines like grain harvesters, the John Deeres of the salt world. A *récolteur* harvests 600 to 800 cubic meters an hour, leading to a daily harvest of around 12,000 tons of salt.

Freshly harvested, the salt is washed in brine to rid it of impurities, sand, vegetable debris, and so forth, then rinsed, dried, and deposited in *camelles*, so-called because each of these small mountains of salt looks from a distance like a camel's back, but a luminescent white camel that glows even at night. By mid-October, the last of the harvested salt will be stocked in its *camelle*, salt that is now 99.5 percent sodium chloride and ready for sale.

Except in a few artisanal sites, like Dr. d'Alí's Ettore e Infersa, most Mediter-

# Garum

THE ODDEST PRODUCT THAT Greeks and Romans produced from salt, at least to modern tastes, was the thick syrupy liquid called *garum*, made from various parts of fish (some authors say from the intestines, others from small whole fish, still others from a combination of the two—and probably all of these methods were used at one time or another). The fish, layered in terra-cotta jars with lots of salt, sometimes with aromatic herbs added, was left in the sun to ferment to a rich and heady brew.

Modern apologists spend a good deal of time trying to persuade us that *garum* was not just total yuck. "A sort of mustard," says one, similarly concentrated and used in small quantities. At one rather modest Pompeiian dwelling, archaeologists discovered a small jar containing, to their surprise, barely half a liter (about two cups) of *garum*—not at all the quantity one would have expected if *garum* was used with abandon in every dish, as is often stated. The closest comparison in the contemporary world is the fermented fish sauce, like Vietnamese nuoc mam, that's used widely in Southeast Asian and Philippine cooking. Like salt, fish sauce is sprinkled on almost every dish, and like salt, it adds depth and integrity to flavors that might otherwise not succeed in coming together.

Eventually *garum* was made all over the Mediterranean to gratify the insatiable Roman palate, but it was the Greeks who invented it before it was taken up by Carthaginians and Romans. And it didn't end with the fall of Rome either. Years later, it was still being produced in Greece and on the eastern Adriatic coast for the Byzantine court. We know this because when Liutprand, bishop of Cremona, paid a long, disastrous diplomatic call on the Byzantine emperor in the year 968, he complained bitterly about the food that was served him, especially the oily sauces, he said, that stank of *garum*.

One could also argue that *garum,* one way or another, is still with us. Take, for instance, *pissala* from Nice—from which we get the niçoise "pizza" called pissaladière. *Pissala* is a paste made of tiny fish, fry really, that are now illegal to harvest but were once a delicacy off the coast of Nice. Like the fish used to make *garum,* they were layered with salt and other aromatics and left to ferment slightly. Unlike *garum,* it was the fish mashed to a paste, not the liquid they exuded, that was consumed. The traditional pissaladière was made of bread dough topped with a mixture of tomatoes and onions and the *pissala* spread over it all. Nowadays, anchovies are used instead.

Or take anchovies themselves, for that matter, or rather the liquid they produce. Called *la colatura,* the clear, amber-colored liquid is poured off salted anchovies as they exude their own brine. It is still used to dress pasta in the province of Salerno in Southern Italy, and, like so many products that were once disparaged as a food of the poor, it is actually experiencing a revival in fancy restaurants where the aromatic concentrate is mixed with fine local olive oil to make a simple dressing for spaghetti. It sounds like a direct descendant of ancient Mediterranean *garum,* and I'd be willing to bet it tastes a lot like *garum,* too.

ranean sea salt is harvested by machine. But machine-harvesting, Dr. d'Alí had told me, scrapes up mud and other impurities from the bottom of the *saline* and the salt, like that from the Salins du Midi, must be washed and then dried in kilns. In the process of washing, Dr. d'Alí said, almost all the magnesium is rinsed away. And magnesium is what makes his salt so special. As for kiln-drying, it makes the salt too dry so that it lacks that delicious humidity at the center of the crystal that lets sun-dried salt melt like butter on the tongue. Still, the salt from the Salins du Midi, widely marketed in North America under the label La Baleine, is delicious and holds its own when tasted against ordinary, everyday Morton's. Best of all was the salt product Dupeux gave me as I left: a box of soft, rich, buttery caramels, each mixed with a judicious quantity of *fleur de sel* that crunched between the teeth in a decidedly pleasant way and at the same time flooded the palate with salt, a startling contrast to the sweetness of the candy.

### 13 GREAT RECIPES USING SALT

Salt-Baked Fish

Salt-Baked Chicken

Spanish Salt-Cod and Red Pepper Salad
   *Ajoarriero*

Sicilian Salt-Cod and Orange Salad
   *Insalata di Baccalà e Arancie*

Provençal Salt-Cod Purée
   *Brandade de Morue*

Provençal "Fresh" Salt-Cod and Potato Pie with Tomato Confit
   *Tarte Tatin de Demi-Sel aux Pommes de Terre et Confit de Tomates*

Pasta with Anchovies and Salted Capers
   *Pasta all'Isolana*

Anchovy Sauce for Toast or Raw Vegetables
   *Anchoïade*

Anchovy-Garlic Dip
   *Bagna Caôda*

Tapenade

Bottarga and Cheese Crostini
   *Crostini di Bottarga al Caciocavallo*

North African Salt-Preserved Lemons

Moroccan Chicken with Black Olives and Salted Lemons

## COOK'S NOTES

If you don't believe that salt makes a difference, try this: Get together a group of half a dozen different kinds of salt. Be sure to include some common commercial salt, the kind you find on supermarket shelves, and kosher salt, as well as some of the super-expensive *fleur de sel* from the Atlantic coast of France. In between, try to have at least two Mediterranean sea salts. Of the ones I've mentioned, La Baleine is quite readily available in gourmet shops; the salt from the Ettore e Infersa salt works in Sicily is a little harder to find, but Zingerman's Deli in Ann Arbor, Michigan (see Where to Find It, page 415), stocks Ravidà salt, which comes from the same area. You might also want to look for Maldon salt, England's finest, and the red salt from Hawaii, just to have some points of comparison.

Don't cheat and don't peek: Number the boxes of salt and put some of each in a plain brown-paper bag with a corresponding number on the front. Set the bags out on a table and put a little of each salt in a plain white saucer in front of each bag so tasters can compare color, grain size, and clarity. You can, and should, taste each salt in two different ways, by crunching the grains between your teeth and by letting the salt melt on your tongue. You'll have a slightly different taste sensation from each method. Then, if you wish, serve wedges of fairly firm tomatoes to be sprinkled with each salt—which will give yet another sense of its worth.

How to clear your palate between tastes? Plain water is just about the best, but if you wish, a piece of sweet fruit, like an apple or orange wedge, helps to rid your mouth of too much saltiness.

## SALT-BAKING

This technique, which I first encountered years ago at a seafood restaurant in Seville, Spain, that was famous for the presentation, is both dramatic and satisfying. Is it traditional? I don't think so. The closest thing to it in traditional Mediterranean cooking is probably the *kleftiko* style of cookery in Cyprus, where lamb is wrapped in clay and baked in an underground oven. But this salt technique is entirely different—dramatic and glamorous, too! To bring a mound of firmly baked salt to the table, then rap it smartly with a knife handle so that the salt cracks and drops away revealing the whole fish inside, is a memorable moment of triumph for the cook. But it is also a superb way to concentrate all the savory juices within the fish, or a chicken, giving it a succulence that will also linger long in the memory.

Isn't it awfully salty, though? Well, no, not really. The salt acts as a case for the roast and because both chicken and fish are protected by their skins, it doesn't really penetrate very far into the flesh, just enough to give it a pleasantly briny flavor.

A few cautions for beginners: Don't try to do this with a bird or a fish that weighs more than about 4 pounds as the cooking time is tricky and you cannot put it back in the oven if it isn't done. Make sure you have a proper-sized baking or roasting pan before you begin—the food being roasted has to fit inside the pan with the salt piled on top. A shallow roasting pan won't do unless you can line it with heavy-duty aluminum foil to come up high over the sides and keep the salt from spilling all over the oven.

Of course you won't use *fleur de sel* for this treatment. The most ordinary sea salt will do just fine and is not terribly expensive—my local whole-foods market has it for 69 cents a pound.

# Salt-Baked Fish

PREHEAT THE OVEN to 425°F.

RINSE THE FISH, inside and out, and dry thoroughly with paper towels. Measure the thickness of the fish at its thickest part.

POUR THE SALT into a large bowl, add the egg whites, and stir vigorously with a spoon until all the grains of salt are well coated with egg white. Spread about a third of the salt mixture over the bottom of an oval or rectangular baking dish large enough and deep enough to hold the whole fish. The bottom layer of salt should be about an inch thick. Set the fish on top and cover it completely with the remaining salt—this is important; no part of the fish should be visible and the top of the fish should be covered by at least 1 inch.

SET THE DISH in the oven and lower the heat slightly to 400°F. Bake for 45 minutes for a 3-pound fish, 60 minutes for a 4-pounder.

ONCE THE FISH IS DONE, remove it from the oven and, for a dramatic presentation, take it right to the table in its baking dish. Crack open the salt (a knife handle is handy for this). As you remove the salty crust, you will pull away the fish skin and scales.

SERVE THE FISH very simply, if you wish, with just lemon wedges and a cruet of your finest extra-virgin olive oil; or try a Sicilian *salmoriglio* for a slight elaboration.

**Makes 6 servings**

1 whole 3- to 4-pound firm, white-fleshed fish, such as snapper, wolffish, or sea bass

4 pounds (8 cups) coarse sea salt

2 egg whites

Lemon wedges, for serving (optional)

Extra-virgin olive oil, for serving (optional)

For serving: Salmoriglio (page 69) (optional)

# Salt-Baked Chicken

Use flat-leaf parsley and rosemary, basil, sage, or thyme to flavor the chicken. Slip some of the herbs between the skin and the flesh, chop most of the herbs to mix with the salt, and reserve a few sprigs to garnish the finished dish.

**Makes 4 to 6 servings**

1 whole 3½- to 4-pound chicken, giblets removed

1 whole head garlic, separated into unpeeled cloves

1 tablespoon crushed black peppercorns

½ lemon

Sprigs of fresh flat-leaf parsley

Sprigs of fresh rosemary, basil, sage, or thyme

1 cup finely chopped fresh herbs (use the same herbs as in the garnish)

3 pounds (6 cups) coarse sea salt

PREHEAT THE OVEN to 450°F.

RINSE THE CHICKEN and dry thoroughly, inside and out, with paper towels.

PEEL TWO OF THE GARLIC CLOVES and cut them in half. Drop into the cavity of the chicken, along with the crushed pepper. Push the lemon in, cut side toward the inside of the bird, squeezing it slightly to release a little juice. Do not truss the chicken.

PICK OVER THE FRESH SPRIGS of parsley and other herbs and set aside a few leaves or tender sprigs to garnish the finished dish. Slide your fingers in between the skin and flesh over the breasts of the chicken and insert the leaves or sprigs. The herbs will impregnate the breast meat with their aromas and also form a pattern under the skin—it will be more visible when the bird is cooked.

LINE A ROASTING PAN with aluminum foil, bringing the foil up the sides of the pan to make a collar that stands up at least an inch or so and will keep the salt from spilling out in the oven.

MIX THE CHOPPED HERBS thoroughly with the coarse salt. Lay a bed of this salt about an inch or so thick on the bottom of the roasting pan and set the chicken on top of it. Scatter the remaining, unpeeled cloves of garlic around the bird. Spoon the rest of the salt all over the chicken and down the sides, so that the bird is completely covered with the herbal salt. Pat it down slightly but don't pack it too tightly. If necessary, raise the excess aluminum foil around the edges of the pan to hold the salt in place.

SET THE PAN in the center of the preheated oven and roast, uncovered, for 1½ hours.

REMOVE THE CHICKEN from the oven and let it sit undisturbed for an additional 30 minutes. The chicken will continue cooking in the heat of the salt.

TRANSFER THE CHICKEN to a big platter and, if necessary, break the salt crust (a knife handle is useful for this). Discard all the salt, brushing the skin to get rid of any that may cling. Use a spoon to scrape out any salt that may have slipped inside the chicken.

SERVE IMMEDIATELY, or let it cool to room temperature if you prefer. Garnish the chicken with the reserved herbs.

## SALT COD

There was a time when the only fish eaten by most people in the western Mediterranean world, except for those who lived right on the coast, was salt cod. They ate a lot of it, too, because the Catholic church deemed almost half the year to be days of abstinence from meat. Besides the great fast of Lent, there was a smaller fast before Christmas at Advent, plus Fridays throughout the year and the vigils or eves of major feast days. Moreover, salt cod was light and dry, and unlike cumbersome barrels of pickled meat, easily transported. It would keep for a long time without spoiling. So salt cod took the place of meat, and, typical of the Mediterranean, clever cooks took this symbol of deprivation and turned it into a whole series of delicious preparations that became greatly in demand. The salt trade developed symbiotically with the fish trade: Basque, Breton, and Scandinavian fishermen needed Mediterranean sea salt to preserve their fish, while Mediterranean cooks needed salt cod to preserve their piety. Back and forth went the crates of salt and the barrels of salt fish, up the Rhône, over the canals, and into the North Sea, and then back down again.

Nowadays, salt cod is almost wickedly expensive, and great chefs often put it on their menus as a luxury item. "After the *Guerra Civil*, it was only for poor people," said my Catalan friend Jose Puig, "and now it's almost as expensive as lobster." You get the best salt cod, he advised, in the Sant Antoni market (the Boquería) in Barcelona.

It isn't always easy to get good salt cod in this country. I scorn outright the little wooden boxes of hard, yellowish, and smelly bits of cod that come in from Nova Scotia, but in a Portuguese, Italian, or Greek neighborhood you may well come upon a fishmonger like Sal Fantasia at the New Deal Market in Cambridge, Massachusetts, who has superb, heavy, meaty, pure white sides of North Atlantic salt cod. And Browne Trading in Portland, Maine, makes its own sides of salt cod that can be shipped all over the country (see page 415 for addresses).

### SALT-COD SALADS

Don't be put off by the idea of using "raw" salt cod in a salad. It's a venerable tradition with variations in many parts of Spain and Sicily—the Sicilian version, I suspect, is a Spanish import dating from the centuries when southern Italy and Sicily were ruled by that nation. The salt cod isn't really raw at all, since it has been thoroughly salted and dried. But once it's been soaked for 24 to 48 hours, it is used as is, without further cooking, for an unusual and interesting first-course salad.

To make either of these recipes, you will need about 8 ounces of salt cod—or a quarter of a 2-pound boneless fillet of dry salt cod. It's not necessary to soak the entire fillet to get this. You can simply cut off what you need and wrap the rest in paper or aluminum foil to store in a cool, dry place for a couple of weeks. Don't store it for longer than that; the cod tends to dry out excessively and shrivel. Cover the piece of cod with cool water and set aside to soak for 24 to 48 hours, changing the water every 6 to 8 hours. When the cod has lost its intense saltiness and is plumped with water, drain it and pat it as dry as you can with paper towels. Use a sharp knife to cut the skin off the fillet. Then shred the cod flesh, tearing it into thin strips with your hands—this is easier to do than it sounds because the texture of cod naturally lends itself to shredding. You should have about 1 cup of shredded salt cod.

# Spanish Salt-Cod and Red Pepper Salad

**AJOARRIERO**

*Ajoarriero* refers to the muleteers who were once responsible for transporting goods by mule caravan all over Spain. They are said to have developed a cuisine based on easy-to-carry ingredients, such as salt cod.

In Valencia's beautiful Mercat Central, a pepper farmer whose stall was heaped with huge, fleshy, sweet red peppers gave me a recipe for the Catalan version of this salad, which he called *esgarrat*—nothing but shredded salt cod and roasted red peppers cut into long thin strips, all tossed together with olive oil and vinegar. Later I had a similar salad, but considerably refined, at El Bohio, a restaurant on the Toledo road outside Madrid. The shredded cod was arranged on a serving platter, potatoes, tossed with oil and vinegar, were distributed over it, and roasted red peppers, cut into wide strips, were arranged on top and garnished with toasted slices of garlic.

**Makes 6 to 8
first-course servings**

1 pound small Yellow Finn or fingerling potatoes

5 tablespoons extra-virgin olive oil

1 tablespoon aged sherry wine vinegar

Sea salt and freshly ground black pepper

2 fresh sweet red peppers

1 cup shredded soaked salt cod (see page 27)

2 garlic cloves, thinly sliced

PEEL THE POTATOES, cut them into chunks, and add them to a pan of rapidly boiling salted water. Cook, covered, for 10 to 12 minutes, until the potatoes are tender. Drain. As soon as you can handle the potatoes, slice them about ¼ inch thick into a salad bowl. While the potatoes are still warm, add 3 tablespoons of the oil, the vinegar, and salt and pepper.

ROAST AND PEEL the red peppers (see page 410). Core the peppers, discarding the seeds and white inner membranes. Slice the peppers about ½ inch thick and add them to the potatoes.

ADD THE SALT COD and toss gently to mix. Cover with plastic wrap and set aside for an hour or so to meld the flavors.

WHEN YOU ARE READY TO SERVE, if you wish, transfer the salad to a serving platter. Brown the garlic slices in the remaining 2 tablespoons of olive oil over medium heat and pour them, oil and all, over the salad.

# Sicilian Salt-Cod and Orange Salad

**INSALATA DI BACCALÀ E ARANCIE**

 This version of a salt-cod salad is reminiscent of the Spanish salad called *remojón,* which also calls for the odd but delicious combination of oranges, black olives, and onion. If you can't find blood oranges, use small navel oranges, but add the flesh of one peeled lemon to give tartness to the mix.

PEEL THE BLOOD ORANGES and cut away all the pithy membrane that surrounds them. Slice the flesh into small chunks—you should have about 1 cup of orange chunks. Combine the orange chunks in a bowl with the olives, onion, chili, oil, vinegar, salt cod, and oregano. Toss to mix well. Set aside, covered with plastic wrap, for at least 1 hour to meld the flavors.

TO SERVE, arrange the greens, if using, on a serving platter and mound the salad on top.

**Makes 6 to 8
first-course servings**

2 blood oranges

⅓ cup pitted coarsely chopped black olives

1 small red onion, very thinly sliced

1 small fresh red or green chili pepper, roasted (see page 410), seeded, and thinly sliced

¼ cup extra-virgin olive oil

1 tablespoon red wine vinegar

1 cup shredded soaked salt cod (see page 27)

Pinch of dried Sicilian or Greek oregano (*rígani*), crumbled

Salad greens, such as escarole or frisée (optional)

# Provençale Salt-Cod Purée

**BRANDADE DE MORUE**

This Southern French favorite is traditionally served with triangles of fried bread, but you may use toasted bread if you'd rather. It makes a delicious "dip" or finger food for cocktail parties, but it's also served plated as a first course—always with fried or toasted bread to go with it.

Allow time for the cod to soak—at least 24 and up to 48 hours.

You might be tempted to puree all the brandade ingredients in a food processor, since it looks easier, but I caution against it for two reasons:

1. The consistency of the final product should not be a homogeneous puree. It should still have a sense of the fibrous texture of the salt cod, which you will get by processing at least part of the fish in a traditional mortar and pestle.

2. Any time you process a potato in a food processor, you risk turning it into a gluey mess.

You may do the whole thing in a mortar, but few of us have mortars that size in our home kitchens—though if you're traveling in the Mediterranean, it's worth looking for a hefty stone or ceramic mortar, especially in the little shops around the markets. I find that doing part of the fish in a mortar and the rest of it in the food processor is a nice compromise.

**Makes about 8 servings as a first course, 16 servings as an appetizer (4 to 5 cups)**

1 boneless (2-pound) fillet salt cod

4 to 5 cups whole milk

1 bulb (Florentine) fennel, leaves included, trimmed and quartered

Zest of 1 lemon, organically raised

1 large potato

1 cup extra-virgin olive oil

3 to 4 plump garlic cloves, chopped

For serving: Slices of bread, toasted or fried in olive oil

RINSE THE SALT COD under running water to remove loose surface salt. Cut it into two or three pieces. Place it in a basin, and fill the basin with fresh cool water. Soak the salt cod for 24 to 48 hours, changing the water every 6 to 8 hours. Taste the cod—it should be pleasantly salty. Continue soaking, if necessary, for 4 to 6 hours longer, then drain the cod and discard the water. (If the salt cod finishes soaking before you are ready to use it, simply remove it from the soaking water, pat it dry, wrap it in plastic or aluminum foil, and store it in the refrigerator until you are ready to use it.)

PLACE THE COD in a pan large enough to hold the pieces and add up to 4 cups milk to cover them completely. Add the fennel and lemon zest. Set over low heat and bring to a very gentle simmer. The cod should never boil fiercely. As soon as the milk is simmering, cover the pan and turn off the heat. Gently poach the salt cod in the hot milk for about 20 minutes, or until the fish is soft but not falling apart. Drain and discard the milk.

WHILE THE COD IS COOKING, peel the potato and boil it in lightly salted water to cover until it is tender.

HEAT THE REMAINING 1 cup milk in a small saucepan until it is very hot, but not boiling. Heat the olive oil in a small saucepan until it is very hot, but not boiling.

USING A MORTAR AND PESTLE, pound the garlic to a paste. Add about a third of the fish to the mortar, a little at a time, and pound with the garlic, pounding and turning until it is a homogeneous mass. Slowly, a little at a time, pound in about ¼ cup of the very hot milk, followed by a similar quantity of very hot oil.

IF YOU WISH, and if your mortar is large enough, continue to add about a third of the fish, pounding in hot milk and oil alternately, until all of the ingredients have been combined, reserving ¼ cup each of milk and oil to add to the potato. But it is easier to process the remaining fish in a food processor, adding hot milk and oil in small quantities through the feed tube while the processor is running—again, reserving a few tablespoons of milk and oil for the potato. Remove the processed fish from the food processor and combine it with the pounded fish.

MASH THE POTATO in a small bowl with a potato masher, gradually working in the reserved hot milk and oil. Using a wooden spoon, combine the potato with the fish. Stir and beat it vigorously to amalgamate all the ingredients thoroughly while still maintaining the texture of the fish.

SERVE THE BRANDADE on a tray with slices of toasted or, for a more authentic touch, fried bread. Brandade is often served as a first course, plated and with the fried croutons of bread on the side.

**NOTE:** Old-fashioned cooks would never add potato to a true brandade, but I like it because it smooths out the flavors. If you want to be 100 percent authentic, however, leave it out.

**VARIATION:** Brandade de morue is similar to Venetian *mantecato,* a tradition in the *baccari,* the little wine bars that add so much to the charm of Venice. Do' Mori, behind the Rialto fish market, is one of the best, and best-known, of these. At 11 o'clock in the morning, the bar is lined with market workers, tourists, and well-dressed Venetian lawyers and academics, all tossing back sparkling chilled prosecco wine with a mid-morning snack of crostini piled with *mantecato.* Note that Venetian *mantecato* is made with a notable quantity of garlic and salt cod and olive oil—no milk and never any potatoes. It is almost always garnished with chopped flat-leaf parsley, sometimes so much that the creamy mixture is tinged with green. In Venetian homes and traditional restaurants, *mantecato* may be served as a first course with slabs of grilled polenta.

# Provençale "Fresh" Salt-Cod and Potato Pie with Tomato Confit

## TARTE TATIN DE DEMI-SEL AUX POMMES DE TERRE ET CONFIT DE TOMATES

When good-quality salt cod is not available, try this method of salting cod (or haddock, or other firm-textured, white-fleshed fish) for a few days. Salting the fish firms up the texture and changes the flavor subtly and in an interesting way. The presentation is similar to a dish on the menu at the lovely restaurant La Fénière in Lourmarin, where Reine Sammut presides over the kitchen. It's called a "tatin" because, like a tarte des demoiselles Tatin, it is baked and then inverted for service.

Could you make this with fresh fish, without salting it? No, because the firm texture of salted fish holds up better in baking.

If you can find small enough baking dishes, make individual tatins for each serving. Otherwise, make one big one in a deep cake or quiche pan with a removable bottom.

RINSE THE FISH and pat dry with paper towels. Sprinkle liberally on both sides with 1 teaspoon of fine sea salt. Wrap the fillet in plastic wrap and set in the refrigerator for 3 to 4 days.

AT LEAST A DAY IN ADVANCE of cooking, prepare the tomato sauce. Combine the onion, garlic, and olive oil in a heavy, non-reactive skillet over medium-low to low heat. Cook, stirring frequently, until the onion has sweated out most of its liquid and is melting into the oil.

IF YOU ARE USING FRESH TOMATOES, dip them in boiling water and peel, then halve the tomatoes and squeeze out as much of the seeds and juice as you can. If you are using canned whole tomatoes, drain them thoroughly in a sieve. Add the tomatoes to the onion in the pan, along with 1 teaspoon salt and the sugar, ½ teaspoon of the pepper, and thyme. Raise the heat to medium-high and cook the sauce rapidly, chopping the tomatoes with a wooden spoon as the sauce cooks down. Cook for 20 minutes or so, until you have a thick, jammy sauce. Remove the sauce from the heat, taste, and adjust the seasoning. The sauce

**Makes 6 first-course servings**

1 pound fillet of haddock, cod, or similar white-fleshed fish

Fine sea salt

1 cup finely chopped yellow onion

4 garlic cloves, finely chopped

¼ cup extra-virgin olive oil

1½ pounds canned, drained plum tomatoes (1½ twenty-eight-ounce cans), or fresh ripe tomatoes, peeled, seeded, and juiced

2 teaspoons sugar

Freshly ground black pepper

½ teaspoon dried thyme, crumbled

1 leek, trimmed and slivered lengthwise (including some of the green top)

1 medium fresh sweet red pepper, roasted (see page 410)

1 pound small yellow-fleshed fingerling potatoes

Short-crust pastry (see page 409, or use frozen pastry)

2 to 3 tablespoons unsalted butter

should be refrigerated until you are ready to use it; heat before adding to the dish.

RINSE THE LEEK after slivering, then drop it into a small pan of rapidly boiling water. Blanch for 1 minute, then drain immediately and rinse under cool running water. Set aside.

SLICE THE ROASTED PEPPER into long thin strips. Set aside.

BOIL THE POTATOES in lightly salted water for about 10 minutes or until just barely tender. Drain and set aside.

PREHEAT THE OVEN to 400°F.

ROLL OUT THE PASTRY to a thickness of about ⅛ inch. Cut rounds to fit the top of the baking dishes. Set the pastry disks aside.

REMOVE THE FISH from the refrigerator, rinse off the salt, and pat dry with paper towels. The fish will be quite a bit firmer in texture than when it was fresh. Slice each fillet on the diagonal, as you would smoked salmon, in slices about ¼ inch thick.

LIBERALLY BUTTER the baking dishes, thoroughly coating the bottoms and sides.

PEEL THE STILL-WARM POTATOES and slice about ¼ inch thick. Distribute the potato slices among the dishes. Arrange the red pepper slices on top. Then arrange the fish slices in an overlapping pattern. Spread the slivered leeks over the fish and sprinkle with black pepper.

SPOON THE WARM TOMATO SAUCE over the top to cover the other ingredients completely, then top with a pastry disk, making a few little holes in the pastry to let out the steam.

BAKE FOR 30 MINUTES (40 minutes if you are using a quiche pan rather than individual molds). Remove from the oven, let rest about 5 minutes, and invert over warm plates or a warm service platter. Serve immediately.

## SALTED ANCHOVIES, CAPERS, AND OTHER FINE THINGS

One of salt's most important uses, apart from the natural human need for it in the diet, is in preserving other foods, for example, anchovies and capers, which are so important in the Mediterranean that one couldn't imagine most of the region's cuisines without them. Anchovies, which are delicious fresh, reach a kind of culinary apotheosis when salted. In Greek and Italian food shops in North America, you'll often find a big open tin of salted anchovies, from which you are invited to select as many as you need. Often this is the best buy for high-quality anchovies. But if the shopkeeper is not careful, his anchovies may be old, dried out, and rather smelly. In that case, it's better to stick with a good brand of oil-packed anchovy fillets. In any case, oil-packed fillets were once salted fish themselves before they were stripped, rinsed, and packaged in oil.

Salt-packed anchovies should be rinsed under running water to rid them of any chunks of salt, then split apart in your hands and the center spine lifted out, along with any fins or tail pieces. Don't worry if you don't get every tiny bone out of the fillets. Softened by processing, the bones are easily digested and a good source of calcium.

In Catalonia, anchovy spines are deep-fried in olive oil to make a crispy snack to serve with a glass of wine. Try it—you'll be surprised at how delicious it is.

Capers grow wild all over the Mediterranean on stony, inhospitable land close to the sea. Their beautiful mauve flowers with yellow pistils, which look vaguely like passionflowers, sway from crannied walls in June. These are caper blossoms, but since the part that is most often preserved is the immature bud, every lovely caper flower represents a missed opportunity. Caper berries, on the other hand, are the fruit that forms after the flowers have gone by, and while they're spectacular for presentations, the flavor lacks the intensity of the small buds.

The best capers, without question, are those from Greece, southern Spain, and the islands of Salina and Pantelleria off Sicily. The unopened buds are carefully harvested, dried, and packed in salt to preserve them. Some regions favor preserving capers in vinegar or brine, but the flavor of salted capers is so superior to the brine- or vinegar-cured ones that it's a wonder to me that the latter continue to find a market.

Salted capers should be thoroughly rinsed in a sieve until all the salt is gone before using.

# Pasta with Anchovies and Salted Capers

## PASTA ALL'ISOLANA

Graziella Crivello owns, with her husband, Franco, a great fish restaurant, Franco U Piscatore (Frank the Fisherman) in the little village of Porticello outside Palermo. She told me about this quick and easy pasta recipe, which is made on the dozen or more little islands scattered off the coast of Sicily.

Use high-quality canned tomatoes to make the pulp needed for this recipe. Or, in season, peel, seed, and finely mince ripe raw tomatoes.

**Makes 4 servings**

Extra-virgin olive oil

3 garlic cloves, chopped

2 whole salted anchovies, rinsed and stripped to fillets, or 4 oil-packed anchovy fillets (see page 411)

¼ cup salted capers, rinsed under running water, drained, and coarsely chopped

½ cup finely chopped canned tomatoes

Pinch of sugar

⅓ cup coarsely chopped pitted black olives (salt-cured are best)

Pinch of dried Sicilian or Greek oregano (*rígani*)

12 ounces short, stubby pasta, such as penne or rigatoni

1 tablespoon minced fresh basil

1 tablespoon minced fresh flat-leaf parsley

Freshly ground black pepper

COMBINE 2 TABLESPOONS of the oil in a pan with the garlic, anchovies, and capers. Cook over medium-low heat, crushing the ingredients with a fork as they soften. (It's important not to let the garlic brown, but just to melt in the oil, along with the anchovies and capers.) You should end up with a coarse paste. Stir in the tomatoes, sugar, and olives, along with a good pinch of oregano, crumbling the herb in your fingers. Cover and let cook over a very low heat for about 10 minutes.

WHILE THE SAUCE IS COOKING, bring a large pot of unsalted water to a rolling boil. (The sauce will be quite salty on its own.) Add the pasta and cook until it is just tender. Remove the pasta from the cooking water with a strainer and transfer to the sauce along with a little of the pasta water—no more than ½ cup. Continue cooking the pasta in the sauce until the added water has been absorbed or boiled away and the pasta is tender. Taste the sauce and add salt if necessary.

TURN THE PASTA AND SAUCE into a heated serving dish and dress with the minced fresh herbs and plenty of black pepper. Serve immediately.

# Anchovy Sauce for Toast or Raw Vegetables

## ANCHOÏADE

 A Provençal favorite that mixes olive oil with anchovies and garlic, *anchoïade* is traditionally served as a thick topping on toasted French bread. If you can only get oil-packed fillets, by all means use them, but salt-packed anchovies, available in Greek and Italian markets, have more flavor and a better texture than oil-packed ones.

COMBINE THE ANCHOVIES with the garlic in a food processor and pulse until they are pureed. Add the butter and blend it in. With the blade spinning, add the olive oil, 1 tablespoon at a time. Lastly, add the vinegar. Transfer the *anchoïade* to a serving bowl and stir in lots of black pepper.

CUT A BAGUETTE (or similar crusty bread) in two the long way, then cut each half into chunks about 4 inches long. Lightly toast the cut side of each chunk on a grill or under the broiler. Spoon lots of anchoïade on each toast, letting it sink in. Or, if you prefer, assemble a tray of raw vegetables and serve the *anchoïade* as a dipping sauce in the middle.

**Makes 8 to 10 servings**

10 whole salt-packed anchovies, rinsed, filleted, and coarsely chopped (see page 411)

4 garlic cloves, coarsely chopped

2 tablespoons unsalted butter, at room temperature

½ cup extra-virgin olive oil

1½ teaspoons aged red wine vinegar

Freshly ground black pepper

For serving: baguette or raw vegetables

# Anchovy-Garlic Dip

## BAGNA CAÔDA

I debated whether to put *bagna caôda* here with the salt recipes or in the olive oil chapter, since that, too, is a primary ingredient in this delicious combination. In thinking it over, I saw how very close this sauce from Piedmont of northwest Italy is to the *anchoïade* of neighboring Provence, so it seemed to fit quite naturally here. But it's served in quite a different fashion: Traditionally, *bagna caôda* is wintertime food from the high mountains where the hot sauce in its terra-cotta pot is set over a fondue or spirit lamp to keep it bubbling, while convivial diners dip raw vegetables (mostly—although I'm told that in some areas they dip cooked beets, potatoes, onions, turnips) in the hot sauce. The de rigueur vegetable for an authentic *bagna caôda* is cardoons, which are almost unfindable in North America and usually damned poor in quality when you do find them. If you happen to have cardoons blanching away in your backyard garden, strip them of their tough, celery-like fibers and soak them in acidulated water for an hour or so before serving them. Otherwise, serve this with a selection of raw carrot and celery sticks, pepper strips, small cabbage leaves, cauliflower and broccoli florets, strips of bulb (Florentine) fennel, scallions, daikon radish wedges—whatever is fresh and crisp and strikes your fancy.

A *bagna caôda* sauce is also delicious poured boiling hot over a dish of roasted and peeled red and yellow peppers to be served as a first course, and it makes an elegant dressing for spaghetti. On winter nights, up in the snowy Alps of Piedmont, they often scramble eggs in any sauce left in the bottom of the pan—following that idea, I like to fry farm-fresh eggs with their upstanding yellow yolks in the sauce for Sunday breakfast, with the extra sauce dribbled over toasted slices of country bread.

The sauce was originally made with walnut oil, once more prevalent than olive oil or butter in the region. Walnut oil is quite expensive, but a few tablespoons added at the end, or a handful of peeled, crushed walnuts, will contribute to the authenticity of the sauce. Buy walnut oil in a shop that has a high turnover, because it rapidly loses its fresh flavor if stored too long.

To serve this as a traditional, center-of-the-table dip for raw vegetables, you will need a fondue pot, preferably the kind that sits directly over the flame of a spirit lamp instead of over a boiling water bath. This is not as hard to find as you might think—most of the mail-order kitchen suppliers have a range of fondue pots available.

**Makes 4 servings**

4 salted anchovies, or 8 oil-packed anchovy fillets

6 garlic cloves, very thinly sliced

3 tablespoons unsalted butter

¾ cup extra-virgin olive oil

3 tablespoons walnut oil, or a handful of crushed, peeled walnuts (optional)

Freshly ground black pepper

RINSE THE SALTED ANCHOVIES and remove the bones. Chop coarsely. (If you are using oil-packed anchovies, simply chop them.)

COMBINE THE GARLIC AND BUTTER in a small deep saucepan or fondue pot. (The traditional pot is made of glazed terra-cotta, but a metal pot will do just as well.) Set over very low heat, using a Flame Tamer if necessary, and melt the butter. Let the garlic slices melt and soften in the butter, always keeping the heat very low and never letting the garlic brown. When they are quite soft, add the anchovies and olive oil, along with the walnut oil or crushed walnuts, if using. Bring the oil to a very soft simmer and just barely simmer for about 10 minutes to meld the flavors very well. Add a good dose of black pepper and serve immediately.

# Tapenade

Why is tapenade, the magnificent paste of black olives, here and not in the olive section? Because tapenade gets its name from *tapéno,* which is Provençal for capers—and that's the critical ingredient. This recipe is based on one in "Reboul," the cookbook that's otherwise known as *La Cuisinière Provençale,* first published in Marseille in 1897. The best olives to use for a tapenade are the ones Provençal cooks use—small, black niçoise olives (which aren't necessarily from Nice). But if you can't find them, other high-quality black olives will do, even the wrinkled salt-cured olives from North Africa or the juicy Kalamatas from Greece. Given the dryness of the former and the juiciness of the latter, you may have to adjust the quantity of olive oil used to compensate. Do, please, avoid the kind of black olives that come in a can and are often marked "California style"—these are green olives that have been processed to turn black and should be avoided. Period.

Tapenade can be made with a mortar and pestle or in a food processor. If you are using the latter, however, be careful not to overprocess the mixture—it should have a good texture and not be a paste or puree.

**Makes 1⅓ to 1½ cups**

1 cup (about 8 ounces) pitted, coarsely chopped niçoise olives

½ cup salted capers, rinsed under running water and drained

¼ cup canned tuna, drained

2 anchovy fillets, rinsed (if salted), drained, and coarsely chopped

1 teaspoon French-style mustard

½ cup extra-virgin olive oil

1 teaspoon Cognac

Freshly ground black pepper

Grilled or toasted bread, for serving

COMBINE THE OLIVES, capers, tuna, anchovies, and mustard in a mortar or food processor. Work with the pestle or process with brief spurts to make a coarse mixture. Gradually add the oil, continuing to process or to work with the pestle, until it has been thoroughly incorporated. If you are using the food processor, transfer the mixture to a bowl and stir in the Cognac and plenty of freshly ground black pepper. (If you're using a handsome mortar, simply stir in the Cognac and pepper and serve in the mortar itself.) Accompany it with grilled or toasted bread on which to spread the tapenade.

**VARIATION:** Reboul suggests an hors d'oeuvre of hard-cooked eggs, split in half and the yolks mixed with tapenade, then piled back into the whites. But it's prettier if you arrange the egg halves yolk side down on a little bed of tapenade, then spoon a little more of the sauce over them.

## BOTTARGA

Another salted product traditional in the Mediterranean is *bottarga*, made from the roe of either tuna or a Mediterranean lagoon fish called grey mullet. *Bottarga* in Italian, it's *boutarekh* in Egyptian Arabic, *putargo* in Turkish, *poutargue* in French, and *avgotáracho* (the original of them all) in Greek. The eggs, removed in their intact membrane, are salted, pressed, and dried, then coated with wax to preserve them—think pressed, sun-dried caviar, and you're pretty close.

*Bottarga* is available from fine gourmet-products stores, either as a block, like a small brick, or in bottles of already grated *bottarga*. The former is much to be preferred. *Bottarga* need not be refrigerated until the wax covering has been removed. To use, peel the wax from one end, exposing the actual *bottarga*, and either slice or grate enough for your purpose. Keep the unused portion as you would cheese, that is, in the refrigerator, with the exposed edges wrapped in plastic wrap to keep it from drying out. As long as it doesn't dry out, it will keep for several months; even if it does dry out at one end, the remainder is still usable. Simply remove and discard the dry parts. *Bottarga* is very salty, so no additional salt is used in any recipe that calls for it; for that reason, look for a cheese that is not overly salted for the recipe that follows.

Another way to use *bottarga* is as an antipasto on its own, very thinly sliced off the brick-shaped block. Fan the slices on a plate and dribble over it your finest extra-virgin olive oil and a few drops of lemon juice. Serve with thin slices of dark bread (rye or pumpernickel, although not typical of the Mediterranean, would be fine) spread with unsalted butter and lots of pepper.

# Bottarga and Cheese Crostini

## CROSTINI DI BOTTARGA AL CACIOCAVALLO

Like a glorious Mediterranean take on the humble grilled cheese sandwich, these crostini could be a first course at a rustic dinner, or they could be the main course for a simple lunch or supper. The *bottarga* adds a note of luxury. (See page 415 for information about where to find *bottarga*.)

Depending on the size of the bread, you'll need one or two slices for each serving. I like to make this with a long, slender baguette, slicing the bread on the diagonal as thinly as I can manage. Two such slices will make one serving.

**Makes 4 servings**

About 2 ounces (50 grams) imported *bottarga* of tuna or mullet (*bottarga di tonno* or *bottarga di muggine*)

8 ounces fresh ripe tomatoes

Sea salt

8 slices crusty country-style bread, about ¼ to ½ inch thick

8 ounces Caciocavallo or Pecorino Toscano cheese, thinly sliced, plus 2 tablespoons, grated

¼ cup extra-virgin olive oil

Freshly ground black pepper

1 small bunch fresh basil, leaves only

REMOVE THE MEMBRANE from the outside of the block of *bottarga*. Using the fine holes of a grater, grate enough *bottarga* to make about ⅓ cup. Set aside.

BRING A PAN OF WATER to a rolling boil and dip the tomatoes in, holding them in the boiling water for 15 seconds. Remove, peel, and seed. Dice the tomatoes, sprinkle with a very little salt, and set in a sieve over a small bowl to drain for 15 to 20 minutes.

TOAST THE BREAD SLICES in a toaster or under the broiler just long enough to turn them a little golden, but not long enough to make them crisp and crunchy all the way through. Once the bread has been toasted, preheat the oven to 300°F. Put the toasted bread (crostini) on a sheet pan, cover each slice with a very thin slice of cheese and return to the warm oven, leaving it just until the cheese has softened and melted slightly around the edges—about 10 to 15 minutes.

IN A SMALL BOWL, combine the olive oil and 1½ tablespoons of the drained tomato juice. Add lots of pepper. Set aside a few small basil leaves to use as a garnish and sliver the remaining leaves—you should have about ⅓ cup. Add the basil to the oil.

SET THE OVEN on broil.

PILE EACH SLICE OF CHEESE TOAST with the chopped tomatoes and sprinkle a good teaspoon of grated *bottarga* on top of each one. Spoon the oil mixture liberally over the top, then add a little grated cheese. Run the pan of toast under the broiler just long enough to melt the grated cheese and warm the tomatoes. Remove from the oven, garnish with the reserved basil leaves, and serve immediately.

NOTE: You can also turn this into a delightful pasta dish. Grate the *bottarga* and separately grate the cheese. Prepare the tomatoes and the oil mixture. Use a short, stubby pasta shape, such as penne, and cook enough for four people. As soon as the pasta is done, drain and dress it immediately with tomatoes and oil, sprinkle the grated cheese and grated *bottarga* over the top, and pass more of each at the table. Serve immediately.

# North African Salt-Preserved Lemons

Salted lemons are an important ingredient in North African cooking, with a flavor that is unmistakeable. Their use, however, should not be restricted to North African recipes as their characteristic, rather exotic flavor adds interest to many meat and vegetable combinations and their bright yellow color contrasts well with the dark hues of a lamb ragoût or a ratatouille with lots of eggplant. Or try them as an ingredient in a winter bean or lentil salad.

Salted lemons are very easy to make, but for best results wait until midwinter when organic lemons are in season and fill several big Mason jars to last through the rest of the year.

Use a 4-pint (1 half-gallon) glass canning jar or any similar lidded jar. It does not need to be self-sealing since it is the salt that preserves the lemons.

24 fresh whole lemons, preferably organic, plus more for juice, if necessary

1 cup pickling, kosher, or sea salt

IF YOU CAN'T FIND certified organic lemons, scrub the lemons very well with a brush under running water to remove any traces of pesticides or other chemicals.

FILL A CLEAN PRESERVING JAR with boiling water, first standing it on a layer of newspapers or kitchen towels. Leave it for 10 minutes or so to sterilize it, then pour the water out. Do this immediately before you're ready to fill the jar in order to have it as clean as possible.

HOLD A LEMON UPRIGHT on a cutting board and slice down carefully from the bud end to the stem end, stopping about ½ inch from the stem end. Give the lemon a quarter turn and slice again. The lemon will be quartered, but the quarters will be firmly attached at the stem end. Open the lemon slightly and pack the insides with salt, then press the lemon down into the bottom of the jar. Do this with all the lemons, pressing them very firmly so that they yield up a considerable quantity of juice. Fill the jar up to the top with an inch to spare.

YOU PROBABLY WON'T USE ALL THE LEMONS. Squeeze the excess lemons thoroughly and add the juice to the jar, along with ⅓ cup salt. The lemon juice should fill the jar right up to the top. Add another 2 tablespoons of salt to the top of the jar and screw the lid on tight. Set the jar aside to pickle for at least 3 weeks. Every couple of days, invert the jar and leave it standing on its head for a couple of days to redistribute the salty juice over all the lemons, then right it again.

TO USE, REMOVE A LEMON from the jar, rinse it briefly, then scrape the seeds away and discard. Slice or chop the lemon, depending on the use.

NOTE: Tunisian cooks make salted lemons with a brine that is half salted lemon juice and half salted water. It makes a milder pickle. Simply substitute heavily salted water (enough salt to float an egg) for half the liquid in the directions above.

# Moroccan Chicken with Black Olives and Salted Lemons

🌿 This is a deservedly famous Moroccan dish, simple in its ingredients but refined in its flavor combinations. It is the best way I know to show off the aromatic delicacy of salted lemons.

Note that the first step, rubbing the chicken parts with lemon and salt, is a typical North African technique to freshen the flavor of the bird.

**Makes 6 to 8 servings**

4 to 5 pounds chicken, preferably free-range, cut into parts

1 fresh lemon, quartered

Sea salt

½ cup finely chopped flat-leaf parsley

½ cup finely chopped cilantro

3 garlic cloves, finely chopped

Freshly ground black pepper

Big pinch of saffron threads

2 whole salt-preserved lemons (see page 44), 1 chopped, 1 sliced into strips

¼ cup water, or more as needed

½ cup extra-virgin olive oil

4 medium onions, halved and thinly sliced

4 chicken livers, carefully trimmed

1 tablespoon sweet Spanish *pimentón* or Hungarian paprika

1 tablespoon unsalted butter

1 cup pitted black olives, preferably salt-cured wrinkled ones

RINSE THE CHICKEN PARTS thoroughly, then rub the pieces all over with the lemon quarters. Take a handful of salt and rub this over the chicken pieces. Set aside in a cool place for 30 minutes, or refrigerate, covered, overnight.

WHEN YOU ARE READY TO COOK, rinse the chicken parts under cool running water, and pat them dry with paper towels.

IN A HEAVY POT large enough to hold all the ingredients, combine the parsley, cilantro, garlic, and black pepper. Crumble the threads of saffron into the herbs. Add the chopped preserved lemon along with ¼ cup of water. Add the chicken parts to the pot and stir to mix well and cover the chicken pieces with the herb mixture. Add the olive oil and set the pot over medium-low heat.

AS THE CHICKEN STARTS TO SIZZLE, stir in the onions and shake the pan to distribute them all around the chicken pieces. Cover the pan and cook very slowly, checking from time to time to be sure there is enough liquid in the bottom of the pan to keep the ingredients from burning, and adding a very little water, if necessary. After 30 minutes, add the livers to the center of the pan, along with the paprika. Cover again and continue to simmer until the chicken is thoroughly cooked and the onions have almost melted into the sauce, about 1 hour.

USING TONGS, remove the chicken from the sauce and transfer to a warm serving platter. Keep warm while you finish the sauce. Use a fork to crush the chicken livers into the sauce. Stir in the butter and the olives. Swirl the pan to emulsify the sauce and distribute the olives throughout.

POUR THE SAUCE over the chicken on the platter and garnish with strips of peel from the second preserved lemon. Serve at once.

# Olives and Olive Oil

THE SHAKESPEARE OF OLIVE OIL," is what Majid Mahjoub's friends call him, and they're only half-joking. It is with Shakespearean eloquence, they claim, that Majid speaks of the unctuous, apple-green balm that flows from his family orchards in the Mejerda Valley west of Tunis, through the family *huilerie*, the oil mill in the town of Tébourba, and out again in little green bottles to avid consumers in other parts of the world.

"Olive oil is like music," Majid says as he steers a little group of visitors through the pristine complex of white stucco buildings, trimmed, naturally, in olive green, where the oil is produced. It is early February, late in the season for olive-oil production, but the Mahjoubs have held back a small quantity of olives to be able to show these visitors from North America how the crush-and-press system works.

Like music? "Well, yes, you see, because music is an expression of time, it's a way of controlling time. And there can be no quality extra-virgin olive oil without controlling time—the time of harvest, just when the olives are turning from green to black, the time between picking and pressing, the time the oil sits before it is used." Slim and attractive despite a perpetually furrowed brow, Majid looks—and speaks—like an eager but anxious graduate student, stretching his simile to make a point. Shakespearean it may not be, but it is imaginative to say the least.

Olive oil is one of the hottest commodities to have arrived in the ever-shifting world of gourmet food preferences in the last fifteen or twenty years. Tunisian oil-producers like the Mahjoub family, however, have been late arrivals at this costly banquet, which was dominated until very recently by Italians and, among Italians, by Tuscans. In the United States alone, the volume of olive-oil imports more than doubled in the last decade, while the dollar value of extra-virgin olive-oil imports doubled just in the five years between 1995 and 2000. Much of the market is still dominated by high-priced Italian estate-bottled oils. Spanish, Greek, and Tunisian producers are quick to point out, though, that lots of the cheaper, mass-market "Italian" oil comes from orchards and mills in Spain, Greece, and Tunisia, transported in bulk containers to Italy, there to be bottled and labeled Italian.

Not from Moulins Mahjoub, however. Extra-virgin olive oil, when it's this high in quality, commands an equivalent high price. And more and more Tunisian producers are beginning to wake up to that fact. As the world's appetite for extra-virgin olive oil grows exponentially, they—along with their colleagues in places including Lebanon, Greece, and Turkey, whose olive oil was once scorned by connoisseurs—are finding their oils in demand. Tunisian growers, moreover, have a further incentive: Since the liberalization of the Tunisian olive-oil market in 1993, they are once more free to sell their oil wherever they can and at whatever price they can command. For many years before that, all oil that was not used locally had to be sold at a set price through the government oil office as a commodity product for export. Tunisians themselves, surrounded by olive groves as vast and productive as any in the Mediterranean, used margarine or cheap industrially produced vegetable oil from northern European factories. There was no reason to aim for high-quality oil since it all got dumped into the same barrel and shipped off to a refinery.

That was the kind of olive oil my mother used to buy at the pharmacy in small bottles and kept in the medicine cabinet to rub into the baby's scalp (a cure for something called "cradle cap," sort of baby dandruff). It's a far cry from the extra-virgin oil that is now slopped liberally ("drizzled" is the food writer's term, in French, more discreetly, "*un filet d'huile*") and somewhat indiscriminately over salads, grilled or poached meats and fish, bean stews, soups, and breads—everything, it seems, except desserts and sometimes even then. North Americans, Germans, English, Japanese, and others in the international marketplace where rank is displayed through expensive and esoteric food choices can't get enough of the stuff. And that's just fine with Majid and his eight siblings, who share in this family fortune that is counted not in gold coins but in olive trees—thousands of them.

From a height of land northeast of Tébourba, battalions of olive trees, the variety called *chetoui* for the most part, stretch in every direction, rolling across the countryside as far as we can see, the groves intersected by streambeds and the silver thread of river that broadens as it flows north into the Gulf of Tunis and the Mediterranean. This is the Mejerda Valley, scene of some of the heaviest fighting in the North African campaigns of World War II. Its rolling uplands, carpeted with silvery olive groves and punctuated by wetlands where European storks find a winter refuge, remind visitors of places like Andalucia (but it's much greener) and Tuscany (but it's much more open).

It's not surprising to learn that this part of Tunisia was settled five hundred years ago by Spanish Moslems, kicked out of their beloved Andalucia in 1492 (and again in 1502, in 1525, and lastly from 1609 to 1615, when a final 300,000 Moriscos were expelled) in one of history's first great acts of ethnic cleansing. Reaching this valley from the opposite shores of the Mediterranean, they must have been reminded immediately of their cherished homeland. Like many families in the valley, the Mahjoubs trace their ancestry in part back to these Andaluzi olive farmers. (On their mother's side, the Mahjoubs are Oueslati, from a tribe that was famous for the cultivation of fruit trees—Oueslati agronomy and Andaluzi engineering, they say, are responsible for the success of the family firm.)

We know how important olive culture was back in Arab Spain because, even though the Phoenicians and Greeks probably brought olive trees west to Iberia, and the Romans certainly made Baetica, as they called southwestern Spain, a major oil supplier for the empire, nonetheless, all the words having to do with olives and oil in modern Spanish are derived from Arabic—*aceite* and *aceituna*, meaning oil and olive, for instance come from Arabic *ẓeyt*, while *almaẓara*, Spanish for an oil mill, is a direct transliteration of Arabic *al-maẓara*.

Olive culture in Tunisia goes back much further than that, however, possibly back to Phoenicians who may have brought olive trees with them from Lebanon when they established their colony at Carthage on the coast west of here in the early ninth century B.C.E. Later, under Roman rule, Tunisia's immense agricultural potential began to be realized. In the second and third centuries of our era, when the great colosseum was built at El Jem in central Tunisia, thirty thousand bushels of wheat were shipped out annually to Roman markets. And olive oil was even more important. It remained that way down through Tunisian history: When French colonists began arriving in the late nineteenth century, a fertile land covered with groves capable of producing high-quality olive oil was one of the major attractions.

In fact it was a French *colon* who established the mill now owned by the Mahjoubs in Tébourba, back in the days when the little country market town was far more French than it is today. "After Khomsi Mahjoub, my grandfather, bought it in the early 1930s," Majid explains, "he exported oil to France. He had a good market there, especially among Jews."

Why Jews in particular? Because olive oil is pareve, meaning it doesn't conflict with kosher dietary laws that prohibit the use of pork fat entirely and butter with any kind of meat cookery. Mediterranean Jews are noted for their olive oil–based cuisine.

The Mahjoub mill has changed very little since the days of the French, although the steam engine that once ran most of the machinery is silent now, a museum piece kept in impeccable order but unused since electricity took over. But the olives are still picked by hand. A lot of the work is done by women; dressed in the brightly checked and striped robes that Tunisian country women favor, they climb sturdy ladders built like tripods to stretch up into the trees, then rake the olives off the branches using an odd but efficient tool, a pair of goat horns hollowed out to fit over the index and middle fingers, that protects their hands as they strip down the olive branches. (In a market in Sfax, over on Tunisia's east coast, I bought a modern version of this traditional implement, made of neon purple plastic—easy to find because it practically glows in the dark.)

The olives are picked at just the right stage of maturity, when their green color starts to turn to purple and black, although, given the propensity of olives to mature at different rates, even on the same tree, the harvest is usually a mix of green, black, and in-between. Within 24 hours of harvest, the olives are rushed to the mill where they are given a quick rinse of cold water to remove leaves and any field dust or mud, then dumped into a broad, shallow basin to be crushed by giant granite millstones that stand on edge like stone wheels and revolve slowly on their axes at the same time that they turn around the basin that holds the olives. Less than an hour later, the basin is filled with a thick, shiny, unctuous black paste in which the hard little pits of the olives stand out like almonds.

Not all olives make the cut at Moulins Mahjoub, which has expanded production to the extent that the family now buys in olives from neighboring farmers who grow to the family's specifications. At the loading dock, Raouf Mahjoub, Majid's older brother, is supervising the arrival of a load from a small farmer who hopes to sell the two burlap sacks of olives that straddle his motorbike like saddle bags. Raouf says nothing, but he looks glum as he silently extends an index finger and moves it back and forth in the universal gesture: Negative. Why? Too old, he explains, and too dirty. "I could press them for him but it would just mess up my own oil. And he shouldn't keep them in burlap bags. The olives heat up and start to spoil."

Once the olives are reduced to a paste by the crushing stones, the paste is spread in thick ribbons on circular plastic mats—they used to be woven of hemp—called *scourtins*. The mats, which are about four feet in diameter, are then stacked one atop the other to make a tall column that is then transferred to a hydraulic press. The press exerts a gentle pressure—so gentle the olive paste doesn't risk heating and spoiling—and then, slowly, slowly, slowly, the oil begins to ooze out and trickle, drop by precious drop, down the sides of the stack. What actually exudes is a combination of oil and vegetable water, for an olive can be as much as 80 to 90 percent liquid, apart from the oil, depending to some degree on how much rain fell during the growing season. That water has to be separated from the oil, either by centrifuging it the way skim milk and cream are separated, or simply letting the oil rise to the top and skimming it off.

The process of making oil could not be simpler: Crush, press, separate, then store the finished oil in a cool, dark place, a stainless steel or cement tank or, at old-fashioned mills like the Mahjoubs', in immense glazed terra-cotta jars. Some producers filter the oil before the final storage, others prefer to leave it thick and slightly cloudy (with both arguing that their own way preserves the oil longer). This is the way olive oil has been produced all over the Mediterranean from time immemorial. If you go to one or another of the great Roman sites in Tunisia—to Sbeitla in the heart of the country, or Dougga and Bulla Reggia, in the far west near the Algerian border—you will see remains of Roman mills that in essence are not very different from the Mahjoub mill in Tébourba. The source of power for crushing and pressing, however, has evolved. Once upon a time, it was slaves who turned the wheels, and later donkeys and horses. At the desert oasis of Matmata, I've even seen a blindfolded camel turning the wheel that crushes the olives. But the process itself remains unchanged.

There are two critical elements in all of this. One is speed, for olives, like any fruit, begin to deteriorate as soon as they are harvested. Pressing within 48 hours of harvest is the standard for extra-virgin oil, but less is better as the Mahjoubs have shown. And while a peach with a slight bruise may still be a pretty good peach, an olive similarly afflicted will very quickly affect the entire batch of oil, giving it the unmistakable flavor of mold and rancidity and rendering it useless for anything but the refinery. The other crucial factor is temperature, for nothing damages the quality of an oil faster than high temperatures. This may be where the misleading term "first cold pressing" originated. For extra-virgin oil, which is the only kind of oil worth considering, there is one pressing and only one, and it is always at ambient temperatures, which is to say, the natural temperature of the mill. There was a time when unscrupulous producers, or poor farmers whose families depended on oil for their daily needs, went back to the mill again and again, pouring boiling water over the olive paste to heat it in order to extract every last molecule of oil, oil which was degrading a little more each time it went through this process. But that time, fortunately, is in the past.

And with the very latest milling technology, it is no longer necessary at all. Moulins Mahjoub in fact is something of a relic in itself, although there are still hundreds of similar mills, dotted all over the Mediterranean. More and more, however, those who can afford it, either alone or in a cooperative with other growers, are turning to continuous cycle machinery made of stainless steel that operates something like a giant bread machine—you put olives in one end, push a button, and, after a discreet period of time, out the other end comes olive oil.

As a general principle, I tend to favor artisanal technologies over anything that smacks, however lightly, of industrial processing. Yet this continuous-cycle oil press is revolutionizing olive-oil production, and making more and more high-quality oil available for consumers for a number of reasons. It's fast, meaning there are fewer delays at the mill when growers arrive and have to wait, with the traditional process, sometimes for days for their place in line to come up. It's easy to clean between pressings, meaning that the producer doesn't risk having his fine oil contaminated by a neighbor's bad stuff, which might have impregnated the mats used in the traditional pressing. Finally, it's easier to control the temperature of the entire pressing from start to finish and make certain it stays at the low end of the thermometer, whereas with the traditional process, friction alone, if not scrupulously controlled, can sometimes raise the temperature to unacceptable levels.

Jean-Benoît Hugues, in partnership with his wife, Cathérine Brunier, makes an exquisite extra-virgin olive oil called Castelas in the Maussanes region of Provence in southern France. He prefers a modern, closed-circuit, continuous-cycle press over the traditional, old-fashioned stone mills that are still used in much of this oil-producing region. "The closed circuit prevents oxidation," he said, "and it keeps the oil very, very clean. In the old way, with granite rollers, you get 45 minutes of exposure to air. Using this system, we take just 24 hours from hand-picking the olives to turning out oil."

The Hugues' oil, which has a deliciously herby flavor, almost like green artichokes but with a nutty almond-like roundness to it, is unfiltered, Cathérine explains, the better to preserve its character, and, no, to the contrary, unfiltered oil does not go rancid more quickly. Their farm is small, compared to the Mahjoubs', just 12 hectares (about 30 acres), spread over the sunny southern slopes of the Alpilles at Mouriès and Saint-Rémy-de-Provence. These are mostly *salonenque* olives with some *verdale, aglandau* (also called *beruguette*), and *grossane* included. All four varieties are permitted in the Appellation Contrôlée for the Vallée des Baux de Provence where their groves are located. (These *appellations contrôlées*, like the *denominaciones de origen* in Spain and the *denominazioni di origine* in Italy, are official designations of quality from the European Community, an attempt to bring the same rationality to olive oil production that has helped make sense of wine.)

Not everyone agrees with the Hugues and me about the virtues of modern processing. Traditional producers, the Mahjoubs among them, are firmly convinced that the old style produces superior oil. "As with all delicate aromas," Majid said, "whether tea or tobacco or olives, the first perfumes that emerge are the best, richest in aroma and flavor." But an olive mill, whether traditional or new-style, is an expensive investment and all that heavy machinery, not to mention the land it sits on, is used, moreover, only about three months out of the year. If the new system allows oil producers to make more oil better and faster, it stands to reason that more of them will be turning to this in the future.

In any case, Jean-Benoît is fully as close to his traditions as Mahjid is to his own. I said good-bye to the Hugues in a grove of salenenques, big old trees with trunks as gnarled as any in a van Gogh landscape. In the moment before departing, Jean Benoît spread his arms, then turned them palms up, like an Old Testament prophet: "When I'm out here with these old trees," he said, "I think a lot about the generations who came before me, those who tended these groves. And then I think about the generations to come. There's a continuous line that runs from the past into the future, and I see myself as a guardian, a keeper, just a link between the generations. I'm the keeper for the moment, that's all."

WITH ITS KNOBBY, TWISTED BRANCHES and silvery leaves, the olive tree is embedded as deep in the history and mythology of the Mediterranean as it is in the landscape. Wherever you go around the shores of the Inner Sea, whether hill country, desert, or coastal plain, you come across olives—sometimes single trees, half-wild with neglect, clinging to bleached hillsides, their trunks split and warped with time, at other times, a whole landscape of pristinely pruned and regimented olive groves springing from bare earth and marching to the horizon, row upon row until the mind grows dizzy at the prospect.

Olive trees are symbols of longevity, and they truly can grow to be very old, perhaps not going quite back to the time of Christ, or the time of Homer, or the time when Athena gave the gift of the olive to her adopted city Athens (though trees of that age have all been pointed out to me at times), but often decades old and sometimes many centuries. Although they're probably not original to the Mediterranean, the nature of the tree is well adapted to a Mediterranean climate of long, hot, dry summers and brief, cool, rainy winters. And they eventually recover even from extremes of heat or cold. In the terrible January of 1986, olive trees in many parts of Tuscany froze so hard their branches snapped, and some growers despaired of ever producing oil again. Yet, within a few years, a decade at most, the stunted stumps had thrown up sturdy new branches that, when properly pruned, completely disguised the scars of trauma. Drought is less of a problem since olive trees are able to reduce transpiration through their leaves, conserving precious moisture during the dry Mediterranean summer; moreover, the main or tap root of the tree goes deep down, ten or twelve feet into the soil, where even during the dryest months there's still some moisture to be found.

If the olive tree symbolizes the Mediterranean landscape, nothing symbolizes Mediterranean culture and cuisine quite like olive oil. Since ancient times it has been not just food, but balm for the sick, the victor's prize (at the original Olympic games, the winner's award was often liquid gold in the form of a jug of oil), unguent for cleansing the skin, and a principal source of light, for lamps were fueled with olive oil. The Mediterranean's three great religions all recognize its importance. It's no accident that olive oil provides the chrism for Christian baptism and anointing the dying, or that the miracle celebrated at the festival of Hanukkah commemorates the supply of olive oil found to light the temple lamps. A sura from the Koran praises the olive: "A sacred tree, the olive," the Prophet says, "which has an oil so clear that it would give light even if no spark were put to it."

Archaeology confirms the importance of olive oil in the ancient Mediterranean. At the palace site of Knossos, just outside modern Iráklion on the island of Crete, the great terra-cotta storage vessels, their walls three inches thick, in which the Minoan dynasties stocked their wealth of olive oil, still stand. Olive oil was one of the early words translated from the ancient Linear B texts, those warehouse inventories written in the proto-Greek language of the Mycenaeans from Pylos on the Greek mainland. Recently Israeli archaeologists uncovered the archaic Palestinian site of Ekron, which in about 700 B.C.E. was one of the largest olive oil–producing centers in the entire Mediterranean. (The methods used at Ekron, which can be seen with unusual clarity, are not very different from those used at Moulins Mahjoub.) Even in early antiquity, olive oil was transported all over the Mediterranean and beyond, thousands of miles from production centers like Pylos and Ekron and Knossos. Much later, huge quantities of oil were shipped from Spain to Rome: Monte Testaccio, along the Tiber in Trastevere, within the present city limits of Rome, is an artificial mountain of pottery shards from some 40 million amphorae, most of them from Spain, shipped to the imperial capital to provide oil for both aristocratic and common tables—as well as to light lamps and cleanse bodies.

S PAIN IS STILL THE WORLD'S largest producer of olive oil, and within Spain, the province of Jaén in Andalucia is the largest production area. Columela, the Latin agronomist from the first century C.E., himself a native Andalucian, described Spanish olive oil thus: "It has a pleasant taste and smell; it is not greasy; greenish in color, it is reminiscent of the fragrance of a fresh olive." This is still a good overall description of Spanish oil today. But within Spain there are hundreds of varieties, some of which are entirely feral and may number no more than a half dozen trees, relics of a more productive past. (Because of the olive's natural longevity, even on farms that have been abandoned for centuries, old olive trees may survive if not flourish.) Others are standard varieties, like the *picudo/picual* that gives Andalucian oils a typically intense, almost aggressively grassy flavor with a characteristic bitter finish, or the *arbequina* olive that is almost universal in the northeastern region of Catalonia and makes oils with a rounded fruitiness and a distinctive nutty flavor, as if the almonds that are interplanted in the olive groves had lent the olives some of their perfume.

Olive oils have a wide range of flavors, varying from one region to the next, sometimes from one valley to the next, and as with fine wines, the particular variety of fruit is only part of the story. In fact, in most regions, oils are a blend of local varieties. Most Tuscan oil, for instance, is blended from at least three (*frantoio, moraiolo, leccino*) with sometimes a fourth, *pendolino*, added. In Andalucia, the *hoji-blanco* adds sweetness and softness to the sometimes too robust *picudo/picual*. But beyond variety, oils vary, like wine, with climate and terrain, with cultivation methods, and, of course, with the way the olives are handled from harvest through to the final bottling. *Terroir* is not as significant with olives as it is with wine, but it certainly plays its part. Minerals in the soil, the amount of rain that fell, or the temperature during blossoming (too much rain, too great a cold spell, will inhibit pollination by bees), the maturity of the individual berries at harvest—all are factors that go into the final flavor mix.

Once upon a time, people knew only their own oil, that is, the oil produced in their own region or provided by their own grocer who bought his oil year after year from the same producer. In oil-producing regions that is still true, and a kitchen in the southeastern Italian region of Puglia would no more think of using a Tuscan oil than a Spanish cook would use an oil from Morocco or Provence. Away from the Mediterranean, though, there's a strong appreciation of the great variety of oils from all over the Mediterranean, as well as from California, New Zealand, Australia, South Africa—all regions of the world with the Mediterranean-like climate that is ideal for olive trees.

The reason for this spread of olive cultivation is simple. Olive oil is in demand and not just as a chic ingredient. It also has been shown conclusively that olive oil is a healthful product, one that is at least in part (but a major part) responsible for the extraordinarily low rates of chronic diseases in places like Crete and Puglia, where the consumption of olive oil is traditionally very high and that of other types of fat almost nil. As a monounsaturated fat, olive oil lowers harmful LDL (low-density lipoprotein) cholesterol and maintains or increases the good HDL (high-density lipoprotein) cholesterol. Moreover, extra-virgin olive oil (but not refined oil—see box, page 60) is rich in polyphenols, indicators of antioxidants present in the oil that act as scavengers in the blood, scooping up the free radicals that we all produce just by the very act of being alive, but that increase with activities like smoking or breathing polluted air.

With so many oils to choose from, how is an ordinary consumer to distinguish among them? It isn't easy. The best advice, to my mind, is simply to experiment, trying many different oils over a period of time, buying in small quantities when possible and keeping in mind that price is no guarantee of quality—often, in fact, price represents the high cost of fancy packaging. Tuscan oils have a high reputation among North American consumers, at least in part because Tuscan producers have been smart marketers of their finest oils. But there are many other regions of Italy—I think of Puglia and Sicily, two southern regions that are producing excellent oils now after years of selling oil as a bulk commodity. Beyond Italy, there are magnificent oils available in North American markets from Spain and Greece, and often at much more reasonable prices than Italian estate-bottled oils. The Mahjoub oil, under the brand Moulins Mahjoub, can be found in gourmet-products stores.

A good extra-virgin olive oil should carry the taste of healthy, sound, fresh olives, whether it's made from green or mature fruit. Since the process of making oil is so simple, it's impossible to improve on the flavor of the olives themselves—unlike wine, which can be manipulated during fermentation or aging to add complexity. Beyond fruitiness, a sensitive palate will recognize other flavors in olive oil, like the green tomato flavors that are characteristic of some southern Italian oils, or the fresh, grassy flavors of Spanish oils, especially from Andalucia, or the artichoke flavors found in many Tuscan oils.

Bitterness and piquancy are two other positive notes to look for in extra-virgin olive oil. For olive oil beginners, these are the most difficult flavors but they are absolutely not defects. The piquancy of immature olives can be especially strong and, when the oil is fresh, it may give a prickly sensation in the back of the throat—Tuscans, who love this flavor, call it *pizzica*. An ideal oil will have all three of these flavor characteristics—fruitiness, bitterness, piquancy—in balance, but there are many, many fine oils that will be more forward, as wine tasters say, with one characteristic or another. All these flavors, however, diminish over time; an oil that is two years old will have lost most of them. If the olive oil you buy tastes flat and flavorless, it is no doubt an oil that's too old. As long as it's not rancid, it won't be harmful to use in cooking, but it will lack the complexity and flavor interest that makes extra-virgin olive oil the fine product it ought to be.

## OLIVES FOR THE TABLE

Not all olives go to make oil, by any means. In fact, large numbers of olives are harvested, whether as unripened green olives, fully mature black ones, or somewhere in between (when they may be a delightfully mottled rose-streaked green or green-speckled brown) and cured by a variety of methods to make olives for eating, or table olives. Anyone who has ever had the misfortune to pop an olive, green or black, off a tree and into her mouth will understand why curing is necessary. Olives in their natural, uncured state are just plain horrid—there's no other word to describe them. The flavor, from a substance called oleuropein, is so bitter and acrid that it's a wonder anyone every figured out olives could be made edible.

And yet someone did, back in the dim reaches of time, and thereby created a product that became a fundamental food throughout the Mediterranean world, a magical thing to eat on its own and one that lends magic to dishes in which it's an ingredient.

Traditional cures for table olives can be as simple as salt or the sun. Fully ripened black olives are layered with great handfuls of salt in a basket or colander. Or they're simply laid out on wicker trays in the sun. Gradually, over the course of 10 to 14 days, the olives shrivel and yield up the vegetable water that makes up a large percentage of their weight. The flavors become concentrated, more intense, sweeter. Once cured, these wrinkled black olives may be lightly rubbed with oil, which gives them the name "oil-cured olives," but in fact they are salt-cured or sun-cured, pure and simple.

More elaborate ways of curing olives use salt brine, flavored brine, vinegar, citrus juice (bitter orange juice on the island of Crete), olive oil, or various combinations of oil and vinegar, oil and citrus, or oil and brine. Almost always, however, the olives are first slit or cracked and soaked in plain cold water for anywhere from six days to six weeks in order to leach out the bitterness. (If not leached in water, they may be soaked in a wood ash solution to achieve the same result.) The cure helps develop flavors through fermentation, just as in wine or cheese.

The flavor and texture of olives vary enormously depending, first of all, on the variety of olive and its maturity when harvested. Beyond that, however, the method of leaching and the length of time will affect the olives, as will the cure itself and the way the olives are treated after curing. Niçoise olives, small, black, and brine-cured, come mostly from North Africa, not from Nice, and vary in

THREE KINDS OF OLIVE OIL can be found on the shelves of groceries, gourmet shops, and ethnic food markets in North America:

- EXTRA-VIRGIN OLIVE OIL. Extra-virgin olive oil has been obtained mechanically, simply by crushing and pressing the olives. No chemicals or solvents are used during the extraction process, which may be similar to the one used at Moulins Mahjoub, or it can be a more sophisticated continuous-cycle process, or any other mechanical method that simply presses the olives to release the oil and the vegetable water the fruits contain. To qualify as extra-virgin, the oil is submitted to laboratory analysis and to a taste test. The analysis determines the level of free oleic fatty acid, which is a measure of oxidation in the oil; extra-virgin must have 1 percent or less of free oleic fatty acid. To pass the taste test, conducted by a panel of experts, the oil must be organoleptically "perfect," meaning free from any defects of taste or aroma. Earthy, muddy, musty, metallic, soapy, greasy, flat, old, or rancid flavors are all considered defects (with good reason) and even a trace of any of these will disqualify the oil.

- "LIGHT" OLIVE OIL. This is a thoroughly misleading product, invented by marketing experts to suggest that it has fewer calories and grams of fat than other oils, which it does not. It is a refined olive oil that is lighter in flavor and aroma—you could, in fact, say that it is distinguished by neither taste nor smell. As such, it isn't worthy of consideration.

- PURE OLIVE OIL. The final type of oil is usually marketed as just plain olive oil, or sometimes as "pure" olive oil. Oil with less than perfect aroma and flavor, or oil that is too high in free oleic fatty acids to be called extra-virgin, is stripped of aroma and flavor, leaving a tasteless, odorless, colorless oil to which a small amount of extra-virgin is added back to give it some character. There's nothing inherently wrong with this oil—I often use it for deep-fat frying because it's a lot cheaper than extra-virgin—but it's an industrial product, produced for consistency so that the oil you buy today will taste the same as the one you buy tomorrow or next year.

quality, but ideally they are small, rather sweet, and firm-textured. Bella di Cerignola olives, on the other hand, are huge, green (sometimes an alarming green), brine-cured olives from the Pugliese town of Cerignola and only from Cerignola. Purple-black Kalamata olives, from the town of the same name in the Greek Peloponnisos, are steeped in red wine vinegar after curing. In the olive country of southern Spain, every farmwife has her own recipe for *aceitunas aliñadas*, marinated olives. There is even a process, disconcertingly labeled "California style," for magically turning green olives into black ones by soaking them in a lye solution (don't be alarmed—lye-curing is a benign process that has been used in food preparation in many traditional cultures for centuries), then treating them with ferrous-gluconate to give them a uniform dull black color. This process is the source for most industrially canned black olives, often labeled California style, and a good reason for rejecting them since they have very little flavor and a rubbery texture.

When buying olives, look for sound, healthy fruit, and reject any that are wrinkled (unless, of course, they're the deliberately wrinkled black ones) or mushy, and, of course, any that have a film of mold. Most supermarkets now have a selection of olives in the deli section. Ask for a sample before buying to make sure you're getting what you want. Olives can be kept in a cool place outside the refrigerator for several weeks. They should be covered in brine or, if you wish, rinse them of the brine and transfer them to a clean jar. Then add olive oil to cover—with some of the flavorings described on pages 70 and 71, if you wish.

To use olives in cooking, in general and unless the recipe specifies otherwise, it's best to use olives that have had no other flavors added to them in the cure or after. Of course, there are certain specific olives that are indisputably part of a dish—like Kalamata olives in a classic Greek salad—but a salade niçoise is just as good with niçoise olives as it is with Gaeta olives from Italy or wrinkled black sun-cured olives from Morocco.

## 18 GREAT RECIPES USING OLIVES AND OLIVE OIL

Garlic Mayonnaise
*Aïoli*

Monkfish Chowder with Catalan Garlic Mayonnaise
*Gazpachuelo con Allioli*

Middle Eastern Lemon Dressing for Salads

French Mustardy Vinaigrette for Salads

Sicilian Oregano-Spiced Dressing for Grilled Fish
*Salmoriglio*

Marinated Green Olives

Marinated Black Olives

Aintab Meze Salad of Green Olives and Walnuts

Tunisian Grated Carrot Salad with Feta and Black Olives

Turkish Green Beans and Olive Oil

Gazpacho

Elizabeth David's Artichokes

French-Fried Potatoes in Olive Oil
  *Pommes Frites à l'Huile d'Olive*

Tunisian Spicy Meat-Stuffed Olives
  *Marqat Zeitoun Mehshi*

Deep-Fried Battered Shrimp

Tunisian Fried *Briks* with Spiced Meat and Spinach

Oil-Poached Salmon Fillet

Tunisian Orange–Olive Oil Tea Cake
  *Gâteau à l'Orange de Madame Mahjoub*

## COOK'S NOTES

All around the Mediterranean, the best restaurant chefs cook with extra-virgin olive oil, even for deep-fat frying—to the surprise of North American food professionals. "You can't fry with extra-virgin," a top California chef told me flat out. "The smoke point is too low."

That is simply not true.

Exact smoke points are always difficult to measure because particular oils and fats vary greatly, but in general animal fats smoke at lower temperatures than vegetable oils—butter, for instance, especially unclarified butter, smokes at 250° to 300°F, which is why butter is never used for deep-fat frying. While it's true that peanut, canola, and sunflower oils all have higher smoke points than olive oil, the smoke point of extra-virgin olive oil is comfortably above the range of 350° to 380°F that is considered optimal for deep-fat frying.

Home cooks in Mediterranean countries tend to use one oil for every purpose, whether cooking or garnishing, typically an oil produced in the cook's own region, often by the cook's own family. But restaurant chefs, like cooks in North America, often have a couple of different oils at their disposal—one for garnishing, one for general cooking, and often a cheaper one for the oil-consuming process of deep-fat frying. Obviously, cost alone prohibits the use of fine estate-bottled olive oils for cooking; in any case, much of the subtlety and complexity of those oils will be destroyed by heat. Fine, expensive oils should be saved for salads and garnishes. It would be a waste to use these oils for deep-fat frying, or any other kind of cooking for that matter.

But that doesn't mean you should avoid extra-virgin olive oil for cooking altogether. To the contrary, nothing lends more panache to any sort of food preparation than the use of extra-virgin olive oil. To avoid taking out a second mortgage before you start cooking, however, look for less expensive extra-virgin olive oils in health-food stores or shops in ethnic neighborhoods and buy in quantity. A 10-liter tin of good Greek extra-virgin, if bought in a Greek neighborhood shop, will often cost less than half the price of a liter of Tuscan estate-bottled oil, and it will last a long time.

Apart from cooking, there are other uses for extra-virgin olive oil, most often as a garnish for other dishes, everything from hot vegetable soups to cool summer salads. Spanish chefs, noted for their zany ideas, sometimes chill olive oil until it's solid and serve it as a quenelle on a chilled dish, and Martin Berasategui in San Sebastián actually makes olive oil ice cream. I prefer my olive oil in more conventional ways—a tablespoon of oil dribbled over toasted country-style bread is my idea of an ideal breakfast, while fresh green oil on a crisp baked potato, sprinkled with coarse sea salt, is close to heaven.

# Garlic Mayonnaise

## AÏOLI

Traditionally, Provençal aïoli was made with whatever local olive oil was available. Nowadays cooks tend to cut the olive oil with vegetable oil—a bow to modern tastes that find 100 percent olive oil overwhelming. Certainly if you like the taste (and I *do!*), use nothing but olive oil, but make sure it's extra-virgin.

This is the way the Romana sisters, Lucie and Marie, made aïoli one summer afternoon at a family farm near Ampus in the Vars region of eastern Provence. They served it with the Provençal feast called *le grand aïoli,* an enormous spread comprised of poached salt cod, chickpeas, artichokes, hard-cooked eggs, beets, carrots, potatoes, cauliflower, green beans, and speckled snails that had been harvested three weeks earlier, then purged and steamed in white wine, Cognac, and garlic. The feast was served on long tables set up under the cork oaks in front of the farmhouse, and the guests included a poet who, after the third glass of a robust and tannic local red, began to declaim his verses in authentic Provençal and then fell asleep at the table.

The aïoli should be served like a mayonnaise (which in fact it is), with *le grand aïoli,* or more simply with a poached fish or a roasted bird. It's also quite wonderful with boiled new potatoes, and a dollop atop each serving of a traditional Mediterranean seafood stew (see page 360) will add immeasurable depths of flavor.

One caution: All sauces made with raw eggs carry the potential for salmonella infection. If you are worried about this, or if you are preparing a meal for someone who ought to be (infants, old people, pregnant women, etc.), it's best to avoid this and all other preparations made with uncooked eggs. For normal, healthy people, however, there should be no problem.

**Makes about 1⅔ cups**

8 garlic cloves, coarsely chopped

Sea salt

3 large egg yolks, at room temperature

1 to 1½ cups extra-virgin olive oil

POUND THE GARLIC CLOVES with about 1 teaspoon of the salt in a mortar until you have a thick paste. Scrape the mixture into a glass or stainless steel bowl, stir in the egg yolks, and let stand for 5 minutes or so.

SET THE BOWL on a damp kitchen towel to keep it steady and start to whisk in the olive oil, a few drops at a time. Slowly add up to ½ cup of the olive oil, whisking constantly; as the aïoli begins to thicken, you can add the oil in a thin stream. When the aïoli is very thick, stir in 2 teaspoons of the lemon juice. Still whisking, gradually add another ¼ cup of olive oil and 2 more teaspoons of lemon juice, then ¼ cup of olive oil and the remaining lemon juice. Finally, whisk in the vegetable oil, or continue with another ½ cup of olive oil if you prefer. When all the oil has been added, adjust the seasoning of the aïoli, adding lemon juice and/or salt.

2 tablespoons fresh lemon juice, or more to taste

½ cup vegetable oil (optional)

NOTE: If you have a food processor, you can make a lighter aïoli by using 2 whole eggs instead of the 3 egg yolks. It's difficult to make a whole-egg sauce by hand, but the food processor makes it a breeze. Pound the garlic cloves in a mortar with the salt and stir them into the eggs at the end. (Processing garlic in the food processor often makes it bitter.)

VARIATIONS: The above is a modern recipe but Provençal cooks have told me that in older times the aïoli was often thickened with a boiled potato, mashed to a pulp, or with stale bread, softened in water and wrung dry, instead of with eggs. This makes it more like Greek *skordalia*, a garlic sauce that was used especially during Greek Orthodox Lent when eggs were forbidden.

A TRADITIONAL CATALAN ALLIOLI is made with garlic and oil and nothing more. When properly made (but it isn't easy) the sauce is much paler in color than a rich, gold aïoli, and it has an almost waxen texture that is very pleasing. The process is exactly the same as that described above, minus the egg yolks. Most Catalan cooks that I know, however, add at least one egg yolk to help the sauce set up, but traditionalists call that cheating.

IN THE CERDANYA, the mountainous region of Catalonia that stretches across the Pyrenees between France and Spain, an aïoli or allioli is sometimes enriched by the flesh of a couple of quinces, roasted in the oven, then peeled and cored before the flesh is pounded in with the pounded garlic.

BY THE WAY, garlic pounded in a mortar is said to be more digestible than minced garlic.

# Monkfish Chowder with Catalan Garlic Mayonnaise

## GAZPACHUELO CON ALLIOLI

*Gazpachuelo* usually indicates a very plain soup simply enriched with mayonnaise or allioli. This one, from Granada, is quite different—but delicious. It's made with a fish called *cazón*, a kind of small shark that doesn't exist on this side of the Atlantic. I use monkfish instead.

**Makes 6 servings**

6 cups water

2 large yellow-fleshed potatoes, such as Yukon Gold, thickly sliced

2 medium yellow onions, coarsely chopped

Sea salt

Freshly ground black pepper

3 bay leaves

1 tablespoon fresh thyme leaves

1 pound monkfish, cut into chunks

1 teaspoon crushed red ñora peppers, or use New Mexico or ancho peppers

⅔ cup Aïoli (page 64) or home-made mayonnaise

1 teaspoon fresh lemon juice

3 or 4 small scallions, coarsely chopped

1 hard-cooked egg, chopped, for garnish

1 garlic clove, finely minced, for garnish

2 tablespoons finely minced flat-leaf parsley, for garnish

BRING THE WATER TO A SIMMER in a soup kettle. Add potatoes, onions, a big pinch of salt, pepper, bay leaves, and thyme. Cook gently over low heat until the potatoes are just barely tender, about 15 minutes. Add the fish and crushed red peppers and continue cooking until the fish is done—about 6 to 8 minutes.

MEANWHILE, MAKE THE allioli, aïoli, or mayonnaise, according to the recipe directions. When the sauce is thick, whisk in the extra lemon juice. If the sauce is too thin, continue whisking or processing while you add a little more olive oil to bring it to the right consistency.

REMOVE THE SOUP from the heat. Stir about a tablespoon of hot soup stock into the mayonnaise and keep adding tablespoons of stock until the mayonnaise is close to the temperature of the soup. (If you add the hot stock all at once, you risk curdling the mayonnaise.) When the mayonnaise is quite hot, stir it into the soup, using a wooden spoon to blend it in thoroughly. Return the soup to the stove over very low heat and gradually, stirring frequently, heat the soup until it is very hot. Watch the soup carefully and do not let it come to a boil as the egg will curdle. Keep cooking the soup, stirring constantly, until it has thickened to a smooth cream.

SERVE IMMEDIATELY, garnished with the hard-cooked egg, garlic, and parsley.

**VARIATION:** Instead of the aïoli or mayonnaise, add ⅔ cup Rouille (page 274) or Romesco (page 276).

## SALAD DRESSINGS: VINAIGRETTE AND SALMORIGLIO

In the olive oil world of the Mediterranean, ranch, blue cheese, and Thousand Island dressings are unknown. It is considered sufficient to dress a salad with three parts of fine, fresh extra-virgin olive oil and one part of good red wine vinegar or freshly squeezed lemon juice. The only additions tolerated are salt and pepper, and perhaps a bit of garlic; sometimes in France a dollop of good mustard is stirred in too.

# Middle Eastern Lemon Dressing for Salads

 This is the way I learned to make salad dressing in the Middle East where, because of Islamic prohibitions, wine vinegar is not much used. It's the best dressing I know of. This will make enough for a green salad for four.

COMBINE THE GARLIC AND SALT in a salad bowl. Using the back of a soupspoon, crush the garlic and salt to a paste. Stir in the olive oil and the lemon juice; taste and adjust the seasoning. Pile the salad ingredients on top and mix with the dressing just before serving.

**Makes about ¼ cup, enough for a salad for 4**

½ small garlic clove, finely minced

1 scant teaspoon sea salt

3 tablespoons extra-virgin olive oil

1 tablespoon freshly squeezed lemon juice

# French Mustardy Vinaigrette for Salads

A proper vinaigrette, of course, is made with vinegar. Here are the proportions. Because mustard is often quite salty, salt should be added at the end, after tasting.

**Makes ¼ cup, enough for a salad for 4**

1 scant teaspoon Dijon mustard

1 tablespoon aged red wine vinegar

3 tablespoons extra-virgin olive oil

Salt (optional)

Freshly ground black pepper

MIX THE MUSTARD AND VINEGAR to a cream in the bottom of the salad bowl. Using a fork or a small wire whisk, vigorously beat in the olive oil. Taste and add salt, if necessary, and pepper. Pile the salad ingredients on top and mix them with the dressing just before serving.

**VARIATION:** Connoisseurs like to add a very few drops of balsamic vinegar to the dressing—not the fiercely expensive condiment, *aceto balsamico tradizionale*, which should be reserved for strawberries, ice cream, and Parmigiano-Reggiano cheese, but the less costly substitute (see page 199), called just balsamic vinegar (*aceto balsamico*).

# Sicilian Oregano-Spiced Dressing for Grilled Fish

**SALMORIGLIO**

 A Sicilian *salmoriglio,* in my experience, is served with fish and only with fish, especially with grilled fish.

COMBINE THE OIL AND LEMON JUICE, beating with a fork. Add salt and pepper to taste, then beat in a big pinch of dried oregano, crumbling it with your fingers to release the flavor and aroma. Serve immediately.

**Makes about ¼ cup, to serve 4 to 6**

3 tablespoons extra-virgin olive oil

1 tablespoon fresh lemon juice

Sea salt and freshly ground black pepper

Dried Sicilian or Greek oregano (*rígani*)

## MARINATING OLIVES

Marinating cured olives is an old tradition. In *De Agri Cultura*, his treatise on agriculture, the Roman statesman Cato, who lived in the third and second centuries B.C.E., has directions for "a confection of green, ripe, and mottled olives" (*epityrum album nigrum variumque*): "Remove the stones from green, ripe, and mottled olives, and season as follows: chop the flesh, and add oil, vinegar, coriander, cummin, fennel, rue, and mint. Cover with oil in an earthen dish, and serve."

# Marinated Green Olives

The following is my own recipe, but feel free to vary flavors to suit your palate with any number of aromatics. Just remember that less is always more—don't use more than three or four flavors in any one batch; otherwise you risk confusing the palate. The point of the marinade is to accentuate the flavor of the olives, not to disguise it.

**Makes 1½ to 2 cups olives**

About 8 ounces brine-packed green olives, with the pits

3 to 4 bay leaves

Big pinch of dried Greek oregano (*rigani*), wild thyme, or *za'atar* (Middle Eastern wild thyme)

1 teaspoon sea salt

Big pinch of fennel seeds, lightly crushed in a mortar to crack them

2 to 3 garlic cloves, peeled and cut into 2 to 3 pieces each

½ cup white wine vinegar

Extra-virgin olive oil

DRAIN THE OLIVES and discard the brine.

WASH A WIDE-MOUTH 2-cup glass canning jar (a Ball or Mason jar) by filling it with boiling water and letting it stand for 5 to 10 minutes, then draining it. (You can also sterilize a jar, if it's convenient to do so, by putting it through the rinse cycle of an automatic dishwasher.)

DROP A BAY LEAF into the jar, then add about one-third of the olives. Combine the oregano, salt, and fennel seeds in a mortar and crush gently to release the flavors. Add a good pinch of this to the olives along with a scattering of garlic pieces. Add another bay leaf and another third of the olives, then crushed aromatics and garlic as above. Continue until you've added all the olives and all the aromatics. Bring the wine vinegar to a boil and pour it over the olives in the jar. Add olive oil to top up the jar, making sure the olives are completely covered with liquid. Screw the jar lid on very tight, give the jar a shake, and set it aside in a cool place. Marinate for 10 days or so, tipping the jar every now and then to redistribute the aromatics.

THE OLIVES SHOULD BE CONSUMED within 3 to 4 weeks.

# Marinated Black Olives

Use either salt-cured (sometimes marketed as "oil-cured") or brine-cured olives with this recipe. Salt-cured olives will plump somewhat with the marinade.

IF NECESSARY, DRAIN THE OLIVES, and discard the brine. Wash a wide-mouth 2-cup glass canning jar (a Ball or Mason jar) by filling it with boiling water and letting it stand for 5 to 10 minutes, then draining it. (You can also sterilize a jar, if it's convenient to do so, by putting it through the rinse cycle of an automatic dishwasher.)

FILL THE JAR WITH OLIVES—8 ounces of olives should almost fill a 2-cup (1-pint) canning jar, leaving a little space for the aromatics. Add the cumin and dried thyme, crumbling it in your fingers to release the flavors. In a small saucepan, combine the garlic, orange zest, vinegar, salt, and 1 cup water. Bring to a rolling boil. Fill the canning jar to within an inch of the top (you may not need all the liquid). Top off with olive oil. Screw the jar lid on very tight, give the jar a shake, and set it aside in a cool place. Marinate for 10 days or so, tipping the jar every now and then to redistribute the aromatics.

THE OLIVES SHOULD BE CONSUMED within 3 to 4 weeks.

**Makes 1½ to 2 cups olives**

8 to 12 ounces black olives, with their pits

½ teaspoon ground cumin

1 teaspoon dried thyme, crumbled

3 whole garlic cloves, peeled

Zest of 1 orange, slivered

2 tablespoons red wine vinegar

1 tablespoon sea salt

Water

Extra-virgin olive oil

# Aintab Meze Salad of Green Olives and Walnuts

Aintab, the old Arab name for Gaziantep, is a Turkish city that sits in the triangle of land between the Syrian border and the Euphrates, a region rich with historical and culinary interest. This green olive salad or dip, served on the meze table with wedges of flat Arab bread for dipping, is typical of the region—indeed, it's hard to say whether it originated in Arab or in Turkish kitchens. Maybe both.

Pomegranate syrup (*dibsl roumann*) and Middle Eastern red pepper paste, as well as crushed and ground red peppers, can be found in shops in Middle Eastern neighborhoods, or by mail order from Adriana's Caravan or Kalustyan's (see pages 415–16).

The olives and walnuts should be chopped finely enough to be easily scooped up with a bit of flatbread but not reduced to a mince or puree. Toast the bread, if you wish, to make it more scoopable. This olive salad is often served with a meze selection that includes hummus bi tahini and baba ghanouj.

If the olives are very salty, cover them with boiling water, let them sit for 30 minutes, then drain.

CHOP THE OLIVES AND WALNUTS together to blend them.

COMBINE THE OLIVE-NUT MIXTURE in a bowl with the roasted pepper, parsley, scallions, and onion. In a separate small bowl, combine the olive oil, pomegranate syrup, and lemon juice. Add the cumin, red pepper paste, sugar, and black pepper and beat with a fork. Pour this dressing over the olive-nut mixture and mix well. Taste and adjust the seasoning, adding more pomegranate syrup or lemon juice, if necessary. Cover the bowl with plastic wrap and set aside in a cool (not refrigerated) place for several hours or overnight.

MEANWHILE, TASTE THE CHEESE. If it's very salty, let it soak in tepid water until you are ready to serve. When you are ready to serve, drain the cheese and crumble or grate it. Add the cheese to the olive mixture and toss with a fork to mix well. Serve at once.

VARIATION: If you can find fresh pomegranates in good condition, add pomegranate seeds to the mix for an authentic touch.

**Makes about 2½ cups**

1 cup coarsely chopped pitted green olives

⅔ cup coarsely chopped walnuts, or combined walnuts and pistachios

1 fresh sweet red pepper, roasted (see page 410) and finely chopped

½ cup minced flat-leaf parsley (leaves only)

6 scallions, chopped (¼ cup)

1 tablespoon chopped red onion

2 tablespoons extra-virgin olive oil

2 tablespoons pomegranate syrup, or more to taste

1 tablespoon fresh lemon juice, or more to taste

½ teaspoon ground cumin

½ teaspoon Middle Eastern red pepper paste, or ½ teaspoon ground red Middle Eastern pepper (Aleppo pepper, Turkish pepper), or to taste

Pinch of sugar

Freshly ground black pepper

4 ounces Lebanese white cheese, or use Greek feta

# Tunisian Grated Carrot Salad with Feta and Black Olives

**Makes 6 servings**

5 to 6 medium carrots, peeled

1 garlic clove, chopped

1 teaspoon ground caraway seeds

Sea salt to taste

1 tablespoon freshly squeezed lemon juice

1 tablespoon harissa (see page 280) or hot red pepper paste, or to taste

¼ cup extra-virgin olive oil

¼ cup chopped, pitted black olives, preferably dry-cured

¼ pound feta cheese, crumbled

USING THE LARGE HOLES of a grater, grate the carrots into a bowl. In a mortar, pound the garlic to a paste with the caraway seeds and salt. Stir in the lemon juice and harissa, mixing well; then add the olive oil. Beat with a fork or a small wire whisk to amalgamate and immediately pour over the grated carrots. Set aside at room temperature for about 30 minutes to develop the flavors.

JUST BEFORE SERVING, stir in the olives and cheese.

# Turkish Green Beans and Olive Oil

Although we don't see much Turkish olive oil in North American shops, the country is a major producer, so it's no wonder that an entire branch of Turkish cuisine, called *zeytinyağlilar,* is given over to the art of cooking vegetables in olive oil—eggplant, beans, leeks, stuffed peppers, grape leaves, and tomatoes, even pumpkin and Jerusalem artichokes. Green beans prepared this way are a favorite. Don't be put off by the quantity of oil in this recipe—it lends a great deal of flavor and is not at all oily.

If you use canned tomatoes, which is perfectly acceptable, drain them well before and after chopping to avoid excess liquid in the pan.

COMBINE THE ONIONS, garlic, and olive oil in a saucepan and set over medium-low heat. Cook, stirring occasionally, until the onions are soft, about 5 minutes. Do not let the onions brown. When the onions are soft, stir in the tomatoes and green beans and mix well. Cover and cook for about 10 minutes, or until the beans are just starting to get tender, shaking the pan occasionally. Add the water to the pan, along with a pinch of sugar and a pinch of salt. Cover again and continue cooking over low heat until the beans are very tender, about 30 minutes. Don't worry about overcooking as the beans should be almost falling apart in the rich tomato sauce.

NOTE: This combination is delicious as a topping for pasta.

**Makes 4 servings**

1 cup yellow onions, finely chopped (about 8 ounces)

1 garlic clove, finely chopped

½ cup extra-virgin olive oil

1 cup chopped, peeled tomatoes

1 pound slender, young green beans, cut into 2-inch lengths

½ cup water

Sugar

Sea salt

# Gazpacho

The most famous soup, possibly the most famous dish, in Andalucia, is gazpacho. Today, it is made with tomatoes, but when British writer Richard Ford was traveling through Spain in the mid–nineteenth century, it was made of "onions, garlic, cucumbers, chilies, all chopped up very small and mixed with crumbs of bread, and then put into a bowl of oil, vinegar, and fresh water. Reapers and agricultural laborers could never stand the sun's fire without this cooling acetous diet.... In Andalucia, during the summer, a bowl of gazpacho is commonly ready in every house of an evening, and is partaken of by every person who comes in."

Actually, there are many gazpachos, not all made with bread (some, like *ajo blanco*, the white gazpacho from Malaga, are made with crushed almonds), not all served cold (*Gazpachuelo*, which is thickened with mayonnaise—see page 66—is usually hot). The following is a version I learned to make in Jerez, the sherry capital of southern Spain; it is blended with an immersion blender to make a delicious cream that still has some texture to it; if you want a smooth cream like that served in restaurants, use a liquidizing blender, and strain through a sieve afterward to make it even smoother.

**Makes 8 servings**

Two 1-inch-thick slices stale country-style bread, or more as needed

1 fresh sweet red pepper, roasted and peeled (see page 410), or 1 canned imported pimiento de Piquillo

3½ pounds ripe tomatoes, peeled and coarsely chopped

2 plump garlic cloves, coarsely chopped

1 small red onion, coarsely chopped

1 cucumber, peeled, seeded, and coarsely chopped

IF THE CRUSTS ON THE BREAD are very firm, cut them off. Tear the bread into chunks and combine in a bowl with cold water to cover. Leave for about 5 minutes, then remove the bread and squeeze it hard to rid it of excess water. Tear apart the bread into shreds and set aside.

COMBINE THE RED PEPPER, tomatoes, garlic, onion, and cucumber in a bowl. Blend with an immersion blender while you gradually beat in the oil and then the vinegar.

ADD THE SOFTENED BREAD to the vegetables, continuing to mix with the blender. Blend in the cumin, pimentón, and chili. Continue blending until the mixture has reached the consistency you want. (If it's too thick, add a little cold water; if too thin, add more softened bread.) Taste and add salt and sugar. Adjust the flavor by adding more vinegar or seasonings, as needed.

THE SOUP CAN BE SERVED immediately, or it can be refrigerated for 30 minutes or more before serving. Just before serving, top with the garnishes, if using. Or serve the soup with the garnishes in separate bowls for guests to add their own.

VARIATION: *Salmorejo,* the version of gazpacho served in Córdoba, is similar but very thick, more like porridge than soup, but still something you eat with a spoon. To make it, simply double or triple the quantity of softened bread in the recipe above. It is always garnished with chopped hard-cooked eggs and thin strips of Spanish serrano ham.

1 cup extra-virgin olive oil

2 tablespoons aged sherry vinegar, or to taste

½ teaspoon ground cumin, or to taste

1 teaspoon sweet *pimentón* (Spanish paprika), or to taste

1 small dried hot red chili pepper, crushed

Water (optional)

Sea salt

Sugar

A dribble of olive oil

Chopped hard-cooked eggs; chopped green peppers (sweet ones or fresh chilies); diced tomato, cucumber, or red onion (optional)

# Elizabeth David's Artichokes

Mrs. David called these *artichauts à la barigoule,* though they are very different from recipes in Provençal cookbooks—better, too, I think.

This is best with very fresh and rather small artichokes (best of all are the ones in which the choke has yet to develop), but they are devilishly hard to find in North America. If you can find the small artichokes, count on two to a serving; with larger ones, one to a serving will do. Very large artichokes should be cut into quarters. The most important thing, however, is that the artichokes should be as fresh as possible and uniform in size.

Be sure to rub the cut surfaces of the artichokes with a lemon to keep them from blackening. And keep a bowl of acidulated water (water into which the juice of half a lemon has been squeezed) to hold the prepared artichokes until you're ready to cook.

**Makes 6 servings**

12 small or 6 large artichokes
1 lemon, halved, plus more for garnish (optional)
Extra-virgin olive oil (at least 2 cups)
Coarse sea salt

TRIM THE ARTICHOKES, rubbing the cut surfaces with half the lemon. Cut off the stalks, leaving about ½ inch of stem. Remove the outer two or three layers of leaves to get to the tender ones inside. Cut the tops back about an inch or so and if the leaves are very prickly, use scissors to cut the top off each leaf. If the artichokes are very large, with well-developed chokes, you can pull apart the inner leaves and with a serrated grapefruit spoon scrape out the thorny choke. Or cut each into quarters and remove the choke. As each artichoke is prepared, toss it into a bowl of cool water into which you have squeezed the juice of the other lemon half.

WHEN ALL THE ARTICHOKES ARE TRIMMED, set them in a deep, heavy saucepan in which they will all fit comfortably in a single layer. (Be sure the pan is deep enough to accommodate all the oil and water, with room to spare so that oil doesn't spit out all over the stove.) Add olive oil to come halfway up the artichokes, then add water to cover. Set over high heat, uncovered, and bring to a boil. Boil fiercely for 15 to 20 minutes, until the water evaporates and the artichokes start to turn golden and crisp in the oil. (There'll be a good deal of sputtering as the water boils but the noise will stop when it has boiled away.) It's important to maintain a high temperature; otherwise the artichokes will get too soft and fall apart before browning. When the water is all gone, and the sputtering has stopped, turn the artichokes over to brown their tops a little, and continue cooking for no more than 90 seconds.

REMOVE THE ARTICHOKES and arrange them on a serving platter, sprinkling them with salt. Serve immediately. Garnish the platter, if you wish, with lemons.

VARIATION: Medium potatoes, scrubbed but unpeeled, can be cooked in the same way. Six medium potatoes will take approximately 30 minutes.

# French-Fried Potatoes in Olive Oil

## POMMES FRITES À L'HUILE D'OLIVE

Some people claim the best French fries are fried in beef tallow, but I don't think anything beats olive oil, which imparts a subtle, more refreshing flavor to the fries. Obviously, you shouldn't use expensive estate-bottled oil for this. A run-of-the-mill oil will do, as long as it's extra-virgin. Once the oil has been used, let it cool, then strain it and keep it in the refrigerator to use a second and a third time, after which it should be discarded.

Don't try this with new potatoes—they just don't work. Older, starchy potatoes are what you want.

Do use a candy or frying thermometer to make sure of the temperature of the oil. It's important.

**Makes 4 to 6 servings**

2 pounds russet potatoes
4 cups extra-virgin olive oil
Sea salt

HAVE READY A LARGE BOWL OF WATER with several ice cubes in it. Peel the potatoes and cut them with a knife into French fries, that is, about ⅜ inch thick, and put them in the bowl of icy water to soak for 20 to 30 minutes.

HEAT THE OIL in a deep saucepan to 320°F. Drain the potatoes and dry them thoroughly, wrapping them tightly in several layers of paper towels or dish towels to get them very dry.

WHEN THE OIL HAS REACHED 320°F, drop in the potatoes, working in batches so as not to cool down the oil too much, and cook for 3 minutes. Remove and set aside in a colander or on a rack covered with paper towel to drain. You can proceed immediately with the next step or, if it's more convenient, you can wait a couple of hours before continuing, even refrigerating the half-fried potatoes if it's necessary to do so.

WHEN YOU ARE READY TO CONTINUE, heat the oil to 360°F. Again working in batches, drop in the potatoes. This time they should brown and crisp very quickly, in about 1 minute. Remove them as they brown and drain.

SPRINKLE THE FRENCH FRIES liberally with salt and serve immediately.

# Tunisian Spicy Meat-Stuffed Olives

**MARQAT ZEITOUN MEHSHI**

 This is a specialty of the Mahjoub family, often served to honored guests at the family's olive mill in Tébourba, in the countryside west of Tunis. You'll need plump green olives to make the dish—the best are from Moulins Mahjoub, but you could use Bella di Cerignola olives from Puglia or, in fact, any plump brine-cured green olives, as long as they have a good olive flavor. The olives should be opened up and the pits removed, which is easy to do by slitting the fruits lengthwise and gently easing the pit out with a small paring knife. (You can also sometimes find good-quality large green olives already pitted.) The olives should remain intact, but opened out like a book, so that each one can be wrapped around a little of the savory meat and ricotta mixture. If the olives are very salty, cover them with boiling water and set aside for 30 to 40 minutes, then drain. If you don't have any salt-preserved lemon on hand, substitute 1 teaspoon of fresh lemon juice.

**DRAIN THE BEANS.** In a small pot, combine the beans with enough water to cover them by 1 inch. Bring to a boil and simmer gently, covered, until the beans are just tender, 20 to 40 minutes.

**WHILE THE BEANS ARE COOKING,** soak the feta, if using, in cool water to get rid of excess salt.

**MAKE THE TOMATO SAUCE.** Combine the sliced onion and garlic with ½ cup of the oil and sauté very gently over medium-low heat until the onion is soft, about 5 minutes. Add 1 teaspoon of the *tebbil*, the paprika, and salt and pepper to taste. Mix well. Stir in the tomatoes and 1 cup of hot water. When the mixture begins to simmer, cover and cook very gently for about 20 minutes, or until the sauce is quite thick. Add the cooked beans, drained of excess liquid, and mix well. Continue cooking, covered, until the beans are very tender, about 10 minutes longer. Then stir in the lemon and the capers. Remove from the heat and set aside. (This sauce can be made a day ahead of time and

**Makes 6 to 8 servings
(36 to 48 olive balls)**

½ cup dried small white beans, soaked overnight

Water

8 to 12 ounces ricotta salata or feta cheese

½ cup thinly sliced onion (one small onion, sliced)

3 garlic cloves, minced (1 heaping teaspoon)

1¼ to 1¾ cups extra-virgin olive oil

1 teaspoon plus 2 tablespoons *tebbil* (recipe follows)

1 teaspoon sweet Spanish, Tunisian, or Hungarian paprika

Sea salt and freshly ground black pepper

½ cup canned crushed tomatoes

½ salt-preserved lemon (page 44), thinly sliced

1 heaping tablespoon salted capers, rinsed under running water, drained, and chopped

2 cups chopped flat-leaf parsley

1 medium onion, chopped (about ¾ cup)

8 ounces finely ground very lean veal

1 cup fine dry bread crumbs, or more as needed

2 tablespoons freshly grated Gruyère or Emmentaler cheese

4 to 5 large eggs

36 to 48 large green olives, pits removed

¾ cup unbleached all-purpose flour, or more if needed

1 fresh green pepper (poblano is best, but a sweet bell pepper will do)

refrigerated, then brought up to simmering temperature before continuing with the recipe.)

COMBINE THE PARSLEY and chopped onion with ¼ cup of the oil in a small skillet and sauté gently over medium-low heat for 5 to 10 minutes, or until the vegetables are very soft and wilted. Transfer the vegetables to a mixing bowl to cool. When the vegetables are cool enough to handle, add the veal, bread crumbs, grated cheese, and 2 of the eggs. With your hands, knead the mixture well. Drain and crumble the ricotta salata or feta and add to the meat. If the mixture is too wet, add another tablespoon or so of bread crumbs. If it's too dry, beat another egg well and add a tablespoon at a time until it's the right consistency to hold together.

ASSEMBLE THE STUFFED OLIVES by taking a generous tablespoon or so of the stuffing mixture and shaping it over and around the individual fruit. Don't worry if it looks more like a meatball with an olive inside, rather than a perfect olive with a discreet stuffing of meat. The former is better than the latter. When the olives are stuffed, place the flour in one soup plate and beat the remaining 2 eggs in another soup plate. Add ½ cup of the oil to a frying pan and heat to a good frying temperature (about 350°F). Roll each olive in the flour, then in the beaten egg, then in flour again and drop it into the preheated oil. Turn the olives with a fork until thoroughly browned on all sides, 10 to 15 minutes. Remove the olives from the oil and drain briefly on a rack. If the oil blackens and burns because of residue, discard it, wipe out the pan with paper towel, and start again with fresh oil.

MEANWHILE, bring the tomato-bean sauce back to a simmer, adding another 1 cup hot water to the mixture. When all the olive balls have been fried, drop them in the simmering sauce. Cover and let simmer for a final 10 minutes.

WHILE THE OLIVE BALLS are simmering, roast the green pepper over charcoal or gas fire until the skin is thoroughly blackened (see page 410). Peel away the blackened skin and slice the pepper into strips, discarding the seeds, core, and white membranes. Add to the sauce for the last 5 minutes or so of cooking.

TO SERVE, arrange the olive balls on a serving platter and spoon the sauce over the olives.

NOTE: Although not traditional in Tunisia, these olive balls, minus the tomato-bean sauce, also make a delicious appetizer to serve with drinks before a meal.

# Tunisian Aromatic Spice Mixture

### TEBBIL

Every Tunisian family has its own formula for making *tebbil*, an aromatic blend that goes into almost every savory dish. The following is based on the recipe I was given by the Mahjoub sisters. If you live in a dry, sunny climate, you can sun-dry the mixture, but in a humid climate it should be dried in a very low oven. When it is properly dried, the blend can be kept, like any spice mixture, in a glass jar away from heat and light for several months. The proportions, of course, may be varied in any way that pleases your own taste.

COMBINE THE GARLIC, onion, and chili peppers with about a third each of the coriander and caraway seeds. Grind to a coarse mixture in a blender or spice or coffee mill, then combine with the unground remainder of the whole coriander and caraway seeds. Spread in a thin layer on a tray and, if possible, dry in the sun for at least three days, stirring the mixture from time to time and bringing it inside at night to protect it from the evening dew. After three days of sunshine, the mixture should be thoroughly dried.

YOU CAN ALSO DRY THE SPICE mixture in a very low oven (200°F.) with the door set slightly ajar to let the damp air escape. Stir the mixture frequently. It may take six or eight hours to dry thoroughly.

**Makes about 1 cup**

5 to 6 garlic cloves, chopped

1 small onion, chopped

2 dried hot chili peppers, stems discarded

8 tablespoons coriander seeds

2 tablespoons caraway seeds

YOU MAY ALSO COMBINE the two methods, starting off with sun-drying; then, if rain or clouds threaten, bring the tray inside and set it in the oven.

THE ONION AND GARLIC part of the blend must be thoroughly dried; otherwise they risk becoming moldy in storage and spoiling the whole thing.

WHICHEVER METHOD YOU USE, once the mixture is completely dry, it should be ground again to a fine powder. Store it as you would any spices, in tightly sealed glass jars.

PLEASE NOTE that if you don't wish or haven't time to make *tebbil*, you can substitute a mixture of dried chili peppers, coriander seeds, and caraway in proportions more or less as in the recipe above—for instance, a small dried chili pepper, 4 tablespoons of coriander seeds, and a tablespoon of caraway seeds, grinding them in a miniblender or a coffee grinder as described. It won't be quite the same, but it will still be a fragrant addition to stews and sauces.

# Deep-Fried Battered Shrimp

 The batter used is the one Italian cooks call *pastella*, the simplest batter of all. Use it in early summer to make a *fritto misto di verdura*, a mixed fry of vegetables, with sliced zucchini, zucchini blossoms, very tender green beans (haricots verts), snow peas, and immature tomatoes cut into wedges. Radish leaves are deliciously spicy done this way. In winter, I use this batter to fry small, sweet Maine shrimp in their season, but it's also a good batter for scallops. Large scallops should be cut into quarters, but the exquisite, small Nantucket scallops are delicious whole on their own.

RINSE THE SHRIMP and pat dry on paper towels.

MIX TOGETHER the warm water and ½ teaspoon salt in a bowl and set aside until the salt is dissolved. Place about ½ cup of flour in a flour sifter. Gradually sift the flour over the salted water while you stir it with a wire whisk or a fork. Keep sifting and stirring until you have a batter that is about the consistency of heavy cream. There should be no lumps in the batter.

IN A FRYING PAN, heat the olive oil to 360°F, or until a small cube of bread, dropped in the hot fat, rapidly turns golden and crisp.

ONE BY ONE, dip the shrimp in the batter, let the excess drip off, and drop into the hot fat. Don't overcrowd the pan—too many shrimp will lower the oil temperature below optimum frying heat. Small shrimp will cook very quickly, in a minute or less. When they are light gold and crisp, remove with a slotted spoon and transfer to a rack covered with paper towels to drain.

SERVE IMMEDIATELY, as soon as all the shrimp are done, sprinkled with salt and with lemon quarters to squeeze over them, if you wish.

**NOTE:** To make a special garnish, take sprigs of flat-leaf parsley, just the upper parts where the three leaf stems come together, dip in the batter and deep-fry. Scatter over the top of the fried shrimp.

**Makes 4 servings**

2 pounds fresh unfrozen shrimp, peeled

1 cup warm water

Sea salt

Unbleached all-purpose flour

1 cup extra-virgin olive oil

Lemon quarters, to garnish (optional)

# Tunisian Fried *Briks* with Spiced Meat and Spinach

A *brik* (sometimes spelled *brique*) is a Tunisian snack food that is related, in name and in style, to Turkish boreks. If you were to make these in Tunisia, you'd use a special type of exquisitely thin, unleavened pastry called *malsouqa*. If, on the other hand, you were to make them in Turkey, you would use either a regular short-crust pastry (page 409) or thin phyllo dough. Since good-quality frozen phyllo is readily available in North American markets, that's what I opt for in this recipe.

**Makes 12 to 16 *briks***

1 tablespoon unsalted butter

1 small onion, finely chopped

8 ounces lean ground beef, veal, or lamb

Coarse salt and freshly ground black pepper

¼ teaspoon ground cinnamon

½ teaspoon ground red Middle Eastern pepper (Aleppo pepper, Turkish pepper)

¼ teaspoon ground allspice

1 pound spinach

4 medium eggs

½ cup finely chopped flat-leaf parsley, leaves only

Extra-virgin olive oil for deep-frying

1 one-pound package frozen phyllo dough

Lemon quarters, to garnish

TO PREPARE THE STUFFING, melt the butter in a skillet over medium-low heat and gently cook the onion until it is tender but not brown, about 5 minutes. Add the ground meat with the salt, black pepper, cinnamon, red peppers, and allspice. Mix well and continue to cook over medium-low heat for about 10 minutes, until the meat has lost its red color, stirring frequently and breaking the meat up. Use a slotted spoon to drain the meat from the fat in the pan. Transfer the meat to a bowl.

RINSE THE SPINACH WELL, trim away tough stems, and cut into slivers. Transfer to a clean skillet or saucepan and cook, covered, over medium-low heat in the water clinging to the leaves until very soft and tender. Drain thoroughly, pressing to release excess juices, and mix with the meat.

BEAT THE EGGS with the parsley. In a small skillet, heat 1 tablespoon of the oil, swirling it around the pan. Add the eggs and swirl them to cook thoroughly, making a flat omelet that is about ¼ inch thick and cooked all the way through. Cut the omelet into rectangles about ½ inch by 1 inch.

THE MEAT, spinach, and omelet may be prepared ahead and refrigerated until you are ready to make the *briks*.

OPEN A PHYLLO DOUGH SHEET and cut it into rectangles approximately 8 inches by 4 inches. At the edge of a rectangle, place a heaping tablespoon of the meat-spinach stuffing, topping with a piece of omelet. Fold the top over the stuffing once, then fold in the two sides and roll toward the opposite end to make a fat roll. Repeat until all the filling mixture is used. Phyllo dough that is not in use should be covered lightly with plastic wrap or a dampened kitchen towel to keep the dough from drying out. Any dough that is unused at the end, may be returned to the freezer, well wrapped for storage.

IN A FRYING PAN, heat 1 cup of oil to frying temperature, about 360°F, or when a small cube of bread dropped into the hot oil rapidly turns golden and crisp. Add the rolls, a few at a time, and fry, turning once, until golden on both sides, 5 to 7 minutes to a side.

SERVE IMMEDIATELY, with lemon quarters to squeeze over.

IF YOU WISH to use short-crust pastry instead of the phyllo, see page 409. Chill the dough for 30 minutes before rolling it out as thinly as possible between two sheets of waxed paper. Cut the dough into circles about 3 inches in diameter. Put 1 heaping tablespoon of stuffing on one side of a circle, top with a piece of omelet, then fold the other side of the dough over to make a crescent, moistening the edges of the pastry to seal it. Fry the pastry as above.

# Oil-Poached Salmon Fillet

Oil-poached salmon is a rich dish and needs no garnish unless it's a few drops of lemon juice. To offset the richness, serve the fish on a bed of bitter greens (such as broccoli rabe) or spinach, lightly steamed, then sautéed in a little olive oil with some finely minced garlic and red chili pepper. The contrast between the succulent, rosy flesh of the salmon and the deep color of the greens is as delicious as the flavors. But you don't have to use salmon with this—cod, haddock, or any firm-textured fish will do just as well.

You will need to use a frying or candy thermometer with this recipe because it's important that the temperature never go above 115°F.

**Makes 6 servings**

2-pound fillet fresh salmon

Sea salt and freshly ground black pepper

2 cups extra-virgin olive oil, or more as necessary

Lemon quarters, for garnish

Steamed, sautéed bitter greens or spinach (optional)

RUN YOUR HANDS LIGHTLY over the salmon fillet to find any pin bones that might be left behind. They're easiest to remove using ordinary tweezers. Sprinkle both sides of the fish with salt and pepper and set it on a rack while you prepare the oil.

POUR THE OLIVE OIL into a saucepan large enough to hold the fish in one piece and set it over low heat. Heat the oil gently until it reaches 120°F. Slip the salmon fillet into the oil, which should entirely cover the fillet. Cook very carefully, watching the temperature constantly. It should never go above 115°F—but it should not go much below that temperature either. The point is truly to poach the salmon, rather than to fry it. Cook the fish for just about 9 minutes, at which point the thinner end of the fillet will be done all the way through and the thicker end will still have a little rareness in the middle. If you want the whole fillet done all the way through, poach for about 11 minutes.

WHEN THE SALMON IS DONE, remove it, draining the oil over the pan. Set the fish on a platter on its own or on the bed of greens. Serve it immediately with a few cut quarters of lemon for a garnish.

# Tunisian Orange–Olive Oil Tea Cake

## GÂTEAU À L'ORANGE DE MADAME MAHJOUB

 This unusual cake, made with olive oil and whole ground oranges, is a Mahjoub family recipe. It's made with a particular blood orange called *maltaise de Tunisie,* which gives the cake a beautiful red blush of color, but I've also made it with small, sweet Florida juice oranges. (Thick-skinned navel oranges won't work.) It's important to use organically raised oranges, since the whole fruit, skin and all, is called for; otherwise, scrub oranges very thoroughly with warm soapy water to get rid of any pesticide residue or wax.

PREHEAT THE OVEN to 350°F. Butter and flour a 9-inch cake pan. A springform pan works best.

SLICE OFF THE TOPS and bottoms of each orange where the skin is very thick, and discard. Cut the oranges into chunks, skin and all, discarding the seeds, which will make the cake bitter.

IN A FOOD PROCESSOR, process the oranges to a chunky puree. Add the oil, pouring it through the feed tube while the processor is running to mix thoroughly.

IN A BOWL, sift together the flour, baking powder, baking soda, and salt.

IN A SEPARATE LARGE BOWL, beat the eggs until very thick and lemon-colored, gradually beating in the granulated sugar. Add the vanilla and almond extract, if using, and mix well.

USING A RUBBER SPATULA, fold about a third of the flour mixture into the eggs. Then fold in about a third of the orange mixture, continuing to add and fold in dry and liquid mixtures until everything is combined in a batter.

POUR THE BATTER into the prepared pan. Bake for 60 minutes, or until cake is brown on top and has pulled away from the sides.

REMOVE THE CAKE from the oven and let it sit about 5 minutes on a cake rack. Then invert the cake onto the rack and leave to cool. When thoroughly cooled, dust lightly, if you wish, with confectioners' sugar.

**Makes 8 to 10 servings**

Butter and flour for a 9-inch cake pan

2 small blood oranges

⅓ cup extra-virgin olive oil

2 cups unbleached all-purpose flour

1 teaspoon baking powder

½ teaspoon baking soda

½ teaspoon sea salt

4 large eggs

1½ cups granulated sugar

1 teaspoon pure vanilla extract

½ teaspoon almond extract (optional)

Confectioners' sugar (optional)

# Wheat

AN INTRODUCTION

Late in autumn, just before the winter rains begin in earnest, all across the Mediterranean the wheat crop is sown, pale seeds broadcast across rich brown soil that has been turned and turned again to prepare a dark, moist, and nourishing bed. Not everyone knows how to do this. In older times, the sowers of seed were certain members of the community, almost always men, often very old men, who had memorized these age-old ritual gestures: Seed basket balanced on the left hip, the sower strides across the naked field, his right arm dipping, then thrusting and flinging in an arc of grace and power, driving the seed home. At its heart, each small grain contains its own genetic code, a message that tells it precisely what it is to become—hard durum wheat, softer bread wheat, or ancient, hulled emmer.

The seeds sprout quickly, but they don't grow much in the chill of winter, just enough to cover the soil with a thick nap of green. Then, as the March sun strengthens, the shoots quicken and begin to develop, stretching up toward the light, while the roots go down, down, reaching for moisture and minerals in the soil that will give the grain character and flavor. And then, all across the Mediterranean, from the broad and treeless plains of Anatolia and northern Tunisia to the fields of southern Spain and the narrowly terraced hillsides of Italy and Greece, green wheat ripples on the April breeze like billowing waves on a grassy sea.

On the third day of May, the feast of Santa Croce or Holy Cross, my Tuscan neighbors, like many Italian farmers, used to set up a cross made of olive branches (or, less often, of palm fronds) in the midst of their wheat fields. (They no longer grow wheat, have not done so in years, but that's another story.) The cross, blessed by the priest in the village church on Palm Sunday, was ancient and powerful magic, a protection during the critical period when, the stalks having achieved their maximum growth, all the plant's energy turns to swelling and ripening the burgeoning kernels. This is the most delicate time in the whole cycle, when windstorms or a sudden burst of hail can lodge the grain stalks, toppling them over and spoiling the crop, when insects, attracted by the ripening kernels, may invade the fields, devouring the wheat just before it's ready to harvest. So the wheat needs all the magic it can get. Small wonder that May, the month of Mary, is the month devoted to Magna Mater, the Great Mother, protective goddess of the grain.

As if by magic, then, the wheat ripens and turns a pale toasted gold, like the crusted surface of a fresh-from-the-oven loaf of bread, and there's a bready, yeasty fragrance in the air over the wheat fields. One year I stood in a broad field of Taganrog, a hard durum wheat variety from the Ukraine that Carlo Latini, wheat farmer and pasta maker in the Marche region along the Adriatic coast of Italy, had planted as an experiment. It was just before the harvest and the stalks were thick and tall, up to my shoulders, stiff yet supple, and almost as big around as my little finger, supporting ears loaded with grains that were the color of antique amber. Carlo's wife, Carla, who is as involved in the wheat business as he is himself, broke off a bearded ear and stripped the grains, cracking the glumes with a fingernail to reveal the seeds inside. "Here," she commanded, "taste it," and passed me a few kernels. They shattered between my teeth, releasing a fragrance that was part grassy and part that same flavor of a fresh-baked loaf.

In most parts of the Mediterranean, the grain is harvested by machine, but some small farmers still cut it by hand, the harvesters, men, women, and children, bending from the waist, their backs bowed like the sickles they wield. Modern sickles are made of steel, of course, with wooden handles, and the harvesters stop periodically to pull out a sharpening stone and hone the blades razor-thin. Eight or nine thousand years ago, early Neolithic farmers, working their wheat fields in Syria and southern Anatolia used similar sickles, curved bone tools, the inside of the curve coated with bitumen in which were embedded sharp flints to cut the stalks of primitive wheat. When I see these tools in archeological museums like the one in Aleppo in northern Syria, I think how comfortably they'd fit in the roughened hands of my farming neighbors in Tuscany, or anywhere else around the Mediterranean for that matter. Often the flints carry traces of sickle gloss, an indication, archaeologists tell us, of their use by those long-ago farmers to harvest their crops.

In times gone by, the annual threshing of the wheat, which follows the harvest by a few weeks, was a cooperative effort involving whole villages or groups of neighbors working together to insure the grain supply for the months ahead. It was hot, dusty, exhausting but necessary labor, made easier by the joy that came both from working together for the benefit of all and from the satisfaction of knowing at the end of the day that the granaries were full once more.

There aren't many places left in the Mediterranean where wheat is still hand-threshed, but thirty years ago, in a Spanish village near the town of San Martín de Valdeiglesias, I happened on an amazing harvest scene that seemed as if it could have taken place anytime in the last five hundred years or so. Like an animation of a Brueghel landscape-with-peasantry, two-wheeled wooden carts, drawn by mules driven by straw-hatted farmers, brought the sheaves of sun-dried wheat to the village threshing floor or *era*, a clean circle of earth that had been beaten to concrete over decades of treading animal hooves and the sweep of the threshing sledge. The wheat stalks, heavy with grain, were spread in a golden pool over the surface of the *era* while another mule was driven briskly round and round the threshing floor, pulling a heavy wooden sledge on which the thresher sat. Sharp stones in the base of the sledge cut the harvested sheaves and separated grain from chaff. Later the womenfolk winnowed the wheat, using wooden pitchforks to toss grain and chaff over their heads, patiently, repetitively, rhythmically, over and over, until the light chaff and straw were blown away on the summer breeze and the heavier grain sank in a golden pile. The gestures they used went back, from generation to generation, to the very beginnings of Mediterranean agriculture.

THAT AGRICULTURE SEEMS to have begun about ten thousand years ago, somewhere in the Levant, possibly in the corner of the Mediterranean where southern Anatolia and northern Syria embrace the coast, at the edge of the sickle-shaped region we learned in grade school to call the Fertile Crescent. The rolling north Syrian steppes, historically one of the great wheat-growing areas of the Mediterranean, are still a prime region for wheat production, and in Syria, as in much of the Mediterranean, the wheat grown is hard durum, with kernels that characteristically shatter into tiny glassy shards when the grain is ground into flour.

Durum is Mediterranean wheat par excellence. "It has to see the Med to grow really well," Miloodi Nachit tells me, laughing because from where he sits, at ICARDA, an international agricultural research station south of Aleppo, you can't see the sea at all, even from the highest hill, though vast fields of durum stretch like the sea in all directions. He's speaking metaphorically, this son of a Berber farmer who is one of the world's leading experts on durum, but the meaning of his metaphor is not hard to tease out. Durum is prized above all other wheats because its vitreous kernels yield the gritty flour called semolina in English. Durum semolina is what goes into high-quality, high-protein pasta, couscous, and dozens of other foods that are important on Mediterranean tables, including many breads, despite its undeserved reputation as "too hard" a grain for bread making. (Try telling that to the bakers of southern Italy, eastern Anatolia, and North Africa who make their best bread from durum semolina.)

Some food historians claim that durum is not an ancient wheat at all, or rather not ancient to the Mediterranean. Instead, they say, it came late, brought by Arabs who, according to one theory, discovered it in East Africa and carried it into the Mediterranean shortly before the time when pasta starts to be mentioned in written texts—around the mid–twelfth century, long after Islamic armies, moving across North Africa, had established themselves in Sicily and Spain. According to this theory, pasta made from hard durum is an Arab "invention" and the two phenomena, hard-wheat pasta and the arrival of durum in the Mediterranean are closely linked.

Ethnobotanists, wheat geneticists like Dr. Nachit, and many archeologists aren't so certain. "Durum is a very ancient wheat in the Mediterranean," Dr. Nachit told me. It has been found in many Neolithic sites, he emphasized, including in eastern Spain, suggesting it was a very early import, since we know it didn't originate there.

The Triticum or wheat family, Dr. Nachit explained, is large and complex, but most members fall into one of three great branches or species:

- *Diploid wheats* with 14 chromosomes. The only significant member of this branch is *Triticum monococcum*, or einkorn, one of the earliest wheats to be domesticated and rarely found today.

- *Tetraploid wheats* with 28 chromosomes. A very important branch, especially in the Mediterranean, this is the *Triticum turgidum* group of so-called hard wheats, with vitreous, somewhat translucent kernels that shatter when milled into a very gritty flour. This branch includes emmer (*T. turgidum*, subsp. *dicoccum*, another very early domesticated wheat, often know by its Italian name, *farro*), durum (*T. turgidum*, subsp. *durum*, also called macaroni wheat because it's used in pasta making), and kamut, among others.

- *Hexaploid wheats* with 42 chromosomes. *Triticum aestivum*, the major modern wheat (as much as 90 percent of all the wheat grown world-wide) for flour and flour products, including bread, cakes, pastries, and some pasta, except that made in countries such as Italy and France where laws require commercial pasta to be made of durum wheat. *T. aestivum* is primarily bread wheat or common wheat, but also includes varieties like spelt and club wheat. The softer kernels of *T. aestivum*, unlike durum wheats, are opaque and can be crushed into fine powdery particles, or flour. When bread wheat is used to make pasta, eggs must be added to the dough to give it elasticity.

There's lots of genetic diversity within these branches, Dr. Nachit said, but there is one indisputable fact: The more chromosomes a living thing has, the later its place in the chain of evolution; so bread or common wheat, with more chromosomes, is a later development than durum. Common wheat probably came about when a domesticated member of the durum-turgidum branch, either emmer or durum itself, crossed with a wild cereal grass from the Aegilops family. Thus, wheat geneticists can almost pinpoint where and when common wheat evolved— somewhere near the Caspian Sea, and sometime between 6000 and 5000 B.C.E., or after Neolithic wheat farming had spread out from the Fertile Crescent and into the Caspian belt where wild Aegilops was at home.

And how old is durum? Miloodi Nachit is unequivocal: very old indeed. As further evidence of its place at the heart of Mediterranean agriculture, he cites the great number of landraces to be found all around the inner sea. A landrace is a local adaptation, a variety that evolves when a plant (or animal) species has a long history in one region. There are said to be seven hundred landraces of durum in Spain alone. Another indication of durum's antiquity is the enormous range of traditional products that depend on the hard grain, from couscous in Dr. Nachit's native Berber country of North Africa to Italian pasta to Lebanese and Turkish *burghul* (bulgur) and Syrian *frik* (durum that's harvested while still green and fired to rid it of its husk and give the grain a pleasantly smoky flavor).

Another wheat variety grown in the Mediterranean since time immemorial is an ancient cousin, perhaps an ancestor, of durum called emmer (*T. turgidum*, sbsp. *dicoccum*), or in Italian *farro*, a word that comes almost directly from Latin. The *confarratium*, the cake that was presented as an offering in the Temple of the Vestal Virgins by Roman couples planning to marry, was always made of very fine, highly bolted, pure, white *farro* flour, a recognition of the importance of the ancient grain as a foundation of family and domestic life. (Our modern wedding cakes are direct descendants of the *confarratium*.) Emmer (or *farro*) has died out in many parts of the Mediterranean, replaced centuries ago by durum and high-yielding modern strains of bread wheat. But in parts of Italy, such as Tuscany and Umbria, where it never quite disappeared, *farro* has become popular recently with regional restaurant chefs.

Emmer is a hulled wheat, meaning each kernel has a tough hull or glume that adheres to it and makes the grain difficult to digest. Early on, cooks learned to get rid of the hulls by parching the grains or by pounding lightly dampened grains in a deep mortar just long enough to release the hull without cracking the grain. That kind of processing isn't necessary with durum or bread wheat since they are both naked or free-threshing wheats, meaning that they thresh clean without that outer hull. Nonetheless, the process of pounding wheat lingers in places such as Puglia in southern Italy, where the wheat, once it's hulled, is called *grano pestato*, pounded or peeled wheat, or in Turkey where it's called *yarma* or *dovme*. There are still delicious traditional dishes that use pounded emmer, but modern machinery makes the processing easier. In Spain, where the pounded grain was known as *trigo picado*, or beaten wheat, the wheat berries have long since been replaced by rice; still, many of the most famous Spanish rice dishes have their origins in these combinations of pounded wheat with pork, with fish, with vegetables.

Despite durum's ancestry, there is plenty of common wheat, *Triticum aestivum*, in the Mediterranean, produced locally or imported from elsewhere to satisfy the demands of modern home and commercial bakeries alike. The egg-based pastas of northern Italy always use flour made from common wheat, and most breads and pastries need common or bread wheat to give the dough the lightness required by modern tastes. American all-purpose flour is made from bread wheat, primarily a variety called hard red winter wheat, the most widely grown and profitable variety in the world. Although it is called a "hard" wheat, it is *not* a durum wheat.

## WHEAT AS BREAD

Bread is astonishing in its variety, even though it comes from the simplest combination of ingredients. If you leave out all those breads made distinctive by the addition of olives or walnuts, mashed potatoes, rosemary or raisins, if you discount all the many different shapes from long, skinny grissini to little round two-bite bunlets to great loaves weighing ten or twelve kilos, even so the variety—like the quantity—of bread consumed in the Mediterranean is staggering—most of it made simply from flour, water, yeast, and, more often than not, salt.

Go to Altamura, a bustling medieval hill town in the heartland of Puglia, the region that makes up the heel of Italy's boot, and you will find some of the most elemental bread imaginable—and some of the best, as almost every Italian connoisseur, myself included, will tell you. If bread this good were made in America, it would be shipped out to meet demands from all over the country; if bread this good were made in France, it would be shipped to America, like the bread from Lionel Poilâne's bakery in Paris. But to eat bread this good in Italy, you have to go to the source, to Altamura itself.

Altamura bread is made from creamy yellow, slightly gritty durum semolina, the same stuff that makes Italian pasta so good. Many authorities—wheat scientists, bakers in other parts of the world, food writers—assert that you can't make good bread from durum wheat. It doesn't rise well, they say, it doesn't make as fine and fluffy a loaf as bread wheat. But when you break open a sturdy loaf of Altamura bread, all that seems beside the point. Durum has always been grown on the grassy uplands of central Puglia, and bakers here have always made bread from it, most often in great, dense, crusty wheels that weigh as much as fifteen kilos and may be sold by the quarter instead of by the whole loaf. This bread has all the nutty aroma and flavor of the wheat; plus a chewy crust; an interior crumb so yellow from the natural carotene in the wheat that you would think, if you didn't know better, that eggs had been added; and a dense, supple, and chewy texture. Bread this good gives new meaning to the term "staff of life."

The process of making the bread is simplicity itself. Flour, water, and leaven are mixed in the early morning hours, when darkness still veils the town. The flour is 100 percent semolina, and for leaven the bakers of Altamura use nothing more than dough from the day before, freshened with a little added commercial yeast. The dough is set to rise, knocked down, a little sea salt is added, and the shaped loaves rise again. Meanwhile, the dark, cavernous ovens, low masonry domes reaching far back into the wall, are set ablaze with faggots of wild broom and trash wood that burn hot until the oven walls give off a uniform incandescent white glow. Then the ashes are raked out and the first loaves put in. The baker's long wooden peel reaches to the innermost recesses of the cavern and, with a confident jerk, he sets the loaf exactly where it belongs—one after the other after the other, until the cavern floor is full and the oven door is sealed. Ninety minutes later, the transformation is complete, the door opens once more, and in a reverse motion, the baker extracts the loaves, now brown and crackling with stored heat. And the aroma, they say in Altamura, would wake the dead.

What makes this bread so special is something of a mystery, though surely it has to do with a combination of factors, including the high-quality, locally raised durum semolina that's the bread's principal ingredient, and the leaven whose ancestry goes back in this same place, year after year, perhaps century after century, like one of those ancient sourdoughs (though there's nothing sour about it) that pretend to pharaonic ancestry. Locals say the quality comes in part from the water of Altamura which, they claim, is exceptionally pure and sweet. Then, too, there's the factor of the cavernous wood-burning oven, for it's well-known that anything—bread, cake, pizza, baby lamb, or apple pie—tastes better baked in a wood-fired oven than using any other fuel.

Herodotus claimed that the Egyptians invented bread, or rather the baking of fermented dough to make bread, but logic alone tells us that, like many of the great historian's claims, it simply isn't true. Bread isn't something that was "invented," the way the internal combusion engine was "invented."

Picture this: a Neolithic farmwife, having pounded her grains of emmer wheat to remove their hulls, grinds them to a gritty flour using a saddle quern, something like a Mexican *metate*. In a pottery bowl that she made three weeks earlier and fired in her temporary oven, she mixes the grits with water to make a porridge for her family and sets it aside until cooking time. But the goats break out of their stockade and run off, and she spends the rest of the day tracking them over the hillsides behind the settlement. By the time she gets the goats back, many hours have passed and the uncooked porridge, which she had left in a sunny corner of her cooking area, has done something funny, bubbled and burbled and expanded—in fact, in something approaching a miracle, there is apparently twice as much porridge in the bowl as what she left that morning. Not only that: It has developed an odd but not at all unpleasant smell.

Should she throw it out and start over again? It's late and besides, in a Neolithic village you do not waste food unless it has gone dangerously bad. And so, in the impatience born of frustration, she slings the bowl into the fire, whereupon another miracle takes place and the porridge, on contact with heat, puffs and expands further and cooks to a solid cake that releases such an overpoweringly enticing aroma that the entire family gathers round demanding more, more. And she never makes porridge again.

Something similar must have happened, over and over, wherever wheat grew and people harvested it and prepared it for their food. Fermentation takes place when yeast spores, naturally present in the air around us everywhere, even on the wheat itself, infect the dough and in its humid and tepid environment begin to grow. But that could not have happened in corn-growing America or rice-growing south Asia, because wheat alone, of the three major cereals, produces the gluten that traps gases released by fermentation—the very process that makes the dough expand. From there to bread is just a question of patience.

And an oven. Of course you can bake perfectly decent bread in the embers of an open fire, as our Neolithic farmwife has discovered, and even better bread if you set the dough on a flat stone, terra-cotta or metal griddle that has been heated over the embers. But the best bread comes from an oven. And once our clever farmwife, having fired pottery in her kiln, decided to use the heat remaining in the kiln to bake her bread dough, well, the rest is—what is it they say? history?

Actually, archeological evidence of ovens shows up in such scattered places that it's obvious that oven-baking was not a technology readily adopted by every Mediterranean culture that came in contact with it. We know of little model ovens, intended as grave goods or perhaps even as toys, from seven thousand to eight thousand years ago, in Bulgaria, Kosovo, and Serbia. The remains of full-sized once-working ovens have also been found in these places as well as in Macedonia and in Anatolia. In the mid–third millennium, production bakeries flourished in Egypt (see sidebar, page 101). But the Minoans on the island of Crete, an otherwise highly advanced society, seem not to have had ovens until very late, around 1500 B.C.E.

More common, possibly because it used less fuel, was the griddle, which produced, quickly and easily, fresh bread for family use. Moreover, griddles were easy to transport (easier at least than ovens) and could be carried from camp to camp by nomads, or up into the hills in the summer as families followed their transhumant flocks of sheep and goats, then brought them back down to the plains again in the winter. And in a part of the world where forest cover was not abundant, a griddle was a more economical use of available firewood. A slightly domed metal griddle called by its Turkish name *saç* (pronounced satch) is still widely used throughout the eastern Mediterranean to produce a variety of savory breads and griddle cakes, often with toppings or stuffings that are as delicious as any pizza. It looks like an upside-down wok, which makes an ideal substitute, and can be set, if necessary, over an open fire right out in the fields.

Griddle breads are the most elementary hearth breads; Italian *focaccia* and Provençal *fougasse* began life as hearth breads, too. You can tell that from the name (in modern Italian the *focolare* is the hearth) even though today they are oven-baked. A hearth bread always used to mean a bread baked in the fireplace on the hearth, although nowadays it indicates an artisanal bread cast directly onto the oven floor. In parts of Turkey, Syria, and Lebanon, bread is baked in a *tannur* or *tannir* (a word related to Indian *tandoor*), like a big terra-cotta oil jar set into the ground. In effect it's somewhere between a griddle or *saç* and a proper oven. A fire is built in the bottom of the jar and when it's white hot, lightly leavened doughs are clapped to the inside walls to toast as if they were on a griddle.

But a proper bread oven, a round, low-domed space built of masonry, stone, brick, or a combination, is what bakes most of the bread consumed around the Mediterranean today, as it has for centuries. It was fired with wood because that was the only fuel available. Lately, however, these old ovens are being replaced by modern production ovens that operate like a piece of machinery and turn out loaf after loaf of perfectly formed, perfectly risen, all-too-often perfectly tasteless bread with all the texture and heft of styrofoam. Lately, too, even where old-fashioned masonry ovens persist as they do in Italy, they are likely to be gas-fired. This is largely a response to European environmental and health regulations that find the dark, smoky, dusty atmosphere of an old-fashioned bread oven extremely hazardous to human life, even when it's heated to above 500°F at least once every 24 hours, allowing precious little of a biological nature to survive.

At the same time that EU health commissars have spread out across Mediterranean Europe in search of ovens to shut down or convert, a countermovement has sprung up of consumers and bread lovers who are demanding a return to a full-flavored loaf. It may be too late in Spain where good bread simply disappeared during the long, bleak years of Franco's government, and for a while in the 1990s it looked as though France would go the same route. Industrially produced baguettes—often freshly baked from fast-rising dough that had been produced and frozen, preservatives and all, hundreds of kilometers from the ovens in which they were baked—had penetrated deep into even the most redoubtable Provençal villages. As usual, however, when French food traditions are threatened, the government stepped in and now, throughout France, a *boulangerie* cannot be called a *boulangerie artisanale* unless it actually produces the dough from which its bread is baked. It may not be very good dough, but at least there's a minimal degree of honesty to the production.

The best bread is still, and probably always will be, the most traditional. In Tunisia, it may be made all or in part of barley; in Morocco it will have durum semolina added; in southern Italy, it may be 100 percent semolina; in Provence, it isn't unusual to find a small amount of rye flour added to good bread made from common wheat flour; and in parts of Greece, the bread may have cornmeal mixed in. But apart from local flour choices, wheaten bread is still what's generally preferred, made from a fairly high-extraction wheat flour at that, even with some flecks of bran in it. The remaining ingredients are equally fundamental—good leaven, often based on a piece of dough set aside at the last baking whether that was a week ago or only yesterday; sea salt, not out of any pretensions, but because that's the salt most readily available; and water, local water from the spring or the well, or, failing that, from a bottle because urban water is too heavily chlorinated to make good-tasting bread. Such bread is the foundation of every meal—breakfast, lunch, and supper—around the Mediterranean.

But I wouldn't be doing bread justice without mentioning that this most ordinary, fundamental food is also often a symbol of celebration, whether of Christmas, Easter, the Eid il Adha, or the Sabbath. Sometimes, as with Sabbath breads, it's an everyday bread dough made special by adding rich ingredients—eggs, sugar, olive oil, and fragrant orange-blossom water. In the holiday breads of Turkey and the Greek islands, fragrances like cassia, grated orange peel, and mastic and *mahlab* (see page 112) are incorporated in a simple bread dough. At other times, it's the dough itself that's used to shape elaborate, fanciful decorative breads, as if the dough were fine potter's clay. Cretan women make exquisitely complex decorated ring-shaped breads for baptisms and weddings—so elaborate that it's hard to conceive how they could be made from leavened dough with its unpredictable elasticity. Equally fancy breads decorate Easter arcades, elaborate triumphal arches set up in sequence along the streets of a Sicilian village. Breads like these are evidence of Sicily's ancient ties to Greece, but they're also a reminder that for the most ancient Mediterranean civilizations, bread was not just the staple of the daily diet, it was—and is—a potent symbol of life itself.

# The World's Oldest Bakery?

ENCOUNTERING THE THREE Old Kingdom pyramids rising on the Giza plateau west of Cairo can take your breath away no matter how many times you come upon them. Massive relics, haunting witnesses of the ancient world, they were erected more than 4,500 years ago by a civilization that had not yet even discovered the wheel. Along with the pyramids themselves a city quickly grew up in the surrounding desert, populated by the workers who built the pyramids and later furnished the mortuary temples that continued on the site for centuries after the monuments had been completed.

As head of the Giza Plateau Mapping Project, Harvard archaeologist Mark Lehner has directed for the last dozen years or so the documentation of this Old Kingdom workers' city which, Herodotus tells us, had a population of 100,000. (Modern archaeologists believe it was more like 10,000 to 20,000—still, Lehner says, "comparable to . . . sizable cities in the Near East in the third millennium.") Among the intriguing artifacts Lehner's team has uncovered is a series of ancient bakeries southeast of Cheops's Great Pyramid. They date from the reign of King Menkaure (sometimes called Mycerinus), late in the Fourth Dynasty (around 2500 B.C.E.), and they show us that even if Egyptians did not invent bread, as Herodotus claimed, they were among history's earliest production bakers—although their technique seems to have been unique to Egypt and not exported elsewhere.

In and around the bakeries, Lehner's team found a great quantity of bell-shaped terra-cotta jars, each more than a foot in diameter, about 15 inches deep, and weighing, because of the thick walls of the jars, up to 26 pounds. These cumbersome vessels, called *bedja* in Ancient Egyptian, were pots for baking bread. We know this from Old Kingdom tomb scenes that show, as in a cartoon strip, the entire process of making bread, from the initial grinding of the grain to the presentation of the finished cone-shaped loaves, as a scribe records the baker's output. Now, with Lehner's discoveries, we have a clearer picture of what the tomb scenes really mean.

Once the dough—which was probably made from barley or emmer or a mixture of the two—had been set to rise, the *bedja* jars were stacked in a circle or pyramid around a steadily burning fire in order to heat their interiors; then the jars were transferred, probably balanced on sticks because they would have been very hot, to a bed of ashes and embers, and the dough, more liquid than what we think of as bread dough today, was poured into the hot pot. Another jar was inverted over the filled one, and ashes and embers were piled around so that each loaf of bread, in a sense, baked in its own individual oven.

The bakeries in the Giza workers community were big businesses, with adjacent grain silos and breweries. Bread and beer were complementary in Egypt, lightly baked bread helping to start the brewing process, and brewer's yeast put back into the dough to help the bread rise, in a kind of closed-cycle technology. They were complementary in Egyptian beliefs too: throughout three thousand years of ancient Egyptian history, the tomb inscriptions intone, over and over again, offerings to or for the deceased of "thousands of bread and thousands of beer."

## 16 GREAT RECIPES FOR BREAD OR USING BREAD

How to Make Bread with a Spontaneous or Natural Leaven

Classic Mediterranean-Style Bread Made with a Sponge
*Poolish or Biga*

Eastern Mediterranean Holiday Bread with Mastic or *Mahlab*

Mediterranean Tunafish Salad Sandwich
*Bruschetta al Tonno*

Pan Bagnat

Tunis Market Sandwiches

North African Breakfast Buns
*Mlaoui*

Halise's Griddle Bread with Cheese or Scallions
*Saç Börek*

Anna Tasca Lanza's Sicilian Pizza
*Sfincione*

Syrian Pizzas
*Lahm b'Ajiin*

Catalan Pizzas
*Cocas*

Twice-Baked Bread Salad
*Cialda Pugliese*

Sardinian Crisp Bread Layered with Tomato Sauce and a Fried Egg
*Pane Frattàu*

Tuscan Bread Soup from the Casentino
*Acquacotta Casentinese*

Eggplant and Lamb *Fatteh*

Chicken and Chickpea *Fatteh*

## COOK'S NOTES

All bread is made in the same way from the same four ingredients: flour, water, leavening, and salt. There is no mystery to this. Sometimes salt is omitted, as in the common household bread from central Italy. More rarely leavening is left out to make a genuine flatbread—like piadine, round griddle-baked breads from Italy's Po Valley. Other ingredients (eggs, butter, nuts, olives, seeds, and so forth) are added for variety. The flour is usually some kind of wheat, whether hard or soft, more or less bolted to leave more or less of the bran. Barley flour is used in parts of the Mediterranean (North Africa, the island of Crete, southern Puglia, and elsewhere) and rye flour is used in a few others, but even when these other flours are used, they are almost always mixed with wheat flour because only wheat has the quality of gluten that will make dough rise.

The leaven is, in many respects, the most variable part of the formula. Most bread bakers today, whether at home or in a professional bakery, use commercial yeasts to leaven their doughs, but some still use a spontaneous leaven that grows up naturally when wheat flour and water are combined under the right circumstances. And many bakers throughout the Mediterranean still use the old-dough method of leavening: Each time bread is made, some small part of the dough is set aside before salting to be used as the starter leaven for the next baking. (This is often called sourdough because the dough will develop a certain acidity over time. It was not invented by forty-niners on the westward trail to California, but is one of the oldest traditions in domestic kitchens, a way for women literally to pass on culture.)

Because the old dough that has been set aside from an earlier baking has to be reactivated before it is ready to use, another tradition grew up alongside, that of the *poolish* (in French) or *biga* (in Italian) or starter sponge (in English). Warm water and flour are mixed with the old dough from the previous baking, then the mixture is set aside overnight in a cool place to activate, rise, and develop flavors. This long, slow fermentation contributes a good deal of character to the finished bread. You can mimic this with a small quantity of yeast, mixed with flour and water and set aside overnight or for several hours. Of course, it's no way to get bread on the table in a hurry—but if this book were about hurrying things up, it would be a very different book indeed.

## HOW TO MAKE BREAD WITH SPONTANEOUS OR NATURAL LEAVEN

A spontaneous leaven is a natural yeast that grows when flour and water are combined under appropriate conditions of warmth and humidity. Given the right setting, it's not difficult to do, but it's easier in a country kitchen where fruits, especially grapes, are ripening outside. Easiest of all is in a kitchen in which bread is made frequently and regularly; in these conditions, natural spores floating invisibly through the air will fix themselves to a flour and water sponge and start to work their magic. With neither orchard nor vineyard nor regularly baked bread, however, a person can still try. If it fails, it's a good lesson in how bread gets made; if, on the other hand, it succeeds, you could be set up for life with a source of delicious homemade leaven from which to make your bread.

I don't want to suggest that the system is foolproof, however. In my own experience, I make great leaven in a Tuscan farmhouse with grapes growing right outside the kitchen window, but in a chilly Maine kitchen, on the other hand, I've not had much success. My friend Karen Mitchell, who owns The Model Bakery in St. Helena, in the heart of the Napa Valley wine country, customarily makes spontaneous leavens from unsprayed grapes in nearby vineyards and uses this kind of leaven in most of her baking. But she's in an ideal situation.

If you want to try your luck with this, you will need a good big bunch of organically raised grapes, the fresher the better—they don't have to be wine grapes. Pull the grapes off the stems and, using a potato masher or a sturdy kitchen fork, crush the grapes in a bowl to release some of the juice. Wrap a single layer of cheesecloth loosely around the grape residue (to keep grape seeds out of your bread dough). Add a good half-cup of unbleached, all-purpose flour and 2 tablespoons of very warm water (about 75°F) to the juice in the bowl and mix it with a wooden spoon, pushing the bundle of grape residue down under the batter. (If your tap water is heavily chlorinated, use noncarbonated bottled water.)

Cover the bowl with plastic wrap and set it aside in a very warm place (70° to 80°F) for 48 hours. The wet dough should rise, develop lots of sponge (in other words, it should look yeasty) and double in volume. If you cannot maintain a warm temperature throughout that time, don't worry—it will simply take longer for the leaven to develop. Do, however, avoid extremely cold temperatures, such as you might find in an unheated pantry in the winter.

This is the beginning, but the dough must be refreshed several times to build up its strength. Here's how to do that:

After 48 hours, add about ⅔ cup flour and ⅓ cup warm water, and stir them into the sponge. Cover again and leave to rise and double, which this time should take about 12 hours. Now you should be able to fish out the bundle of grape residue and discard it. Add another ¼ cup flour and 2 tablespoons warm water. (Don't be too finicky about exact weights and measures—if you happen to put in a little more or less, it won't matter.)

At this point the dough should rise and double in just four or five hours and have the characteristic sweet, slightly acid tang (like slightly fermented apple or grape juice) of natural yeast. You can keep this in the refrigerator, covered, for quite a long time, but it must be refreshed every 4 or 5 days by adding a little more flour and warm water (about half a cup of each), stirring it in, waiting for the leaven to start bubbling, and then refrigerating again.

To make bread, take 8 ounces (about 1 cup) of the prepared spontaneous leaven and use it in the following recipe. (If the leaven has been refrigerated, allow sufficient time for it to come to room temperature before using it to make bread.) The rest of the leaven should be refreshed by adding a little more than ½ cup flour, and a little less than ½ cup of warm water.

# Classic Mediterranean-Style Bread Made with a Sponge

## POOLISH OR BIGA

 This bread takes 2 or 3 days to make, but most of that time is spent waiting while the dough rises. It's worth it because when dough is given a long, slow rise at cool temperatures, the bread develops both texture and flavor.

I use unbleached flour from the King Arthur Flour Company in Vermont; they will ship all over the country (see Where to Find It, page 415), but if you have a good source in a local mill or supplier, by all means use it. Flour made from organically raised grain is best but not always available.

If your tap water is hard or tastes of chemicals, use bottled spring water or leave the tap water in an open measuring jug for several hours to disperse some of the chemical flavors.

Parchment paper spread on a baking sheet helps to achieve an even, golden-brown crust, and a spritz of water from a simple plastic spray bottle as the loaf goes in the oven will give the crust good texture.

**Makes about 3 pounds of bread (three 1-pound baguettes or two 1½-pound boules)**

**For the starter:**

1 cup (8 ounces) sourdough or spontaneous leaven; or use ¼ teaspoon active dry yeast or ¼ packet fresh yeast mixed with ⅓ cup warm water and ½ cup unbleached, all-purpose flour

1 cup warm water

1 cup unbleached, all-purpose flour

TO MAKE THE STARTER SPONGE, put the leavening in a bowl and add the warm water, stirring it gently with a wooden spoon. Add the flour and mix well, beating for about 30 strokes with a wooden spoon to activate the gluten. The mixture will be a thick slurry, more like a batter than a dough. Cover with plastic wrap, and set aside in a cool place to rise overnight and form a sponge.

THE NEXT DAY, combine the starter sponge with 4 cups of the flour, including, if you wish, 1 cup of barley, rye, or whole-wheat flour, or cornmeal or semolina to give the bread slightly different character and flavor. Add the yeast to 1 cup tepid water and, when it has dissolved completely, stir this into the flour, along with another ¼ cup water. Stir this very well with a wooden spoon. It will be a raggedy and unpromising looking mass. Cover with plastic wrap and set aside for 20 minutes to rest. Now check the texture of the dough, and if it seems too wet, add a little more flour. If it seems too dry, add a little more water. Make these additions in ¼-cup increments to avoid tipping the balance too far. A wetter dough will make the kind of bread the French call "*bien alvéolé*," meaning full of holes; a dryer dough will be more compact. It's hard to describe what a perfect texture looks and feels like at this point—experience is the best teacher—but it should be neither so wet that it doesn't hang together nor so dry that it looks and feels powdery.

KNEAD THE DOUGH, either in an electric mixer with a dough hook (this is best for wet doughs which are hard to handle) for 6 or 7 minutes, or by hand for 10 minutes on a lightly greased board to keep from adding too much flour to the dough. (To grease the board, tip a little olive oil into the palms of your hands and rub them over the board.) Knead until the dough has reached a good springy consistency and is no longer sticky. Once the kneading is done, transfer the dough to a lightly greased bowl, cover with plastic wrap, and set aside in a cool place for several hours or in the refrigerator overnight, to rise and develop flavor. A couple of times during this rising period, deflate the dough by gently punching it down.

WHEN THE DOUGH HAS DOUBLED in size, remove 1 cup, if you wish, to serve as the starter for the next time you bake. Put it in a plastic or glass container, cover it well, and refrigerate until you are ready to use it.

ADD THE SALT to the dough and knead to mix it in well. Divide the dough in three or four pieces, depending on what kind of bread shape you want, and let it rest, lightly covered with plastic wrap, for 20 minutes.

SHAPE THE DOUGH PIECES into long baguettes or round boules

**For the bread:**

4 to 5 cups flour, including, optionally, 1 cup rye, barley, or whole-wheat flour, or cornmeal or semolina, as well as unbleached, all-purpose flour

½ teaspoon active dry yeast, or ½ packet fresh yeast

1½ to 1¾ cups water

1 tablespoon sea salt

Extra-virgin olive oil

About ¼ cup cornmeal or semolina, if needed

(or a couple of each, if you wish). To shape baguettes, take ⅓ of the dough and pat it on the board into a roughly rectangular shape, about twice as long as it is deep. Roll the dough into a long, thin, jelly-roll shape, tucking the ends in and keeping the roll as tight as you can manage. To make boules, take ½ of the dough and roll it on the board to make a tight, compact ball with no loose ends.

BOULES MAY BE PUT TO RISE in baskets, if you have them, or in colanders; baskets and colanders should be lined with clean dish towels that have been dusted liberally with flour. Baguettes are usually put to rise in a *couche*, a long, thin basket, or series of baskets, lined with cloth that should be liberally dusted with flour before the baguettes are set into it. You may also improve a *couche* with a liberally floured dish towel that you pull up between each dough baguette to keep the loaves from merging into each other as they rise. Whichever method you use, dust the dough shapes very lightly with flour, cover lightly with plastic wrap, and set aside to rise for 2 hours.

(IF YOU WISH, you may also set this dough to rise in lightly greased rectangular bread pans, covering each pan lightly with plastic wrap before setting it aside to rise.)

PREHEAT THE OVEN to 475°F. If you're using terra-cotta baking tiles or a baking stone, put them in the cold oven to avoid cracking them and let them heat for a good 45 minutes before putting in the bread loaves. If you're using sheet pans, spread a sheet of parchment paper to cover each pan. Transfer the fully risen loaves to the sheet pan, or, if you're using baking tiles, to a wooden peel sprinkled with cornmeal or semolina. Using a very sharp knife or a baker's *lame*, slash the tops of the loaves, making several diagonal cuts about ½ inch deep in the top of each loaf. (You can make these in a pattern running down the length of a long baguette loaf, or cross-hatching a round boule.) Have ready a plastic kitchen spray bottle with clean warm water in it.

SET THE SHEET PAN in the oven, or use the peel to transfer the loaves directly to the terra-cotta tiles or baking stone. Quickly spray the loaves in the oven with a spritz or two of water and close the door. Let bake for 1 minute, then open the door and again spray the loaves quickly. Let bake 2 minutes and spray again. Close the oven and continue baking for a total of 15 minutes. Then lower the heat to 350°F. Continue baking another 30 to 40 minutes, or until the loaves are nicely golden on top. Remove and set on a rack to cool.

NOTE: *The Baker's Catalogue,* produced by the King Arthur Flour Company (see page 415), offers a French product called Lalvain du Jour Artisan Bakery Starters. These dried starters are various formulations of *Lactobacillus, Saccharomyces,* and other yeasts that help develop good flavor. They're sold as "French sourdough starter" and "*pain de campagne* starter," and I've found them very useful used in small quantities instead of yeast in the first step above, making the starter sponge. I'm grateful to the folks at King Arthur for their help, in both written publications and telephone conversations, in developing this recipe.

## VARIATIONS

CIABATTA. Divide the dough into four pieces for the final shaping. Stretch each piece out, using your hands or a rolling pin, into a slipper shape (which is what *ciabatta* means), longer than it is wide and approximately 1 inch thick. Bake as above, on a sheet pan covered with parchment paper, spraying with water. The baking time will be considerably reduced, as the dough is so much thinner—15 to 20 minutes at 400°F should be sufficient to make the surface golden.

FOCACCIA. Add a tablespoon of extra-virgin olive oil to the basic dough mixture when you add the salt. Spread the dough out on a parchment-covered sheet pan (or two, if necessary) in a rectangular shape. Dimple the top surface with your fingers, or use the handle of a wooden spoon to make irregular dimples in the surface. Sprinkle with a little extra-virgin olive oil and, if you wish, large grains of sea salt and some chopped fresh rosemary leaves. Ag. in, 20 minutes should be sufficient baking time. (Note that focaccia in Italy is much thinner than what's marketed as focaccia in North America. The dough in the pan should be no more than ½ inch thick for best results.) Bake for 15 to 20 minutes at 400°F.

**FOUGASSE**. To make the thin French bread elaborated with a pattern of holes, add a tablespoon of extra-virgin olive oil to the basic dough mixture when you add the salt. After the final rise, divide the dough into three or four pieces. Shape each piece by flattening it into a rectangle or lozenge. Place it on a sheet pan covered with parchment paper. Use scissors to cut a pattern in each piece, cutting right down through the dough. A traditional pattern is a herringbone of three or four slanted cuts, but use your imagination. Once the cuts have been made, pull them apart gently so that they don't bake together again. Bake for 15 to 20 minutes at 400°F.

**GRISSINI**. To make the long breadsticks from northern Italy, roll the dough out and cut into thin strips, twisting each strip slightly before placing on a baking sheet. (A baker I know makes grissini by putting them through the tagliatelle setting on his pasta machine.) Bake for 10 to 15 minutes at 425°F. If you wish, sprinkle the rolled-out dough with some finely grated Parmigiano-Reggiano cheese and/or coarsely cracked black pepper, before you cut and twist the strips.

**WALNUT BREAD**. Add 2 cups of coarsely chopped walnuts to the dough and knead it well before you shape it.

**OLIVE BREAD**. Add 1½ cups pitted, chopped black or green olives. The best black olives to use are the wrinkled, salt-cured ones (sometimes called oil-cured olives) as they add no excess moisture to the dough. Drain brine-packed olives very well before adding, as the additional moisture will affect the dough.

**OTHERS**. You may also top the bread with sesame seeds or poppy seeds, first painting the surface very lightly with a little egg white beaten with water to make the seeds adhere to it. Or you can add a little handful of fennel seeds to the dough and knead it well before you shape it into loaves.

**FRENCH BAKERS** customarily add a healthy pinch of cumin when they're making the levain or sponge. You will not be able to detect cumin itself but it will taste different from plain dough.

**TUSCAN AND UMBRIAN BAKERS** add no salt—bread without salt tastes very different indeed. Various reasons are offered for the lack of salt, but the one that makes sense to me is that the bread keeps better and firms up in a pleasant manner that makes leftover bread (*pane raffermo*, in Tuscany) a useful ingredient in bread soups and bread-based salads.

**NORTH AFRICAN BREADS** are often made with 50 percent or more of barley flour and customarily include fennel and nigella seeds in the dough.

## FESTIVE BREADS FROM THE EASTERN MEDITERRANEAN

Festival breads, made for Christmas and Easter in Orthodox communities, for the Sabbath among Jews, and for Islamic feast days among Muslims, differ from normal everyday breads in the quantity of enrichment that is added to them—everything from eggs, butter, and sugar to fragrant aromatics like mastic, *mahlab*, cinnamon, and mace. Greek Easter breads are often decorated with brilliant red-dyed hard-boiled eggs, while at Christmastime the breads sometimes seem like nothing more than a dough casing to hold all the dried fruits and nuts in the baker's dispensary.

# Eastern Mediterranean Holiday Bread with Mastic or *Mahlab*

The following recipe evolved from a bread that was made in a Turkish Aegean village home to celebrate the arrival of relatives from the city, or Istanbul. It was sent to the neighborhood baker to be baked and picked up just before lunch. Mastic is a resin produced on the Greek island of Chios from trees in the pistachio family. It is a favorite in the Aegean islands. You may find it already ground to a powder, but if it comes in little crystals, crush them in a mortar before adding to the dough. If you can't find mastic, you may be able to find *mahlab*, the seeds of a type of wild cherry, crushed or whole—again, to be crushed in a mortar. The flavor of *mahlab* is much softer and sweeter than the wild, piny fragrance of mastic.

**Makes 6 individual buns or 2 braided loaves**

**For the starter:**

1 teaspoon active dry yeast
½ cup warm water
½ cup tepid milk
1 cup unbleached all-purpose flour

TO MAKE THE STARTER, combine the yeast, water, milk, and flour in a small bowl and stir to make a thick cream. Cover and set aside for several hours or overnight to develop the flavor.

COMBINE THE OIL with the sugar in the bowl of an electric mixer and beat until thick. Then add 3 eggs, one at a time, beating well after each addition. Stir in the mastic or *mahlab*, cinnamon, orange-blossom water, orange zest, and orange juice. Mix to combine well. Add 1 cup of the flour and beat just long enough to combine well.

CHANGE THE MIXER ATTACHMENT from the beater to the dough hook and start to knead at the slowest speed while you gradually add the remaining flour. If the dough seems too dry, add ¼ cup of warm water. Knead with the dough hook for 7 to 10 minutes, or by hand for 10 to 12 minutes. When the dough is soft and resilient, transfer to a lightly greased bowl, cover with plastic wrap, and set aside in a cool place for several hours or overnight to let the dough rise and develop flavor.

WHEN YOU ARE READY to make the bread, knock the dough down and knead briefly to get rid of any air pockets. Divide the dough into six pieces. Sprinkle some sesame seeds on a bread board and roll a piece of dough in the sesame, continuing to knead it to distribute the sesame seeds throughout the bread. Shape the dough into a long serpent and then coil the serpent, setting an uncooked egg in its shell in the center of the coil if you wish. (For Orthodox Easter, dye the egg red beforehand.)

SCATTER CORNMEAL or semolina over a baking sheet and set the coil of dough on the pan. Proceed with the rest of the dough pieces. (For a variation, take three dough serpents and braid them together to make one loaf.) Paint the tops of each bread lightly with the egg wash and scatter a few more sesame seeds on top.

PREHEAT THE OVEN to 425°F. Lightly cover the breads with plastic wrap and set aside for 30 minutes to rise while the oven heats. Bake the coiled breads for 40 minutes and the braided breads for 50 minutes, or until the tops are golden and shiny.

REMOVE FROM THE OVEN and let rest on a rack for 30 to 60 minutes before serving.

**For the bread:**

½ cup extra-virgin olive oil or ½ cup butter, at room temperature, plus a little more for bowl and board

½ cup sugar

3 large eggs, lightly beaten

½ teaspoon crushed mastic or powdered *mahlab*

½ teaspoon ground cinnamon

1 tablespoon orange-blossom water

1 tablespoon finely grated orange zest

Juice of ½ orange

3½ cups unbleached all-purpose flour

½ to ¾ cup sesame seeds

6 whole raw large eggs in their shells (optional)

cornmeal or semolina for baking sheet

1 large egg mixed with 1 tablespoon of cool water to make a wash

## SANDWICHES, MEDITERRANEAN-STYLE

Tuna always seems to be a feature of Mediterranean sandwiches, which is just fine with me, as long as it's a high-quality canned tuna, preferably packed in olive oil. You could also use cooked fresh tuna when you happen to have leftovers.

# Mediterranean Tunafish Salad Sandwich

### BRUSCHETTA AL TONNO

**Makes 1 sandwich**

Two thin slices Mediterranean-style bread

1 garlic clove, cut in half

½ cup tuna, preferably canned in olive oil

1 medium very ripe tomato, seeded and roughly chopped

1 tablespoon coarsely chopped flat-leaf parsley

1 tablespoon coarsely chopped fresh mint

1 tablespoon salted capers, rinsed under running water and drained

2 tablespoons extra-virgin olive oil

1 teaspoon fresh lemon juice

Sea salt and freshly ground black pepper

LIGHTLY TOAST the bread slices, then rub them with the cut clove of garlic. Arrange them side by side on a plate.

DRAIN THE TUNA and flake it in a bowl. Combine with the tomato, parsley, mint, and capers. Stir in the olive oil and lemon juice. Taste and add salt and pepper as necessary.

PILE THE TUNA MIXTURE on the toasted bread and serve.

# Pan Bagnat

 This famous sandwich from the French Riviera is usually made with round breads about 5 or 6 inches in diameter, but I have also had pan bagnat on baguettes cut about 6 inches long. If you're making the bread yourself, use the Classic Mediterranean-Style Bread recipe (page 106) and shape it into baguettes or small rounds. Either way, some of the crumb is pulled out of the top and bottom halves to make more room for the delicious filling. The Niçois always say you should rub the insides of the bread with a cut clove of garlic, but that doesn't make it nearly garlicky enough for my taste. I prefer my system.

Don't feel you must stick to the following ingredients or that they must be in the quantities I've given. Feel free to use more or less of anything you fancy.

CUT THE BREAD in half and pull out and discard some of the inside crumb. Put the cucumber slices in a colander, salting them liberally.

IN A SMALL BOWL, crush the garlic cloves with the sea salt, using the back of a spoon, until you have a smooth paste. Mix in the vinegar and olive oil and beat with a fork to emulsify. Dribble this mixture liberally over both halves of the bread rounds. Pile the tomatoes, onion, sweet pepper, tuna, eggs, anchovies, and olives on the bottom halves of the bread rounds. Rinse and dry the cucumbers and set them on top along with the basil leaves and pepper. Set the top halves on, then wrap the sandwiches in plastic wrap and weight them for at least 15 minutes, so that some of the juices ooze into the remaining crumb. Then serve.

**Makes 4 sandwiches**

4 small (½-pound) rounds Classic Mediterranean-Style Bread (page 106) or four 6-inch lengths of baguette

1 cucumber, peeled and thinly sliced

2 garlic cloves, smashed with the flat blade of a knife

Sea salt

1 tablespoon red wine vinegar

3 tablespoons extra-virgin olive oil

2 medium firm ripe tomatoes, thinly sliced

1 medium red onion, very thinly sliced

1 fresh sweet green or red pepper

½ cup flaked tuna, preferably canned in olive oil

2 hard-cooked eggs, sliced

6 to 8 anchovy fillets (see page 411)

½ cup pitted black olives

Fresh basil leaves

Freshly ground black pepper

# Tunis Market Sandwiches

Tunisians distinguish between *cuisine tunisoise* and *cuisine tunisienne,* the latter being the cuisine of the country, the former that of the great city of Tunis. This type of sandwich, stuffed with a spicy salad, is served all over the country but is most associated with Tunis itself and especially with the area around the Marché Centrale and the medina. It is made with similar round buns as those used for *pan bagnat,* but they are sliced open at one end, to make a kind of pocket sandwich, instead of being cut in half. The ingredients should be added to taste.

### Makes 4 sandwiches

4 small (½ pound) rounds Classic Mediterranean-Style Bread (page 106), or a similar crusty bread

Tunisian Carrot Salad, minus the olives and feta (page 74)

Harissa (page 280)

*Mechouia* (page 283)

2 medium yellow-fleshed potatoes, boiled, peeled, thinly sliced

1 salt-preserved lemon (see page 44), rind only, thinly sliced

Large black and green olives, pitted

Salted capers, rinsed under running water and drained

Flaked canned tuna, preferably canned in olive oil

Extra-virgin olive oil

CUT A SLICE OFF one edge of a bread round (about a third of the whole bread round) and reach into the larger portion to pull out some of the crumb and make room for the other ingredients. Dip the edge you pulled out in a little of the carrot salad to moisten it and set it aside. Slather harissa all over the inside of the bread. Stuff in the potatoes, *mechouia,* lemon, olives, capers, and tuna, a little at a time, ending with the tuna. Sprinkle on enough olive oil to drizzle down inside, then cap the sandwich with the edge piece that was dipped in carrot salad to hold everything else in place.

SERVE IMMEDIATELY.

# North African Breakfast Buns

## MLAOUI

 These breads, called *mlaoui* (or *mlawi*), with a little honey to spread on them and a cup of mint tea to wash them down, are favorite breakfast companions throughout North Africa. Sometimes they're made simply with semolina, oil, and water, but this version, rich with egg, yeast, oil, and butter, is the kind of *mlaoui* that would be served to break the fast of Ramadan. You can make this dough the evening before and set it aside in a cool place overnight.

MIX THE YEAST in ½ cup of the warm water and set aside to dissolve.

COMBINE THE ALL-PURPOSE FLOUR and semolina in a bowl and stir in the dissolved yeast. Add the olive oil and egg and combine to mix well. The mixture should be about the consistency of mashed potatoes at first. If it seems too dry, add a little more warm water, in increments of ¼ cup in order to avoid adding too much all at once. (If you do add too much, stir in a little more semolina.)

ADD THE SALT and knead the dough on a lightly greased board for about 5 minutes, or until you feel the yeast and gluten start to come together and make a springy dough. Transfer the dough to a lightly greased bowl, cover with plastic wrap, and set aside for a couple of hours or overnight.

WHEN YOU ARE READY to make the buns, punch the dough down and divide it in half. Oil your hands with olive oil. Take one of the dough halves in your left hand (assuming you're right-handed) and squeeze out between your thumb and index finger a lump about the size of a Ping-Pong ball, and pull it off with

**Makes about 24 small buns**

⅛ teaspoon active dry yeast

1 cup warm water

2 cups unbleached all-purpose flour

1¾ cups semolina

1 tablespoon extra-virgin olive oil, plus a little more to work the dough

1 large egg

Sea salt

½ cup unsalted butter, at room temperature, plus additional butter for serving

Honey, for serving

your right hand. Roll it in your oiled palms and set aside. Continue until you've formed all the dough into balls.

TAKE A PING-PONG BALL OF DOUGH and roll it into a snake between your palms. Using a rolling pin, roll the snake on a lightly greased board into a long, thin strip of dough, about 1 inch wide and 4 to 5 inches long. Using your fingers, spread a small dab of butter in a thin smear over the dough, then roll the dough up in a tight cylinder. Continue until all the dough balls have been rolled.

MIDWAY THROUGH THIS PROCESS, set a cast-iron griddle on the stove over medium heat and let it heat up while you continue to shape the buns. When all the buns are formed, take the first cylinder and pat it between your oiled palms into a disk. You can use the rolling pin to help with this, but it should not be rolled too flat—about ⅛ to ¼ inch is plenty. Set the disk on the hot griddle and let it bake for about 2 minutes to a side, or until the sides are toasted brown and the inside is cooked through. It will look like a small, squat English muffin and the inside should be rather flaky because of the layers of butter. Check the first bun to be sure your temperature is correct and adjust accordingly. Continue cooking until they're all done, keeping the finished ones warm in the oven until you are ready to serve.

SERVE WARM with plenty of honey and additional butter for the greedy.

# Halise's Griddle Bread with Cheese or Scallions

## SAÇ BÖREK

*Saç börek* is an unleavened pancake bread, made from a simple flour and water dough called *yufke* and usually stuffed with something—onions, poppy seeds, scallions, or a mixture of white cheese and herbs. It is baked on a griddle called a *saç*, which looks like an inverted wok set over a live fire. Near Bodrum in southwest Turkey, a favorite *saç* bread is *hashhashli ekmek*, made with the seeds of opium poppies (the seeds are not narcotic), lightly crushed to release their oil and make a spread with the consistency of peanut butter. They roll out the *yufke* dough into a circle, spread it with poppy seed paste, then fold the dough over several times and roll it out again before grilling it on the *saç*.

This is the way the eighty-year-old aunt of a Turkish friend made *saç börek,* in the town of Ula, not far from Bodrum. You can use a black iron skillet or a griddle in place of the traditional *saç*. If the feta cheese you buy is very salty, soak it in cool water for a couple of hours before grating it.

**Makes 1 12-inch *börek*, 2 servings**

TO MAKE THE DOUGH, combine the whole-wheat flour, all-purpose flour, semolina, and salt in a bowl and toss with a fork to mix. Stir in about half the water and work with your hands. Add more water in small amounts as needed (you may not need the entire ½ cup) until the dough is soft and somewhat sticky. Lightly grease your hands with olive oil and knead the dough in the bowl. As soon as you can work the dough on a board, smear a few drops of olive oil across a pastry board and knead the dough on the board until it is smooth and elastic. Set aside, covered to keep it from drying out, for about 30 minutes.

TO MAKE THE STUFFING, in a small bowl, combine the cheese, parsley, and egg. Add black pepper to taste and mix together with a fork.

HAVE READY A SMALL BOWL with about ¼ cup olive oil in it.

**For the *yufke* dough:**

½ cup whole-wheat flour

1 cup unbleached all-purpose flour

½ cup semolina

½ teaspoon sea salt

½ cup warm water

Extra-virgin olive oil

**For the stuffing:**

1 cup grated feta cheese

½ cup minced flat-leaf parsley

1 large egg

Freshly ground black pepper

Unsalted butter

ONCE THE DOUGH has rested, divide it into eight pieces. Roll a piece out to a circle about 6 inches across. Dip your hand in the oil and very lightly smear it across the circle, then set the circle aside. Proceed with another three circles, each time smearing them lightly with oil and laying them on top of each other so that at the end you have a little stack of four oiled circles of dough. Do the same with the other four pieces of dough, to make two stacks of four each.

NOW TAKE ONE OF THE STACKS and roll it out to a larger, thinner circle, about 12 inches across. Sprinkle the cheese and parsley filling all over the circle, keeping a margin of about ¼ inch around the edge. Roll out the other stack to make the top for the *börek*. Dampen your fingers in a little water and press the top and bottom around the edge to seal.

SET A LARGE SKILLET (preferably a heavy black iron skillet) or griddle large enough to hold the *börek* over medium-high heat. When a few flicks of water dance on the surface, transfer the *börek* to the skillet. Bake for 8 to 10 minutes, turning once, or until the dough is cooked and starting to turn golden and the filling is soft and hot. Remove the *börek* from the skillet and butter the top lightly. Serve immediately.

NOTE: If you don't have a skillet large enough to accommodate a 12-inch *börek*, make two smaller 6-inch *böreks*. Or do as some Turkish cooks do: Roll out a 12-inch circle of dough as described above, cover half of it with the cheese filling, then fold the other half over it, sealing the edges, to make a crescent. Cook in the skillet or on a griddle as described.

VARIATION: Instead of the cheese-parsley stuffing above, try the following. Roll out the circle of dough and spread half of it with lightly beaten egg. Sprinkle with about ¼ cup sliced scallions, both white and green parts, and ¼ to ½ teaspoon crushed red chili pepper, preferably Middle Eastern or Turkish pepper, such as Urfa or Aleppo pepper. Fold over the other half of the circle, seal the edges, and cook on a skillet or griddle as described above.

## PIZZA'S COUSINS

Something like pizza exists in one form or another all over the Mediterranean, from Niçoise pissaladière to various open tartlike pastries from the eastern Mediterranean. A true Neapolitan pizza is rather different from and a good deal simpler than the incredible concoctions of ingredients that are to be found in North American pizzerias. In fact, in my favorite Neapolitan pizza shop, da Michele on the via Cesare Sersale, only two kinds of pizza are served—marinara, the classic, topped with a plain tomato sauce with garlic and oregano, and Margherita, an embellishment that includes cow's milk mozzarella (buffalo milk mozzarella doesn't work so well, they say) and fresh basil over the top.

Other Mediterranean versions of flatbread-with-a-topping, which is a basic definition of pizza, follow. Note that flatbread does not necessarily, and not often, mean unleavened bread.

# Anna Tasca Lanza's Sicilian Pizza

### SFINCIONE

 *Sfincione* is Sicilian-style pizza with a thick crust, baked in a large rectangular pan—it's a favorite street food in Palermo. The version made by Anna Tasca Lanza, a great Sicilian cook and tireless investigator of Sicilian traditions, has both a richer dough and a more elaborate topping than the Neapolitan classic. Here's how Anna makes *sfincione* for her cooking classes at Regaleali, her family's winery in central Sicily. The use of Swiss cheese (Emmentaler) may come as a surprise, but it is a long-standing tradition in the Tasca family.

TO MAKE THE DOUGH, add the yeast to ½ cup of the warm water and set aside to dissolve.

COMBINE THE FLOUR, semolina, and salt. Make a well in the center and pour in the dissolved yeast. Add the butter and mix together, adding another ¼ cup warm water. Add the egg and mix, adding more water as necessary—up to 1 cup in all—to make a soft, dense dough. (You can also do this using an electric

**Makes 12 to 18 servings**

**For the dough:**

1 teaspoon active dry yeast

1 cup warm water

3 cups unbleached all-purpose flour

1 cup semolina

1 teaspoon sea salt

2 tablespoons unsalted butter or lard, cut in pieces, at room temperature

1 large egg

**For the topping:**

2 medium onions, thinly sliced

¾ cup extra-virgin olive oil

4 salted anchovy fillets, rinsed and coarsely chopped (see page 411)

8 ounces Emmentaler or Swiss cheese, thinly sliced

8 ounces fresh goat's cheese, crumbled

4 pounds tomatoes, peeled, seeded, and roughly chopped; or 3 (28-ounce) cans whole tomatoes, drained well

2 teaspoons dried Sicilian or Greek oregano (*rígani*)

2 tablespoons grated Pecorino Sardo or Parmigiano-Reggiano

2 tablespoons dried unflavored bread crumbs

mixer with a dough hook.) Knead by hand for at least 10 minutes, or for about 6 minutes using the electric mixer. Set the dough aside, covered, to rest for about 30 minutes.

WHILE THE DOUGH IS RESTING, make the topping. Gently sauté the onions in ½ cup of the oil over medium-low heat until they are golden, about 30 minutes. Remove from the heat and set aside.

LIGHTLY OIL a 12 by 17-inch baking sheet. Or cut a piece of parchment paper to fit the baking sheet. Roll the dough out on the baking sheet to cover it entirely, patting the dough to push it into all the corners of the sheet.

SCATTER THE ANCHOVIES over the dough, then cover them with the sliced cheese. Crumble the goat's cheese over the top. Mix the tomatoes into the browned onions and spread over the cheese. Sprinkle with oregano, grated Pecorino cheese, and bread crumbs. Lightly press all the toppings into the dough, using the palms of your hands, then raise the dough a little all around the edge to create a border. Generously dribble the remaining ¼ cup oil over the top and set aside, lightly covered with plastic wrap, to rise for about an hour.

PREHEAT THE OVEN to 400°F. Bake the *sfincione* for about 30 minutes, or until the dough is thoroughly cooked and the topping is bubbling.

REMOVE THE *SFINCIONE* from the oven and cut into squares. Serve immediately.

# Syrian Pizzas

## LAHM B'AJIIN

The name *lahm b'ajiin* means simply "meat pastry." These little tarts are popular as street food and home-baked snacks all over the Middle East. Peddlers sell them piping hot along the sea-front corniche in Beirut. In the old stone-paved alleys of Aleppo, every bakery worth its salt displays a tray full of hot *lahm b'ajiin* in the window at midmorning, just when energies are beginning to flag.

If you don't want to make the bread yourself, use Middle Eastern flatbread (Arab bread, pita), simply splitting the breads in half and topping them with the meat mixture. Just be careful to spread it in a thin layer right out to the very edge of the bread; otherwise the exposed edges of the bread may burn in the hot oven.

In Gaziantep, in southeastern Turkey, these little pizzas are made with pomegranate syrup (*dibsl roumann*) and/or sumac. In other regions, ⅓ cup of strained yogurt with a tablespoon of lemon juice is added to the meat mixture to give it the desired tartness.

TO MAKE THE DOUGH, add the yeast to the water and set aside to dissolve.

COMBINE 1½ CUPS of the all-purpose flour and the semolina in a bowl. Add the salt. When the yeast has dissolved, make a well in the middle of the flours and pour in the yeast mixture. Mix together, using a wooden spoon at first and then, as the dough comes together, your hands. When the dough is malleable, turn it out onto a board and knead, incorporating a little more flour if necessary. (You can also do this with an electric mixer and a dough hook. Combine the yeast and water in the mixer bowl and when the yeast has dissolved, add 1 cup flour. Mix with the dough hook for about 1 minute or so, then add another ½ cup flour and the semolina. Continue mixing until the dough is well-kneaded and has formed a ball—about 5 minutes should do it. Add a little more flour if necessary.)

**Makes 6 to 8 servings
(16 small tarts)**

**Dough:**

1 teaspoon active dry yeast

¾ cup warm water

2 cups unbleached all-purpose flour

1 cup semolina

1 teaspoon salt

Extra-virgin olive oil

**Topping:**

½ cup pine nuts

4 teaspoons extra-virgin olive oil

1 cup peeled, seeded, chopped fresh (or canned) tomatoes

½ fresh sweet red pepper, chopped

1 cup finely chopped flat-leaf parsley

2 tablespoons finely minced cilantro

⅓ cup strained yogurt and 1 tablespoon fresh lemon juice or 1 tablespoon pomegranate syrup and 2 teaspoons ground sumac

1 teaspoon ground cumin

1 teaspoon ground cinnamon

½ teaspoon ground allspice

½ teaspoon hot red chili pepper flakes

Freshly ground black pepper

1 medium onion, finely chopped

1 pound ground lean lamb

SET THE KNEADED DOUGH ASIDE in a lightly greased bowl, covered with plastic wrap, to rise and double—30 to 60 minutes.

WHILE THE DOUGH IS RISING, make the topping.

COMBINE THE PINE NUTS with 1 teaspoon oil in a sauté pan and gently toast them over medium-low heat, being careful not to burn—pine nuts will burn very quickly. As soon as they start to turn golden, remove them from the heat and set aside.

COMBINE THE TOMATOES in a bowl with the chopped pepper, parsley, cilantro, yogurt and lemon juice mixture, cumin, cinnamon, allspice, chili pepper flakes, and black pepper. Mix well and set aside.

ADD THE REMAINING 3 teaspoons oil to the pan in which you cooked the pine nuts. Add the onion, and cook over low heat for 10 minutes or so, until it has sweated out all its liquid and softened. Do not let it brown. When the onion is done, transfer it to a bowl and add the meat. Taste the tomato mixture and adjust the seasoning, then stir it into the onion and meat. Add the pine nuts and mix well, using your hands or a wooden spoon.

WHEN YOU ARE READY TO BAKE, preheat the oven to 450°F. Punch down the dough and knead it briefly. Divide the dough into sixteen equal pieces, each about the size of a golf ball. Roll each piece into a ball and set aside, covered with plastic wrap, to rest for 10 minutes or so. Then take a ball and roll it out on a lightly greased board into a thin disk, not more than ⅛ inch thick. Lay the disk on a lightly oiled baking sheet and proceed with the rest of the balls.

SPOON SOME OF THE TOPPING over each disk, spreading it right out to the edge, leaving just a very thin margin exposed. Let rest, lightly covered with plastic wrap, for 10 minutes.

BAKE FOR 10 MINUTES or so, or until the pastries are golden but still rather soft. Remove from the oven and serve immediately.

# Catalan Pizzas

### COCAS

The Catalan version of pizza is often a sweet dough with a sweet topping, but I much prefer the savory variation. When you find red peppers used in abundance, as in the following recipe, it's almost always an indication of a link with the Balearic Islands (Majorca, Minorca, Ibiza), where plump, flavorful red peppers are a local favorite.

TO MAKE THE DOUGH, combine the warm water and the yeast and set aside until the yeast has thoroughly dissolved. Transfer the mixture to the bowl of an electric mixer and add the olive oil, salt, and 1 cup of flour. Using the dough hook, mix until well-blended, about 1 minute. Add the remaining flour and the semolina. Mix again until the dough forms a ball. Or mix the yeast, water, oil, salt, and flours in a bowl and knead by hand, first in the bowl then on a lightly greased board, until it is a smooth, elastic dough.

TURN THE DOUGH into a lightly greased mixing bowl. Cover and set aside to rise until double, about 1 hour.

WHILE THE DOUGH IS RISING, make the red pepper–tomato topping. Roast the red peppers and peel them (see page 410). Discard the seeds and white membranes and cut them into long strips.

COMBINE THE ONIONS and garlic with the oil and gently sauté over medium-low heat until the vegetables are very soft, 10 to 12 minutes. Add the red peppers, tomatoes, a little sugar, and salt and pepper. Cook over medium-high heat until most of the liquid in the tomatoes has evaporated.

TURN THE DOUGH out onto a board, punching it down. Divide the dough into four equal pieces. Sprinkle cornmeal or semolina over a 12 by 17-inch baking sheet. Roll each piece of dough out into a long oval and set it on the baking sheet.

## Makes 8 servings (4 cocas)

**For the dough:**

1½ cups warm water

1 teaspoon active dry yeast

2 tablespoons extra-virgin olive oil

1 teaspoon sea salt

3 cups unbleached all-purpose flour

1 cup semolina

Cornmeal or semolina for the baking sheet

**For the topping:**

4 large fresh sweet red peppers

2 thinly sliced onions

3 to 4 garlic cloves, coarsely chopped

¼ cup extra-virgin olive oil

4 large ripe tomatoes, peeled, seeded, and chopped

Sugar

Sea salt and freshly ground black pepper

8 ounces chorizo, coarsely chopped

¼ cup pine nuts, toasted

PREHEAT THE OVEN to 450°F.

DIVIDE THE TOPPING into four portions and spread a portion over each of the dough ovals, spreading it out to about ¼ inch from the edge. Sprinkle the chopped chorizo and toasted pine nuts on top.

BAKE FOR ABOUT 20 MINUTES, or until the edges of the cocas are golden brown and the topping is simmering.

REMOVE THE COCAS and set aside on a rack to cool slightly before serving.

## USING LEFTOVER BREAD

Because bread is such an important part of the Mediterranean diet, none is ever wasted. Leftover bread, stale bread, bread that has lost its original oomph is turned into delicious soups and salads. It may be grated into bread crumbs to add to a stuffing or fried in olive oil to sprinkle over pasta in place of cheese; it may be cubed into croutons that are then fried in garlicky oil to garnish and add crispness to a salad; it may be simply sliced and set at the bottom of a bowl of fish or bean soup to add substance to the dish. In Tuscany, leftover bread is not considered stale; instead it's called *pane raffermo*, firmed-up bread, and used as the base of crostini, little crusts, that could be piled with a mash of chicken livers or, in season, an impromptu salad of chopped tomatoes and basil fresh from the garden.

Often, too, bread may be sliced while still fresh, then returned to the oven for a second baking at lower temperatures, which dries it out thoroughly for long-keeping. This is typical of island cultures where fuel is not readily available and a single firing of the village or family oven has to produce bread to last many days or weeks.

# Twice-Baked Bread Salad

### CIALDA PUGLIESE

 This recipe begins by making *friselle*, a Pugliese barley bread that is shaped in small buns and baked twice. If you don't want to make bread first, take an ordinary Mediterranean-style bread, one you've made yourself or bought from a good bakery, slice it in ½-inch slices, and set the slices in a low (200°F.) oven until they are very hard—40 to 60 minutes. Then proceed with the salad part of the recipe.

TO MAKE THE *FRISELLE,* first make a sponge. Sprinkle the yeast over ¾ cup water and leave to dissolve thoroughly. Stir in ¾ cup all-purpose flour, mixing the flour and water thoroughly. Cover with plastic wrap and set aside to develop for at least

**For the friselle:**

½ teaspoon active dry yeast

Very warm water
(100° to 120°F.)

2¼ cups unbleached
all-purpose flour

1 cup barley flour

½ cup whole-wheat flour

Sea salt

About ¼ cup extra-virgin olive oil

Cornmeal or semolina

**For the salad:**

8 friselle halves

½ cup red wine vinegar

1 cup water

1 pound potatoes, preferably
yellow-fleshed, boiled and
peeled

4 large, firm ripe tomatoes,
coarsely chopped

1 red onion, halved and
thinly sliced

2 tablespoons salted capers,
rinsed under running water,
drained, and coarsely chopped

10 to 12 large green olives, pitted
and coarsely chopped

¼ cup slivered fresh basil leaves

1 teaspoon dried Sicilian or Greek
oregano (rígani)

1 (3¼-ounce) can oil-packed
tuna, drained and flaked

¼ cup extra-virgin olive oil

Sea salt and freshly ground
black pepper

1 hour—but the bread will have more flavor if you can let the sponge develop for several hours or overnight in a cool place.

WHEN THE SPONGE IS READY, combine it with 2 cups warm water, ½ cup all-purpose flour, ½ cup barley flour, and all the whole-wheat flour. Mix together well and leave to rise, covered, for several hours or overnight.

WHEN THE DOUGH IS WELL RISEN, add another ½ cup warm water, ½ cup all-purpose flour, the remaining ½ cup barley flour, and ½ teaspoon, more or less, of salt. Mix together well.

SPREAD THE REMAINING ½ cup all-purpose flour on a board and knead the dough, gradually kneading in the flour on the board. Once all the flour has been incorporated, if the dough must be kneaded further, rub a very small amount of oil on the board—this, to avoid adding too much flour to the dough. When the dough is sufficiently kneaded and has lost its stickiness and become soft and resilient, transfer the dough to a bowl that has been rubbed with about a teaspoon of olive oil. Cover and set aside to rise for 2 hours, or until double.

PUNCH DOWN THE DOUGH and divide it into two pieces. Roll each piece out in a long thick roll, like a snake, and cut it into four pieces. Roll each of the four into a thinner snake, then bring the two ends of the snake together to make a ring. As you finish each ring, set it aside on a board lightly dusted with cornmeal or semolina.

WHEN ALL THE DOUGH has been shaped, cover the rings lightly with a dry towel and let them rise until almost doubled. Don't worry if the rings close, leaving just a dimple in the center.

PREHEAT THE OVEN to 450°F, letting it preheat for at least 30 minutes.

WHEN YOU ARE READY TO BAKE, lightly oil a 12 by 17-inch baking sheet. Have ready a bowl filled with cold water to which you've added a couple of ice cubes. Dip the risen dough rings in the icy water, then place on the sheet. Bake for 15 minutes, then lower the temperature to 350°F. and continue baking for another 45 minutes, or until the friselle are crisp and golden.

REMOVE THE SHEET from the oven and turn the oven temperature down again to 225°F. As soon as you can handle the *friselle*, slice them in half and lay the halves, cut side up, on the baking sheet. Return to the oven for 1 hour, to dry out thoroughly. Properly stored, in a biscuit tin or similar container, they will keep for weeks.

ONCE THE *FRISELLE* are ready and thoroughly dried out, proceed with making the salad.

BREAK THE *FRISELLE* into pieces and crumble them into a bowl. Add the wine vinegar and water and let soak for 15 minutes or until the *friselle* have absorbed the liquid. Then squeeze the *friselle* gently to release as much of the liquid as possible. Transfer the friselle to a salad bowl. Slice the potatoes and add, along with the tomatoes, onion, capers, olives, basil, oregano, tuna, oil, and salt and pepper. Taste and adjust the seasoning, then set aside at room temperature to let the flavors develop for at least 30 minutes before serving.

VARIATION: Feel free to add other ingredients to this basic mixture. Hard-boiled eggs, roughly chopped, are sometimes substituted for the tuna, and small, very fresh cucumbers, their skins intact, are a seasonal addition. Arugula or other bittersweet salad greens will contribute an interesting flavor, or you might consider serving the salad on a bed of dark-green lettuces and red chicory when available.

# Sardinian Crisp Bread Layered with Tomato Sauce and a Fried Egg

### PANE FRATTÀU

To make *pane frattàu,* you'll need *pane carasau,* the traditional crisp flatbread of Sardinia, known in other parts of Italy as *carta da musica* (music paper) for the thin, fine paper on which musical compositions are written. In North America, a good-quality *pane carasau,* made in commercial bakeries in Sardinia, is available in 500-gram (approximately 1-pound) packages from Todaro Brothers (see Where to Find It, page 415).

Nowadays *pane carasau* is made almost entirely in industrial bakeries, but one traditional wood-fired bakery still exists in the town of Oliena, where the three Bette sisters produce *pane carasau* for the town and a nearby resort hotel, Su Gologone. The bread is made in big flat disks that puff up like Arab bread in the oven's heat. They cook quickly and are then extracted from the oven and, while still hot, split into upper and lower portions. These two flat rounds are put back in the oven briefly to crisp and dry out, after which the bread may be kept for weeks and probably for months. Traditionally, *pane carasau* was the very definition of a flatbread, since no leaven was used; today, most bakers, including the Bette sisters, use a small amount of leaven to raise the dough.

Served with tomato sauce and poached or fried eggs, pane frattàu makes wonderful comfort food for a late-night supper. In Sardinia, each serving consists of a single large *pane carasau,* but, because the fragile bread breaks up when it's shipped here, I've made it by layering several large broken pieces.

### Makes 4 servings

**For the tomato sauce:**

1 medium onion, coarsely chopped

2 tablespoons extra-virgin olive oil

1 (28-ounce) can whole plum tomatoes, or 2 pounds fresh ripe seasonal tomatoes

Tomato concentrate or paste (optional)

THE TOMATO SAUCE may be prepared well ahead of time. Combine the onion and oil in a saucepan over medium-low heat and cook until the onion is soft and golden, but not brown—10 to 20 minutes. If you are using canned tomatoes, drain them, reserving the liquid, and chop coarsely. If you are using fresh tomatoes, skin and seed them, then chop coarsely. Add the tomatoes to the onion and stir to combine well. Cook, uncovered, stirring frequently, until the tomatoes are thoroughly melted into a sauce, about 30 minutes. From time to time, add a little liquid from the can or plain water, to keep the tomatoes from sticking to the pan. (If you are using fresh tomatoes, you may wish to add a tablespoon or so of tomato concentrate or paste to boost the flavor.) When the tomatoes have dissolved into a sauce, taste and add salt and pepper and, if the sauce is acid, a little sugar. Then add the red pepper flakes and basil. Set aside. (You should have about 2½ cups of tomato sauce.)

OPEN THE PACKAGE of *pane carasau* and select three good-sized pieces of flatbread for each serving—twelve pieces in all. Heat the stock until it is very warm. Have four dinner plates warming in a 200°F oven. If the tomato sauce is no longer warm, heat it until it is just below simmering.

IF YOU ARE POACHING the eggs, add the vinegar to 3 cups of water in a poaching pan and bring to a boil. If you are frying the eggs, add oil to a frying pan to a depth of about 2 inches and set over medium heat to reach a frying temperature of 350° to 360°F.

ONCE YOU HAVE all your ingredients in place, proceed with the recipe.

REMOVE A DINNER PLATE from the oven. Dip a piece of *pane carasau* in the very warm stock, turning it once, until it starts to soften. Using a spatula or slotted spoon, remove the bread from the stock and set it on the plate. Immediately spread the bread with a layer of tomato sauce and sprinkle it with about a tablespoon of grated cheese. Do the same thing with the next two pieces of *pane carasau*, then return the plate to the oven while you continue with the remaining three servings.

WHEN ALL THE PLATES have been prepared, start to poach or fry the eggs, two at a time. Each time you finish a pair of eggs,

Salt and freshly ground black pepper

½ teaspoon sugar (optional)

Pinch of hot red chili pepper flakes, or to taste

About ¼ cup slivered fresh basil leaves

1 (500-gram) package *pane carasau*

2 cups rich meat or chicken stock (vegetable stock may also be used)

¼ cup white wine vinegar (optional)

Oil for deep-fat frying (preferably Sardinian extra-virgin olive oil) (optional)

1½ cups grated cheese, preferably aged Pecorino Sardo or Pecorino Toscano; otherwise use Parmigiano-Reggiano

8 large eggs

arrange them atop a stack of layered bread and sprinkle with another tablespoon or so of grated cheese. When all the eggs are done, serve the *pane frattàu* immediately, passing more cheese at the table.

**VARIATION:** Sardinian cooks also serve *pane guttau,* brushing the bread on one side only with extra-virgin olive oil into which a clove or two of garlic has been crushed, then sprinkling it with coarse sea salt and putting it in a hot oven just long enough to warm it thoroughly. It is usually served at the beginning of the meal as something to nibble on while more sustaining fare is prepared.

# Tuscan Bread Soup from the Casentino

## ACQUACOTTA CASENTINESE

 The Casentino is the mountainous region north of Arezzo, still not well known to the foreigners who have flocked to Tuscany in recent years. It preserves many of the old Tuscan traditions, including this *acquacotta*, or "cooked water," one of the many uses to which thrifty Tuscan peasants put their leftover bread. In essence, it's more like a savory bread pudding than a soup and is thick enough to eat with a fork.

If you can't get pancetta, use a thick slice of bacon, but blanch it in boiling water for 10 to 12 minutes to get rid of the smoky flavor.

**Makes 4 main-course or 6 first-course servings**

1 thick slice pancetta, coarsely chopped

1 garlic clove, coarsely chopped

1 small celery stalk, including the green top, coarsely chopped

1 medium carrot, coarsely chopped

1 bunch flat-leaf parsley, coarsely chopped (about 1/2 cup)

2 tablespoons extra-virgin olive oil

4 to 5 medium red onions (about 1 1/2 pounds), very thinly sliced

2 tablespoons tomato concentrate or tomato paste

Sea salt

1 small dried hot red chili pepper, broken in two (stem discarded)

4 to 5 cups light chicken broth

About 1 pound stale country-style bread, very thinly sliced

1 cup grated cheese, preferably aged Pecorino Toscano, Pecorino Sardo, or Parmigiano-Reggiano

MAKE A *BATTUTO* by mixing together the pancetta, garlic, celery, carrot, and parsley on a board and further chopping them to make a mince. Add to a heavy saucepan or deep skillet, along with 1 tablespoon of the oil, and cook gently over medium-low heat for 10 to 20 minutes or until the vegetables are very soft and the fat in the pancetta has started to run.

STIR IN THE ONIONS and continue to cook, stirring frequently, until they are very soft and translucent, about 30 minutes. Do not let the onions brown.

WHEN THE ONIONS ARE THOROUGHLY SOFT and wilted, stir in the tomato concentrate. Add a good pinch of salt and the chili pepper, then pour in some of the chicken broth. There should be just enough liquid to cover the onions to a depth of about 1/2 inch. (You may not need all the broth to start with.) Let the soup come to a simmer, cover the pan, and cook very gently for about 30 minutes.

TURN THE OVEN ON to 375°F. Spoon a little of the hot onion broth into the bottom of a baking dish—a 4-quart soufflé dish will do just fine. Cover the bottom of the dish with bread, cutting the slices to fit in as many as you can in a single layer. Spoon about a third of the onion broth over the bread, then sprinkle about a third of the grated cheese on top. Add more bread slices, again cutting them to make one layer, then another third of onion broth and another layer of cheese. Make a final layer of bread, add the rest of the onion broth and the rest of the cheese. Fill the casserole with any broth you have left over—the liquid should come just to the top of the bread slices. Dribble the remaining 1 tablespoon oil over the top. Bake for 30 minutes, or until the flavors are well blended and the top is golden.

SERVE IMMEDIATELY, passing more grated cheese if you wish.

VARIATION: Some Casentino cooks add a bunch of green chard, thinly sliced to make about 3 cups, to cook gently with the onions.

## FATTEH

This preparation, which evolved as a way of using up stale bread, is unquestionably one of the glories of Levantine cuisine. I've always found it odd that it's not better known outside the region. Perhaps it's the name, *fatteh* (pronounced FAHT-tay), which might get mispronounced as fatty—which it most definitely is not unless you heap on the melted butter at the end. There's really no way to translate the name in English so *fatteh* it is, and *fatteh* it shall remain.

*Fatteh*s exist in a number of different variations, based on meat, chicken, eggplant, other vegetables, or just plain chickpeas. What unites them all is the way they're constructed: a bottom layer of toasted Arab pita bread soaks up a rich stock made of meat, chicken, legumes, or vegetables. Then the solid part, the part that was cooked in the stock, is ladled over the top, yogurt (often but not always strained yogurt) is poured over that, and the dish is garnished with toasted pine nuts or sometimes with crushed dried mint, fresh parsley, or crushed red chili peppers mixed into warm olive oil and melted butter.

*Fatteh* is a countryman's dish par excellence, but I've seen it avidly scooped up for Friday lunch at open-air restaurants outside the great *souqs* of Aleppo. In Christian mountain communities in Lebanon, it's the dish served on the festive autumn day when they slaughter fat-tailed sheep to make *qawarma*, confit of mutton, and render the tail fat for winter stores. Lamb is at the basis of *fatteh* on that day and *samneh*, preserved butter, is poured over it at the end.

All of these ways of making *fatteh* are so delicious that, remembering my kitchen dictum that less is always more, I've had to restrain myself from putting them all together in one dish. Note, before you begin these recipes, the yogurt should be strained or drained several hours or overnight.

# Eggplant and Lamb *Fatteh*

**Makes 6 servings**

2 medium onions, finely chopped

Extra-virgin olive oil

1 pound boneless lamb (shoulder is best), cut into small cubes

¼ teaspoon ground cumin

¼ teaspoon freshly ground black pepper

¼ teaspoon ground coriander seeds

1 (2-inch) cinnamon stick

6 whole cloves

Water

Chicken or meat broth (optional)

2 pounds eggplant, sliced about ½ inch thick, salted, and put in a colander to drain

1 cup chopped, drained canned plum tomatoes

Three 6- to 7-inch rounds Arab pita breads

2 cups strained yogurt, made from 3 to 4 cups unstrained yogurt (see page 410)

1 tablespoon unsalted butter

1 tablespoon minced flat-leaf parsley

1 teaspoon ground red Middle Eastern pepper (Aleppo pepper, Turkish pepper)

TO PREPARE THE LAMB STEW, in a small (2-quart) heavy-duty stockpot, gently sauté the onions in 2 tablespoons of olive oil over medium-low heat, 20 to 30 minutes, or until the onions are soft and translucent, but not brown. Add the lamb and continue cooking gently until the meat has changed color. Stir in the cumin, black pepper, and coriander, mixing well. Add the cinnamon and cloves and water to cover the lamb to a depth of 1 inch. Bring to a simmer, cover, and simmer very gently until the lamb is very tender—about 1 hour. Discard the cinnamon and cloves and set the lamb aside in its broth to keep warm. You should have at least 1½ cups broth left with the lamb. If not, add some chicken or meat broth to make up the quantity needed.

PREHEAT THE OVEN to 375°F.

RINSE THE EGGPLANT SLICES thoroughly under running water and dry well using paper towels. Use a little olive oil to grease a baking sheet large enough to accommodate all the eggplant slices in one layer. Arrange the slices on the sheet and paint each one with a little more olive oil. Bake until the tops are golden, 15 to 20 minutes. Turn the slices over and continue baking until the undersides are golden. Remove from the oven and transfer to a bowl. Add ¾ cup of chopped tomatoes to the eggplant and mix thoroughly. Some of the eggplant will break up as you mix, but that's no problem.

LOWER THE OVEN HEAT to 300°F. Separate the bread rounds into top and bottom halves and set in the oven. Bake until crisp—10 to 15 minutes. Break the bread up into smaller pieces. Warm six soup plates in the oven (or use a single large platter).

WARM THE YOGURT very gently, but do not let it boil because it will separate. When warm, stir in the remaining ¼ cup chopped tomatoes and set aside.

MELT THE BUTTER in a small saucepan with 1 tablespoon olive oil. When it is thoroughly melted and very hot, stir in the parsley and red pepper. Set aside.

WHEN ALL THE INGREDIENTS ARE READY, assemble the dishes. Remove the six soup plates from the oven. Divide the crisped bread among the plates. Arrange the eggplant-tomato mixture on top and use a slotted spoon to distribute the pieces of lamb over the eggplant. Now spoon some of the spicy lamb broth over each serving—no more than ½ cup per serving. You may not need to use it all—the idea is not to create a soup that must be eaten with a spoon, but a soupy dish that can be eaten with spoon and fork together. Spoon the tomato-yogurt sauce generously on top of each dish and garnish with the parsley–red pepper combination. Serve immediately.

# Chicken and Chickpea *Fatteh*

**Makes 6 servings**

¾ cup dried chickpeas, soaked several hours or overnight

Water

2 bay leaves

½ small chicken, or about 2 pounds chicken parts

1 small onion

5 garlic cloves

1 medium carrot, coarsely chopped

1 celery stalk, coarsely chopped

Sea salt and freshly ground black pepper

Three 6- to 7-inch rounds Arab (pita) bread

2 tablespoons unsalted butter, melted

¼ cup pine nuts

2 cups strained yogurt, made from 3 to 4 cups unstrained yogurt (see page 410)

1 tablespoon dried mint

1 tablespoon ground cumin

DRAIN THE CHICKPEAS and transfer to a saucepan. Add enough water to cover by 1 inch. Add the bay leaves, bring to a simmer over medium-low heat, and continue simmering, partially covered, until the chickpeas are very tender, about 40 minutes. Add boiling water from time to time if necessary. When the chickpeas are done, discard the bay leaves and set the chickpeas aside in their cooking liquid.

WHILE THE CHICKPEAS COOK, place the chicken in a small heavy-duty stockpot, combining it with the onion, 2 cloves of the garlic, the carrot, and celery. Add salt and a good quantity of black pepper and bring to a simmer over medium-low heat. Simmer, partially covered, until the chicken is very tender, 40 to 60 minutes. Remove the chicken and vegetables from the stockpot. Discard the vegetables and strip the chicken meat from the bones, discarding the bones and skin. Chop the chicken meat in rather large pieces and return it to the stock in the pot to keep warm.

PREHEAT THE OVEN to 300°F.

SPLIT THE ARAB BREADS in half. Arrange the halves on a cookie sheet and dribble the melted butter over them. Toast the bread halves in the oven until they are crisp, then remove them and break up into smaller pieces.

PUT THE PINE NUTS in a small baking dish and toast in the oven until they are golden, about 10 minutes. Be careful not to burn them. When they're done, remove them from the heat immediately and set aside. Warm 6 soup plates in the oven. (You may also assemble the fatteh on a single deep serving platter.)

CHOP THE REMAINING 3 garlic cloves and crush them in a bowl with a small amount of salt, using the back of a spoon to make a garlic paste. Stir some of the strained yogurt into this, then add it all back into the rest of the strained yogurt. Crumble the dried mint and cumin into the yogurt and stir to mix well. Warm the yogurt over very low heat but be careful not to let it boil, because it will separate.

WHEN ALL THE INGREDIENTS ARE READY, assemble the dishes. Divide half the crisped bread among the plates. Spoon half the chickpeas with some of their liquid over the bread. Top with the rest of the bread. Now divide all the chicken among the servings, along with some of the chicken stock. Top with the remaining chickpeas, again with some of their liquid, remembering that you're not making a soup as such, but rather a soupy combination. Finally, spoon the flavored yogurt over everything and garnish with the toasted pine nuts. Serve immediately.

# Pasta and Couscous

## OTHER WAYS WITH WHEAT

*For us [Sicilians], as you know, pasta is a religion, we eat it "tutto d'un fiato"*
*[all in one breath], like we drink coffee! My nephew Filiberto and my father too, when*
*they sat down in front of their pasta dish for supper, they wouldn't even answer*
*a question. Filiberto says: "Don't disturb me, I am eating pasta!"*

—Anna Tasca Lanza, Sicilian food authority

WHERE DOES PASTA COME FROM? The quick and easy answer is Italy, of course! Pasta is so strongly identified with the cooking of the Italian peninsula—with the very history of the Italian peninsula—that it's no wonder that to the entire rest of the non-Mediterranean world, the word pasta conjures up something like spaghetti or macaroni or tortellini or ravioli, boiled in water and sauced in a manner that recalls, if sometimes only vaguely, an Italian progenitor. Even way back in fourteenth-century England, when the chefs of King Richard II compiled a manuscript cookbook called *The Forme of Curye*, they included recipes for "macarouns" (macaroni) and "rauioles" (ravioli)—clearly reflecting a strong Italian influence (possibly even an Italian presence?) in the royal kitchen.

The quick and easy answer, however, belies all the multiple ways that cooks in other cultures all around the Mediterranean have devised to cope with this fundamental wheat product. If we use the food manufacturers' rather gross terminology, pasta is an "alimentary paste," which allows us to include couscous in the definition. Whether couscous or pasta, though, it's made simply by combining flour and water, shaping and drying it, then cooking it, primarily by boiling but also, especially with North African couscous, by steaming. The flour most often used is durum semolina, another indication of how important that type of wheat is in the Mediterranean context, but other flours can be added; indeed, as is well known, the tradition in Northern Italy is for pasta made with soft flour from bread wheat mixed with eggs. And in Liguria, on Italy's northwest coast, chestnut flour may be added to the basic dough (see page 164).

But it isn't just Italian.

In Turkey, for instance, two deeply traditional dishes, *tutmaç* and *mantı*, can be traced back to the Central Asian origins of modern Turks. *Mantı* are meat-stuffed dumplings, like smaller versions of the more familiar Italian capelletti or tortellini, but the meat is lamb for the most part and the sauce is yogurt-based. *Tutmaç*, "part of the courtly cuisine of the Seljuqs," says Ayla Algar, Mellon Professor of Turkish at Berkeley, are more like tagliatelle noodles, served with a sauce based on fried meat, yogurt, mint, and garlic, very fitting to the Turkish flavor profile. If *tutmaç* have fallen somewhat from favor, seldom prepared at home these days, mantı still play a major role in celebratory meals. Pasta dishes like these, touchstones for Turkish culinary identity, might suggest that pasta is Turkish. Dr. Algar notes simply that "Turks have prepared noodle dishes throughout their recorded history, and with one or two exceptions, these dishes cannot be ascribed to outside influences."

Greece, too, has long respected pasta traditions, very different from Italy's and more regionally based than Turkey's. If Turkish pasta identifies the cook as a Turk, pure and simple, Greek pasta identifies the cook as someone from the Aegean, or the Dodecanese, or from Crete. In the northeastern Aegean, *moustokoulika* is a hand-made pasta cooked in sweet grape must, while on the island of Limnos, where wheat has been grown since at least 3000 B.C.E., home cooks, according to Diane Kochilas, still make *flomaria*, short stringy or flat noodles, from a particularly aromatic variety of durum grown on that island. Unlike Italian pasta, which is boiled, drained, and then sauced separately, Greek pasta is often cooked right in the sauce that will adorn it. On the island of Rhodes, flat noodles called *matsi*, flavored with cinnamon and allspice, are baked in the oven with chickpeas, a combination that, apart from the aromatics, recalls similar dishes from southern Italy—just one of many southern Italian culinary traditions that are similar to Greek island cooking. Do these go back to Greece itself or are they evidence of a common Byzantine ancestor to both traditions?

Spain's pasta vocabulary, if not always the dishes themselves, can be traced back to Arab and Berber cooks who lived in Iberia for seven hundred years. *Fideos* (the name comes directly from Arabic *fidawsh*) are thin, fine, short noodles that used to be cooked in their own sauce, like the Greek pastas mentioned above. In modern times, *fideos* are often cooked apart, like Italian pasta, then sauced before serving, but in Catalonia, things take a different course, one more closely related to the old ways of preparing *fidawsh:* The uncooked pasta is fried gently in olive oil until it has turned golden-brown, then sauce or stock is added, a little at a time, until the pasta has thoroughly absorbed the liquid. Colman Andrews, passionate student of Catalan cuisine, points out the difference: These are not noodles covered with a sauce, like Italian pasta, he says, rather "they are noodles which have *drunk* a sauce, absorbed it, become one with it."

In a thirteenth-century Arabic Spanish cookbook known as the *Manuscrito Anónimo,* translated into English by Charles Perry, "*fidaush*" is quite different. There the pasta might be shaped "in thin sheets, as thin as paper," but more characteristically it is formed into long grains like wheat, or round ones like coriander seeds, and "cooked like *itriyya*"—boiled in a rich meat broth flavored with coriander seeds, then served up with the meat, which has been pounded to a paste, and sprinkled with cinnamon and ginger.

Pasta that is round like coriander seeds sounds like nothing so much as couscous, and it's interesting that the *Manuscrito Anónimo* also has a recipe for *kuskusu fityani*, which Perry translates as "soldiers' couscous." This is one of the earliest references to couscous in a cookery text, although the preparation was already well-known, as the introduction to the recipe reminds us: "The usual moistened couscous is known by the whole world." In this case, the cooked couscous, like *fidaush*, absorbs a rich meat broth and is then served with the meat and vegetables of which the broth was made, sounding very much like many North African couscous preparations today.

Couscous is probably as North African as pasta is Italian, which is why it would have been familiar to Muslims in Spain, most of whom had come from North

Africa originally and were familiar with the process of steaming couscous over a fragrant stew of vegetables, meat, or fish.

So couscous is steamed and pasta is boiled. And yet, and yet . . . I think of *nwasser,* little squares of pasta, made in Tunisia and cooked, like couscous, by steaming over a stew. Or the *kuskus* made in far-off Anatolia by Turkish village women, who roll fine bulgur wheat and semolina in a mixture of egg and water, then dry the little beads of alimentary paste and toss them in water to boil until they're done. Or *fregola* from the island of Sardinia which is really a large-grain couscous that is toasted in the oven, then boiled and sauced, just like pasta.

It's easy to see why the question of origins for all these pasta and couscous preparations has bedeviled food writers and culinary historians alike, tied them in knots of gnarled reasoning, sent them scurrying through libraries in search of obscure manuscripts, of dusty and elusive printed texts, had them quoting slender bits of evidence, chapter and verse, back and forth. But given the present state of knowledge (or lack of knowledge) of Old World food traditions, the question is almost impossible to answer.

One camp currently in favor says Arabs brought pasta to Sicily when they settled there in the ninth century. Another school claims an Etruscan origin, citing as evidence an Etruscan wall relief that shows what is said to be a *spianatoia,* the wooden board on which pasta is rolled out in Tuscan kitchens to this day. (Others say it's a sort of proto-chessboard.) Some scholars hint at a Greek origin for the product, which is plausible since several old Italian words for pasta (*tria; laganum/lasagna*) stem from Greek originals (*itrion,* pl. *itria; laganon,* pl. *lagana*), and Greeks had a forceful impact on Italian ideas about food, diet, and gastronomy that continued over many centuries from the Bronze Age through Byzantium. Perhaps Jews may have been involved in pasta's dissemination since there's a reference to *itriyah* (the Aramaic form of the Greek word) in the Jerusalem Talmud from the sixth century C.E. Yet another school of thought, but one that grows smaller and less credible with time, harks back to the tattered old canard that Marco Polo brought pasta back to Italy from China, ignoring the fact that pasta was known in Italy long before Ser Marco set off on his twenty-four-year journey in 1271, else how, indeed, would he have had a word to describe what he found—and found, as it turns out, not in China (where a type of pasta was, to be sure, well known at the time), but on an island in the Indonesian archipelago?

Because the gluten that forms when wheat flour is mixed with water naturally traps microbes that cause carbon dioxide gases to expand in the dough, bread must have been a spontaneous discovery that occurred almost by accident, probably not just once but over and over again in wheat-growing cultures. But pasta is something else. You have only to look at the pasta section of any modern supermarket in Italy—or elsewhere in the world for that matter, so popular has it become—to see that pasta is a product of sheer fantasy. (One British supermarket chain claims there are at least six hundred different shapes of fresh, dried, and egg-enriched pasta from which to make one's selection—and that, presumably, in England, which is not exactly Pasta Central.)

That it is also an extremely useful product is not in doubt. Couscous and pasta, especially dried commercial *pasta secca* made from hard durum semolina, share many virtues: The product can be stored, in pantry or warehouse, for very long periods of time; it is light, which means it's cheap and easy to transport; pasta itself is almost infinite in the variety of shapes which makes it a delight for the cook; and, not least, both products are quick and effortless to prepare, requiring nothing more than a pot of rapidly boiling water and 5 or 10 minutes of time—longer if it's a question of steaming couscous.

Of course, there is pasta, and then there is pasta, even in Italy. If, for instance, you're speaking of *pasta all'uovo* (*pasta fresca* or *la sfoglia*), it's a very different product with a very different history from *pasta secca*. *Pasta all'uovo* is sheet pasta, traditional in central and northern Italy. Freshly made from eggs and the fine flour of bread wheat, the dough is rolled out on a board and cut into noodley strips or made into ravioli, tortellini, or other dumpling shapes that are stuffed with a dab of minced meat, cheese, or pureed vegetables. Pasta made this way can be dried, it is true, but because of the eggs, which are essential to give tenacity and suppleness to a dough made with low-gluten flour, it does not have a long shelf life.

When my next-door neighbor Mita Antolini makes pasta in her Tuscan kitchen for her family's Sunday lunch, she uses a flour made from bread wheat (*grano tenero,* or *Triticum aestivum* to give its botanical name), the kind sold in Italy as 00 or "*doppio zero,*" the equivalent more or less of American all-purpose flour (see recipe, page 157). To this she adds as many eggs as the flour will absorb and no other liquid except sometimes a dab of olive oil. (The more eggs the better and the richer the pasta: a point of pride with northern cooks. Mita uses eight or nine eggs from her own yard hens for a kilo [2.2 pounds] of flour, but I was once told, with evident awe, of a woman who could get thirty eggs to a kilo of flour, which is practically scrambled eggs with a little flour to bind them.) When the dough has been mixed and kneaded to a smooth, silky texture, Mita rolls it by hand in a broad, thin sheet called *la sfoglia,* which she then cuts into rectangles for lasagna, or rolls up and slices, jelly-roll fashion, into ¼-inch-thick tagliatelle noodles.

*Pasta secca,* on the other hand, is mostly factory-made, although the factories vary in size from giants like Barilla, which supplies a huge 35 percent of the Italian market for commercial pasta, to small artisanal producers like Carlo Latini in the Marche and Benedetto Cavalieri in southeastern Puglia, both great durum wheat–growing regions. *Pasta secca* is made only from water and hard durum semolina, a gritty, high-protein flour, richly colored from carotene, that nowadays is produced almost exclusively for pasta making. This commercial pasta is what Mita uses for her everyday meals—not because it's secondary or lesser, but because the time and effort, not to mention the eggs, in the Sunday pasta give it a special distinction that's appropriate for this singular day.

(An aside: In Italy and France, laws require that commercial *pasta secca* be made only with 100 percent durum semolina. But a European Union decision in 1998 permits the use of flour from softer *Triticum aestivum,* or bread wheat, to make spaghetti, macaroni, etc., as is done normally in northern Europe and the United States. This is not good news for those of us raised on Gresham's Law who believe that, as with money, bad pasta will eventually drive out good, and we will have to travel ever greater distances to find pasta made with high-quality, high-protein durum wheat.)

Mita's method of making *la sfoglia,* which she learned from her mother, is not very different from that followed by Italian cooks going back over the years, even over the centuries; her use of commercial *pasta secca,* however, is something the mother of this 70-year-old Tuscan cook would not have known, much less her grandmother, for factory-made *pasta secca* made from semolina, though long a staple in the Italian south, only became widely distributed throughout the rest of the peninsula in the years since World War II. In a world where pasta has become synonymous with Italian cooking, this may seem incredible. Nonetheless, throughout northern Italy, even in wheat-growing regions, until at least the mid-1950s, bread was the staple food, and handmade *pasta all'uovo,* rich with eggs, was the holiday special, while commercially produced *pasta secca* was almost unknown.

W HETHER PASTA originated with the Jews or the Arabs, the Greeks, Etruscans, or Turks, it seems clear that Italy had been evolving into a pasta culture since far back in culinary history—though not all kinds of pasta and not in all regions. If handmade egg pasta became the norm in the north, if machine-made *pasta secca* was a more southern tradition, that is because of the kinds of wheat that were grown in these places. Durum wheat, *grano duro,* grows well, exceptionally well, in the classic Mediterranean climate of southern Italy and the islands—long, hot, dry summers with brief, cool, rainy winters. Bread wheat, *Triticum aestivum, grano tenero,* grows better in the continental climate of northern Italy, as well as throughout Europe where, except in the far north, it is the farmer's grain of choice.

Not all freshly made pasta uses softer *grano tenero,* however. There are many regions of Italy, especially in the south, where fresh pasta continues to this day to be made from hard-wheat semolina. One such is Puglia, in the heel of the Italian boot, where many old, traditional ways of cooking and eating thrive, and chefs like spunky little Concetta Cantoro think nothing of making up their daily pasta each morning from semolina and water, nothing more. "Oh, sometimes I might sneak in an egg or two, if I think it's not going to hold together properly," Concetta confessed to me in the kitchen of her restaurant, "but that's only when the weather's really dry." Concetta, who was an accountant in another life, opened the restaurant, which she calls forthrightly Cucina Casalinga (Home Cooking), when she despaired of finding decent food in a public place in her home town of Lecce. The menu is exactly what you would find in the kitchens and dining rooms of prosperous Leccesi families, hard-wheat bread and hard-wheat pasta, lots of vegetables, lots of seafood, all of it lavishly bathed in the region's fragrant olive oil.

All pasta, of course, was once made by hand. Commercial pasta production began to evolve only with the development of machinery that enabled it to be produced cost-effectively—that is by men working in factories rather than by women working at home. In fact, it was a long time before industrial pasta production took off. In sixteenth-century Naples, macaroni, as hard-wheat pasta came to be called, was still a luxury product prohibited by law when flour was scarce and otherwise reserved for urban and aristocratic tables, where it was often served as part of the sweet course, sprinkled with sugar, strewn with cinnamon, or drizzled with honey and butter, at a banquet.

The actual recipes that have come down to us from that time are for what modern chefs call presentation dishes, dishes that call attention to themselves, not the kind of food that appears on peasant tables or, truth to tell, on bourgeois tables except for special occasions. Maestro Martino Rossi, who was as renowned for his kitchen skills in fifteenth-century Italy as Gianfranco Vissani is today, gives us a recipe for Sicilian macaroni, made by mixing flour with egg whites and rosewater, simple enough in its ingredients but with a demanding technique. This is his recipe: "Take the best flour and make a dough with egg whites and rose water or, in truth, ordinary water. And if you want to make two servings, don't put more than one or two egg whites. And when the dough is nice and firm, make batons as long as your palm and as thin as a straw. Then take an iron wire and put it on top of the baton and on a tabletop give it a turn with both your hands. Then extract the wire and leave behind the macarone pierced through the middle."

Maestro Martino's macaroni, dried in the sun, would last, he says, two or three years, especially if made during the August full moon. It was to be cooked in meat broth for two full hours. Can this be? Yes, given the still fairly primitive methods of milling in the fifteenth century, I am told, it's entirely possible that pasta made from coarsely ground flour could cook for two hours without dissolving to porridge in the cooking water.

What Martino lacked, what would come along within another 150 years or so, was both better mills to make a more finely ground flour and a machine to extrude the pasta to overcome the tiresome labor of making it, spaghetto by spaghetto, rolling dough around a wire and pulling the wire out again. The machine, called an *arbitrio* in Sicilian, an *'ngegno* in Neapolitan dialect, and a *torchio* elsewhere, worked like a big cake-decorating syringe: you put a hole-punched disc in the bottom, filled the tube with pasta dough, then turned the handle to force the dough through the tube and out in the shape of the pasta you wanted. (Thomas Jefferson, apparently, sent just such an *'ngegno* back to Monticello from Napoli in 1789.) It remained in use in parts of Italy well into the last century. Pina Coppola, a Sicilian friend, remembers her grandmother still using an *arbitrio* to extrude pasta during Pina's childhood in the 1960s.

In the late nineteenth century, continuous cycle machinery began to make it possible to produce pasta on an automated, industrial scale, but it was still very much local to the Italian south. It was not until the late 1950s and the introduction of Teflon dies for extruding pasta, along with the simultaneous use of fast, high-temperature drying methods, that commercially produced pasta became a national institution. Large factories could turn out thousands of kilos of pasta daily and a new national network of highways meant that crates full of pasta could be distributed rapidly throughout the Italian peninsula, not just in cities where pasta had always been strong but to the countryfolk who, now armed with a cheap little Fiat 500, could drive to urban markets and buy a box of this convenience food to take home. The growth of commercial *pasta secca* from a local Sicilian product to a southern Italian product was slow and incremental, but the diffusion of *pasta secca* on a national scale after the 1950s was rapid, even explosive, so much so that it's hard to believe now that there was once a time when every Italian cook didn't reach for the pasta box as the first step before preparing dinner.

Couscous is the great "grain" of North Africa, but it's a grain only in the metaphoric sense; in fact, it's more appropriate to describe couscous as a technique, a process, rather than a product. Typically it's made in a large wooden or terra-cotta dish with a flat bottom and sloping sides. Gritty semolina made from durum wheat is placed in the bottom of the dish and gradually mixed as it's dampened with very small amounts of water, sometimes very small amounts of oil as well (often just a drop or two of oil rubbed on the cook's hands). The couscous maker uses a regular sweeping motion of the right hand, rolling the particles of semolina with the fingertips and at the same time flexing the fingers to gather together and shape them into slightly larger grains. (The metaphorical use of the word "grains" can be misleading—some have mistakenly thought couscous itself was a grain, like wheat or barley, which it is not.) Most often, couscous is made from two different grades of milled flour, the larger grade forming the core of each grain while the finer grade adheres to the outside. Once the grains are shaped, they're spread in the sun for three or four days to dry thoroughly, then stored to be used later.

Although most couscous, like most commercial pasta, is made with semolina, it can also be made from a variety of other grains and beans. Abderrazak Haouari, a great chef and student of the foodways of his native Tunisia, told me that in his grandparents' day on the island of Djerba, couscous was sometimes made from barley grits and lentil flour, rolling the grits in the flour to shape the couscous, an intriguing take on that old vegetarian idea, combining a bean and a grain to make a whole protein. But it has to be eaten right away, he said. It's not for long-keeping or storage.

Haouari made semolina couscous for me one breezy afternoon in his dining room—usually, he said, the couscous would have been made outside but the blustery wind made it difficult. "My mother always said to roll the couscous in a clockwise direction," he said, as he moved the grains with a slow, graceful motion. "And my grandmother always said to roll the couscous in a counterclockwise direction." He paused, then reversed the motion. "And so," he continued, with the shy smile he gets when he knows a joke is coming, "sometimes I do it one way" . . . pause . . . "and sometimes the other."

Haouari is one of the very few Tunisians whom I've seen actually making couscous by hand, apart from a couple of women in colorful garb who are installed in the courtyard of the big couscous factory outside Sfax whenever a delegation of foreign journalists is expected. Most Tunisian women (and couscous, throughout the Maghreb, is primarily the product of women) simply don't have time or can't be bothered, since good-quality commercial couscous appeared on the scene some years ago. Whether made by hand or store-bought, however, couscous is always prepared in the same way, first sprinkled with salty water, then placed in the top of a couscoussière in the bottom of which a stew or broth is cooking, and steamed in the vapor from the broth. At least twice, and more often three times, during this cooking, the couscous is turned out onto a tray or flat dish and gently rubbed and tossed to insure that the grains are light and tender, not heavy or gummy. If it all sounds desperately complicated, it really isn't at all; once you've done it a first time, you'll find it very easy to do again.

Couscous is primarily identified with North African cuisines, but it does exist in other places—in France nowadays, where it was brought by immigrants and returning *colons* from Algeria and Morocco, and in the Middle East, where in Lebanon a large-grain couscous called *maghrabiye* (mahgrah-BEE-yah), for its origin in the Maghreb, is popular. When Sakine Koyun made Anatolian couscous for me in Istanbul, her gestures, as she circled the flat bottom of a terra-cotta dish with the palm of her hand and flexed her fingers to rake through the "grains" of couscous, reminded me of precisely the same gestures used by the Tunisians, Moroccans, Sardinians, and Sicilians that I'd seen doing the same thing. Truly, couscous is not just North African, but a Mediterranean product of great ancestry with deep roots in traditional cultures from Spain to the Middle East and back again.

One of the most unusual couscous I found was from the west coast of Sicily, where it's made around the towns of Erice, Trapani, and Marsala. Local historians claim it as a relic of the Arab occupation of Sicily a thousand years ago. Whether it's really that old or not, it's made differently from North African couscous, and almost always served with a seafood sauce. Matteo Giurlanda, chef at the Ristorante Monte San Giuliano in the dizzyingly high hill town of Erice, makes cuscussu ericiana in a flat-bottomed terra-cotta bowl called a *mafaradda* or *mafarda*, another word with Arab roots. Sicilian couscous is a festive, not an everyday, dish, he explained, as he rolled salt, pepper, finely minced onion, and olive oil into the couscous—something that would be anathema in North Africa. Other cooks add finely minced parsley or crushed hot red peperoncini.

Another difference: Sicilian couscous is freshly made and cooked almost immediately. After just an hour or so of drying, it's steamed for at least an hour over a broth that's little more than water flavored with laurel leaves, an onion, cinnamon, and strips of lemon zest. In one variation, the top of the couscoussière is lined with bay leaves before the couscous is added. Then the *cuscussu* is turned hot onto a platter and fish broth, prepared separately, is added to it, little by little so that the couscous absorbs the broth and swells—just like the *fideos* noodles in the Catalan dish above.

But wherever in the Mediterranean world that it's made, couscous is based on two principles: the mixing of different calibers of flour and grits, whether barley or wheat, to produce the grains; and steaming, which causes the resulting grains to swell and soften. It can be eaten plain, as it is at the little Jewish restaurant called Mamie Lillie in La Goulette, the fishing port next to Tunis, where the couscous is as light and delicate as any I've ever had. More often, however, it is sauced, either with an elaborate vegetable, meat, or fish stew or with something as simple as a piquant tomato sauce. In the North African countryside, a daily couscous may be dressed with nothing more than a dollop of *smeen,* or preserved butter; in Anatolia, bulgur couscous is served with melted butter and yogurt; in a Sicilian convent, it may be mixed with crushed pistachios, preserved fruits, and bits of chocolate to create an Easter treat. A spectacular couscous, to celebrate a great feast like the Id al-Adha at the end of Ramadan, may be rich with mutton, meatballs, and sausages, along with brightly colored vegetables, such as red pumpkin and green peppers, plus chickpeas, lentils, and other legumes, the mound of couscous garnished with lines of powdered cinnamon and sugar while hard-cooked eggs and roasted almonds add to the decoration.

The kinship between couscous and pasta is almost too obvious to need pointing out. Both are simple in nature, yet lead to fanciful, elaborate treatments and presentations, foods that are rooted in the fundamental need to maintain a stable subsistence of country people all around the Mediterranean, yet foods that can also challenge the limits of aristocratic chefs—and purses. It is no exaggeration to see them both as the solid foundation of the Mediterranean diet pyramid and of Mediterranean cuisines.

## 12 GREAT RECIPES FOR PASTA, COUSCOUS, AND BULGUR

Orecchiette with Broccoli and Cauliflower

Penne with Garden Vegetables
*Penne al Ortolano*

Spaghetti with Garlic, Oil, and Chili Peppers
*Spaghetti Aglio-Olio-Peperoncino*

Mita's Homemade Pasta with Meat Ragù
*Tagliatelle al Ragù*

Homemade Semolina Pasta with Chickpeas
*Ciceri e Tria*

Chestnut-Flour Pasta with Pesto
*Trenette di Castagna con Pesto*

Haouari's Lamb Couscous with Dried Fruits and Nuts
*Couscous a l'Agneau et aux Fruits Secs*

Sardinian Couscous with Vegetables
*Secondo Borghero's Cascà Tabarkina*

Trapani or Favignana Seafood Couscous

Lebanese Couscous
*Maghrabiye*

Tabbouleh

Bulgur and Lamb Kofte

## COOK'S NOTES

Every well-stocked pantry should contain several boxes and bags of imported Italian pasta in different sizes and shapes from long, skinny spaghetti noodles to short, stubby ones like farfalle (butterflies) or penne (quills). For a quick, easy, nutritious, delicious meal, pasta puts any fast-food outlet to shame. A single box of pasta, plus some anchovy fillets, a clove of garlic, maybe an onion, a can of good whole tomatoes, a splash of extra-virgin olive oil, and a little wedge of Parmigiano-Reggiano for grating is all it takes to put a wonderful meal on the table. And all of these ingredients can be kept in the pantry or the refrigerator.

For best results and biggest flavor, look for a fine artisanal pasta, made by a small firm that shapes its pasta with old-fashioned bronze dies and dries it slowly at low temperatures. Using bronze dies instead of industrial Teflon gives pasta a rough-textured surface to which sauce clings rather than slipping off; and pasta that is dried slowly at low temperatures retains more of the nutty flavor and aroma of durum wheat. You can tell artisanally made pasta by its color—it will be a pale, creamy hue, whereas industrial pasta will be golden yellow from the toasting it undergoes as it dries.

Some of my favorite brands, all of which are available in North America, include Latini from the Marche, Benedetto Cavalieri from Puglia, Setaro from Torre Annunziata outside Naples, Martelli from Tuscany, and Rustichella d'Abruzzo from the Abruzzi. And new (or, more likely, old) pasta firms are constantly being discovered by North American importers. While you're at it, don't forget couscous, both medium-grain and large-grain (the kind called Middle Eastern or Israeli couscous). Although couscous takes longer to prepare than pasta, it's still a useful product to have on hand.

## THREE SIMPLE PASTA RECIPES USING COMMERCIAL *PASTA SECCA*

The most important Italian pasta rule, the one most often broken by North American cooks, is to use plenty of rapidly boiling salted water in which to cook it—5 quarts of water for a pound of pasta is not too much. And don't overcook it. The only way to tell when pasta is done is to test. And test again. At the precise moment the pasta is ready, it must be drained, sauced, and served. So it's important to have a colander, sauce, and a warm serving dish ready as soon as the water is put on to boil.

How do you know when it's done? When, if you cut into a strand of cooked spaghetti, it appears cooked through except for a white ghost, a tiny spot of not-quite-rawness, at the center of the strand. Pasta-maker Carlo Latini calls this the anima, the soul of the pasta.

Immediately, then, dump it into a colander, remembering that residual heat will cook it just a little more. When it's appropriate, you can also try a method favored by Italian cooks called *saltato in padella*, or sautéed in the saucepan: Cook the pasta until it is about 3 minutes away from being done, then drain it well and finish cooking in the pan with the sauce.

There are many other recipes in this book that will make an appropriate sauce for pasta—especially the tomato sauce recipes in the Peppers and Tomatoes chapter. And the recipes that follow, for ragù and pesto, need not be served only and always with handmade, homemade pasta. They are quite acceptable to dress commercial *pasta secca* as well.

# Orecchiette with Broccoli and Cauliflower

This is one of my all-time favorite recipes for a quick, easy pasta dish that gratifies hungry stomachs without wearing out the cook. In Puglia, the region that occupies the heel of Italy's boot, it's usually made with pungent local broccoli rabe, but the green is not always easy to find in North American markets. When it's not available, I combine broccoli and cauliflower as in this recipe.

If you don't have orecchiette ("little ears"), you could use other types of small, round pasta—small shells, for instance, or farfalle ("butterflies").

TRIM THE BROCCOLI and cauliflower and break the heads up into individual florets. Bring about 1 inch of lightly salted water to a rolling boil in a heavy saucepan. Add the vegetables and cook until they are just tender enough to yield to the sharp point of a paring knife and only a few tablespoons of liquid are left in the bottom of the pan, 8 to 10 minutes. Set aside, but keep warm.

IN A SMALL SKILLET, combine the garlic and oil over medium-low heat and cook gently until the garlic is soft but not brown. Coarsely chop the anchovy fillets and add to the garlic, crushing them into the oil with the back of a fork. Break open the chili (use more than 1 chili if you like a very spicy sauce) and discard the top and core. Crumble the chili into the pan and stir to mix well. Pour the oil mixture over the vegetables and toss to coat the vegetables with the oil.

BRING 5 QUARTS of lightly salted water to a rolling boil and add the pasta. Stir with a wooden spoon and cover. When the pasta water has come back to a boil, remove the lid and cook furiously until done. Drain the pasta immediately and turn it into a warm bowl, and toss with the vegetable mixture. Add pepper to taste and serve immediately. No cheese.

**Makes 4 to 6 servings**

1 medium head broccoli

1 small head cauliflower

Water

Sea salt

2 garlic cloves, finely minced

¼ cup extra-virgin olive oil

6 anchovy fillets, or 3 whole salted anchovies, rinsed and deboned (see page 411)

1 small dried red hot chili pepper, or to taste

1 pound orecchiette or similar small pasta

Freshly ground black pepper

# Penne with Garden Vegetables

**PENNE AL ORTOLANO**

Other seasonal vegetables can be substituted for the ones in this recipe. Lightly steamed green beans, broccoli, or cauliflower, broken into small pieces, work well in place of the zucchini; shredded spinach or other greens can take the place of the eggplant. Adjust your cooking times accordingly, steaming the vegetables until tender then tossing them in the hot, herby oil.

Penne is my suggestion, but any kind of short stubby pasta will work well with this treatment.

**Makes 4 to 6 servings**

1 medium or 2 small eggplants, cubed, salted, and put in a colander to drain

Sea salt

2 medium fresh sweet peppers, red or yellow, cored and coarsely chopped

1 garlic clove, coarsely chopped

½ cup extra-virgin olive oil, or more if needed

3 small or 2 medium zucchini

⅓ cup minced fresh green herbs, such as flat-leaf parsley, basil, chives, or a combination

1 pound penne or other short, stubby pasta

⅓ cup light cream or half-and-half

For serving: freshly grated Parmigiano-Reggiano (optional)

CUT THE EGGPLANT into cubes of ½ inch or smaller. Set in a colander and sprinkle with salt, tossing to mix well. Set aside in the sink for 30 minutes, to drain some of the liquid and soften the eggplant before frying. After 30 minutes, rinse the eggplant cubes thoroughly and dry on paper towels.

BRING 5 TO 6 QUARTS of water in a large saucepan or stockpot to a rolling boil over high heat while you cook the vegetables.

IN A LARGE SKILLET, combine the peppers and garlic with 2 tablespoons of the olive oil. Sauté gently over medium-low heat until the vegetables are very soft. Remove the peppers and garlic and set aside in a bowl. Add the remaining 6 tablespoons oil to the pan, and raise the heat to medium-high. Add the rinsed and dried eggplant cubes and brown them quickly, removing them as they brown and adding them to the peppers.

WHILE THESE VEGETABLES COOK, cut the zucchini in half lengthwise, then slice about ½ inch thick. Add more oil to the pan if necessary, then add the zucchini pieces and brown them quickly on both sides. Mix the browned zucchini pieces with the eggplant and peppers.

REMOVE THE PAN from the heat, and immediately stir the minced herbs into the hot oil. Return the vegetables to the pan, stirring to mix well, and keep warm while you cook the pasta.

ONCE THE WATER has come to a rolling boil, add 2 tablespoons salt and the pasta. While the pasta is cooking, warm the cream to just below simmering in a separate small pan.

START TESTING THE PASTA at 6 minutes. When the pasta is almost done, add 2 tablespoons of pasta water to the vegetables and start to simmer them over medium-low heat. Drain the pasta and turn it immediately into the vegetables to finish cooking. Mix rapidly with the hot cream.

SERVE IMMEDIATELY, passing, if you wish, some grated Parmigiano-Reggiano cheese.

# Spaghetti with Garlic, Oil, and Chili Peppers

## SPAGHETTI AGLIO-OLIO-PEPERONCINO

 This is the kind of quick, simple dish Italian cooks might throw together after an all-night party, or when spirits are flagging and an infusion of food is called for. It is made with the kind of ingredients that should be at hand in every pantry. Other types of long, thin pasta, like vermicelli, linguine, or taglierini, can be substituted. If you leave out the anchovies, be sure to adjust the salt in the sauce.

**Makes 4 to 6 servings**

4 to 6 plump garlic cloves

½ cup extra-virgin olive oil

Sea salt

1 pound spaghetti

4 to 6 anchovy fillets, coarsely chopped (see page 411) (optional)

1 small dried hot red chili pepper, crumbled, or ½ teaspoon hot red chili pepper flakes, or more to taste

½ cup minced flat-leaf parsley

IN A LARGE SAUCEPAN or stockpot, bring 5 to 6 quarts of water to a rolling boil over high heat.

WHILE THE WATER IS HEATING, peel and coarsely chop the garlic. In a pan large enough to hold all the drained pasta, cook the garlic in the oil very, very gently over low heat, just until the garlic softens and starts to turn golden. Do not let the garlic brown. (If it browns, throw it out and start over.)

ONCE THE WATER has come to a vigorous boil, add 2 tablespoons salt and then the pasta, stirring the pasta to separate the strands.

IF YOU'RE USING ANCHOVIES, add them to the oil and garlic. Cook briefly, mashing the anchovy pieces into the oil with a fork. Stir in the chili pepper and ¼ cup of the parsley, and add a ladleful of the pasta cooking water. Let this sauce simmer and reduce slightly while the pasta cooks.

START TESTING THE PASTA after it has cooked for 4 minutes. When it is still a little chewy in the center, drain it and add it to the pan with the sauce. Turn up the heat slightly, and cook, mixing the pasta and sauce together well for 1 to 2 minutes, until the pasta is done to taste. Adjust the flavoring, adding more salt or chili pepper, if desired.

TURN THE PASTA INTO a preheated serving bowl, sprinkle with the remaining ¼ cup parsley, and serve immediately.

# Mita's Homemade Pasta with Meat Ragù

## TAGLIATELLE AL RAGÙ

A traditional ragù, as prepared in farmhouse kitchens all over northern Italy, is a rich and meaty affair, made for the long Sunday lunch when families gather from distant parts around ancestral dining tables. Often, as at my neighbor Mita Antolini's house, that table sits right in the great room of the farmhouse, with a big fire on the central hearth, and kitchen activities going on as children run in and out and their parents greet each other over glasses of home-made wine and snippets of home-cured prosciutto while they wait for the *primo*, the pasta, to appear. Because it's Sunday, the food is deliberately made as distinctive as it can be from the more restrained daily fare. Often, there'll be two kinds of pasta, one served *in brodo*, in a flavorful stock, and the other almost always accompanied by this ragù.

Sunday pasta is different, too, in that it's made at home by hand, whereas the daily pasta may be a good commercial brand. The supple, elastic nature of pasta dough made with softer bread flour and as many eggs as the cook can work into the dough, is one of the chief charac-teristics of northern Italian cuisine, whether in farmhouse kitchens or fancy restaurants.

Make the ragù first, even a day ahead, and then the pasta. The sauce will improve if it sits overnight in the refrigerator.

This sauce may be used on good commercial pasta, preferably an artisanal brand such as those mentioned on page 152. But the true glory of the dish is expressed when it's served with homemade pasta with as many eggs in the dough as you can manage.

FIRST, MAKE THE RAGÙ: In a large, heavy saucepan, gently sauté the pancetta dice in the olive oil for a minute or so, just until the fat starts to run. Add the carrot, onions, and celery and cook very gently until the vegetables are soft, about 30 minutes. Don't let the vegetables brown.

MEANWHILE, put the dried mushrooms in a bowl and cover with the hot water. Set aside to steep and reconstitute for at least 20 minutes.

WHEN THE VEGETABLES ARE SOFT, add the chicken livers to the pan and cook, stirring and tossing, until the livers have lost their color, 15 to 20 minutes. While the livers are cooking, skin

**Makes about 10 servings as a first course, 8 servings as a main course**

**For the ragù:**

2 to 3 ounces pancetta, diced (⅓ to ½ cup)

2 tablespoons extra-virgin olive oil

1 medium carrot, coarsely grated

2 medium red onions, grated or finely chopped

1 celery stalk, including green top, finely chopped

2 ounces dried porcini mushrooms

2 cups hot tap water

2 chicken livers, trimmed and roughly chopped

2 small, sweet Italian sausages (½ pound total)

1 pound very lean ground beef or veal

½ cup dry white or red wine

4 cups whole canned tomatoes, lightly drained

½ cup tomato puree (or use juice from canned tomatoes)

2 or 3 bay leaves

Sea salt and freshly ground black pepper

**For the pasta:**

6 cups unbleached, all-purpose flour, plus a little more for dusting the board

Finely ground sea salt

8 large eggs

Extra-virgin olive oil

Semolina for dusting the pasta

**For the garnish:**

½ cup freshly grated Parmigiano-Reggiano, plus more to pass at the table

the sausages and crumble the sausage meat. Raise the heat slightly and add the sausage meat. As the sausage meat cooks, crumble it further with a fork. When the sausage meat is brown, add the ground beef or veal, again crumbling and mixing with a fork.

WHILE THE MEATS ARE COOKING, drain the mushrooms, reserving their liquid. Rinse the mushrooms under running water to rid them of any residual grit, chop them roughly, and add to the meats. Strain the liquid through a fine sieve and a triple layer of cheesecloth to get rid of any grit.

WHEN THE MEATS ARE BROWN, add the wine, raise the heat to medium-high, and cook, stirring to scrape up any brown bits in the pan. Add the drained tomatoes to the pan, breaking them up with your fingers as you do so. Lower the heat to medium-low, and cook, further breaking up the tomatoes with the side of a fork or spoon. Once the tomatoes have cooked down, in about 10 minutes, add the strained mushroom liquid, the tomato puree or juice from the can, and the bay leaves.

BRING TO A SIMMER, taste the sauce, and add salt and pepper. Continue to simmer the sauce, uncovered, very slowly for at least 30 minutes, adding a little of the tomato juice or plain water if necessary to keep the sauce from sticking to the bottom of the pan.

ONCE THE SAUCE IS DONE, set it aside to cool. If you wish, use a stick blender to puree the sauce a little and give it a smoother texture, but it should still have some heft to it. If you're not going to use the sauce right away, keep it in a cool place or in the refrigerator, and heat it up before serving.

TO MAKE THE PASTA, combine the flour and salt and make a mound in the center of a large cutting board or pasta board. Make a well in the center of the mound.

CRACK THE EGGS and add them, one after another, to the well. Using your fingers, stir the eggs into the well, being careful to maintain the sides but gradually drawing flour into the well to cover and mix with the eggs. Work gently and slowly until all the flour is incorporated. (You may find it easier to add just 5 eggs at first, working them in, then making a well in the rough dough into which you add the remaining 3 eggs.) If the mixture is too wet once the flour and all the eggs have been thoroughly combined, work in a very small amount of flour—no more than a tablespoon or two. If, on the other hand, it seems too dry, run water over your hands and work that moisture into the dough. Keep in mind that, as the dough is kneaded, it will become more supple, but it should not be sticky or slippery with egg.

YOU CAN ALSO MAKE THE PASTA dough in a food processor, using the plastic paddle blade rather than the chopping blade. Add the salt and flour to the processor bowl. Turn the processor on and, with the motor going, quickly add the eggs one after the other. Just as soon as the dough comes together and forms a ball, turn off the motor and remove the dough. Finish kneading, as below, on a cutting board or pasta board.

KNEAD THE PASTA just as you would bread dough, but for less time—you don't want to develop the gluten because it will make the pasta rubbery. After about 5 minutes of kneading, the dough should be supple and elastic. Put a few drops of olive oil in the palms of your hands and rub over the smooth ball of dough. Wrap it in plastic wrap and set it aside for 20 to 30 minutes.

WHEN READY TO CONTINUE, divide the dough into 6 or more portions for ease in rolling it out. Keep the unworked portions covered with plastic wrap. Have ready 4 or 5 clean kitchen towels, liberally sprinkled with semolina, to hold the finished pasta.

ROLL OUT A PORTION of dough on a very lightly floured board, or use a pasta rolling machine, following the machine instructions and gradually decreasing the setting until you reach the thinnest opening. If rolling by hand, gradually roll out the dough into a circle, rolling from the center out to the edge and occasionally rolling up the dough circle around the rolling pin and stretching it very gently toward the ends of the pin. When the pasta is a uniform thinness, no more than $\frac{1}{16}$ of an inch and preferably even thinner, sprinkle the surface with semolina, then roll the dough up loosely, like a floppy jelly roll, and slice in $\frac{1}{4}$-inch ribbons for tagliatelle. Lift each tagliatella strip to let it unfold loosely on the towels to dry slightly before cooking.

FRESHLY MADE PASTA cooks very quickly—in seconds, rather than minutes. Before you cook the pasta, you should reheat the sauce to simmering and make sure you have a warm bowl to turn it into as well as plenty of freshly grated Parmigiano-Reggiano to sprinkle over the top.

BRING ABOUT 6 QUARTS of water to a rolling boil.

WHILE THE WATER IS COMING to a boil, heat the serving bowl by half filling it with very hot water and letting it sit a bit to warm the sides of the bowl, then tipping it out. Add about a cup of pasta sauce to the bottom of the bowl, swirling it around to coat the sides. Sprinkle the bowl with a few tablespoons of the grated cheese.

STIR A COUPLE OF tablespoons of salt into the boiling water, then tip in the pasta and stir it gently with a long-handled wooden spoon. Bring the water rapidly back to the boil and cook for about 1 minute, testing the pasta periodically. Underdone is better than overdone—much better, in fact. When the pasta is done, immediately extract it, preferably by using a wooden pasta extractor or, if this tool is not available, turn it gently into a large colander. (You don't want to smash around and damage the pasta that you have so carefully prepared.) Immediately turn it into the warmed bowl and stir it into the pasta sauce, adding another $\frac{1}{2}$ cup or so as you stir. Top the pasta off with 1 cup of sauce and scatter grated cheese over the top. Send the pasta to the table immediately, along with the grated cheese and a bowl with any remaining sauce to pass.

# Homemade Semolina Pasta with Chickpeas

### CICERI E TRIA

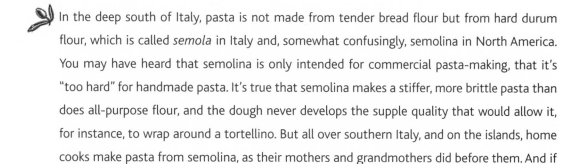

In the deep south of Italy, pasta is not made from tender bread flour but from hard durum flour, which is called *semola* in Italy and, somewhat confusingly, semolina in North America. You may have heard that semolina is only intended for commercial pasta-making, that it's "too hard" for handmade pasta. It's true that semolina makes a stiffer, more brittle pasta than does all-purpose flour, and the dough never develops the supple quality that would allow it, for instance, to wrap around a tortellino. But all over southern Italy, and on the islands, home cooks make pasta from semolina, as their mothers and grandmothers did before them. And if northern cooks are proud of the quantity of eggs they can add to the dough, southern cooks pride themselves on making a pasta dough with no eggs at all!

*Ciceri e tria* is one of several dishes particular to the cuisine of Puglia, the region that stretches down the heel of Italy's boot, where traditional ingredients and cooking methods are treasured and where, I often feel, there's a perceptible link with the kitchens of antiquity. The combination of boiled and fried pasta is unusual and intriguing, and makes this dish very different from its cousin, *pasta e fagioli* (pasta fazool). *Ciceri* is a dialect word for chickpeas, while *tria* comes from that old Greek word for pasta, *itrion* (pl. *itria*), which is often suggested as the origin of all the pastas made from durum wheat. That makes it a very old dish indeed.

DRAIN THE SOAKED CHICKPEAS, transfer to a saucepan, and add enough fresh water to cover them by about 1 inch. Add 1 of the crushed garlic cloves, the onion, bay leaves, and celery and bring to a simmer. Cover the pan and simmer over low heat until the chickpeas are very tender—this should take about 40 minutes, but cooking time depends on the age of the chickpeas. If the chickpeas absorb the water in the pan, add boiling water. They should always be covered by about 1 inch of water, which will become thicker and soupy as they cook.

MAKE THE PASTA while the chickpeas are simmering. Dissolve about 1 teaspoon of salt in ⅔ cup warm water. Put the semolina

**Makes 6 to 8 servings**

1½ cups dried chickpeas, soaked for several hours or overnight

Water

2 garlic cloves, crushed

1 medium yellow onion, quartered

2 bay leaves

1 celery stalk, coarsely chopped

Sea salt

2 cups semolina, for pasta

Extra-virgin olive oil, for deep frying

1 small dried hot red chili pepper

in a mixing bowl and slowly pour the salty water into the flour, a little at a time, gradually mixing until all the water has been added. (You may need a little more water or a little more semolina, depending on the weather.)

KNEAD THE PASTA in the bowl for a few minutes. You will feel the semolina granules start to soften and relax. Once the dough is well mixed, turn it out onto a wooden board. If it feels stiff, brush a little water on the board with your fingers and knead it into the dough. On the other hand, if it feels too loose and wet, scatter just 1 tablespoon of semolina on the board and knead it in. Continue kneading for about 10 minutes, or until the dough has reached a soft, silky texture. Cover the dough with plastic or a cloth and set it aside to rest for 30 minutes.

WHEN YOU ARE READY to roll out the pasta, divide it in half and keep the half you're not working under wraps. Roll the pasta out into the thinnest possible sheet. If you're familiar with working with egg-based pasta, you'll find that you cannot roll semolina pasta as thin. You can, however, use a pasta machine, rolling it up to the #5 setting, which should be sufficient. Let the pasta sheet dry for a few minutes, then cut it into long, straight noodles, about ½-inch wide. Drape the pasta over a rack or a chairback covered with a clean dish cloth, and leave it to dry for 15 to 30 minutes, no more.

WHEN THE CHICKPEAS ARE COOKED, start to assemble the dish. First separate out about a third of the pasta for frying. In a saucepan or deep frying pan about 10 inches in diameter, add olive oil to a depth of 1 inch. Set the pan over medium heat and toss in the remaining garlic clove and the chili pepper, broken in half. As the oil warms up, the garlic will start to brown. When it is golden, but not completely brown, remove it, along with the chili, and add the pasta, a few strips at a time. Quickly fry the pasta in the hot oil until it is crisp and brown. Transfer to a rack covered with paper towels to drain.

REMOVE THE BAY LEAVES from the chickpeas and discard. Raise the heat under the chickpeas to medium-high, adding boiling water to keep them covered to a depth of 1 inch. Gently stir the remaining pasta into the chickpeas and cook until the pasta is done, about 5 minutes. When the pasta is *al dente*, remove from the heat and serve immediately, without draining, garnishing each bowl with a generous handful of fried pasta.

# Chestnut-Flour Pasta with Pesto

**TRENETTE DI CASTAGNA CON PESTO**

All over Italy, in poor, mountainous regions, chestnuts were once used to eke out the meager wheat harvest. Flour ground from dried chestnuts was added to bread doughs so often that the majestic chestnut tree came to be known as *l'albero del pane,* the bread tree. But, like many ingredients that were once symbols of dearth (like farro, like polenta), chestnut flour has had a comeback in recent years and achieved a certain chic status as a product of the land. This unusual pasta, made with half chestnut flour and half all-purpose flour, comes from Liguria, the mountainous region that embraces Genoa on Italy's northwestern coast. Meli Solari, from the Ristorante Ca' Peo in Leivi, a village on the steep heights above Rapallo, made this for me and sauced it with her own handmade basil pesto, the finest kind.

Pesto is basil's leap to immortality. It should be made only when basil is fresh in local gardens, preferably using the small-leaved, fragrant Genovese basil, but any kind will do so long as it's fresh and seasonal.

For years I made pesto ineffectually by pounding the basil with the pestle; Meli Solari showed me the correct technique. You must have a mortar with rough-textured stone or pottery sides, not a smooth, glazed ceramic mortar, because the action of the wooden pestle against the sides is what turns the basil into an unctuous paste. Initially you reduce the garlic, salt, and pine nuts to a paste by a combination of gentle pounding and pressing against the sides of the mortar. Once you've added the basil leaves, you change the stroke, now swiping the pestle diagonally down the sides of the mortar, capturing any basil leaves as they build up around the edges. Keep turning the mortar: if you're right-handed, it works to stroke the pestle down in a counterclockwise direction, while you turn the mortar counterclockwise a little between every second or third stroke. I imagine if you're left-handed, you would do this in the opposite, clockwise direction.

To toast pine nuts, place them in a shallow pie pan in a 350°F. oven until lightly golden, which can take anywhere from 5 to 15 minutes. Toss them from time to time and pay attention that they don't burn, which seems to happen in an instant. Remove and let cool before adding to the mortar.

MAKE THE PASTA as described for the tagliatelle on pages 157–60, but first combine the all-purpose flour and the chestnut flour with the sea salt. Mound the combined ingredients on a large cutting board or pasta board, and make a well in the center of the mound.

CRACK THE EGGS and add them, one after another, to the well. Using your fingers, stir the eggs into the well, being careful to maintain the sides but gradually drawing flour into the well to cover and mix with the eggs. (If you ever made a fortress of mashed potatoes, with gravy inside, you will appreciate what this is like!) Work gently and slowly until all the flour is incorporated. If the mixture is too wet, work in a very small amount of additional flour, either all-purpose or chestnut, but not more than a tablespoon or two. If on the other hand, it is too dry, run water over your hands and work that moisture into the dough. Keep in mind that, as the dough is kneaded, it will become more supple, but it should not be sticky or slippery with egg.

YOU CAN ALSO MAKE THE PASTA dough in a food processor, using the plastic paddle blade rather than the chopping blade. Add the salt and flours to the processor bowl. Turn the processor on and with the motor going, quickly add the eggs, one after another. Just as soon as the dough comes together and forms a ball, turn off the motor and remove the dough. Finish kneading, as below, on a cutting board or pasta board.

KNEAD THE PASTA just as you would bread dough, but for less time—about 5 minutes should be sufficient, after which the dough should be supple and elastic. Rub a few drops of olive oil into the palms of your hands and smooth them over the ball of dough. Wrap it in plastic wrap and set it aside for 20 to 30 minutes.

WHEN READY TO CONTINUE, divide the pasta into two or three portions for ease in rolling it out. Keep the unworked portions

**Makes 6 servings
as a first course**

**For the pasta:**

¾ to 1 cup unbleached all-purpose flour, plus a little more for the board

¾ to 1 cup chestnut flour

1 tablespoon fine sea salt

4 large eggs

Extra-virgin olive oil

Semolina for dusting the pasta

2 packed cups whole basil leaves, rinsed and dried

1 large garlic clove, coarsely chopped

Pinch of sea salt

3 tablespoons lightly toasted pine nuts

½ cup freshly grated Pecorino Sardo or Pecorino Toscano (do not use Pecorino Romano)

½ cup freshly grated Parmigiano-Reggiano, plus more for serving

⅓ to ½ cup extra-virgin olive oil, preferably Ligurian or Provençale

covered with plastic wrap. Have ready 2 or 3 clean kitchen towels, liberally sprinkled with semolina, to hold the finished pasta.

ROLL OUT A PORTION of dough on a very lightly floured board, or use a pasta rolling machine, following the machine instructions and gradually decreasing the setting until you reach the smallest opening. If rolling by hand, gradually roll out the dough into a circle, rolling from the center out to the edge and occasionally rolling up the dough circle around the rolling pin and stretching it very gently toward the ends of the pin. Because chestnut flour has no gluten, the pasta will be more frangible than that made with 100 percent wheat flour, so handle it carefully.

WHEN THE PASTA IS a uniform thinness, no more than $\frac{1}{16}$ of an inch, sprinkle the surface with semolina, then roll the dough up loosely, like a floppy jelly roll, and slice in ¼-inch ribbons. Lift each ribbon to let it unfold loosely on the towels to dry slightly before cooking.

WHEN THE PASTA IS COMPLETED, make the pesto.

PICK OVER AND WASH THE BASIL, discarding any blackened or shriveled leaves. Use only the leaves, discarding the stems. If the leaves are very large, discard the firm central veins as well. Completely dry the basil leaves before you start making the paste.

ADD THE CHOPPED GARLIC, salt, and pine nuts to a mortar and crush to a paste with the pestle. When the mixture is homogeneous, if still a little grainy in texture, start adding the basil leaves, about ½ cup at a time, working each addition into the garlic-nut paste well, as described above.

ONCE ALL THE BASIL HAS been worked in, the paste will be rather liquid but viscous in texture with discernable bits of basil in it. Continue working it with the pestle, adding the cheeses, a little at a time, in the same fashion. When all the grated cheese has been worked in, start to add the olive oil, again a little at a time. You may find that ⅓ cup or a little more is sufficient to arrive at the viscous texture of a well-made pesto, or you may need to use the entire ½ cup—a lot depends on the quality of the basil itself. The sauce should be a dense green well sprinkled with bits of darker green, but it will always have more texture than a pesto made in a blender or food processor.

ONCE THE PESTO has reached the right consistency, it can be used immediately, or stored, tightly covered with a couple of layers of plastic wrap, in the refrigerator for 2 to 3 days. It's often suggested that pesto can be frozen, but I have never found this is truly successful. Pesto is something to be enjoyed as it is on its home ground, when the season is right, in the fullness of summer, when the flavor sometimes seems like the very definition of summer itself.

YOU CAN ALSO MAKE this in a food processor by whizzing the garlic, salt, pine nuts, and basil leaves together until they are reduced to a fine mince. Then whirl in the cheeses and finally, with the motor running, slowly pour the olive oil in a thin thread through the feed tube. This pesto will be bright green, with a homogeneous texture that is not unpleasing but is a far cry from the unctuous viscosity of the real thing—which every cook should make at least once in his or her lifetime, just to appreciate the difference.

ONCE THE PESTO IS FINISHED, cook the pasta in 5 quarts of rapidly boiling lightly salted water, as described in the recipe for tagliatelle. Swirl a little of the pesto in a warm serving bowl. Carefully drain the pasta and add to the serving bowl. Add the remaining pesto and toss gently to mix well.

SERVE AT ONCE. If you wish, pass more grated Parmigiano-Reggiano at the table.

VARIATION: No rule says you must make pasta from scratch to enjoy pesto. A well-made commercial pasta is excellent with this. You could also copy Ligurian cooks, adding 2 or 3 potatoes, cut into chunks and boiled until not quite tender, to finish cooking with the pasta. Pasta and potatoes sounds odd together, but it is delicious, with a delightful contrast in textures.

## ABOUT COUSCOUS

You don't have to have a special pot, called a couscoussière, to make couscous; although if you're planning to make it often, it's worth investing in one. But you can improvise the two-layer vessel with a colander and a deep stockpot, into which the colander should just fit so that the bottom of the colander will sit well above the liquid in the stockpot. For proper steaming, it must be above the liquid by a good 3 inches, otherwise the couscous will boil, which is not desirable. You bring liquid or stew to a simmer in the bottom layer, set the colander on top, pressing aluminum foil around the edge to seal it tightly, and there you are!

But it's easier with a proper couscoussière, which is not an expensive piece of equipment and not difficult to find from mail-order kitchenware suppliers like Williams-Sonoma or Sur la Table (see Where to Find It, page 415).

You can also avoid the couscoussière altogether and simply make your couscous the way various recipes suggest, by pouring boiling water over couscous grains and setting them aside to swell. But you will never get the extraordinary lightness and delicacy of a North African couscous by preparing it that way. The proper way to do it takes a little time, but the technique is not complicated, and most of the time is spent waiting for the couscous to swell and/or steam.

# Haouari's Lamb Couscous with Dried Fruits and Nuts

## COUSCOUS A L'AGNEAU ET AUX FRUITS SECS

Most North African cooks buy their couscous ready-made, just like buying commercial pasta, but my Tunisian friend and occasional traveling buddy Chef Abderrazak Haouari sometimes makes it from start—just to keep in practice, he says. In the old days, he says, they always made the couscous in August, well after the harvest, when there was lots of sun for drying it rapidly. Then it was stored and used throughout the year.

For ease of preparation, make the basic lamb stew a day ahead and refrigerate it when done; the fat will rise to the top and can be easily removed before continuing with the cooking, making a lighter stew.

Use medium-grain couscous, which is what is generally available in health-food stores, gourmet shops, and supermarkets. Do *not* use the large-grain couscous variously called Middle Eastern or Israeli couscous or *maghrabiye* (mahgrah-BEE-yah).

To toast the nuts, spread them on a sheet pan or cookie sheet and set in a preheated 350°F. oven for about 10 minutes, or until they turn golden.

USING YOUR HANDS, combine the lamb in a bowl with salt and pepper to taste, 1 teaspoon of the cinnamon, and the saffron. Toss to mix. Set aside, covered, to marinate for at least an hour.

WHEN YOU ARE READY to prepare the lamb stew, combine the onions and garlic with the olive oil in the bottom part of a couscoussière or a heavy stew pot. Set over medium-low heat and cook, stirring occasionally, 20 to 30 minutes, or until the vegetables are soft but not brown. Add the marinated meat and raise the heat slightly. Cook, stirring frequently, until the meat has completely changed color, about 15 minutes. Add water to cover—at least 6 cups—and bring to a simmer. Cover the pan and let simmer for at least 1 hour. The stew may be prepared ahead up to this point and refrigerated until you are ready to

**Makes 8 servings**

3 pounds lamb shoulder meat, cut into stewing-sized pieces

Sea salt and freshly ground black pepper

2 teaspoons ground cinnamon

¼ teaspoon saffron threads, crumbled

2 medium onions, coarsely chopped

3 garlic cloves, coarsely chopped

¼ cup extra-virgin olive oil

Water

6 large carrots, cut into chunks

6 medium white turnips, peeled and cut into chunks

1 tablespoon harissa, plus more for serving (page 280)

4 ounces dried figs

4 ounces dried apricots

2 cups whole milk

¼ cup blanched almonds, toasted and chopped

¼ cup shelled pistachios, toasted

¼ cup pine nuts, toasted

2 to 3 tablespoons golden raisins or black currants

3 tablespoons unsalted butter, melted

1 pound medium-grain couscous (about 2½ cups)

continue cooking. If you wish, remove the fat from the top of the stew before continuing.

WHEN YOU ARE READY TO CONTINUE cooking, return the meat stew to the bottom of the couscoussière. Add another 1½ cups of water and heat the stew to simmering. Mix in the carrots, turnips, and harissa. Cover the pan and let simmer gently while you prepare the rest of the ingredients.

COMBINE THE FIGS and apricots in a bowl and cover with boiling water. Set aside to soften.

SIMMER THE MILK very slowly in a small pan until it has reduced by half.

COMBINE THE CHOPPED TOASTED ALMONDS with the toasted pistachios and pine nuts. Set the raisins or currants in a separate small bowl and cover with boiling water. Set aside to soften for about 10 minutes, then drain thoroughly and add to the nut mixture. Add 1 tablespoon of melted butter to the nut mixture, mix well, and set aside to keep warm.

DISSOLVE 1 TEASPOON SALT in 1 cup of warm water.

SPREAD THE COUSCOUS out in a thin layer, about ¼ inch thick, in a sheet pan. Sprinkle the couscous with a little of the salty water, raking your fingers through the grains in order to distribute the water evenly throughout. The grains of couscous will quickly absorb the water, but continue sprinkling, using all the salty water, and raking and rubbing gently so that no lumps form in the couscous. Then let the couscous rest for about 30 minutes while the grains swell slightly.

TRANSFER THE PREPARED COUSCOUS to the top of the couscoussière (or the colander). Set the top over the stew in the bottom, sealing the join well with a length of aluminum foil. (Traditionally, the join is sealed with a thick flour-and-water paste, but this is messy and time-consuming.) Do not cover the top of the couscoussière, otherwise steam will condense inside the lid and drip back inside, making the couscous lumpy. When you see steam begin to rise through the grains, start to time the cooking.

MEANWHILE, prepare another cup of warm salty water, using 1 teaspoon salt.

AFTER 15 MINUTES OF STEAMING, remove the top of the couscoussière and tip the partially cooked couscous back onto the sheet pan. As soon as it is cool enough to handle, start to toss, rake, and stir the couscous with your fingers to make it more fluffy and airy, breaking up any lumps that may have formed. Sprinkle the salty water over the couscous as you do this, using the entire cup.

RETURN THE COUSCOUS to the top of the couscoussière and set once more over the boiling liquid, again sealing the join between top and bottom well. Let it steam for 10 minutes, then turn again into the tray and repeat the previous step, again sprinkling the couscous with 1 cup warm salty water and tossing and raking it.

RETURN THE COUSCOUS to the top of the couscoussière for the third and final steaming, which should last for 7 to 10 minutes. Turn the couscous out onto the sheet pan and add half the buttery nut mixture, tossing the grains with a fork to distribute the nuts throughout. Continue to toss the couscous, using a fork and your hands, while you mix in the reduced milk and then about a cup of the rich juices from the lamb stew. Use a very light touch as you mix in these additions, tossing the couscous gently. The point is to enrobe it with these savory ingredients and not to mash it to a paste.

WHEN THE COUSCOUS IS READY, mound it on a platter. Mix the remaining 2 tablespoons of melted butter with the remaining 1 teaspoon cinnamon and dribble it all over the couscous. Arrange the meat and vegetables around the couscous and garnish the top with the remaining nut mixture. Serve immediately.

# Sardinian Couscous with Vegetables

## SECONDO BORGHERO'S CASCÀ TABARKINA

Secondo Borghero, who owns the Ristorante al Tonno di Corsa in Carloforte, Sardinia, says this Sardinian version of couscous is typical of "*la cucina tabarkina*," Tabarka being a town on the coast of northwestern Tunisia from which the original settlers of Carloforte came. They were Genovese in origin and had founded the Tunisian colony in the 1500s after the port was received in ransom for the pirate Barbarossa by a Genovese banking family. The Genovese stayed in Tabarka until 1741, when they were expelled by the Bey of Tunis.

Tabarkina, or Sardinian, couscous is quite different from North African couscous, however, since it's steamed for a long time over plain water rather than a rich meat-and-vegetable broth. Like its cousins, however, ideally it should be cooked in a couscoussière.

Secondo uses large-grain couscous, but not so large as *maghrabiye*, Lebanese or Israeli couscous. If you can't find large-grain couscous, use the regular medium-grain couscous available in most shops and health-food stores.

Pork rind (called *cotiche di maiale*) is available in Italian groceries and butcher shops. If you can't find it or don't wish to use it, substitute 1 tablespoon extra-virgin olive oil, rubbing it well into the swollen couscous before placing it in the top of the couscoussière.

**Makes 6 to 8 servings, depending on whether it's served as a first course or a main course**

1 pound couscous (about 2½ cups)

6 ounces dried chickpeas, soaked several hours or overnight

Water

6 to 8 tablespoons extra-virgin olive oil

1 garlic clove, finely chopped

1 sun-dried tomato, rehydrated if necessary, finely chopped

IN A SIEVE, thoroughly rinse the couscous under running water; then spread it out on a tray to swell while you prepare the chickpeas.

DRAIN THE CHICKPEAS, discarding any husks. (A Sardinian trick for a nicer presentation: rub the drained chickpeas with handfuls of coarse salt to remove the husks, then rinse the salt off and drain again.) In a saucepan combine the chickpeas with water to cover to a depth of 1 inch and bring to a simmer.

MEANWHILE, heat 2 tablespoons of the olive oil in a small saucepan over medium-low heat and add the garlic and dried tomato. Cook, stirring, until the garlic softens, about 10 minutes. Add the tomato concentrate and cook briefly, less than a minute, stirring to mix it in. When the chickpeas are simmering, stir this mixture into them, cover, and leave to cook gently until the chickpeas are tender, about 40 minutes, but the cooking time depends on the age of the chickpeas. Add a little boiling water from time to time if necessary.

FILL THE BOTTOM of the couscoussière, whether genuine or improvised, with enough water to come two-thirds of the way up the sides. Set the top part of the couscoussière over the water and make sure the water doesn't touch the top, even when it's boiling vigorously. When the couscoussière is properly set up, bring the water to a boil, then turn it down to a controlled, steady simmer. Rake your fingers through the couscous, stirring it up so that no lumps form. Using your hands, mix the pork rind squares or the olive oil with the couscous and pile it into the top part of the couscoussière. Cover with a lid, set over the boiling water, and leave the couscous to steam for 2 to 3 hours, or until it is completely tender. After the first hour, remove the lid and fluff the grains with a fork, turning so that what was on the bottom is now on top and vice versa. Stir it again, gently, every 30 minutes or so until done.

WHILE THE COUSCOUS IS COOKING, prepare the vegetables to go with it. In a large skillet, combine 2 tablespoons of the olive oil with the cabbage, carrots, and onions and stew gently over medium-low heat until the vegetables are softened but not brown, about 20 minutes.

MEANWHILE, rinse the salt off the eggplant cubes and dry well with paper towels. Heat the remaining 2 tablespoons of oil in a sauté pan over medium heat and quickly sauté the eggplant cubes until they are brown on all sides. Do this in batches, adding more olive oil if necessary. When the eggplant is brown, set aside, with any pan juices, until the other vegetables are done.

1 tablespoon tomato concentrate or tomato paste

2 ounces pork rind, cut into little squares (if unavailable, use 1 tablespoon olive oil instead)

½ small green cabbage, trimmed and slivered

2 medium carrots, cubed

1 large onion, coarsely chopped

1 small eggplant, cubed, salted, and put aside in a colander to drain (see page 411)

2 to 3 small artichokes, trimmed and quartered or sliced

1 cup fresh shelled green peas

1 cup fresh shelled fava beans (optional)

½ teaspoon dried marjoram, or 1 teaspoon chopped fresh

Sea salt

STIR THE ARTICHOKES, peas, and fava beans into the cabbage, carrots, and onions. Add a small amount of water, not more than ½ inch, to the pan. Mix together, adding salt to taste, and leave to stew gently over low heat for 20 minutes, until all the vegetables are tender, stirring frequently but gently. When the vegetables are soft, stir in the marjoram.

WHEN THE VEGETABLES ARE DONE, remove from the cooking pan using a slotted spoon; reserve any cooking liquid. Combine the eggplant with the other vegetables. Drain the chickpeas and combine their cooking liquid with that from the vegetables.

WHEN THE COUSCOUS IS DONE, bring the vegetable cooking liquid to a rolling boil. Spread out the couscous on its tray and sprinkle with the cooking liquid, tossing the couscous with a fork so it absorbs all the liquid, letting each spoonful be absorbed before another is added.

TO SERVE, mound the couscous on a platter. Arrange the vegetables around the couscous and spread the chickpeas over the top. The *cascà* may be served hot, but it is more typically served at room temperature, especially in early summer when all these vegetables are in season. Cover the dish lightly and set aside for an hour or two to let the flavors meld before serving.

# Trapani or Favignana Seafood Couscous

The couscous made on the Sicilian island of Favignana, famous for its fishing fleet, is made with a rich seafood stew that in fact could be served on its own, if you don't care for the couscous part. Rosa Ponzio, the cook in a little restaurant in the main square of Favignana, showed me how to make this, but I have adapted her recipe to ingredients available in North America. Make the seafood stew ahead of time, even a day ahead, and reheat it, stirring in the basil pesto, when you are ready to serve. Use either the Sardinian recipe on page 358 or the Provençale recipe on page 360.

Sicilian cooks proudly make their couscous from scratch, but it's perfectly acceptable to use a good-quality, packaged commercial couscous. Note, however, that the couscous does not cook over the seafood stew, but rather over its own broth of lemon and bay leaf.

**Makes 6 to 8 servings**

1 pound couscous (about 2½ cups)

2 lemons, coarsely chopped, peel and all

6 bay leaves

1 small onion, very finely minced

⅓ cup very finely minced flat-leaf parsley

⅓ to ½ cup extra-virgin olive oil

Seafood stew

½ cup slivered fresh basil leaves

Sea salt

Freshly ground black pepper

IN A SIEVE, thoroughly rinse the couscous under running water; then spread it in a shallow layer, not more than ¼ inch thick, on a tray to swell for at least 30 minutes, while you prepare the cooking liquid.

FILL THE BOTTOM of the couscoussière, whether genuine or improvised, with enough water to come two-thirds of the way up the sides. Set the top part of the couscoussière over the water to be sure the water doesn't touch the top, even when it's boiling vigorously. When the couscoussière is properly set up, add the lemons and bay leaves to the water and bring it to a boil, then turn it down to a controlled, steady simmer.

RAKE YOUR FINGERS through the couscous on the tray, stirring and rubbing it so that no lumps form. Sprinkle the minced onion and parsley over the couscous and gradually, using your hands, work the olive oil into the grains. (Use at least ⅓ cup of oil, but you may not need to use all of it.) When the couscous grains have absorbed as much oil as they can, transfer to the top of the couscoussière and set it over the simmering water. Steam the couscous for 30 minutes. Using a fork, gently fluff the grains in the top of the couscoussière, turning so that what was on the bottom is now on top and vice versa. Stir it again, gently, after another 30 minutes or so. If the couscous is not tender, let it cook another 15 minutes. It should be completely tender.

WHEN THE COUSCOUS IS ALMOST DONE, bring the seafood stew to a gentle simmer. Extract ⅔ cup of the flavorful broth from the stew and set aside.

COMBINE THE BASIL and 1 teaspoon salt in a mortar and grind them together to make a coarse pesto. (If you don't have a mortar and pestle, mince the basil very fine and crush with the salt in a small bowl, using the back of a spoon.) Stir the basil pesto into the simmering stew and remove from the heat.

WHEN THE COUSCOUS IS DONE, tip it onto its tray and gently dribble the reserved seafood cooking liquid over it, tossing with a fork to make sure the couscous absorbs as much as possible, adding a little more salt and freshly ground pepper to taste.

TO SERVE, mound the couscous on a platter and serve the seafood stew apart. Guests help themselves to the stew and the couscous in whatever balance they wish. It's not traditional on Favignana, but you could also spoon the seafood over the couscous and serve the broth apart in little bowls for guests to add to the couscous or to sip as an accompaniment.

# Lebanese Couscous

## MAGHRABIYE (MAH-GRAH-BEE-YAH)

The Lebanese style of couscous is very different from that made in North Africa, although the name, *maghrabiye,* means "from the Maghreb," or North Africa. In the Levant, however, couscous grains are quite large, more like small peas than the tiny, fluffy grains of Tunisian or Moroccan couscous. Moreover, the grains, after being gently sautéed in butter, are not steamed but simmered in water until tender. In North America, this type of couscous is sometimes called Israeli—although it's an old-fashioned and deeply traditional Arab dish.

This is a long recipe, most definitely not something to throw together for dinner in half an hour. But it is worth the effort because the result is aromatic with warm, round Middle Eastern flavors of cinnamon and cumin, and delicious—well worth the trouble.

**Makes 6 to 8 servings**

1 cup dried chickpeas, soaked for several hours or overnight

Water

5 tablespoons extra-virgin olive oil

4 tablespoons unsalted butter

1 whole chicken, weighing about 4 pounds

2 (1-pound) lamb shanks

1½ pounds small white onions, peeled

3 small cinnamon sticks

3 bay leaves

Sea salt

DRAIN THE CHICKPEAS and transfer to a saucepan. Add enough water to cover the beans by 1 inch and bring to a simmer. Simmer over low heat, stirring occasionally, until tender, 40 to 60 minutes. Add more boiling water from time to time if necessary to keep the chickpeas covered.

WHILE THE CHICKPEAS COOK, heat 3 tablespoons of the oil over medium heat in a large enameled cast-iron casserole. Add 3 tablespoons of the butter and when it has melted, add the chicken and brown it well on all sides.

WHEN THE CHICKEN IS WELL BROWNED, remove it and set aside. Add the lamb shanks to the casserole and brown on all sides. Remove and set aside.

ADD THE ONIONS to the casserole and lower the heat to medium-low. Brown the onions, stirring occasionally, until they are golden all over, about 20 minutes. Set aside. Discard all but 2 tablespoons of the fat in the casserole.

ADD 6 CUPS OF WATER to the casserole, along with the cinnamon sticks, bay leaves, and 1 tablespoon salt. Return the chicken and lamb shanks to the casserole and bring to a simmer. Cover and cook over low heat until the chicken is done, about 1 hour.

1 pound *maghrabiye* or Israeli couscous, about 2½ cups

2 teaspoons ground cinnamon

2 teaspoons ground cumin

⅓ cup plus 2 tablespoons finely minced cilantro

Lemon wedges, for garnish

For serving: toasted pita or Arab bread triangles

Remove the chicken from the liquid in which it has cooked and set aside. Continue to cook the lamb shanks until very tender, about 40 minutes longer.

MEANWHILE, as soon as the chicken is cool enough to handle, pull off all the meat in as large pieces as possible. Discard the skin and bones. Put the chicken pieces in a baking dish with a little of the liquid in which they cooked and cover the dish with foil to keep warm.

IN A LARGE BOWL, combine the couscous with 1 tablespoon of the oil, tossing to coat the grains of couscous. Bring a kettle of water to a boil and pour boiling water over the couscous to a depth of 1 inch. Cover the bowl and set aside for 45 minutes.

WHEN THE LAMB IS DONE, remove it from the cooking liquid or broth and set aside. Strain the broth and skim the fat from the surface. You should have about 6 cups of broth.

REMOVE THE MEAT from the lamb shanks and chop it roughly into 1-inch pieces. Combine the lamb with the onions, the drained chickpeas, a big pinch of salt, and 1 teaspoon each of ground cinnamon and ground cumin. Add 2 cups of the strained broth. Bring to a simmer, cover, and cook over medium-low heat until the onions are tender, about 25 minutes. Stir ⅓ cup of the cilantro into the broth.

DRAIN THE COUSCOUS. In a large saucepan, melt the remaining 1 tablespoon butter in the remaining 1 tablespoon oil over medium heat. Add the couscous and the remaining 1 teaspoon cinnamon and 1 teaspoon cumin, with a pinch of salt. Cook, stirring, until most of the butter has been absorbed, about 3 minutes. Stir in the remaining 4 cups broth and bring to a simmer. Cover and cook over low heat until the couscous is very tender and most of the liquid has been absorbed, about 30 minutes.

PREHEAT THE OVEN to 350°F. Set the chicken in its baking dish in the oven to warm up. Reheat the lamb stew. Mound the couscous on a large platter and arrange the hot chicken pieces on top. Spoon the lamb stew over all and sprinkle with the remaining 2 tablespoons cilantro.

SERVE IMMEDIATELY, garnishing the platter with lemon wedges and the toasted triangles of bread.

## BULGUR OR BURGHUL

*Bulgur* is the Turkish name, *burghul* the name in Arabic for this product, a traditional staple throughout the Middle East and some parts of North Africa. More recently, bulgur has become known in North America, primarily through that robust salad tabbouleh, in which bulgur is the chief ingredient. But why is bulgur in a group of recipes for pasta and couscous? Because, like them, it's a method that has evolved over the centuries as a way to preserve wheat from harvest to harvest, creating a staple for the family pantry that is quick and easy to use. A brief soaking in water softens bulgur into a grain that can be used in dozens of ways—in pilafs, as stuffings for vegetables, mixed with lamb to make all the glorious variations of kibbeh, and, of course, in tabbouleh.

I often see bulgur mistranslated as cracked wheat. It is not. Cooks would make a serious mistake to substitute cracked wheat in any recipe calling for bulgur. Bulgur in fact is precooked—the whole grains of wheat are brought to a boil in salted water, drained as soon as they start to expand, then spread in the sun and left to dry for a week or so. Once the swollen grains are thoroughly dry, they are then pounded in a mortar or taken to a special bulgur mill where the husk is removed and the grains are cracked according to what their final use will be—fine for kibbeh, coarse for tabbouleh and pilafs.

Apart from Syrian countryfolk who still make bulgur by hand, modern processing is thoroughly industrialized. As there is no set standard for bulgur, bread wheat may be used instead of durum, especially with bulgur made in North America. Try to find bulgur made in Lebanon or Turkey, although shops in Middle Eastern neighborhoods usually sell bulgur from unlabeled bulk containers. Buy fine bulgur to make kibbeh and coarse or medium bulgur for tabbouleh and pilafs.

# Tabbouleh

In North America, tabbouleh is often made with a great deal of bulgur, far more than is used in the Middle East, so that the dish becomes a sort of porridge garnished with parsley and mint, rather than vice versa, a salad of parsley and mint, garnished and made more robust with bulgur. Modern Lebanese cooks sometimes serve a tabbouleh made with minimal bulgur and they don't soak it at all, since the bulgur grains soften, they say, with the juices from the vegetables. That may be so, but I still prefer the slight softening the grains get from a brief soaking.

Resist the temptation to chop the vegetables in the food processor as it simply turns them to mush and the dish really needs the texture that comes from hand chopping.

Tabbouleh is usually served as a centerpiece of a meze table, with other little dishes of appetizers, but it's fine to serve it on its own as a first-course salad. Guests help themselves from the center platter, scooping up tabbouleh with the lettuce leaves, or with pieces of Arab (pita) bread, but it's perfectly acceptable to eat it with a fork, too.

**Makes about 3½ cups, 4 to 6 servings as a first course, more if part of a meze**

½ cup coarse- or medium-grain bulgur

6 scallions, diced

1 to 2 bunches flat-leaf parsley, chopped to make 1–1½ cups

1 bunch fresh mint, chopped to make 1 cup

1 pound ripe but firm tomatoes, seeded

Extra-virgin olive oil

Fresh lemon juice

Sea salt and freshly ground black pepper

1 head romaine lettuce

RINSE THE BULGUR in running water until the water runs quite clear, then transfer the bulgur to a bowl. Add enough water to cover the bulgur by 1 inch. Set aside for 5 minutes, then drain in a sieve and set aside, in the sieve, while you prepare the rest of the salad ingredients.

COMBINE THE SCALLIONS, parsley, and mint in a deep salad bowl. Remove excess water from the bulgur by squeezing it dry with your hands. (Some cooks wrap the bulgur in a kitchen towel and squeeze it to extract as much water as possible.) Add the bulgur to the salad bowl and mix with your hands, gently squeezing the greens and onions to release their fragrance and flavor.

CHOP THE TOMATOES and add them to the salad, again, squeezing gently with your hands.

ADD 4 TABLESPOONS OLIVE OIL and the juice of half a lemon to the salad. Mix in salt and pepper as desired and toss well. Taste and adjust the seasoning, adding more salt, pepper, or lemon juice, if you wish.

SET THE TABBOULEH ASIDE to let the flavors mix for at least 30 minutes before serving. When you are ready to serve, arrange the romaine lettuce leaves on a platter with the tabbouleh in the center of the platter.

VARIATIONS: Some Lebanese cooks add a very small amount of cinnamon and allspice—just a pinch of each—with the salt and pepper. Others will add a pinch of Middle Eastern dried red chili peppers, ground or flaked, and a hint—just a whisper—of cumin.

# Bulgur and Lamb Kofte

In Gaziantep, in southeastern Turkey, Filliz Hosukoglu makes kofte with twice as much bulgur as meat. In Aleppo, just across the border in Syria, cooks reverse the proportions, using twice as much meat as bulgur, and further south, in Lebanon, most cooks add no bulgur at all. I've used the Aleppo version in the recipe that follows, but I'm afraid it's impossible to duplicate the wonderfully sweet-tart sour cherry sauce that's served with kofte in Aleppo in the late spring when the local sour cherries are fat and ripe. The yogurt sauce is as close as I can come to that flavor. Or you could serve the kofte as they often do in Turkey, on split rounds of pita bread with a simple mixture of finely slivered white onion, minced flat-leaf parsley, and 2 tablespoons of sumac on top; serve this with lemon wedges to squeeze over the kofte.

Shape the kofte into patties, like small hamburgers, and grill them over charcoal if you are able to do so. You could also make kofte kebab, by shaping the ground meat mixture into thick fingers on lightly oiled skewers, then charcoal grilling them. Otherwise, they're best fried in a little olive oil; an oven broiler dries them out too much.

**Makes 4 to 6 servings
as a main course**

2 cups plain whole-milk yogurt

1 cup fine-grain bulgur

2 medium yellow onions, minced finely

1 cup chopped fresh flat-leaf parsley

1 to 3 tablespoons extra-virgin olive oil

¼ cup crushed red Middle Eastern pepper (Aleppo pepper, Turkish pepper)

1 teaspoon ground cumin

1 pound very lean ground lamb

Sea salt and freshly ground black pepper

1 garlic clove, chopped

STRAIN THE YOGURT in a yogurt strainer or a sieve lined with a double layer of cheesecloth for about 30 minutes, then transfer to a bowl.

RINSE THE BULGUR in running water until the water runs quite clear, then transfer the bulgur to a bowl. Add enough water to cover the bulgur by 1 inch. Set aside for 5 minutes, then drain in a sieve and set aside, in the sieve, while you prepare the rest of the ingredients.

COMBINE THE ONIONS and parsley in the bowl of a food processor and pulse to mix well and chop them to a fine paste. Add 1 tablespoon of the oil, red pepper, and cumin and pulse again.

DISTRIBUTE THE LAMB over the onions and pulse to mix well and grind the meat even finer. Transfer the mixture to a large bowl.

SQUEEZE THE BULGUR DRY and add it to the lamb mixture in the bowl, along with 1 teaspoon of salt and pepper to taste. Using wet hands, knead the bulgur into the lamb, just as if you were kneading bread dough, wetting your hands frequently to keep the mixture from sticking. When the mixture resembles the texture of biscuit dough, cover the bowl and refrigerate until chilled, about 1 hour.

PREPARE A CHARCOAL FIRE, if you are using one. When the coals have turned white and the meat mixture is well chilled, wet your hands again and divide the mixture into eight to twelve balls, using about ⅓ cup of the mixture for each ball. Flatten the balls into thick patties; or torpedoes, or footballs; or mold each ball into a thick finger around a skewer—two balls to each skewer. Grill over the charcoal until done, about 10 minutes to a side, depending on how hot the fire is. Alternatively, shape the balls into thick patties and sauté in 2 tablespoons of olive oil for about 10 minutes to a side.

TO MAKE THE YOGURT SAUCE, crush the garlic with about ½ teaspoon salt in a small bowl, using the back of a spoon to make a paste. Stir in some of the strained yogurt to mix well, then stir the yogurt-garlic mixture back into the bowl of yogurt. Serve cold with the hot kofte, or, if you wish, heat the yogurt very gently until it is quite warm. Do not let it come to a boil as it will curdle.

# Wine

## A QUESTION OF *TERROIR*

FROM THE RUINED CASTLE above the village of Châteauneuf-du-Pape, the view looks down and out on an endless panorama of vineyards, dropping below the pinnacle of the fortress and unfolding to the west across rich bottomland to the silvery ribbon of the Rhône shining in the near distance. Turn to the east, away from the river, and there are vineyards again, deep green and rising, wave after gentle wave of terrain, culminating in the 6,000-foot peaks of Mont Ventoux, high and white in the distance. Turn a full circle and it is all vineyards, punctuated by thin lines of highways and little clusters of villages, interspersed with a few hedgerows and small copses of trees, out to the river and then back again, climbing up to where the steeper slopes of the mountains begin.

In early August, still a month or more away from the *vendange*, the grapes in these vineyards are, astonishingly, almost ripe. In other wine-growing regions on the same latitude, in France and in Italy, grapes won't start to take on this deep coloration for another month at least. It's the combination of climate and terrain that does this, the hot sun of the southern Rhône valley heating the stony soil all day, while an almost constant breeze from the northwest keeps the air over the vineyards dry and pleasantly stirred—and all too frequently strengthens into the merciless gales of the mistral.

The Rhône is broad as rivers go, but once upon a time it was broader still, stretching across the prized terraces where the vineyards of Châteauneuf-du-Pape are sited. Characteristically, the vineyard floors are layered with big, round stones, some like tennis balls, but others as large as soccer balls, even watermelons. Called *galets roulés* or *cailloux*, these quartzite rocks were worn smooth as beach cobbles by the glacier that scoured out the valley millennia ago and the ancient action of the river that succeeded it. The river-washed stones absorb the sun's intense heat by day and release stored warmth by night, just like a Trombe wall in a solar house. While they make the vineyards extraordinarily difficult to work (imagine walking, much less driving a tractor, over this terrain), the stones also transmit from sun to vine the energy that creates the brilliant color and intense flavor for which these wines are so renowned. Châteauneuf-du-Pape is a superb example of what vintners mean when they speak of *terroir*, the peculiar combination of soil, location, climate, environment, cultivation methods, and other imponderables that make a characteristic wine.

There are five villages in the Châteauneuf-du-Pape appellation—Corthezon, Bédarrides, Châteauneuf, Orange, and Sorgues. But the appellation limits don't depend on geography so much as they do on the structure of the soil. Sometimes it's hard even to think in terms of soil here, so stony is the terrain. I was told that some growers actually bring in stones to replenish worn-out vineyards, but when I mentioned this to Daniel Brunier, one of the owners of the prestigious Vieux Télégraphe winery, he scoffed good naturedly at the very idea.

At the Bruniers' winery in Bédarrides, a glass case displays the soil structure, showing a cross-section cut down ten feet or so into the substructure of the Vieux Télégraphe vineyards high on the plateau called La Crau. La Crau is the top of a moraine, a place where the glacier paused in its long, slow retreat northward up the Rhône valley and left this deposit of stones, which were then rolled and smoothed and polished by the great river. Dig deeply into the soil of La Crau and you'll find that the stones diminish only very gradually, Daniel said. He pointed it out to me on the cross-section: "There's no reason for anyone to replenish the stones," he said. "Even 3 meters down, you can see, the soil is still 60 percent stones mixed with sand." After the sand comes a layer of clay that itself runs deep. The clay keeps the soil humid, but good drainage is important for the vineyard too. Sand, interspersed with the clay, keeps it from holding too much water.

"Vines and olive trees share the same characteristic," Daniel said. "They die if they get too much water."

And too little water? "Drought is a different problem. Grapes might stop maturing because of drought, but the plant itself won't die." Average rainfall in this part of Provence is about 1 inch per month during the growing season and it is forbidden to irrigate; the rules of the *Appellation d'Origine Côntrolée* (AOC) prevent it, as they do elsewhere in France as well—too much water dilutes the quality of the grapes.

The Domaine du Vieux Télégraphe gets its name from an "optical telegraph" tower that was erected on the property in 1792, but the Bruniers acquired the terrain only in the early part of the twentieth century. As wineries go, that's not very old (in Tuscany and elsewhere I know of properties where the same family has been producing wine since medieval times). Vieux Télégraphe, however, is exceptionally distinguished, with what Robert Parker, wine expert and impassioned admirer of Rhône wines, has called "one of the most privileged terroirs" and "one of the finest microclimates" in the entire appellation of Châteauneuf-du-Pape. The hot sun that shines on the stony plateau of La Crau means the Bruniers can usually harvest a week or more before other growers. But it does much more. Because the light and warmth of the sun helps to draw out all the opulence that the fruit is capable of producing, Vieux Télégraphe wines, at their best, are exceptional for richness, complexity, and depth of flavor, a sort of quintessence or archetype of what a great Châteauneuf-du-Pape can be—big, jammy, spicy wines that recall, for North Americans, the greatest of California's great zinfandels.

Of course, it takes more than sunlight and warm stones to produce a great wine. It also takes technique in the vineyard as well as in the winery. Like other producers of great wines around the Mediterranean, the Bruniers—Daniel manages Vieux Télégraphe with his brother Frédéric—practice what must seem to micromanaging California winemakers to be an extraordinarily hands-off style of wine production. The philosophy is not to manipulate the wine, not to fiddle it into a predetermined style by raising and lowering temperatures, pumping over the cap that forms on the must in the first days, using wood-aging to manufacture flavor, fining and filtering wines. Rather the Bruniers' goal is to set the parameters that allow the wine to express itself, to yield its own true character, by handling it infrequently and in the simplest manner possible.

The secrets of making a great wine, as the Bruniers describe them, are equally uncomplicated: Keep yields low; de-stem part, but not all, of the grapes to add complexity and agreeably tarry flavors to the wines; crush very lightly and don't pump, both of which actions cut down on the potential for oxidation. They are rigorous about no refrigeration, no fining, and no filtering of the wines. The wines that will become Châteauneuf-du-Pape Vieux Télégraphe spend two weeks in stainless-steel fermentation tanks, then are racked into concrete or stainless vats for a year, and finally, after blending, are stored for six to eight months in old oak *foudres* (wooden barrels that vary greatly in size but are considerably larger than those used in Burgundy and Bordeaux) before bottling. (Larger barrels are preferred because the proportion of wine to wood is greater, meaning less of the wine is in contact with the wood than in smaller casks; this, again, helps to protect against oxidation and allows the fruity flavors in the wine to predominate over oak flavors from the wood.)

I had come to Vieux Télégraphe through Kermit Lynch, who imports the Bruniers' wines to the United States and is also a partner with the brothers in another vineyard, Les Pallières, in the neighboring appellation of Gigondas. I was looking for a wine region that would be suggestive of the important role wine has played in the Mediterranean, a place with a strong sense of history and tradition, that was also deeply, inextricably linked to a sense of its own *terroir*.

That word, *terroir*, is bandied about a lot these days. Chefs and marketers like to talk about everything from lamb to eggs, from strawberries to heirloom apples, having a "*goût du terroir*," a taste of the particular earth in which the particular food was raised. In a sense they're right to do so. It seems altogether obvious that a lamb raised in the high country of Mt. Lebanon, for instance, will taste very different from a lamb raised on Brittany's salt meadows. But the term *terroir* really belongs in the wine world where it originated. The great wine writer Hugh Johnson defines it as "the whole ecology of the vineyard: every aspect of its surroundings from bedrock to late frosts and autumn mists, not excluding the way the vineyard is tended, nor even the soul of the *vigneron*." As a place to explore the connection between wine and *terroir*, Kermit Lynch didn't hesitate to suggest Vieux Télégraphe. He mentioned one thing in particular that he liked about working with the Bruniers—they share his own sense that the goal of the best wine-making should be "to preserve the typicity of a great *terroir*."

Well, but how do you define this? I asked Daniel Brunier. How do you explain the typicity of Châteauneuf-du-Pape?

Never one to rush his words, he thought for a long moment, then said, "The wine must be balanced. It must have body, structure, and fruit, all in just measure, harmonious, one characteristic balanced with another and no one dominating."

But couldn't you say that about *any* wine, I insisted, or at least about any great wine?

We were tasting the 1998 Vieux Télégraphe and comparing it with its cousin, Vieux Mas des Papes, also made by the Bruniers, the same year and the same grapes, but from vines that were no more than 20 years old. (Some of the grenache vines that provide juice for Vieux Télégraphe are as much as 60 to 75 years old, planted by Daniel and Frédéric's grandfather.) "Well," Daniel said, swirling the wine in his glass without really looking at it, "for me the '98 is more reflective of that typicity. That was a good year for grenache," he added, naming the principal grape in the Bruniers' blend. "The '97, on the other hand, is too round, too easy, to be a good expression of that. It might seem a little flabby on the palate compared to the 1998."

But doesn't typicity change over time, I asked. Surely the Vieux Télégraphe made by your father or your grandfather was a very different wine from what you and your brother make today. Yet all three generations share a noble goal, to make a wine that expresses some typical quality of the soil, of this place, of the *terroir*.

Back in his grandfather's day, Daniel admitted, tannins in the wine gave it greener, more aggressive flavors. "We improved the tannins, we made the wines more accessible." Technology of the kind available at this end of the twentieth century, he said, allows winemakers to be more demanding of the fruit than in his grandfather's time. "We have more maturity in the grapes, we can wait longer, we have more experiments and improvements," he said, with a broad gesture that I took to include everything from more precise measurement of sugar in the fruit to more accurate weather predictions.

The biggest concern in making wine here in the valley of the Rhône, Daniel continued, is to keep it from oxidizing. The grenache grape, a hot-climate vine that is a critical element in the blend that makes up Châteauneuf-du-Pape, is particularly sensitive to oxidization. In earlier times, he said, "they lost fruit because they crushed in the vineyard and only moved the wine four times a day," thus exposing the musts to air. "Now the juice is moved out of the vineyard every 15 minutes and temperatures are controlled, although there's still no refrigeration."

As for organic production, called biological production in Europe, the Bruniers are not so much against it as they find it irrelevant to great wine. "I never met a great wine from this thing called biological," Daniel told me. "The big problem with biological agriculture is that they don't really analyze what they do. They may only use copper sulphate [the blue fungicide, also known as Bordeaux mixture, that is acceptable for organic cultivation], but they use it a *lot*. We are cleaner than that. What we do I call *culture raisonné*, rational agriculture." He went on to explain something that sounds like what North Americans call "integrated pest management," a system of carefully measured use of low-impact pesticides and fungicides that are applied very rarely and only when conditions require them. "We don't go into the vineyard because it's Monday morning," Daniel said, "but because the vine needs it."

Actually, others explained to me, organic cultivation in this peculiar environment is not difficult, since the dry mistral, which blows some 150 days a year, acts as a natural fungicide. In his car, as we climbed up through the southeast-facing slopes above the village of Bédarrides, Daniel pointed to little brown tags hanging from some of the vines as his favorite new tool in the struggle against insects and disease. The tags release a pheromone that sows sexual confusion among the bugs. "The little caterpillar doesn't know whether he is male or female," Daniel explained, "so he doesn't know to reproduce." He stopped the car for a moment. "Listen to the cicadas," he said as the shrill sawing, so typical of a Mediterranean summer, flooded the air. "If we sprayed, we would have no cicadas."

What produces quality for the Bruniers is not one but a combination of all these and other factors, a balance, if you will. That word balance was to crop up over and over again in our conversations. It is balance between the region, the soil, and the vine, Daniel explained, that produces great wine. Change any one of those three elements, change the balance, and you change the wine—and, he implied but did not say, diminish its greatness.

I T  I S  S A I D  T H A T  Châteauneuf-du-Pape got its name and its reputation for wines in the fourteenth century with the establishment of papal vineyards after the papacy was transferred from Rome to Avignon. Such, however, is not the case. The village was already known as Castrum Novum by the eleventh century, the name meaning not a castle (*castellum* in Latin) but a fortified village (*castrum*—an open, unfortified village was a *villam*), presumably because it was founded, or new fortifications were built, around that date. The popes didn't come along until three hundred years later, in the early fourteenth century, when Clement V, who was

French, moved the papacy from Rome to Avignon, just 20 kilometers (12 miles) south of here on the Rhône. Avignon remained the seat of the Holy Apostolic Church, the only Christian entity as far as most of Europe was concerned, for most of that contentious century.

It was a period of the bitterest factional disputes. After Clement's death, the church was popeless for two years until the 71-year-old Bishop of Avignon was elected as John XXII in 1316. Expected to reign briefly because of his age, John in fact ruled from Avignon for 18 years, until his death in 1334. A year after his election, he began construction on Châteauneuf's castle, which castle remained in place until August 1944, when it was blown up during the German retreat north. But the "pope" who was most attached to Châteauneuf was the unfortunate Clement VII (1378–94), whom church historians do not recognize as pope at all—the *Catholic Encyclopedia* dismisses him as the first of the "antipopes." When he failed to unseat his rival Urban VI, who had also been elected pope, Clement returned to Avignon in 1379, never again to leave. The castle at Châteauneuf became his favorite residence, presumably because he felt safer there than elsewhere. It still wasn't Châteauneuf-du-Pape, although in later centuries the wines began to be called "*vins du pape,*" wines of the pope. But not until 1893 did the village, and its wine, became officially known as Châteauneuf-du-Pape.

Even so, wine was always important. A census taken in the year 1344 showed that, although there was lots of mixed cultivation in fourteenth-century Châteauneuf—vines and roses, vines and olives, vines and cereal crops—vineyards were well developed, occupying almost half (46 percent) of the agricultural land. Some four hundred years later, in 1789, 49 percent of the land was still devoted to vineyards. So important have vineyards become today, however, that almost 100 percent of arable land is devoted to vines.

All the to-ing and fro-ing of popes and antipopes throughout the fourteenth century may seem irrelevant to the story of wine, but it is so only for those who forget the role played by the church in spreading wine consumption throughout the Mediterranean and from the countries of the Mediterranean north into the rest of Catholic Christian Europe. Wine was essential for the mass: In the miracle of transubstantiation, consecration of the wine (red, of course) miraculously transformed it into the blood of Christ—as bread was transformed into the body of Christ—for the Eucharist or rite of Holy Communion, at the very heart of Christian belief. When Christianity was still new among the trans-Alpine tribes, some among them had tried to introduce a more familiar intoxicant, beer, to the mass, but the church fathers, shocked by allusions to pagan sacrifice, banned it outright, unconditionally, and forever more.

It wasn't surprising that wine was adopted into Christianity, for it had always had sacramental significance throughout the Mediterranean world. For the Greeks, Dionysus (Bacchus to the Romans, and Fufluns to the Etruscans) was the giver of wine, a god who had his origins in the mysterious East and whose character veers between amiable familiarity, like the favorite uncle who always has too much to drink at Thanksgiving, and a dangerous but seductive abandon associated with the more sinister orgies of carnival. Dionysia, festivals in the god's honor, took place throughout the year in different Greek cities and regions; one of the most important was the Anthesteria in late winter, when the wine jars were opened, the new wine tasted for the first time, and libations of new wine offered to the god, somewhat like beaujolais nouveau, which is tasted and shipped on the feast of Saint Martin in November. When animals were sacrificed, part of the offering was almost always a libation, a full measure of wine poured on the ground or directly onto the altar, which is one source of Christian understanding of the relationship between wine and the blood sacrifice of Jesus.

The consumption of wine was a real mark of cultural identity for the Greeks, who considered beer- and milk-drinking evidence of irredeemable barbarity. Wine taken undiluted with water was another indication of rudeness and incivility. One reason the Greeks added water as well as aromatics to their wines was probably because the wines they made were sweet, for the most part, and quite heady with alcohol. In any case, diluted or not, the wines of the ancient world certainly tasted very different from anything we know today. If they were aged at all, it was in terra-cotta pithoi or amphorae lined with pitch or resin, which gave a strong resinous flavor to the wine; moreover, inefficient pressing probably left bits of residue in the wine—skins, stems, and such—that would give it lots of rough tannins. It's no wonder Greek wine merchants customarily added other flavors, everything from salt seawater to honey, from aromatics like rosemary, thyme, and frankincense to outright perfumes.

THE CULTURE OF THE VINE, and the transformation of its fruits into wine, almost certainly began in the east, possibly as far east as the Transcaucasus, the high mountain region between the Black Sea and the Caspian. From there, it spread slowly south into Anatolia and the Levant, and then west, carried by

Phoenicians, Greeks, Etruscans (who were growing domesticated vines by the ninth century B.C.E.), and later by Romans. It wasn't until around the sixth century B.C.E., archaeologists say, that vineyard culture arrived in Provence, most likely through the Greeks at Massalia (Marseilles), although the Etruscans also exported wine to the south of France: An Etruscan ship that was wrecked off the island of Giglio around 600 B.C.E., and another a few years later off Cap d'Antibes, were both carrying heavy cargoes of wine amphorae.

Since ancient times, wine had been one of the most important trade items all over the Mediterranean—the Egyptians imported wine from Syria and Lebanon, while Greek wines were exported from the homeland to the colonies, as well as to Rome. The Rhône became a great trade route largely through the movement of wine, oil, and other Mediterranean products that couldn't be produced in cool climates to the north. Amphorae of wine, whether from Greece, Etruria, or Spain, could be landed at Massalia (Marseilles), transferred to flat-bottomed barges, and then, with great effort, hauled up the swift-flowing river. But very soon it must have dawned on some Greek or Phoenician colonial entrepreneur that life would be easier and trade more profitable by planting vineyards on the spot, rather than importing fragile jugs of unstable and highly perishable wines over great distances.

We know that vines thrived in southern France because, by the early first century B.C.E., the Emperor Domitian, concerned about competition with Italian wineries as well as providing Rome with grain, ordered many Provençal vineyards to be pulled up, destroyed, and replaced by wheat. But with the Pax Romana, which began later in that same century under the reign of Augustus when all the Mediterranean finally came under the rule of Rome, vineyards themselves, rather than jugs of wine, began to move up the Rhône. Later, in the first century C.E., Columella, the great Latin writer on agriculture, tells of Julius Graecinus, a Roman vice-governor of Provence, who not only cultivated vines on his vast estates but also wrote an authoritative two-volume treatise on viticulture in Provence and in Italy—lost, alas, to history.

Two hundred years later, Christianity had arrived in Provence, and there were bishops at Fréjus, Marseilles, and Arles. But it was monks who played the greatest role in developing viticulture throughout the Middle Ages. With the collapse of Rome, what remained of the imperial economy in the western Mediterranean also disappeared. Vineyards, olive groves, and farmlands were abandoned and roads fell into disrepair. Into the breach stepped the monasteries and, from the fifth century on, they grew in strength, expanding into virgin and derelict territories, enlarging their patrimonies through gifts and legacies, and becoming economic powers in their own right. Vineyards, which produced wine for the mass (and for the consumption of the monks who, according to the Benedictine rule, should drink about a liter of wine each day), like olive groves, which produced oil for the chrism, and bees that produced wax for the candles that lit the churches, began once more to thrive. And wine, like oil and fine beeswax, was not entirely destined for the mass and for monastic tables—it was also a commercial product that produced great revenues for the monastery. Right up until the fourteenth century, any piece of abandoned wasteland was converted to vineyards; in later years, even fields planted to cereal grains, were converted to more profitable vineyards.

OUTSIDE THE REGION it's not generally known that Châteauneuf-du-Pape is not only one of the largest *appellations contrôlées* in the Rhône valley, but also one of the oldest. Tavel, over on the other side of the river, is equally old, as both appellations were established on May 15, 1936. But the *appellation côntrolée* system itself, which since its inception has been responsible for quality control in the French wine industry—and has since spread to other European countries and other products than wine—had its rudimentary beginnings, in fact, right here in Châteauneuf-du-Pape.

The idea of *appellations contrôlées* ("controlled names" is the awkward English translation) is often misunderstood by consumers who think that it is, in and of itself, a guarantee of high quality. It is not, and, with the spread of the idea into other countries and other, mostly artisanally produced foods (olive oils, cheeses, vinegars, hams, and sausages), it's important to understand that an *appellation contrôlée* is only an assurance that the product, whether wine or anything else, was made in a specified region from very specific varieties (only arbequina olives, for instance, in Borjas Blancas olive oil; or only the milk of Lacaune sheep in Roquefort cheese), and by using methods that are traditional, or at least time-honored. But it doesn't guarantee that the product is any good, and especially it doesn't guarantee that the product has maintained its inherent qualities in subsequent shipping and handling. We've probably all had the unhappy experience of opening what ought to have been a wonderful bottle of wine only to find that something questionable between the time the bottle left the winery and the time it arrived on our dinner table has rendered it unacceptable.

In the early 1920s when the ravages of phylloxera combined with the human destruction of World War I were still being felt acutely throughout European vineyards, nearly half the present appellation of Châteauneuf-du-Pape remained unplanted or derelict and abandoned. Baron Pierre Le Roy, a World War I fighter pilot who had married into the family of Château Fortia in Châteauneuf-du-Pape, was approached by other vintners to take on the task of developing a system of voluntary controls that, it was hoped, would raise the overall level of Châteauneuf-du-Pape production and put the wine securely on the quality map once more. The regulations he drew up were later adopted and, moreover, are still in force. They include:

- strict delimitation of the geographical area of production, as well as limits on the number of vines per hectare;
- the use of specific grape varieties and cultivation techniques;
- a minimum alcohol level of 12.5 percent;
- mandatory selection of 5 percent of each crop to be discarded, regardless of quality;
- no rosé wines to be produced at all;
- all wines to be submitted to a taste panel.

Only wines that fulfill all these regulations are entitled to bear the name of Châteauneuf-du-Pape.

Such a large appellation, with three hundred producers on more than eight thousand acres, means Châteauneuf-du-Pape varies greatly in quality; only a very few achieve the stature of Vieux Télégraphe. But when Châteauneuf-du-Pape is good, it is very, very good indeed. No less an authority than Robert Parker praises the wine for "its glorious perfume . . . reminiscent of an open-air produce market in a Provençal hill town, expansive, generous, well-endowed flavors, sumptuous texture, and heady alcohol content. . . ."

VINEYARDS ARE CULTIVATED and wine is made all over the Mediterranean world, even in places, Egypt for instance, where the climate would seem to be irrevocably hostile. A very few countries—one thinks of Syria and Libya—don't produce wine at all as far as one can tell, possibly for religious reasons. (It's tempting to think that the lack of wine goes a long way toward explaining the dourness of those two regimes.) Oftentimes, the wine made isn't very good—Turkish and Tunisian wines are not notable, Moroccan wine is only a slight improvement, Israeli wines can be judged a rather passive-aggressive "not bad," but some Lebanese wines—and there are only three or four vineyards, most of them in the Bekaa valley in the interior—are surprisingly well made, easily holding up against better, if not the best, mid-range Spanish, southern French, and Italian wines. The problem with making good wines in the Mediterranean has always been the hot, dry summer climate which, except in higher country, produces heady, heavy red wines and easily oxidized whites.

That problem has been largely solved by modern winemaking technology, especially temperature-controlled fermentation, which keeps the musts from overheating. Italian white wine production, for instance, has been revolutionized in the last twenty to thirty years and sales on the world market of Italian whites have justified the considerable expense to which some wineries have gone to install the latest equipment. International varietals—chardonnay and cabernet sauvignon, especially, but also merlot, sauvignon blanc, pinot noir—are invading vineyards all across the Mediterranean and pushing aside local vines like sangiovese in Tuscany or the grenache that's such an important component in Châteauneuf-du-Pape.

Moreover, the late twentieth-century market for wine all over the Mediterranean has expanded enormously. Not so long ago, the only wine available in a given locale was what was produced locally—and when I say locally, I mean from within the confines of the commune in which you were drinking. Nowadays you can find, even in country towns, a pretty good selection from a whole region, if not a whole country. The supermarket I frequent in Cortona, a Tuscan hill town, once sold bianco della Valdichiana and rosso Cortonese and that was it. Now we find on its shelves wines from all over Italy, including Sicily and Sardinia, as well as a single novelty wine from California. No French wines as yet, and nothing from Australia, but that will change in the years to come. With more wines to choose from, local taste also begins to change and evolve among both the consuming public and their winemaking neighbors.

All of this might seem very positive were it not for the principle that is so valued by the Brunier brothers and their American partner Kermit Lynch—the principle that the greatest wine is the wine that most expresses the "typicity of a great terroir." When all wines are made alike—whether in California or Australia, along the banks of the Rhône or in the hills of Friuli in northwest Italy—and when all wines are made from the same international varietals, then all wines start to taste alike. And that is to the great detriment of wine enjoyment and to the very idea of *terroir.* Elusive though the concept may seem, it is after all simply a combination of influences from the land, the microclimate, and the vine in its vineyard, expressing itself in a balance—a balance that evolves directly from the traditions that govern the way the wine is made.

A criticism I've heard European winemakers make about California wines is an easy censure, perhaps, but it makes an important point. "Yes, they're good," they say, "often very, very good. But even when they're very good, they still all taste alike. From Napa or Sonoma, from Santa Barbara or Carneros—they lack a sense of *terroir.*"

## VINEGAR

I once made an innocent but very serious mistake when I suggested to a Tuscan producer of fine vin santo that his wine would make a very interesting vinegar. My friend Rolando, who knows more about Tuscan wines, and winemakers, than I do, hissed at me: "You don't tell a winemaker he'd make good vinegar!" he screeched (if you can screech sotto voce, which Rolando can). "That's tantamount to telling him he makes bad wine!"

Well . . . perhaps. But I do think that a fine vinegar is one of the great products to come out of a winery. Actually, in Tuscany (and perhaps elsewhere in Europe), vinegar cannot legally be made within a specified distance of a winery, for fear the bacteria that convert wine to vinegar may attack the wine itself. When I told Rolando about the great aged sherry vinegars of Jerez in Andalucia, the rich flavors of aged cabernet sauvignon vinegars from Catalonia, he spread his hands in a *sans-dire* gesture: "Of course! They can't make good wine so they have to make vinegar."

In a certain sense he was right. Excellent wines are made in Catalonia and in Andalucia, but most traditionally made vinegar is, in fact, a delicious form of spoiled wine. That's what the English word means, as you can see in the French from which the word was loaned to us: *vin aigre,* sour wine. But bad wine makes bad vinegar. The people who make fine vinegars these days do so because that's what they intend to do from the start, not because the wine is no good but because vinegar is a fine and complex product in its own right, one that is as useful in the kitchen as it is at the table for dressing a salad. If you don't believe me, next time you have a stew that seems a little *fade,* a little lacking in punch, instead of a spoonful of salt, try adding a spoonful of aged wine vinegar. I think you'll be pleased at the result.

Jose Puig is a Catalan wine producer, a man of restless temperament who is constantly searching for new challenges. A few years ago, he began making an aged vinegar by combining year-old red wine of his own production with about 15 percent of fresh, unfiltered must from the current year's pressing, then letting it evolve into vinegar. The musts are left unfiltered, he said, in order to contribute all the flavor components of the fresh juice to the vinegar, but he has to control the quantity of must carefully. If he adds too much, the wine will start to re-ferment, which is not what he wants. "It's like red wine," he said, "the less you work it, the better it is."

Without knowing it, Puig echoed what I had learned from the Bruniers at Bédarrides. With the right combination of soil and climate, and with a clean vineyard of well-tended grapes, harvested at the peak of ripeness and pressed in a pristine environment, there's not much need for anything more to encourage greatness. In fact, the less you fiddle with it, the more likely you are to produce a great wine. Or a great vinegar.

Puig is primarily a winemaker, with cabernet franc, cabernet sauvignon, merlot, and chardonnay vineyards on land overlooking the sea in Vendrell, south of Barcelona. An old Roman road, the via Augustea, runs along the bottom of his property; because of the road he markets his vinegar under the Forum label (you can find it in fine shops in North America).* To make his vinegar, Puig blends old wine with new grape must, then transfers the blend to big wooden wine barrels that sit outside, in hot summer sunshine and chilly winter rain, for a year or so while the wine turns into vinegar. It's a small fly called *Drosophylla melanogaster* that begins the process, Puig said. The tiny flies that drifted over his vinegar barrels in the strong August sunlight reminded me of fruit flies hovering over bowls of peaches left on a buffet after lunch. Each big barrel also holds part of the "mother," the gelatinous mass created by acetobacter that converts wine into vinegar by consuming the alcohol in the wine and oxidizing it in a controlled fashion. The mothers of Puig's vinegars have been developing for fifteen years. When you start out with vinegar production, he said, it takes a good five years before you begin to get a good vinegar because the mothers are still developing. Now his process is much quicker because the mothers are older and stronger.

After a year or so, the vinegar is transferred to oak *barriques*, smaller barrels, for aging. While it sits in the *barriques*, the vinegar mellows and flavorful esters start to

* Since I wrote these words, Puig has sold his vinegar enterprise and gone on to invest time, money, and expertise in a new winery in the Priorato, Catalonia's hottest new wine region. Forum vinegars are still produced to his exacting standards, however.

develop, from the vinegar itself and from the barrel in which it is held. With the onset of cold weather, solids in the vinegar precipitate, falling to the bottom of the barrel and leaving the clear, deep-flavored liquid on top. Some years ago, Puig persuaded the renowned Catalan chef Ferran Adria to make chocolates filled with intense Forum vinegar. The result was extraordinary, especially if you let the chocolate melt on your tongue like a communion wafer; at a certain point, the wall of chocolate thins enough to let the vinegar through and the rich sweet fat of chocolate is suffused with the acid-sweet sharpness of the vinegar.

Another vinegar that's had lots of press recently isn't really a vinegar at all. *Aceto balsamico tradizionale,* the Italian condiment, I was surprised to learn, does not begin with wine but with fresh, gently pressed grape must of golden trebbiano grapes that mature to an aromatic, autumnal sweetness on low hills near Modena and Reggio just south of the river Po. Once pressed, the must is filtered to remove stems and skins and transferred, just before it starts to ferment, to big open cauldrons where it is simmered for a full 24 hours or more to concentrate its sweetness, slightly caramelizing the sugars in the grape juice and reducing the amount of liquid by half or more. Then the cooked must is added to the first of a series of at least five barrels.

The *batteria,* or battery, of barrels is the most curious and venerable aspect of making *aceto balsamico.* A *batteria,* which can include as many as eight or nine barrels, is as much a treasured family heirloom as the family silver, a symbol of nobility and longevity in the family tree, and handed down from one generation to the next—curiously, always through the female line, even though it seems to be mostly men who are involved in producing *aceto balsamico tradizionale.* The barrels decrease in size from the largest, at 60 liters, down to the smallest, the regina or queen, at 20 liters, each made from a different wood, traditionally beginning with *rovere* (oak) and ending with mulberry for *la regina.* In between there may be barrels of chestnut, cherry, locust, juniper, and ash, each of which imparts special aromatic characteristics to the liquid, which itself gradually condenses, thickening and concentrating its flavors. The fifty or so liters that go into the first barrel (barrels are never completely filled) will reduce over a period of five years to no more than two or three liters. A battery of barrels that has been in operation for a century or more—there are examples of such batteries stored away in the attics of old farmhouses along the via Emilia that connects Reggio and Modena with the Adriatic—means that the *aceto* that comes out may well be carrying drops of liquid that started developing from grape must into *aceto balsamico* two or three generations ago.

*Aceto balsamico* was never intended for commercialization. It was a family product, and a product of upper-class families at that. Bottles of the precious liquid were given as gifts and doled out, drop by drop, on special occasions, and competitions were held among family producers to see who had the best, the oldest, the most syrupy, and so on. Somehow in the 1980s, word of this superb product slipped out to a world that was frantic for the latest gastronomic craze. That's when North American chefs started slopping "*balsamico*" over every other dish, it seemed, that came out of their kitchens. Degradation, inevitably, set in. Today I can buy in my local North American supermarket bottles of something called *balsamico* that is basically commercially produced vinegar—that is vinegar that's produced in days rather than months—that has been infused with caramel syrup and artificial flavorings to reproduce something rather vaguely recalling true *aceto balsamico tradizionale*. And those three words—*aceto balsamico tradizionale*, traditional balsamic vinegar—have been reserved by European law, in a desperate attempt to shore up the tradition, for the product that's produced the old way, over a period of years, even decades, drop by precious drop.

Confusion reigns on the subject of *aceto balsamico*, especially because there is another product called *aceto balsamico di Modena*—but *not*, you will note, *aceto balsamico tradizionale di Modena*. *Aceto balsamico di Modena* is made from true vinegar, that is wine that has been acetified, then turned into *balsamico* by adding either cooked must (this is the best) or caramel syrup (clearly the worst). "*Aceto balsamico tradizionale* sells for $240 a bottle," one traditional producer explained to me. "*Aceto balsamico di Modena* sells side by side at $80 a bottle—and is worth maybe $3. Industrial producers turn out 11,000 bottles an hour, while I make," he said with evident pride, "10,000 bottles a year." Go figure.

## 12 GREAT RECIPES USING WINE OR VINEGAR

Red-Wine Risotto
*Risotto al Vino Rosso*

Oven-Roasted Fish Fillets in White Wine with Almonds

Provençale Rabbit in Wine Sauce

Veal Shanks in White Wine
*Osso Buco Milanese*

Chicken in Wine Sauce
  *Coq au Vin*

Lamb in Red Wine from Avignon
  *Daube d'Agneau d'Avignon*

Pork Braised to Taste Like Wild Boar
  *Stufato di Cinghiale o di Maiale*

Braised Duck Legs in a Sweet-Sour Sauce

Pumpkin in a Sweet-and-Sour Sauce
  *Zucca al' agrodolce*

Oven-Baked Beans with a Red Wine Sauce

Leeks or Onions Braised in Wine

Christmas Dried Fruits in a Spiced Red Wine
  *Zurracapote*

## COOK'S NOTES

Although wine is made and enjoyed with meals all over the Mediterranean, except by strict Muslims, using wine and wine vinegar as an ingredient in cooking is a feature only of the cuisines of southern France, Italy, and Spain. (There are a few Greek dishes that use wine as an ingredient, it's true, but apart from octopus or squid stews, the addition of wine is very restrained.)

Wine and wine vinegar were often the basis of marinades for meats, especially tough cuts of older farm animals, beef cattle, pork, mutton, animals that had outlived their usefulness and were converted to meat for the family stewpot. This kind of meat almost doesn't exist anymore, certainly not in commerce, so the usefulness of the marinade as a tenderizer has disappeared, except for a rare piece of game—I think of the wild boar shot in Tuscany in the wintertime, the meat of which is almost always marinated in spiced wine for days before cooking. A marinade can still offer great flavor to any sauce of which it is a part, but we must be careful with modern butcher meats not to *over*marinate. Too long a soak in the acid of wine or vinegar (or citrus juice or yogurt, for that matter, to mention two other types of marinade, used by non-wine drinking cultures) will soften the flesh of butcher meats to an unacceptable mush. Nowadays, unless you know for certain that a cut of meat is tough, limit the marinating time to several hours; with fish, 30 minutes or so is plenty of time for most marinades.

What to do, then, with recipes for delicious old-fashioned wine sauces that called for days of soaking and/or cooking? One solution I've suggested in the recipe for coq au vin (page 209), which used to be made with a barnyard rooster that only softened up with hours of cooking while the wine reduced to a thick, delicious, almost syrupy sauce, is to reduce the wine ahead of time, with the aromatics, then add it to the browned meat or chicken. This is an especially useful technique with super-tender, modern chickens.

That said, however, I should note that almost all meat ragoûts (but not fish or vegetable stews) in which wine predominates benefit from being served the day after they are made. Sitting overnight in the sauce seems to pull the flavors together in a remarkable fashion. By all means, serve the dish immediately if you must. But remember that, as a boon for the busy host, cooking the stew a day ahead will not damage it in the slightest. *Au contraire!*

What wine to use in these preparations? The old adage is still apt: The better the wine, the better the sauce. But within reason: I'm not about to use a 1968 Barolo riserva to marinate a roast of pork. On the other hand, I would never use in cooking a wine of any sort that I don't consider good enough to serve at the table. In fact, for a first-rate marriage between food and drink, it's a good rule of thumb to serve the wine you use in cooking to accompany the dish.

Most of these saucy preparations, if they don't actually include noodles or rice or potatoes, are served with a starch of some sort to soak up the delicious juices. In days gone by, that starch might well have been a thick slice of rather stale bread, set in the bottom of the plate and with the meat or fish in its sauce spooned on top. That's still an excellent idea, when appropriate, if you have good, country-style bread; toasting the bread in the oven beforehand, rubbing it with a cut clove of garlic, dribbling olive oil over it, will also add considerable interest.

# Red-Wine Risotto

**RISOTTO AL VINO ROSSO**

This used to be called risotto al Barolo, but when the price of a decent Barolo went up to sixty dollars, I decided that a wine with a less stratospheric price would have to do. Do use the best wine you can afford, and make sure it's a robust, well-flavored wine—a cabernet sauvignon would be perfect but so would some of the big-flavored Rhône wines from France, or the new-style Priorato reds from Spain. In fact, this risotto is also a beautiful dish made with a white wine. Just make sure it's a white with lots of forward fruit, not too austere and steely.

The best risotto is made with round-grain rice that cooks slowly and retains its shape while absorbing the flavorful liquid in which it is cooked. Arborio is the most commonly available variety, but Italian restaurant chefs and other knowledgeable cooks insist on varieties called carnaroli or vialone nano because of their shorter, fatter, more resistant grains. These varieties can often be found in fine gourmet-products stores in North America. (Note that these are rice varieties, not brand names.)

**Makes 6 servings**

2 cups hearty red wine

2 cups light chicken stock

1 tablespoon unsalted butter

1 tablespoon extra-virgin olive oil

2 tablespoons minced red onion

1½ cups rice for risotto (arborio, carnaroli, vialone nano)

Sea salt and freshly ground black pepper

½ cup grated Parmigiano-Reggiano, or more to taste

WARM THE WINE in a saucepan to just below the simmering point. In another saucepan, bring the stock to a gentle simmer. Keep these two liquids very warm, just below simmering, while you prepare the rice.

IN A HEAVY-DUTY SAUCEPAN, melt the butter in the olive oil over medium-low heat. Add the onion and cook until the onion is very soft and melting into the fat. Do not let the onion brown.

WHEN THE ONION IS SOFT, add the rice and raise the heat slightly to medium. Cook, stirring, until the rice is translucent and starting to absorb some of the fat. Add ½ cup of the warm wine and raise the heat to medium-high. Cook rapidly, stirring, until all the wine has been absorbed.

NOW, LOWER THE HEAT AGAIN to medium-low and start adding the warm wine in increments of ½ cup or so, stirring slowly. As each addition of wine is absorbed by the rice, add another, but don't let the rice dry out between additions of liquid. When all the wine has been added, start to stir in the simmering stock in the same way. You may not need to use all the stock.

WHEN THE RICE IS SMOOTH and creamy, well coated with the sauce but with each grain still a little resistant at the center when you bite it, remove the saucepan from the heat. Stir in salt and pepper to taste, along with 2 tablespoons of the grated cheese. Cover the pan and set it aside for 5 to 7 minutes to let the rice rest. Then serve immediately, passing the remaining cheese at the table.

# Oven-Roasted Fish Fillets in White Wine with Almonds

Choose thick, meaty fillets from a fish such as haddock or red snapper, and use a dry but flowery wine, like a sauvignon blanc, a vermentino from Sardinia, or a white from the Languedoc region of southern France.

**Makes 6 to 8 servings**

2 large garlic cloves, coarsely chopped (1 tablespoon)

¾ pound yellow onions, coarsely chopped (2 cups)

½ cup extra-virgin olive oil

Sea salt

¼ teaspoon ground red chili pepper

1 teaspoon fennel seeds

2 bay leaves

2 cups dry white wine

1 tablespoon finely grated orange zest

⅓ cup salted capers, carefully rinsed and drained (optional)

1 pound potatoes, peeled and cut into small cubes

1 cup chopped, drained canned tomatoes

1 teaspoon dried thyme or dried Sicilian or Greek oregano (*rígani*)

2 pounds thick fish fillets

⅓ cup dried unseasoned bread crumbs

⅓ cup finely chopped blanched almonds

COMBINE THE GARLIC and onions in a large heavy sauté pan with ¼ cup of the oil and 1 teaspoon salt. Set over medium-low heat and cook gently, stirring often, until the onions are very soft and almost melting into the oil. Add the chili pepper, fennel seeds, and bay leaves and mix well. Pour in the wine and continue cooking at a low simmer for 15 to 20 minutes, until the wine has reduced by almost half. Remove the pan from the heat and stir in the grated orange zest and, if you wish, the capers. Set aside.

BRING A SMALL POT of lightly salted water to a rolling boil and drop in the potatoes. Boil vigorously for 5 minutes, then drain immediately and transfer to a small bowl. Stir in 2 tablespoons of the remaining olive oil and the tomatoes and stir to mix well.

TURN THE OVEN ON to 350°F.

DISTRIBUTE THE POTATOES and tomatoes over the bottom of a rectangular or oval oven dish large enough to hold all the ingredients. Sprinkle with the dried thyme, crumbling the herb between your fingers. Lay the fish fillets on top of the potatoes, then spoon the wine sauce over the fish, covering it with the sauce. Sprinkle liberally with the bread crumbs and chopped almonds and dribble the remaining 2 tablespoons of olive oil over the top.

COVER THE DISH with aluminum foil. Bake for 20 minutes, then raise the heat to 450°, remove the foil, and bake an additional 10 minutes, or until the surface is crisp and brown.

SERVE IMMEDIATELY.

# Provençale Rabbit in Wine Sauce

The original of this recipe is a *civet,* an old French dish in which the blood of the animal being cooked figures largely in the sauce. "Reserve the blood with a half glass of vinegar," the recipes typically say. No one in North America, unless they slaughter their own rabbits, will have access to rabbit blood, or any other kind of blood for that matter, so we may never know what those old recipes tasted like. Serve with steamed new potatoes, rice, polenta, or plain flat noodles dressed with a little of the rabbit gravy.

PUT THE RABBIT PIECES in a bowl and cover with the wine and armagnac. Stir in the minced onion. Break up the bay leaves and add, along with the leaves of the thyme sprigs, the sage leaves, and the savory. Add 1 tablespoon of sea salt and several turns of ground black pepper. Cover and set in a cool place to marinate for 2 to 4 hours. (If you don't have a cool pantry or cellarway, refrigerate the rabbit.)

WHEN YOU'RE READY TO COOK, combine the olive oil, pancetta, chopped onion, and garlic in a large skillet and sauté very gently over medium-low heat until the vegetables are soft and the pancetta has yielded its fat. Remove with a slotted spoon and set aside.

WHEN THE VEGETABLES and pancetta are cooked, remove the rabbit pieces from the marinade and dry well with paper towels. Raise the heat to medium and brown the rabbit pieces on both sides in the oil remaining in the skillet (add a little more oil if it seems necessary). When all the rabbit has been browned, return the sautéed onion-pancetta mixture to the pan. Strain the marinade over the rabbit, discarding the solid bits of vegetables and aromatics. Add the remaining cup of wine to the pan, along with the chopped tomatoes. Cover and simmer for about 1½ hours.

FINELY CHOP THE RABBIT LIVER and kidneys, if present. Toast the flour over low heat in a dry frying pan until it starts to turn

## Makes 4 servings

1 rabbit, weighing 2½–3 pounds, cut into six pieces

**For the marinade:**

2 cups flavorful red wine, such as a red Bandol or Châteauneuf-du-Pape

½ cup Armagnac

1 yellow onion, minced

3 bay leaves

3 to 4 sprigs fresh thyme

3 to 4 sage leaves, slivered

Pinch of dried savory

Sea salt

Freshly ground black pepper

3 tablespoons extra-virgin olive oil, or more as needed

2 ounces pancetta or bacon, diced

2 medium onions, chopped

2 garlic cloves, chopped

1 cup red wine

1 cup peeled, chopped ripe tomatoes

1 tablespoon all-purpose flour

brown, then mash the flour into the chopped liver. Stir this into the sauce and cook for about 10 minutes longer to thicken it.

SERVE IMMEDIATELY, or set aside in a cool place and reheat to serve the next day.

VARIATIONS: Add fresh wild mushrooms, sliced and sautéed briefly in olive oil, or dried reconstituted wild mushrooms, with the tomatoes. Add a handful of pitted small black olives—Nyons, Gaeta, or niçoise, at the end.

# Veal Shanks in White Wine

## OSSO BUCO MILANESE

Milano is the wealthy heart of bourgeois Italy and the home of fine, attentive, bourgeois cooking of rich ingredients. Yet the epitome of *la cucina milanese* is osso buco, bone with a hole in it, which is Italian for the veal shank, surely one of the humblest parts of the animal. As is typical of a dish of such respected tradition, every cookbook, every chef, has a slightly different way of preparing it. The one area of agreement is that osso buco is truly slow food— the browning of the veal must be slow, the simmering in wine must be slow, the wine must be added in slow increments, and the consumption of the finished dish must be slow too— preferably over the course of a traditional, 2-hour Milanese businessman's lunch.

The traditional accompaniment to osso buco milanese is risotto, either a plain one made with flavorful veal stock or a saffron risotto, made simply with water or a light stock colored with a pinch of saffron threads. Use the recipe for Red-Wine Risotto (page 202), substituting veal stock or water with ¼ teaspoon of crumbled saffron threads dissolved in it for the red wine. In either case, whether you use veal stock or saffron water, encourage your guests to take a little of the tender marrow at the center of the veal bones with each bite of rice.

PAT THE VEAL SHANKS DRY with paper towels and cut a few narrow slits around the edge of each shank to keep them flat when they're cooking. Sprinkle each shank liberally on both sides with salt and pepper. Spread the flour on a plate and dredge the shanks on both sides in the flour, tapping to get rid of any excess flour. Set aside.

ADD THE OIL AND BUTTER to a heavy-duty saucepan that's large enough to hold all the shanks in one layer, and set the pan over low heat. When the butter has melted and the foam starts to subside, add the pancetta. Cook briefly, just a minute or so, until the fat in the pancetta starts to melt. Stir in the carrot, celery, onion, and chopped garlic. Continue cooking, stirring occasionally, until the vegetables are very tender and melting in the fat. Do not let the vegetables brown.

**Makes 4 servings**

4 veal shanks, each about 2 inches thick and weighing about 12 ounces

Sea salt and freshly ground black pepper

About ½ cup unbleached all-purpose flour

2 tablespoons extra-virgin olive oil

2 tablespoons unsalted butter

2 ounces pancetta, minced (½ cup)

1 medium carrot, chopped

1 celery stalk, chopped

1 small yellow onion, chopped

1 garlic clove, chopped

1 medium ripe tomato, peeled, seeded, and chopped, or 2 canned plum tomatoes, well drained and chopped

2 bay leaves

1 cup dry white wine, preferably an Arneis from Piedmont

½ cup chicken or veal stock

**For the gremolata:**

Grated zest of 1 lemon

2 tablespoons finely minced flat-leaf parsley

1 garlic clove, finely minced

WHILE THE VEGETABLES ARE COOKING, turn on the oven to 300°F.

USE A SLOTTED SPOON to remove the vegetables from the saucepan and set aside. Raise the heat slightly and in the fat remaining in the pan, slowly brown the veal shanks on both sides—about 10 minutes to a side. Once the shanks are thoroughly browned, return the vegetables to the saucepan. Stir in the tomato. Add the bay leaves, ½ cup of the wine, and the stock. Bring to a simmer, cover, and transfer to the oven to bake for about 2 hours. (You may also cook this on top of the stove, if it is more convenient.)

HEAT THE REMAINING ½ cup wine to just below boiling. Check the meat from time to time and add small amounts of hot wine—a few tablespoons at a time—to the pan as the liquid cooks down. After the first 45 minutes, carefully turn the veal shanks over. The meat is done when it is fork-tender and falling off the bones.

WHILE THE OSSO BUCO IS COOKING, combine the lemon zest, parsley, and minced garlic. Mince together until very fine to make a gremolata. Add the gremolata to the pan at the end of the cooking time and stir in. If you wish, hold back a little of the gremolata to scatter over the *ossi bucchi* as you serve them.

# Chicken in Wine Sauce

**COQ AU VIN**

 This French classic is a dish once found on every bistro menu and in provincial households all over the country. It was originally intended to tenderize a tough old rooster that had outlived his usefulness and could only be made edible by long hours of simmering in a gradually reducing and concentrating volume of robust red wine. Nowadays, it's hard to find a bird like that, nor would we probably want to eat it if we could. The problem with today's chickens, even when they're free-range, is that they cook up very quickly, so it's hard to get the concentration of flavors that the old recipe had without turning the chicken to mush. I solve that by reducing the red wine with its aromatics before adding it to the stew.

In southern France, this kind of stew is often served with wide noodles, steamed and dressed with a little olive oil and a sprinkling of minced flat-leaf parsley. Use oil or butter, or a combination of the two, as your cooking fat. Like most wine-based stews, this is really better if made a day ahead and set aside in a cool place or refrigerated until ready to serve.

**Makes 6 servings**

1 chicken, preferably free-range, weighing 4 to 5 pounds, cut into parts

1 chicken liver, trimmed and coarsely chopped

5 tablespoons extra-virgin olive oil or unsalted butter, or more as needed

1 medium onion, coarsely chopped

1 garlic clove, coarsely chopped

1 bottle red wine, preferably a full-bodied Côtes-du-Rhône

2 bay leaves

Zest of 1 orange

3 allspice berries

½ teaspoon whole black peppercorns

CUT AWAY ANY PARTS of the chicken that are not suitable to serve, such as the wing tips and the back, and combine them in a saucepan with the liver and 1 tablespoon of the oil or butter. Cook over medium heat for about 5 minutes, or until brown on all sides. Add the chopped onion and garlic and continue cooking until the vegetables are soft. Pour in the wine and add the bay leaves, orange zest, allspice, peppercorns, and fennel seeds. Bring to a boil, then lower the heat to a simmer and cook, uncovered, for 20 minutes or longer, to reduce the wine by half. Strain the wine through a fine-mesh sieve, discarding the solids, then combine it with the stock. Set aside.

IF YOU ARE USING BACON, bring a small pot of water to a rolling boil. Add the bacon and simmer for 5 minutes, then drain and rinse with cold water. This will get rid of an excessively smoky flavor. If you are using pancetta, this step is unnecessary.

½ teaspoon fennel seeds

¼ cup veal or chicken stock

3 ounces bacon or
pancetta, diced

¼ cup Cognac

½ ounce dried mushrooms

1 cup very hot water, or
more if necessary

4 ounces fresh mushrooms,
trimmed and sliced

18 to 20 small white onions

1 tablespoon instant flour

Minced flat-leaf parsley,
to garnish

IN A LARGE, HEAVY SAUCEPAN, gently sauté the bacon or pancetta in 2 tablespoons of the oil or butter until the meat is brown. Remove the meat with a slotted spoon and set aside.

DRY THE CHICKEN PIECES thoroughly with paper towels. In the fat remaining in the pan, brown them well on all sides. You may do this in several batches. Once the chicken pieces are all browned, combine them in the saucepan and add the Cognac. Light the Cognac and stir the chicken pieces with a wooden spoon until the blue flames have died out.

ADD THE REDUCED WINE to the chicken, bring to a simmer, and cook, covered, for about 30 minutes.

WHILE THE CHICKEN IS COOKING, immerse the dried mushrooms in very hot water and set aside, weighted to keep the mushrooms under water, for about 20 minutes to soften. When the mushrooms are soft, strain them, reserving the mushroom liquid but discarding any bits of soil that pass through the strainer. Rinse the mushrooms under running water to rid them of any soil, pat dry with paper towels, and slice them. Add to the reserved bacon or pancetta.

IN THE REMAINING 2 tablespoons of oil or butter, sauté the sliced fresh mushrooms over medium heat until they are tender and have given off their liquid, about 10 minutes. Remove from the pan with a slotted spoon and add to the reserved bacon or pancetta.

IN THE FAT REMAINING from the mushrooms (adding another tablespoon, if it seems necessary), brown the small onions over medium heat, turning frequently until they are golden brown. They will still be firm in the middle. Add the instant flour to the pan and continue turning the onions until the flour and fat are well mixed and quite stiff. Carefully pour the reserved mushroom liquid into the pan, holding back any bits of grit or soil. Stir to combine the liquid, which should thicken rapidly.

WHEN THE CHICKEN HAS COOKED for 30 minutes, turn the contents of the onion pan into it, stirring to mix well. Then add the reserved mushrooms and bacon or pancetta. Stir gently to distribute all these ingredients, then cover the pan again and simmer for another 15 to 20 minutes, or until the chicken is cooked through and its juices run clear yellow when the meat is pierced with a fork.

IF THE STEW STILL SEEMS TOO LIQUID, remove all the solids and arrange on a platter. Keep warm while you boil down the liquid until it's the right consistency to nap the chicken pieces with sauce. You should have enough liquid to provide two to three big spoonsful for each serving. You may serve this immediately, but it's better if set aside and reheated and served the following day.

# Lamb in Red Wine from Avignon

**DAUBE D'AGNEAU D'AVIGNON**

If your butcher will bone the lamb shoulder for you, ask him to include the bones in the package. They will lend immeasurable flavor and a rich, gelatinous texture to the finished stew. The stew can be accompanied by a bowl of noodles dressed with a few spoonsful of the juice from the daube. It's not unheard of to grate a little Parmigiano-Reggiano or Gruyère cheese over the top of the noodles.

**Makes 6 to 8 servings**

2½ pounds boned lamb shoulder, cut into large stewing pieces

Lamb bones from the boned shoulder, if available

2 onions, coarsely chopped

2 carrots, sliced

12 garlic cloves, peeled but left whole

3 bay leaves

Zest of 1 small orange

½ teaspoon freshly grated nutmeg

Sea salt and freshly ground black pepper

2 cups dry red wine, preferably a Châteauneuf-du-Pape or other Côtes-du-Rhône

2 ounces pancetta, diced

2 tablespoons extra-virgin olive oil

¼ cup flour

IN A LARGE BOWL, combine the lamb, lamb bones, onions, carrots, garlic, bay leaves, orange zest, nutmeg, salt and pepper to taste, and wine. Stir to mix well. Cover with plastic wrap and set aside to marinate for 4 to 6 hours, stirring the ingredients from time to time; refrigerate the meat in warm weather.

WHEN YOU ARE READY TO COOK, turn the oven on to 275°F

IN A HEAVY OVENPROOF SAUCEPAN, with a tightly fitting lid, heat the pancetta in the olive oil over medium-low heat. When the fat in the pancetta starts to run, use a slotted spoon to transfer the vegetables, meat, and bones in the bowl to the saucepan. Cook slowly, stirring frequently, until the meats have changed color and the vegetables are starting to soften slightly, about 15 minutes. Add the liquid contents of the bowl and bring to a simmer.

COVER THE PAN with a tight-fitting lid and let the ingredients simmer while you combine ¼ cup flour with enough water to make a thick paste. Roll the paste into a long snake and use it to seal the lid on the saucepan, pressing the dough around the edge to make a tight seal.

BAKE VERY SLOWLY for 4 to 5 hours. (The lamb will be done in 4 hours, but becomes more tender with more time.) Remove the pan from the oven and break the seal, discarding the dough snake. Discard the bones and the bay leaves. Serve the daube, preferably in the pot in which it was cooked.

# Pork Braised to Taste Like Wild Boar

## STUFATO DI CINGHIALE O DI MAIALE

 This is a Sardinian way of preparing the wild boar that range over the wild land of the island mountains. If chance brings you a loin roast of boar, by all means use it in preparing this recipe. If on the other hand, boar is hard to find in your local meat market (as it is in mine), you may use a boneless pork loin. High-temperature cooking in a tightly sealed pot results in meat that remains surprisingly succulent, juicy, and very tender.

You can serve the meat with other vegetables to accompany it, but in Italy, where this recipe comes from, the meat is most often served on its own, perhaps with a few (a very few) slices of boiled or sautéed potato, but nothing more.

PREHEAT THE OVEN to 425°F.

IN A HEAVY SAUCEPAN large enough to hold the whole pork roast, melt the salt pork in the olive oil over medium-low heat for a few minutes, until the salt pork slices are transparent and giving off their fat. Do not let the slices brown.

ADD THE ONIONS, garlic, celery, and carrots, stirring to mix well. Mince together the bay, sage, and thyme leaves and stir into the vegetables in the pot.

LIGHTLY SALT and heavily pepper the pork roast, rubbing the seasonings into the flesh. Set the roast, fat side up, on top of the vegetables and sprinkle the peppercorns around the edges. Cover the pot with a tight-fitting lid and bake for 40 minutes. The vegetables should give off plenty of liquid as they soften, but check the pot halfway through this cooking time to make sure nothing is burning. Add a couple of tablespoons of water if the pot seems too dry.

REMOVE THE POT from the oven and pour in the red wine. Cover again and return to the oven for 30 minutes, then remove and turn the roast over, leaving it for an additional 30 minutes. At the end of this time, turn the roast once more so that the fat side

**Makes 8 servings**

2 ounces lean salt pork, cut into very thin slices

3 tablespoons extra-virgin olive oil

2 medium yellow onions, thinly sliced

2 garlic cloves, crushed with the blade of a knife

1 celery stalk, thinly sliced

2 medium carrots, thinly sliced

2 large bay leaves, preferably Turkish

Leaves from 3 to 4 sprigs fresh sage

Leaves from 3 to 4 sprigs fresh thyme

Sea salt and freshly ground black pepper

3-pound boneless pork loin roast

6 to 8 black peppercorns

Water (optional)

2 cups dry, flavorful red wine, such as Sardinian Cannonau or Monica, or use a Spanish Rioja or Italian chianti

is now uppermost and return to the oven, this time without the lid, to let the roast brown and the juices in the pot reduce. This should take 20 to 30 minutes.

WHEN THE ROAST IS CARAMEL BROWN on top, remove it from the pan and set it aside on a platter to let the juices retract. If the pan juices are thin, boil them rapidly over high heat to reduce and thicken. If you wish, you can puree the vegetables with the pan juices to make a thick "gravy." I prefer to serve the reduced pan juices with the vegetables adding texture to the sauce. Let the meat stand for 30 minutes or so, then slice and serve with the juices as a sauce.

# Braised Duck Legs in a Sweet-Sour Sauce

 Sweet-and-sour combinations are typical of many regions of the Mediterranean. They hark back to classical times, long before tomatoes, sugar, and citrus became standard Mediterranean ingredients, when the combination of sweetness and acidity, while prized, was more difficult to come by. Duck, a naturally rich and fatty meat, is often served with something tart and slightly bitter to counteract the richness. Green olives, in this sweet-sour tomato sauce from southern Italy, are perfect.

TRIM THE EXCESS FAT and skin away from the duck legs. (Reserve the fat and skin to render into duck fat and duck cracklings; see note below.)

TRANSFER THE LEGS to a bowl and add the wine, vinegar, pepper, cinnamon, nutmeg, ginger, cloves, and onion. Stir to mix well and set aside, covered, to marinate in the refrigerator overnight.

WHEN YOU ARE READY TO COOK the duck, preheat the oven to 350°F. Remove the duck legs from the marinade and dry well with paper towels. Strain the marinade, reserving both the onions and the marinade. Heat the duck fat or oil in a heavy skillet over medium-high heat until very hot. Drop the duck legs into the hot fat and sear on all sides until they are crisp and brown. As they are done, transfer the legs to a casserole. Sprinkle with salt to taste.

LOWER THE HEAT TO MEDIUM. Add the carrot to the fat in the pan, along with the reserved onions from the marinade. Cook briefly, just 5 minutes, or long enough to soften the chopped vegetables slightly, then transfer to the casserole. Add the marinade to the skillet and bring to a boil. Let it simmer for 5 minutes to reduce the marinade slightly, then pour over the casserole ingredients. Cover with a tight-fitting lid and transfer to the oven to bake for 1 hour.

REMOVE THE CASSEROLE from the oven and add the fennel, stirring to mix it in well. There should be plenty of liquid still in

**Makes 6 servings**

3 pounds duck legs (6 legs)

1 cup dry red wine

¼ cup aged red wine vinegar

Freshly ground black pepper

½ teaspoon freshly ground cinnamon

½ teaspoon freshly grated nutmeg

½ teaspoon ground ginger

¼ teaspoon freshly ground cloves

1 medium onion, coarsely chopped

1 tablespoon rendered duck fat or extra-virgin olive oil

Sea salt

1 large carrot, coarsely chopped

2 fennel bulbs, trimmed and coarsely chopped

Boiling water (optional)

2 cups canned, drained, and chopped tomatoes

2 tablespoons sugar

⅔ cup chopped pitted green olives

1 tablespoon salted capers, rinsed and drained

the casserole, but if necessary, add a small amount of boiling water, not more than ⅓ cup, to the pan. Cover again and return to the oven. After another 30 minutes, stir in the tomatoes, sugar, olives, and capers. Cover again and return to the oven for a final 30 minutes of cooking.

SERVE IMMEDIATELY, with the duck legs napped with the sauce.

NOTE: To render duck fat, chop the pieces of fat and skin and transfer to a small heavy saucepan. Add a little water—2 tablespoons should be plenty, or just enough to keep the fat from burning—along with, if you wish, ½ teaspoon salt and a fat garlic clove, peeled and cut in half. Set over low heat and cook for 20 to 30 minutes, or until the pieces of skin and fat have reduced to little brown nuggets swimming in a bath of duck fat. Remove from the heat and strain. Transfer the fat to a container and refrigerate until you are ready to use it. (Duck fat is the best medium for frying potatoes.) Discard the garlic cloves and use the cracklings as a garnish for a salad made with bitter greens. Or add more salt and serve as something to munch on with drinks.

# Pumpkin in a Sweet-and-Sour Sauce

### ZUCCA ALL'AGRODOLCE

 North American cooks think of pumpkin as pie filling, not as a vegetable. This recipe will convince us of how wrong we are. Botanically, I'm told, there are no such things as pumpkins since they're basically just variations on winter squash. "But we all know a pumpkin when we see one," says my seed catalog. Do look for pumpkins that have been raised for the table, rather than for carving—the spectacular rouge vif d'Estampes variety is often available in farmers' markets in the fall. And if you can't find a satisfactory pumpkin, use any type of hard winter squash (acorn, butternut, etc.), preferably with deep red-orange flesh.

DUST THE PUMPKIN CUBES with flour. The easiest way to do this is to put the flour in a paper bag, add the pumpkin cubes, and shake gently.

HEAT THE OIL in a deep heavy skillet over medium heat. When the oil is hot enough to quickly brown a little cube of bread (about 350°F, if you are using a thermometer), add the pumpkin cubes, in batches, and fry until golden brown and tender in the middle. Remove the cubes as they're done, and transfer to a rack covered with paper towels to drain. Sprinkle with salt and pepper, then arrange the drained cubes on a serving platter or in a bowl.

REMOVE ALL BUT 3 TABLESPOONS of oil from the pan. Add the vinegar and sugar and return to the heat, now set at medium-low. Cook for about 5 minutes, or until the sugar has completely dissolved and the sauce is slightly thicker. Remove from the heat and stir in the garlic and mint. Immediately, pour the hot sauce over the pumpkin. Set aside to cool to room temperature before serving.

**Makes 6 servings**

2 pounds pumpkin or hard winter squash, cut into cubes about 1 inch to a side

1 cup unbleached all-purpose flour

1 cup extra-virgin olive oil

Sea salt and freshly ground black pepper

3 tablespoons red wine vinegar

2 tablespoons sugar

2 garlic cloves, crushed and chopped

2 tablespoons slivered fresh mint

# Oven-Baked Beans with a Red Wine Sauce

🌿 Ordinary stewed beans, delicious in their own right, are made more so if they're baked in the oven and given a finishing touch with red wine. A lidded terra-cotta oven dish is perfect for these, but you can also bake them in any dish that can be safely put in the oven. Use a robust red wine with lots of complex flavors—a barbaresco from Italy's Piedmont, a Côtes-du-Rhône from Provence, a hearty Rioja from northern Spain, or an inky Náoussa from Greek Macedonia would be a good choice. California zinfandel is also excellent.

To soak or not to soak the beans? See page 232 for suggestions.

**Makes 4 to 6 servings**

1½ cups dried white or lightly speckled beans (French haricots, great northern white beans, Maine soldier beans), soaked for several hours or overnight

2 bay leaves

3 or 4 sprigs of fresh thyme, or ¼ teaspoon dried, crumbled

3 garlic cloves, crushed with the flat blade of a knife

Freshly ground black pepper

1 small dried hot red chili pepper (optional)

8 ounces lean bacon or pancetta, in one piece

Boiling water

1 medium yellow onion, coarsely chopped

2 tablespoons extra-virgin olive oil

¾ cup robust red wine

1 tablespoon tomato concentrate or paste

Sea salt

PREHEAT THE OVEN to 325°F.

DRAIN THE BEANS and transfer to a baking dish. Add the bay leaves, thyme, garlic, plenty of black pepper, and the red chili, if desired. Stir to mix the seasonings into the beans. Bury the bacon or pancetta into the middle of the beans. Add enough boiling water just to come to the top of the beans. Bring to a simmer on top of the stove, then cover the dish, and transfer to the oven. Bake until the beans are tender, 1½ to 3 hours, depending on the age of the beans. Check the beans frequently and top up with more boiling water when necessary.

WHEN THE BEANS ARE VERY TENDER, remove the dish from the oven. There should be just a small amount of liquid (½ cup or so) left in it. Remove the piece of bacon or pancetta and set aside to cool. As soon as you can handle it, dice it.

IN A MEDIUM SAUTÉ PAN, gently cook the chopped onion in the oil over medium-low heat until it is soft and golden. Add the diced meat to the pan and continue cooking, browning the meat on all sides. Add the red wine and tomato concentrate and simmer for about 2 minutes, stirring to mix the tomato into the wine. Add the beans, using a slotted spoon. (Do not discard the bean cooking liquid.) Bring to a simmer. Simmer for 10 minutes, adding about ¼ cup of the bean cooking liquid, or more if necessary, to give the beans a nice, thick sauce. Once the beans are well sauced, discard the rest of the bean cooking liquid, along with the bay leaves, the chili, and the remaining twigs of the thyme.

RETURN THE BEAN MIXTURE to the oven dish and keep warm in the oven until you are ready to serve.

# Leeks or Onions Braised in Wine

The cooking process is similar, whether you use leeks or onions. The method is called *á l'étuvée* in French, *in umido* in Italian. In both cases, it usually means long, slow stewing in a winey sauce that gradually reduces and concentrates with the other flavors of the dish, especially with the inherent sweetness of these vegetables, to make a rich, well-focused blend. When properly made, the preparation should have just a few tablespoons of reduced sauce at the end.

**Makes 4 to 6 servings**

12 small leeks (about ¾ inch in diameter); or 12 small to medium yellow onions

2 to 3 tablespoons extra-virgin olive oil

Sea salt and freshly ground black pepper

3 or 4 sprigs fresh thyme or ¼ teaspoon dried

2 bay leaves

3 or 4 sprigs flat-leaf parsley, plus 2 tablespoons finely minced, for garnish

½ cup white wine (preferred for the leeks) or red wine (preferred for the onions)

About ¼ cup beef or chicken stock

TRIM THE LEEKS, leaving about ¾ inch of green tops attached; or peel the onions but leave them whole.

TURN THE OVEN on to 300°F.

HEAT THE OIL in a heavy saucepan or oven dish large enough to accommodate all the vegetables in one layer over medium heat. When the oil is hot, add the leeks or onions and lightly brown them on all sides, turning frequently. When the vegetables are golden brown, add salt and pepper to taste, along with the thyme, bay leaves, and sprigs of parsley. Pour in the wine. Add just enough stock to come about halfway up the vegetables. Bring to a simmer on top of the stove.

WHEN THE LIQUID IS SIMMERING, cover the dish with a lid or aluminum foil and bake until very tender—the leeks should be done in 20 to 30 minutes; the onions will take longer, up to an hour. Keep testing the vegetables with the sharp point of a knife. If the vegetables are tender before the sauce has reduced to a syrupy liquid, transfer the pan from the oven to the top of the stove and boil down rapidly until the sauce is the right consistency.

SERVE THE VEGETABLES, preferably in the dish in which they were cooked, with the minced parsley sprinkled over the top.

# Christmas Dried Fruits in a Spiced Red Wine

### ZURRACAPOTE

 You can make this spicy Spanish dessert with just one or two fruits, say prunes and apricots, if you wish, or try as many dried fruits as you can find, including the above two, plus figs, raisins, and dried peaches. A health-food store with a quick turnover is a great place to find an assortment of dried fruits. Adding roasted nuts at the end is a nice seasonal touch and makes a pleasant contrast with the soft sweet fruits.

COMBINE WINE, sugar, cinnamon, lemon zest, and peppercorns in a saucepan. Bring to a simmer over low heat. Simmer about 15 minutes to concentrate flavors and thicken the sauce. Add the dried fruits, stirring so that each piece of fruit is well-coated with wine sauce, and simmer for 15 minutes longer. When the fruits are tender but not falling apart, remove from the heat and cool. If the sauce seems too thin, strain the fruits out with a slotted spoon, discarding cinnamon, lemon zest, and peppercorns. Return sauce to the stove, on medium heat, and simmer until it has reached the desired thickness.

TURN THE OVEN ON to 350°F. and spread the nuts on a baking sheet. Toast for about 15 minutes, or until the nuts are golden. Almonds will be ready to use at this point, though you can chop them coarsely if you wish. Hazelnuts, however, should be turned into a dish towel and rubbed briskly to get rid of as many of the skins as you can, before chopping them.

STIR THE FRESHLY ROASTED nuts into the fruits, add the thickened sauce, and serve immediately, or let cool to room temperature.

VARIATION: Similar dishes in Turkey are often served with a dollop of sweetened yogurt. Strain the yogurt for a couple of hours to thicken it, then beat in sugar to taste with a wire whisk. If you wish, beat in a few drops of rose water or vanilla extract at the same time.

**Makes 6 servings**

1 bottle medium-bodied dry red wine, such as a Spanish Rioja

1 cup sugar

2 (2-inch) cinnamon sticks

Zest of 1 lemon

1 teaspoon whole black peppercorns

1½ pounds dried fruit (see headnote for suggestions)

½ cup blanched almonds or hazelnuts

# The Oldest Legumes

## CHICKPEAS, LENTILS, AND FAVA BEANS

O N A COOL AUTUMN MORNING in the foothills of the Moroccan Atlas, when the valley mists mingle with blue threads of woodsmoke rising from thousands of cooking fires, the narrow, stone-paved alleys in the medieval medina of Fez teem with traffic, most of it pedestrian. The crowded old streets of Fez, which lies in a cleft in the rolling hills, seem scarcely to have changed since souks were established here late in the first millennium of our era. Donkeys, the preferred means of transportation, are given precedence, and people press flat against dusty walls to let the crabby little beasts pass by. But human backs are used more often, stooped beneath their burdens—sacks of wool for the dye-works and leather for the tanneries, olives for the olive mills, whole carcasses of mutton for the butchers, grain and flour for the bakers, carts of fruits and vegetables, even trays of unbaked flatbreads, each pale loaf marked with its maker's symbol, balanced on the heads of schoolchildren, bound for the ovens that were fired before dawn.

All this press of humanity needs sustenance from time to time, and the sustenance, on these cool days leading up to winter, is most often a bowl of thick, hearty soup, filled with beans and legumes such as chickpeas and lentils, possibly some shreds of preserved mutton, spiced with turmeric, cumin, hot chili-flavored harissa, and a little powdered ginger, and maybe a sprinkle of fresh green cilantro and a splash of lemon juice over the top at the moment it's dished up. This kind of belly-filling provender comes from pots that simmer over braziers on street corners where workmen gather when they can take a break, as well as from slightly more upscale establishments, nothing more than counters open to the street with stools for two or three more leisured diners and a blue-painted bench along the wall where older men can loll over their *harira*, as the soup is called (see page 234).

Minus the New World beans (variously known as haricot, kidney, or French beans), which had to wait for Columbus to sail across the Atlantic and back again, a stew like this—composed of lentils, chickpeas, dried fava beans, maybe some black-eyed peas too—is as old as Fez. Older, even, for despite its Biblical appearance, Fez is just a little over a thousand years old, an upstart town in Maghrebi terms, and this mess of pottage is at least as old as Jacob. The stew exchanged by the patriarch for Esau's birthright was a lentil-and-bread pottage, according to my Jerusalem Bible, and it's a fair bet that it wasn't all that different from the *harira* being served up in the souks of Fez this chilly autumn morning.

Lentils are among the oldest cultivated foods in the Mediterranean, at least as old as wheat and olives, and just as persistent. At Tell Abu Hureyra, an archaeological site on the Euphrates in Syria, now drowned under the waters of Lake Assad above the al-Thawra dam, wild lentils were found in a ninth millennium settlement level, with domesticated ones coming along a mere thousand years or so later. Chickpeas and fava beans were also early introductions to the Mediterranean diet, domesticated from the wild back when agriculture was a very young science indeed. Chickpeas, favas, and lentils are all, like peas (another early domesticate), members of the Vicieae or vetch (*Vicia*) branch of the great family of Leguminosae. New World beans, called by botanists *Phaseolus*, are also members of that family but branched off millennia ago to form the *Phaseolus*.

Various other members of the vetch families were also once much more significant in the Mediterranean soup bowl than they are now. *Cicerchie* (chee-CHAIR-kyeh), grown in Italy and sometimes available in North American gourmet markets, look like a cross between a chickpea and a fava, though their botanical name is *Lathyrus*. Lupines, called *lupini* by Italians, are a favorite snack food, served up in paper cones in street markets in the Italian south. But most of these old-fashioned legumes have fallen from favor and are now grown primarily for fodder or as nitrogen-fixing green manure crops.

In the ancient city of Aleppo, some 80 miles west of the Euphrates, I was drawn to a lunch counter in the beautiful old Jdeideh Quarter (the name, however, means "new" quarter) north of the Citadel. The eating place, which was known by the cook's name, Abu Abdul, served nothing but *ful*. Pronounced *fool*, it's a type of fava bean that's very popular in the Middle East. At lunchtime, hungry crowds gathered at a window counter open to the street to collect deep bowls of stewed beans swirled with sesame-cream tahina and a healthy dollop of the hot and fragrant red pepper paste for which Aleppo is famous. The menu at Abu Abdul was concise: you could have plain *ful*, *ful* with pepper paste, *ful* with tahina, or *ful* with both. Workmen ate their stew while standing outside in the street, but young lads with big tinned copper jars waited patiently, somewhat anxiously, to carry beans home for the family lunch, while I was urged to sit inside at a table with paper placemats, presumably because I was the only woman around. "And is that Abu Abdul?" I asked about the stout and rather cranky old man who was slopping ladle-fuls of beans to all comers. "It's one of them," explained my Syrian host. "But his father was Abu Abdul, too, and also his father before him. Maybe they weren't even really Abu Abdul but that's what they've always been called."

They eat *ful* in Egypt, too. Onions, lentils, and *ful* are what modern Egyptians thrive on, the same fare that gave their ancestors the energy to quarry colossal masses of stone, to move them across desert and river, to erect them into pyramids long before even the invention of the wheel. *Ful*, stewed with garlic and olive oil, cumin, caraway, and coriander (the three Cs of Egyptian cooking) is often served, like Moroccan *harira*, for breakfast, while falafel, made from crushed dried fava beans or chickpeas, shaped into a cake and deep-fried, are a national addiction at any time of the day (recipe, page 238). *Kushari*, a mixture of lentils with rice and pasta, sprinkled with a tart and fiery Tabasco-like chili sauce, another popular Egyptian street food, must have come along somewhat later, for rice was strictly a luxury product until sometime in the first millennium of our era (time is long in Egypt). Kushari is also sold from street corner stands in Old Cairo and Alexandria (recipe, page 254).

In Tunis, the *soupe du jour* in the restaurants along the alleys that climb steeply to the Zeitouna, the city's foremost mosque up at the summit of the medina, is *leblebi,* made from chickpeas stewed with sweet-smelling cumin until they're almost disintegrating, then served with a choice of garnishes—quarters of hard-cooked eggs, slices of pink pickled turnips, salted capers, flakes of canned tuna, olive oil, of course, lemon juice, and the eternal Tunisian harissa, the hot pepper sauce that is added to almost every restaurant dish from fried eggs to lamb chops.

The appeal of these legumes, alone or in combination, is ancient and strong—they are foods of the poor, foods of the teeming streets of ancient cities like Aleppo, Cairo, and Fez, but also foods of national (as opposed to ethnic or social) identity, eaten in these multicultural cities by all religions and all ethnic backgrounds, Christians, Moslems, and Jews, and by all social classes and economic groups. In *A Book of Middle Eastern Food,* Claudia Roden tells of an Egyptian aunt who made a spectacular *mujaddarah,* a combination of rice and lentils, also much loved in Egypt. "Excuse the dish of the poor," she would say as she brought the dish to table. To which the response was always: "Keep your food of kings and give us *mujaddarah* every day!"

"Chickpeas," said Richard Ford, the British traveler who wrote in exquisite detail about his journeys through Spain in the early part of the nineteenth century, "are the potatoes of the land," as essential to the Spanish diet as potatoes were to the English. They were introduced to Spain by the Carthaginians, he claimed, meaning some time around 500 B.C.E., though he doesn't tell us on what authority. Ford praised the Spanish *olla,* or *olla podrida* (the name means "spoiled" or "rotten" pot, but, Ford assures us, "the epithet is now obsolete"), a dish into which "the whole culinary genius of Spain is condensed." Ford's *olla,* like Don Quixote's, was made in an earthenware pot, or rather two pots, the chickpeas, beef or chicken, and bacon cooking in one, while the vegetables steamed in another together with salted pork cheeks and chorizo sausages, colored red with an abundance of paprika, for flavor.

The alliance of legumes and salted meat is encountered so often that it has to be a natural, god-given combination, like tomatoes and basil. In Christian cultures, the meat is always ham, bacon, or some other form of salt pork or pork sausages, while among Moslems and Jews, the salt meat will be mutton or even goose—Italian Jews call salted goose breast "Jewish prosciutto." Dried beans, cooked on their own with nothing but garlic and salt to season them, are hard to get down, even when you're really hungry. But fat meat gives an unctuous quality to beans and when it's preserved meat, it contributes salt and more complex flavors.

Meat isn't always necessary, however. Beans are called the meat of the poor for obvious reasons. As vegetarians know (and the food of the poor, in the Mediterranean as in other traditional cultures around the world, is predominantly vegetarian), olive oil can serve the same function as preserved meat, adding depth of flavor and complexity to a bean dish. Packed with protein and fiber, legumes of any kind are great low-fat additions to the diet, even for committed carnivores like myself. Moreover, dried legumes keep well on the pantry shelf. Lentils especially, since they need no soaking, are a good standby for cooks in a hurry.

Legumes are an essential part of a pattern that Sidney Mintz, a great and thoughtful anthropologist, has written about at length. Mintz calls it the core-fringe-sauce pattern in traditional diets, and it's something he has found almost everywhere in the world, from China to Africa to the Mediterranean and back again. The core is a complex carbohydrate (in the Mediterranean, that means rice, bread, pasta, potatoes); the fringe is a legume that complements the carbohydrate and adds more easily assimilated protein; the sauce is the flavor principle that makes the whole thing go down easily and with great relish. A peanut butter and jelly sandwich on whole-wheat bread is the simplest example of core-fringe-sauce, but so is Egyptian *kushari*, and many, many other of the old combinations, traditional throughout the Mediterranean, of carbohydrates and legumes (*pasta e fagioli* in Italy, *moros y cristianos*, or black beans and rice, in Spain, bulgur pilaf with chickpeas or lentils in Turkey) with a flavor-sizzling sauce of garlic, hot peppers, tomatoes, cumin, and/or dozens of other aromatic flavors to give this essentially bland combination the relish it otherwise lacks.

Lentils and chickpeas are not hard to find—rare is the supermarket that doesn't have sacks of them on its shelves. If you're lucky, you'll find several choices of lentils, both the common, dun-colored larger ones and the smaller, fine-skinned ones that most connoisseurs prefer for flavor, appearance, and ease of cooking—green ones from Le Puy in France's Massif Centrale or dark, shining brown-to-black ones from the Abruzzi region of Italy. Black-eyed peas, an African cultivar that migrated to the Mediterranean long centuries before they arrived in the Americas with the slave trade, are also widely available in North America, especially in the Southern United States. Dried fava beans may take a little more effort, but they're easy enough to locate in Italian, Greek, and Middle Eastern specialty markets. (If you find peeled dried fava beans, which are more difficult to come across, they're worth buying in quantity for the ease with which they can be turned into a robust pureed bean dish, like those served in the south of Italy—see recipe, page 246.)

All of these staple legumes are eaten dried, but fava beans are the only ones that are widely consumed as fresh beans, and eagerly awaited they are throughout the Mediterranean as harbingers of spring. Fresh favas (the name *fava* is Italian—in Spanish, they are *habas;* in French, *fèves*) were once popular in North America, their stiff, unbean-like stalks and pretty black-and-white flowers forming a backdrop in household gardens. Inexplicably they disappeared from our markets and our tables sometime in the nineteenth century, only to come back very recently as fancy restaurant fare. Colonial gardeners on this continent always sowed a plot or two of fava beans, back then called broad or Windsor beans, English names. In early American recipe collections, bean recipes, unless otherwise identified, are often intended to be made with broad beans or favas.

Broad beans may have lost out in the bean popularity contest simply because New World beans were easier to cultivate, but the recent relegation of this extremely humble bean to the status of fancy-restaurant fare is owing at least in part to the mistaken notion that not only must the beans be shelled from the pods, but each individual bean within the pod must be peeled before cooking, a tedious task suitable only for well-staffed restaurant kitchens, and moreover entirely unnecessary if the beans are harvested young—as they should be to be eaten fresh. (Dried favas, on the other hand, *must* be peeled as the skins of the mature beans are unpleasantly tough—but peeling dried beans is considerably easier than dealing with fresh ones.)

Peeling fresh beans actually takes away a good deal of their earthy flavor—you might as well eat peas, I think, as peel the favas. When buying fresh fava beans, you must absolutely reject the big fat pods of overly mature beans and insist, instead, on the smallest, most tender pods. There should be no need at all, in that case, to peel individual beans. Indeed, when the favas are young and tender, Palestinian and other Middle Eastern cooks often add the *whole* pods, cut into inch-long pieces as if they were string beans, to the pot.

Once the season for fresh beans is past—usually by the time in late May or June when the first peas start to come in—the beans are left on their stalks to swell and mature, after which they are dried, husked, and stored as a winter staple. As such, they are prolific throughout the Mediterranean but reach a kind of culinary apotheosis in Puglia, the region at the heel of Italy's boot, where peeled dried favas are simmered, sometimes with a potato for added bulk, until they disintegrate into a thick puree that is then served with steamed wild chicory greens, the bitter pungency of the greens offsetting the earthy sweetness of the bean puree. A similar combination of pureed favas and greens is traditional on the island of Crete, one of many old-fashioned country traditions shared between Puglia and the Greek islands. *'Ncapriata* the Pugliese call it. It's a dish for a feast, though not extravagant, not at all opulent, rather one that combines the traditional products of the region in a manner that is both austere and elegant—and delicious.

Beans were always regarded with some suspicion in the ancient Mediterranean world, and no beans more so than favas. Why this should be so, why a staple leguminous protein, a cheap, valuable, and efficient food, should evoke complex and ambiguous feelings, is something of a mystery.

Pythagoras, the sixth-century B.C.E. philosopher, moral authority, magus, and mathematician (yes, the very one who brought us the Pythogorean theorem and the square of the hypotenuse), out-and-out forbade his followers to eat fava beans. The prohibition is especially weird if you remember that Pythagoras preached a rigorous vegetarianism; beans, one would think, would be an essential source of protein in a vegetarian diet. In other parts of the Mediterranean, in Ancient Egypt and classical Rome, fava beans, while not taboo for the populace in general, were forbidden to the priests of certain cults. No less an authority than Aristotle posited that the prohibition came about because fava beans "have the shape of testicles, or because they resemble the gates of hell, for they alone have no hinges, or again because they spoil, or because they resemble the nature of the universe, or because of oligarchy, for they are used for drawing lots"—favas were used in the Athenian democracy to cast votes, a dried white bean being an aye, while a darker one meant a nay vote.

Many—but not all—modern investigators think the reason for the prohibition is related to an understanding of favism, an inherited nutritional disorder that affects as much as a third of Mediterranean populations, most of them in the eastern half, regions that came under strong Greek influence in classical times, including the Ionian island of Samos where Pythagoras himself was born. Favism can be a lethal allergy. How it works is complicated, but, in brief, susceptible people lack the enzyme glucose-6-phosphate dehydrogenase (G6PD) which is involved in the production of protective antioxidants. Favas are rich in oxidizing compounds (the reason fava bean flour is used, in infinitesimal amounts, in French bread-making— see below). People with favism, lacking the protective enzyme, can be poisoned by the oxidizing compounds when they eat favas (indeed, sometimes when they merely walk through a field when the plants are in bloom); the poisoning takes the form of hemolytic anemia, a severe blood disorder that begins with jaundice and blood in the urine and can lead, in some 10 percent of cases, to a quick and uneasy death.

Curiously, there's a beneficial side to this: G6PD-deficiency is also a marker for resistance to malaria, and malaria, right up until the middle of the twentieth century, was a scourge in many Mediterranean countries, responsible for thousands of deaths in that region annually. (Around the world, two million people still die of the disease each year, though no longer do many of those deaths take place in the Mediterranean.)

The suspicion about fava beans persists. James Chatto, who lived on the island of Corfu for many years, says that modern Corfiote Greeks still consider fava beans poisonous and cook them with great care, boiling them twice with fresh water and never giving them to children or old people. Very young broad beans, they told Chatto, were not so dangerous and could be cooked in their pods, a delicious way to prepare them and, as noted above, one that's typical early in the season in many Eastern Mediterranean kitchens (see recipe, page 248).

But fava beans weren't held in universal disregard, whether in the ancient world or in the modern Mediterranean. In the form of a soup called *panspermia,* made of boiled beans and grains, they were actually part of the offerings at the Pyanopsia, a late autumn festival dedicated to the two solar gods, Phoebus (Bright) Apollo and Helios, the Sun. The festival, which seems to have taken place midway between the autumn equinox and the winter solstice, was both a thanksgiving for the autumn harvest and a propitiation for the autumn sowing of grain. A kind of *panspermia* called *palikaria,* made of fava beans, chickpeas, lentils, wheat, and New World beans all mixed together, is prepared on the island of Crete to this day and traditionally served on the eve of Epiphany, January 6, to all members of the household, including animals. In olden times leftover *palikaria* was thrown up onto the house roof for the birds.

Banned by one cult, hallowed by another, fava beans seem always to have evoked an edgy, ambiguous attitude linked to death and mourning. Pliny tells us that they were used in memorial sacrifices to commemorate dead family members, a practice that continues in one form or another to this day. In the Orthodox Church, sweetened grains of wheat make up the offering, *kolyva,* to be blessed by the priest and distributed to mourners 40 days after a death. But in Turkey, legumes are added, along with nuts, dried fruits, honey, and pomegranate seeds (it was the pomegranate Persephone ate that condemned her to remain in Hades), to make a dish for Ashure, a day of deepest mourning similar to Christian

Good Friday, for Shiite Moslems who commemorate the martyrdom of the Imam Husain.

In Sicily, bean superstition lingers in the form of *cuccia*, traditionally served on the feast day of St. Lucia, December 13. In many parts of the island, *cuccia* is like *kolyva*, a sweetened porridge of wheat grains (with chocolate bits added in modern versions), but in other regions, *cuccia* is a savory stew made of many different beans and legumes, sometimes with rice or wheat grains included. The rationale behind this dish—for there's a rationale, even behind the most obscure sort of folklore— has to do with a famine in the seventeenth century, when, it is said, shiploads of grain miraculously arrived in Palermo—or perhaps Siracusa, the legend is not clear—to feed the populace. Because it happened to be the feast day of St. Lucy, from that day to this, Sicilians have honored her intervention by not eating anything made with flour on St. Lucia's day—hence, no bread and no pasta. Whole grains of wheat are acceptable, however, as are all other sorts of grains and legumes.

Or at least that's the legend. But you don't have to be a folklorist to recognize that Lucia, patron saint of light and protector of eyes, is intimately related to the winter solstice. Her name alone means light (*lux* in Latin, *luce* in Italian, *luz* in Spanish), and the fact that she martyred herself to protect her virginity by tearing out her own eyes and presenting them on a platter to a prospective lover is not just a particularly grisly example of early Christian behavior (and one much loved by Sicilians who, in chapels dedicated to the saint, hang rather alarming small silver ex-votos of eyes on a platter), but also an example of her protective role in bring- ing back the light that, at this time of the year, is fast disappearing from the heavens.

But what does all this have to do with beans? Beans are seeds, and seeds are life. Without light, seeds will not come to life; without seeds, light is merely light and not a force of regeneration. Is it far-fetched to see a connection between the Feast of Saint Lucia, patroness of light, and the Athenian Pyanopsia, dedicated to the sun deities at a time of the year when the days are growing perceptibly short?

That's not the only link to the ancient world: After the bean stew *cuccia* is dis- tributed to family, neighbors, kinfolk, and passersby, I'm told, any leftovers are tossed onto the house roof for Sicilian birds—like the *palikaria* of old Crete.

D RIED BEANS ARE AN ESSENTIAL PART of every family's store for winter. In times of privation, or just to eke out a meager harvest, favas, chickpeas, lentils, and other legumes, including ones that are now grown mostly for forage, were ground to a meal and used on their own, boiled like polenta or porridge or even mixed with wheat or barley flour to make bread. (Chestnuts and acorns were sometimes used to the same end.) It wasn't very good bread; in fact, it was downright stodgy, but at least it filled hungry bellies. Perhaps it was from this experience that French bakers learned that a very small amount of fava-bean meal, even as little as 0.6 to 0.8 percent, actually strengthens ordinary bread dough. How this happens is complex and has to do with a process of oxygenation that braces the gluten network, increasing volume even as it decreases the weight of the finished bread; when it's overused, the additive leads to the kind of puffy, airy, cotton-wool baguettes that are still all too prevalent in French bakeries despite recent efforts at reform.

Another outcome of experimentation in times of dearth was more fortunate, if more limited in distribution. The flat cake called *socca* in Nice, *farinata* in Liguria, and *cecina* in Tuscany is made from chickpeas ground to a fine meal or flour, mixed with lots of water to make a very liquid batter, then poured into an olive oil–slicked flat copper pan and set in a very hot oven—as hot as a pizza oven and similarly fired with wood (olive wood is said to be best) until the sides are glowing white. This thin chickpea tart bakes for 20 minutes or so and is then quickly carved into pie wedges and, still steaming with the oven's heat, served up to eagerly awaiting customers who consume it instantly—cold it's not so great—sometimes topped with a thin slab of salty *lardo di Colonnata*, the cured pork fat from Tuscany, that melts along its edges and perfumes the *farinata* with a fragrance of garlic and rosemary. One can only truly appreciate the filling nature of beans by consuming a tray of *farinata*—the wedges of cake, thinner than New England flannel cakes, thicker than French crêpes, go down all too easily. Moments later, one realizes that one is—absolutely, emphatically, undeniably, and irrevocably—full.

## 14 GREAT RECIPES USING BEANS

Hearty Bean Soup from a North African Souk
   *Harira*

Tunisian Fava-Chickpea-Bulgur Soup
   Yumna Mahjoub's *Burghul Djery*

Clara Maria's Spanish Beef and Lentil Soup
   *Potaje de Lentejas*

Chickpea-Fava Fritters with Tahini Sauce
  *Falafel*

Toasts with Lentil–Green Olive Spread
  *Crostini di Lenticchie con Ulive Verde*

Greek Black-Eyed Pea Salad

Chickpea-Flour Fritters
  *Pannelle/Panisses*

Chickpea-Flour "Pizza"
  *Farinata/Cecina*

Sweet Fava Bean Puree with Bitter Greens from Southern Italy
  *'Ncapriata di Fave e Cicoria*

Fresh Spring Fava Beans, the Classic Way

Spanish Chickpeas and Spinach with Chorizo Sausage
  *Garbanzos y Espinacas con Chorizo*

Catalan Chickpeas with Tomatoes and Toasted Almonds
  *Cigrons a la Catalana*

Great Andalucian Stewpot of Chickpeas, Beef, Pork, and Vegetables
  *Cocido Andaluz*

Egyptian Rice and Lentils with a Spicy Tomato Sauce
  *Kushari*

## COOK'S NOTES

To soak or not to soak? That is a major question in bean cookery, and there are many conflicting answers, all of them seemingly authoritative. I used to feel that all legumes, with the exception of lentils, had to be soaked overnight or given what the Extension Service of the U.S. Department of Agriculture calls the "quick-soak method": Put the legumes in water to cover, bring to a boil, boil for 1 or 2 minutes, then cover and let soak for an hour. In many old-fashioned cookbooks from Mediterranean countries, you will read the further advice that the beans should be soaked in water with a pinch of bicarbonate of soda (baking soda). These methods may well be necessary still with very old beans, ones that might have been kept around a shop for a couple of years, not an unlikely situation back in the days of my youth. Nowadays, for the most part, however, I find all this quite unnecessary.

I don't know whether it's because bean preservation techniques have improved or because more people are eating beans, hence the turnover is greater, but it does seem that beans cook up more quickly than they used to, and without presoaking, too. I seldom bother soaking beans anymore, with the exception of chickpeas.

The real problem is that you never know how old the beans are that you buy, since there's almost never any indication on the package of when they were harvested and dried. Nothing is more disheartening for the cook than to simmer or bake beans for hours and hours only to find them still hard and indigestible. By then, it's usually time to put dinner on the table, too late to make a change.

Fortunately, that's a rare enough occurrence that I don't usually give it a thought. It does point to another question, however, and that is: How long should the beans cook? As you'll see in the recipes that follow, I've been a bit vague about that. I've had chickpeas become tender in 40 minutes without soaking, to my astonishment, and I've cooked other beans for 90 minutes before I thought they were sufficiently soft to eat. Do be sure to allow enough time when cooking beans for the possibility that they may need longer than the recipe indicates. And when using two or more different kinds of legumes, as in the harira recipe that follows, cook the legumes separately and combine them at the end—that way you don't risk having part of them overcooked and mushy while the rest still need to cook more.

Dried beans of any kind are best purchased from a shop that has a fairly rapid turnover of stock. Health-food stores are a good choice because their customers are big bean eaters, so new products are constantly arriving; another good source for a variety of different beans are shops specializing in Greek, Turkish, or South Asian foods, whose clientele are also major consumers of legumes of all descriptions.

Beans should be cooked very slowly, in order to keep them from bursting apart and disintegrating into the cooking liquid. And they should always be covered with liquid, but only to a depth of an inch or so. If you find the beans are thirsty for more, add liquid during the cooking—but it must be boiling hot, whether broth or plain water, to keep the temperature of the beans from dropping below the boiling point.

# Hearty Bean Soup from a North African Souk

## HARIRA

In one variation or another, this is the type of soup served from market stalls in the souks of North Africa, a mixture of whatever legumes the cook has to hand with small amounts of meat and lots of aromatics. In Morocco, the aromatics tend toward the clove-cinnamon-ginger side, while in Tunisia, hot chili seasonings are more popular.

**Makes 6 to 8 servings**

1 cup dried chickpeas, soaked for several hours or overnight

1 pound lean lamb

1 large yellow onion, coarsely chopped

¼ cup extra-virgin olive oil

1 tablespoon freshly ground black pepper, or 1 teaspoon freshly ground black pepper and 1 or 2 small hot dried red chili peppers, plus more black pepper if needed

Sea salt

1 teaspoon ground ginger (optional)

1 (3-inch) cinnamon stick (optional)

Pinch of saffron threads (optional)

1 teaspoon ground cumin (optional)

1 teaspoon ground hot Spanish paprika (not smoked paprika) (optional)

2 bay leaves

DRAIN THE CHICKPEAS and transfer to a saucepan. Add enough water to cover by 1 inch. Bring to a simmer and cook until the chickpeas are tender—anywhere from 40 to 90 minutes, depending on the age of the chickpeas.

WHILE THE CHICKPEAS ARE COOKING, prepare the meat. Cut into very small pieces—so that 2 or 3 pieces will make a single mouthful. Combine the meat with the onion, oil, and the black pepper in a heavy-duty saucepan. Add salt to taste and *either* the ginger, cinnamon, and saffron, *or* the cumin and hot paprika. Stir to mix well, set over medium-low heat, and sauté gently until the meat is brown and the onions are golden, about 20 minutes.

ADD THE BAY LEAVES, parsley, celery, and carrot and continue cooking for about 5 minutes. Add the water or half water and half stock and bring to a boil. Turn the heat down, and simmer, covered, for an hour or so, until the meat is very tender.

ADD THE LENTILS and tomatoes to the meat and continue cooking, uncovered, for about 20 minutes, or until the lentils are tender.

WHEN THE CHICKPEAS ARE TENDER, remove about ½ cup and puree them. Return them to the pan in which they were cooked. (Or use a stick blender to puree the chickpeas slightly right in their pan.) Stir the chickpeas with their cooking liquid into the tomato-lentil-meat soup and mix well. Simmer, covered, very gently for about 20 minutes, or until all the legumes are tender and the soup is slightly thickened. Taste and add salt and more pepper if desired. Stir in the cilantro and remove from the stove. Serve immediately, passing harissa, if you wish.

½ cup finely chopped flat-leaf parsley

2 celery stalks, including leaves, coarsely chopped

1 medium carrot, coarsely chopped

6 cups water, or use 3 cups water and 3 cups meat or chicken stock

1 cup small brown lentils

1 (14-ounce) can whole tomatoes, coarsely chopped, with their liquid

¼ cup finely chopped cilantro

Harissa (page 280), to serve (optional)

# Tunisian Fava-Chickpea-Bulgur Soup

## YUMNA MAHJOUB'S BURGHUL DJERY

 A hearty soup for cool weather, this is remarkably easy since it's made from the basic grains and legumes that Yumna, like every Tunisian housewife, always has in her larder—and North American cooks should have in their larders, too. The seasoning, added toward the end of the cooking time, gives it character and spice appeal.

Coarse bulgur and dried peeled fava beans should be easy to find in any well-stocked Middle Eastern market. Peeled fava beans need no soaking; but if you cannot find them, use the whole dried favas available in Italian and Spanish markets. Soak them overnight (the one time when this is really necessary), then slip the skins off, a much less laborious task than it sounds.

**Makes 4 to 6 servings**

1¼ cups coarse-grain bulgur

1 cup dried chickpeas, soaked several hours or overnight

1 cup small dried peeled fava beans, rinsed

½ cup extra-virgin olive oil, plus more to garnish

Water

3 tablespoons harissa (page 280)

2 garlic cloves, chopped

2 teaspoons mild Tunisian or Spanish paprika

½ teaspoon caraway seeds

2 teaspoons coriander seeds

1 small dried hot red chili pepper

3 tablespoons tomato paste or concentrate

Sea salt

IN A BOWL, combine the bulgur and water to cover. The water will turn cloudy with wheat dust. Pour off the water, holding back the bulgur, and add more water. Rinse the bulgur, over and over, until the water runs clear.

TRANSFER THE RINSED BULGUR to a large heavy soup pot. Add the drained chickpeas, fava beans, and olive oil. Add about 5 cups of water and bring to a simmer. Cover and cook gently for about 3 to 4 hours, stirring every now and then and adding boiling water, up to 2 cups, if the mixture becomes too thick or is in danger of scorching. The fava beans should have melted into a puree by the end of cooking time.

STIR IN THE HARISSA, garlic, and paprika. In a small saucepan over medium-low heat, warm the caraway and coriander seeds with the broken chili pepper until their fragrance starts to rise—about 2 minutes. Transfer the spices and chili to a mortar or spice grinder and process to a powder. Stir this into the soup along with the tomato paste. Add salt to taste and continue cooking for another 15 minutes, to develop the flavors fully. Taste again and adjust the seasoning. Serve, garnishing each soup plate with a dribble of olive oil.

# Clara Maria's Spanish Beef and Lentil Soup

## POTAJE DE LENTEJAS

 As the unofficial ambassador of Spanish gastronomy, Clara Maria Amezua spends her time tirelessly, gracefully, and generously bringing together chefs, winemakers, cookbook writers, and others interested in the foods and wines of Iberia. When she makes this classic Castilian soup, she often uses beef, but lamb would be equally good. Vegetarians, of course, could simply leave the meat out altogether.

**COMBINE THE OIL** and onions in a heavy stockpot over medium-low heat and cook until soft but not brown, about 10 minutes. Stir in the garlic and meat and cook, stirring, for another 10 minutes or so, or until the meat has lost its red color. Add the tomatoes, thyme, and parsley. Add boiling water to cover and bring to a simmer. Cover the pot and simmer for about 45 minutes.

**ADD THE LENTILS**, along with salt and pepper. Cover the pan and bring the soup back to simmering. Cook until the lentils are tender, about 40 to 60 minutes. From time to time, give the pot a shake, instead of stirring, so that the lentils remain whole. Add more boiling water as necessary to maintain a soupy consistency.

**SERVE THE SOUP** with a garnish of scallion tops and a generous spoonful of white rice in the middle of each soup plate. Pass a cruet of extra-virgin olive oil for those who wish to add a dribble over the top of the rice.

**NOTE:** If you happen to have some homemade harissa (page 280) in your refrigerator, a spoonful added to each portion of soup is delicious.

### Makes 6 servings

¼ cup extra-virgin olive oil, plus more for serving

2 large yellow onions, halved and thinly sliced

1 garlic clove, crushed

1 pound stewing beef, cut into small pieces

4 medium red-ripe tomatoes, peeled, seeded, and chopped, or 1 (28-ounce) can whole tomatoes, drained and chopped

Pinch of dried thyme

2 tablespoons minced flat-leaf parsley

Water

2 cups lentils, preferably small green or brown ones

Sea salt and freshly ground black pepper

Sliced green scallion tops, for garnish

For serving: 2 cups hot cooked long-grain white rice

# Chickpea-Fava Fritters with Tahini Sauce

### FALAFEL

This is *the* Middle Eastern street food, wildly popular and available everywhere from Aleppo to Alexandria and back again. It has even been adopted by Israelis, who have popularized it in New York City. Hearty and filling, falafel are eaten at all hours of the day and night, on their own or in a flatbread sandwich, as a pick-me-up or a full-fledged lunch.

If you are unable to find peeled fava beans for this, use unpeeled ones. After they have soaked overnight it will be easy, if a bit tedious, to strip the outer peel off each one. Have the tahini sauce ready and be prepared to serve the falafel immediately—leftovers are not very good.

**Makes about 2 dozen balls**

1 cup dried peeled fava beans, soaked several hours or overnight

¼ cup dried chickpeas, soaked several hours or overnight

1 small onion, finely chopped

⅓ cup minced flat-leaf parsley

2 tablespoons minced cilantro

1 garlic clove, crushed

1 teaspoon baking powder

1 teaspoon sea salt, or more to taste

¾ teaspoon ground cumin

1 teaspoon ground coriander

Pinch of ground hot red pepper (optional)

Freshly ground black pepper

3 to 4 tablespoons cool water

Extra-virgin olive oil or a mixture of olive oil and vegetable oil, for deep-fat frying

Tahini Sauce (recipe follows)

DRAIN AND RINSE THE FAVAS and chickpeas and combine them, uncooked, in a food processor. Add the onion, parsley, cilantro, garlic, baking powder, salt, cumin, coriander, red pepper, and black pepper. Pulse, scraping down the sides of the bowl as you do so, until you have a coarse paste. Add a couple of tablespoons of water through the feed tube as you continue pulsing. The mixture should be quite gritty but should hold together. Add a little more water if necessary. Turn the paste into a bowl. Set aside to rest for 15 minutes or so, to make the batter easier to shape.

HEAT ABOUT 2 INCHES OF OIL in the bottom of a saucepan to 350°F. Scoop out rounded patties of the falafel mix, shape gently into round balls or flatter patties, 1½ to 2 inches in diameter, and drop into the hot oil. Fry in batches until crisp and brown, turning once to brown both sides. Drain on paper towels set on a rack. Serve immediately, piping hot, with Tahini Sauce.

# Tahini Sauce

Tahini is always served with falafel, but it also goes very well with other dishes, especially as it's served traditionally in the Levant, with fried, broiled, or roasted fish.

STIR THE GARLIC and tahini together in a bowl. Add water, 1 teaspoon at a time, stirring well, until the sauce has the consistency of heavy cream. Stir in the lemon juice to taste, then add salt to taste. Oddly enough, the more water you add, the thicker the cream will be.

**Makes about 1¼ cups**

½ teaspoon finely minced garlic
1 cup tahini
Water
Juice of 1 lemon
Sea salt

# Toasts with Lentil–Green Olive Spread

## CROSTINI DI LENTICCHIE CON ULIVE VERDE

Tiny, slate-colored lentils from the Abruzzi, the mountainous region east of Rome, have an earthy, spicy fragrance that acts as a splendid foil for richly flavored olive oil. If you can find an oil from the Abruzzi (which is not at all common), by all means use it; otherwise, use one of the lemon- or orange-spiked oils from Molise.

Small lentils like these cook up very quickly and, salted, peppered, and with a spoonful of good oil stirred in, make a nice *contorno* or accompaniment to fatty meats like duck or pork. But they're also delicious in this unusual topping for toasted bread crostini.

**Makes 6 to 8 servings**

8 ounces tiny lentils from Abruzzi

1 small whole onion, peeled

1 whole garlic clove, peeled

1 bay leaf

½ small dried hot red chili pepper

24 plump green olives, pitted and coarsely chopped

½ cup finely sliced celery

¼ cup finely sliced shallots

1 garlic clove, finely minced

¼ cup extra-virgin olive oil, plus more to serve

1½ tablespoons red wine vinegar or fresh lemon juice

Sea salt and freshly ground black pepper

6 to 8 thin slices crusty country-style bread

1 small fresh sweet red pepper, cored and sliced into very thin rings

PICK OVER THE LENTILS very carefully, discarding any tiny stones or bits of grit. Rinse quickly under running water. Combine the lentils, onion, garlic, bay leaf, and dried pepper in a pot with water to cover by 1 inch. Set over medium-high heat and bring to a boil. Turn the heat down to a simmer, cover the pot, and cook for 20 to 30 minutes, until the lentils are very tender. Drain the lentils, reserving about ¼ cup of the cooking liquid and discarding the onion, garlic, bay leaf, and chili.

REMOVE ABOUT ONE-THIRD of the lentils and mash with a fork or whirl to a puree in the bowl of a food processor. Mix the mashed lentils with the whole lentils and stir in the olives, celery, shallots, garlic, oil, and vinegar. Add salt and pepper to taste. If the resulting paste is too thick to spread, thin it with a few spoonfuls of the reserved liquid.

TOAST THE BREAD SLICES until crisp and brown under a broiler (rather than in a toaster which will leave the bread too soft in the middle) immediately before serving. Drizzle a little additional oil over each slice, then mound with the lentil-olive mixture and garnish each with a sliver of red pepper.

# Greek Black-Eyed Pea Salad

When black-eyed peas are available fresh in midsummer, Greek cooks make this salad with fresh beans. Except in the southern United States, North American cooks are not apt to find fresh ones and must make do with dried beans. But the recipe is eminently adaptable to all kinds of fresh and dried legumes. Speckled cranberry beans, for instance, are often available fresh in season, but you could make this salad as well with dried chickpeas or lentils as well as dried haricot beans. If you are using fresh beans, count on 2½ to 3 cups of shelled beans for the recipe.

The salad is usually served as a first course, but it is also good as an accompaniment to a plain roast of pork or veal, sliced very thinly and served at room temperature.

DRAIN THE SOAKED BEANS—you should have about 2½ cups. Transfer the beans to a saucepan. Add the bay leaves and cover with fresh water to a depth of 1 inch. Set over medium heat and bring to a simmer. Simmer very gently, covered, until the beans are tender, about 40 minutes, though the time will depend on the age of the beans. When the beans are done, drain well. Transfer the beans to a salad bowl, discarding the bay leaves. Add the salt to the beans.

WHILE THE BEANS ARE STILL WARM, add the onion, garlic, carrot, pepper, parsley, dill, oil, lemon juice, cumin, olives, and feta. Toss gently so as not to break up the beans too much. Set aside for about 30 minutes to meld the flavors together. Serve at room temperature.

**Makes 6 first-course servings**

1 cup dried black-eyed peas, soaked overnight

2 bay leaves

1 teaspoon sea salt

1 medium red onion, diced

2 garlic cloves, minced

1 carrot, coarsely grated or chopped

1 fresh red sweet pepper, slivered

2 tablespoons minced flat-leaf parsley

1 tablespoon minced fresh dill

4 tablespoons extra-virgin olive oil

1 tablespoon fresh lemon juice

½ teaspoon ground cumin

½ cup coarsely chopped pitted black olives

½ cup diced feta cheese

# Chickpea-Flour Fritters

## PANELLE/PANISSES

In Nice on the French Riviera and in Palermo on the north coast of Sicily, crisp, salty chickpea flour fritters called *panisses* or *panelle* are a favorite street food. Deep-fried Sicilian chickpea-flour *panelle* are such close cousins to deep-fried Niçoise chickpea-flour *panisses* that I'm persuaded they share a parentage somewhere back in time. My Sicilian informant, Anna Tasca Lanza, says they are "*porto*" food, meaning food that traveled from port to port all over the Mediterranean.

They're made in a slightly different style, however. The Niçoise *panisses* are cut into sticks, like French-fried potatoes, while Sicilian *panelle* are cut into irregular rectangles or lozenges or what-have-you. In any case, both are fried in extra-virgin olive oil and served piping hot with a sprinkling of salt. They're delicious with a glass of crisp-flavored, chilled white wine before lunch in the summertime.

**Makes 8 to 10 servings as a snack or with drinks**

4 cups cool water

2¼ cups (8 ounces) chickpea flour

Sea salt and freshly ground black pepper

2 tablespoons finely minced flat-leaf parsley, or chopped rosemary leaves

Extra-virgin olive oil, for deep-fat frying

BEFORE YOU BEGIN COOKING, have ready the containers in which to cool the chickpea porridge. A marble countertop, if you have one, is ideal. Dip your hands in running water and lightly skim them over the surface, just to dampen it. Without a marble countertop, you can use a couple of large, shallow serving platters or oven dishes, in which case they should be very lightly oiled, again, dipping your hands in a little olive oil and rubbing it over the surfaces.

WHEN YOU ARE READY TO COOK, pour the water into a saucepan and set over medium heat. Gradually, sift in the chickpea flour, a little at a time, stirring with a wire whisk to avoid lumps. By the time all the flour has been added, the water should be hot but not yet boiling. Continue stirring while adding salt and pepper to taste. Once the mixture has come to a boil, turn the heat down to low so that the porridge is just simmering in the saucepan. Simmer for about 30 minutes, stirring frequently, until the porridge is very dense and starts to pull away from the sides of the pan.

WHEN THE PORRIDGE IS VERY THICK, stir in the parsley and pour the porridge out onto the marble work surface or the dishes or platters. Use a spatula to smooth the porridge out to a consistent ⅛-inch thickness.

WHEN THE PORRIDGE IS COOL, it will be quite firm. Cut into triangles or irregular lozenges or whatever shapes suit your fancy.

HEAT 2 CUPS EXTRA-VIRGIN OLIVE OIL to frying temperature—about 360°F. Drop the panelle into the boiling oil, a few at a time, and fry in batches until crisp and lightly golden, turning once. The panelle will be done in 4 to 5 minutes. Drain on a rack covered with paper towels. Serve piping hot, sprinkled with coarse sea salt.

NOTE: If you wish, let the olive oil cool, then strain it through a fine-mesh sieve to be reused two or three more times.

VARIATION: To make panisses, pour the porridge in a slightly thicker layer, about ¼ inch thick. Cut in fingers about 2 inches long and ½ inch wide. Fry as above.

# Chickpea-Flour "Pizza"

### FARINATA/CECINA

All along the coastline, from Genova to Livorno and Pisa, the streets leading down to wharves and beaches in little port towns are lined with hole-in-the-wall shops where hungry customers line up in the early evening to wait for another chickpea-flour confection to come out of white-hot wood-fired ovens. This is *farinata* (in Liguria) or *cecina* (in Tuscany), usually consumed hot from the oven, wrapped in paper to protect the fingers, while standing around outside. The most glorious *farinata* of my life, however, was in a rustic restaurant in Chiavari on the Ligurian coast where the Osteria Luchín, right off the main square of the town, serves *farinata* with paper-thin slices of *lardo di Colonnata,* a gloriously fat and tasty confection from Tuscany, that melts and oozes over the top of the hot pie.

Like real Neapolitan pizza, *farinata* is at its best only when made in a commercial-sized wood-fired oven (*farinata* makers claim the oven temperature is an extraordinary 800°F.), but you can get a pretty good idea of it by making it at home. Chickpea flour can be found in health-food stores and in some Middle Eastern or South Asian food shops. You'll also need a heavy round pan with low sides that can go in the oven—a light aluminum pizza pan will simply warp in the high oven heat. In Liguria, a heavy, tinned copper pan is used, but you can make do with a cast-iron crepe pan, preferably one that is at least 14 inches in diameter. (You could also use two smaller pans but cooking times should be adjusted to reflect the smaller surface area.)

This must be eaten hot from the oven. It really isn't good cold.

IN A LARGE MIXING BOWL, stir the warm water into the salt to dissolve it. Once the salt is completely dissolved, add the cold water. Then, using a flour sifter, stir in the chickpea flour, a little at a time, whisking with a wire whisk so that no lumps form. When the flour is fully incorporated, set the bowl aside, covered, for 3 to 4 hours. The batter should be as liquid as whole milk—if necessary, add a little more water.

PREHEAT THE OVEN to 500°F. Skim the foam off the top of the chickpea batter and discard it. The batter will be very liquid.

USE ABOUT 1½ tablespoons of the oil to grease thoroughly a heavy 14-inch round pan with low sides. Set aside another 1½ tablespoons of oil for the second *farinata*. Whisk the remaining oil into the batter and immediately, before the oil has a chance to separate, turn half the batter into the oiled pan, tilting the pan to cover the bottom to a depth of less than ¼ inch. Slide the pan into the oven and bake for 20 to 30 minutes, until a golden crust, sprinkled with blackened blisters, has formed on the top. (If necessary, finish cooking under the broiler.) Remove, sprinkle liberally with black pepper, cut the pie into serving wedges or rectangles, and serve immediately, while it's still very hot.

CONTINUE WITH THE SECOND BATCH of dough, greasing the pan with the reserved 1½ tablespoons of oil, and whisking the batter thoroughly before pouring it into the prepared pan.

VARIATION: Sometimes a little handful of coarsely chopped rosemary leaves is stirred into the batter before it's poured into the pan.

**Makes two *farinate*,
or about 8 servings**

⅓ cup warm water
1½ teaspoons sea salt
2 to 3 cups cold water
2¼ cups (8 ounces) chickpea flour
½ cup extra-virgin olive oil
Freshly ground black pepper

# Sweet Fava Bean Puree with Bitter Greens from Southern Italy

## 'NCAPRIATA DI FAVE E CICORIA

This is a classic combination from southeastern Puglia, the region in the heel of Italy's boot. The fava bean puree can be served on its own, but is most often accompanied by steamed bitter greens. The Pugliese like to harvest wild greens, but turnip tops, broccoli rabe, collards, and other bitter greens also make a pleasant contrast to the natural sweetness of the fava bean puree.

In Puglia, 'ncapriata is served as a first course, but it also makes a splendid vegetarian main course.

Peeled dried fava beans are worth seeking out for their ease of preparation, but if you can't find the peeled ones, use unpeeled favas. Soak them for several hours or overnight, after which the peels should slip off quite easily.

'Ncapriata is traditionally served accompanied by thick slices of country-style bread, either fried in olive oil or toasted and liberally doused with olive oil. Other accompaniments include: red onions, thickly slivered and steeped in red wine vinegar; whole small green peppers deep-fried in olive oil; black olives sautéed in olive oil; a scattering of thick bread crumbs sautéed in oil until crisp and crunchy.

**Makes 6 servings as a main course, 8 to 10 servings as a first course**

½ pound dried peeled fava beans (*fave sgusciate*), or 1 pound whole (unpeeled) dried fava beans

Sea salt

½ cup extra-virgin olive oil

1 pound bitter greens (wild dandelion greens, broccoli rabe, collards, Chinese broccoli, turnip greens, or other)

SOAK THE *FAVE* for several hours or overnight. Drain and, if using unpeeled *fave*, pull the outer skin off and discard. Transfer the fave to a deep saucepan or, preferably, a terra-cotta cooking pot that is higher than it is broad—an old-fashioned bean pot is perfect for this. Add water to cover the beans and set the pot over medium-high heat (if using terra cotta, be sure to shield the bottom of the pot from direct contact with the heat). Bring to a boil, skimming off the foam as it rises with a slotted spoon.

ONCE THE FOAM HAS STOPPED RISING, add salt to taste, turn the heat down to medium-low, and simmer the beans, stirring them frequently with a long-handled wooden spoon. The beans should gradually dissolve into the cooking liquid. Keep a kettle of water simmering on the stove and, when necessary, add a little boiling water to the simmering beans to keep them from drying out or scorching. The beans should take 40 to 60 minutes to cook, and you will need to stir them constantly during the last 10 or 15 minutes. When they are completely dissolved, without any lumps, they should have the consistency of clotted cream. Away from the heat, beat in ¼ cup of the olive oil with the wooden spoon, then taste, adding salt if necessary.

WHILE THE BEANS ARE COOKING, clean the greens thoroughly in several changes of water. Set the cleaned greens in a large kettle over medium heat and boil in the water clinging to their leaves until they are thoroughly cooked and tender—time will vary from 20 to 40 minutes, depending on the type of greens used. You may have to add a very little boiling water from time to time to keep the greens from scorching.

WHEN THE BEANS AND GREENS ARE BOTH DONE, drain the greens in a colander, turn into a warm bowl, and dress the hot greens with the remaining ¼ cup of olive oil. Salt to taste and toss to mix well.

SERVE THE FAVA PUREE piled on one side of an oval serving platter, with the greens piled on the other. Guests help themselves to both and eat them together.

# Fresh Spring Fava Beans, the Classic Way

This is a Greek recipe from the island of Corfu, described by James Chatto in his memoir of life on that island, but it's very similar to the way fava beans are prepared, early in the season when they are young and tender, in many parts of the Mediterranean. Select beans with firm, moist, slender pods, in which the beans themselves are still quite small and underdeveloped.

**Makes 4 servings**

2 pounds fresh fava beans in pod

4 fresh white spring onions, coarsely chopped

½ cup extra-virgin olive oil

Sea salt and freshly ground black pepper

1 tablespoon chopped fennel leaves (optional)

1 tablespoon chopped flat-leaf parsley

Juice of 1 large lemon

SHELL THE BEANS; or, if you wish, shell half the beans and with the other half, top and tail the pods and cut them into 1-inch lengths.

COMBINE THE ONIONS and oil in a saucepan and sauté very gently over low heat until the onions are tender and melting into the oil, 20 to 30 minutes. Do not let the onions get brown. Add the beans and continue cooking very gently for another 10 minutes, or until the color of the beans changes and becomes more opaque.

ADD SALT AND PEPPER to taste and stir in the fennel, if available, and the parsley. Add a small amount of water, just enough to come to the top of the beans. Bring to a simmer and cook very gently for about 30 minutes, until nearly all the water has boiled away and there are just a few tablespoons left in the bottom of the pan. Stir in the lemon juice, bring to a simmer, remove from the heat, and serve immediately.

VARIATION: Instead of adding lemon juice, remove the beans from the heat and stir in 2 to 3 tablespoons of whole-milk yogurt, preferably made from sheep's or goat's milk.

# Spanish Chickpeas and Spinach with Chorizo Sausage

## GARBANZOS Y ESPINACAS CON CHORIZO

 Chickpeas are ubiquitous in Spanish cooking, as important as fava beans are in the cuisine of southern Italy, and an important vegetable source of protein. In Catalonia, they're often served with the garlic mayonnaise called allioli (page 64), or they may be stewed with pork ribs or sausages, or with salt cod. Another traditional way to serve them is with simply steamed spinach or chard.

Most traditional recipes call for ½ teaspoon of bicarbonate of soda added to the soaking water; this is said to tenderize the beans, but I find that the chickpeas I buy in North American supermarkets don't require this kind of treatment.

**Makes 6 servings**

1 cup dried chickpeas, soaked for a few hours or overnight

Boiling water

2 medium onions, 1 peeled but left whole, 1 coarsely chopped

3 bay leaves

Small handful of flat-leaf parsley

Sea salt

4 tablespoons extra-virgin olive oil

1 pound fresh spinach, cleaned and coarsely chopped

3 garlic cloves, coarsely chopped

1 Spanish-style chorizo, about 6 ounces, coarsely chopped

Freshly ground black pepper

THOROUGHLY DRAIN THE CHICKPEAS and combine in a saucepan with enough boiling water to cover by about 1 inch. Add the whole onion, bay leaves, and parsley and simmer, partially covered, until the chickpeas are tender, 40 to 60 minutes, depending on the age of the legumes. Keep an eye on them and add a little boiling water from time to time as necessary to keep them from scorching. Toward the end of the cooking time, remove and discard the onion, bay leaves, and as much of the parsley as you can conveniently extract. Add a pinch of salt to taste and 1 tablespoon of the oil.

WHEN THE CHICKPEAS ARE TENDER, stir in the spinach and cook briefly, just long enough to soften the spinach—4 to 5 minutes.

COMBINE THE REMAINING 3 tablespoons oil in a large deep saucepan with the chopped onion and garlic and sauté gently until they are quite soft but not brown, 20 minutes or so. Add the chorizo and sauté until the fat runs and some of the color of the paprika in the chorizo is released into the fat in the pan. Add the chickpeas and spinach, with a little of their cooking liquid, and cook, stirring, just long enough to meld all the flavors. Add pepper to taste and serve immediately.

# Catalan Chickpeas with Tomatoes and Toasted Almonds

## CIGRONS A LA CATALANA

 The following recipe is adapted from one in Catalan food-historian Jaume Fàbrega's wonderful compilation, *Traditional Catalan Cooking.* It can be served on its own, but it is very good with a pound or so of spinach or chard, steamed separately and chopped, then stirred into the chickpeas when they're done to make a thick soup.

**Makes 6 to 8 servings**

1½ cups dried chickpeas, soaked for a few hours or overnight

Boiling water

1 onion

3 small, very ripe tomatoes

¼ cup extra-virgin olive oil

Big pinch of saffron threads

3 garlic cloves, peeled but left whole

⅓ cup toasted chopped almonds

About ½ cup chopped flat-leaf parsley

Sea salt

2 hard-cooked eggs, for garnish (optional)

THOROUGHLY DRAIN THE CHICKPEAS and combine in a saucepan with enough boiling water to cover by about 1 inch. Simmer the chickpeas, partially covered, until they are tender, 40 to 60 minutes, depending on the age of the legumes. Keep an eye on them and add a little boiling water from time to time as necessary to keep them from scorching.

WHILE THE CHICKPEAS ARE COOKING, grate or finely chop the onion and peel and grate or finely chop the tomatoes. In a frying pan, lightly sauté the onion in the oil over medium-low heat for 20 minutes, adding the tomatoes when the onion is very soft (this is called a *sofregit*). Stir the tomatoes from time to time. They will stew rather than fry as they give off their liquid, but eventually all the liquid will be given up, and the tomatoes will sizzle in the fat in the pan. At this point, the *sofregit* is done. Add the *sofregit* to the cooked chickpeas and leave to simmer another 5 to 10 minutes to develop the flavors.

TOAST THE SAFFRON by folding it into a piece of clean white typing paper and setting it in a pan over medium-low heat. Keep turning the folded paper, using tongs, until it starts to turn brown. Remove immediately and unwrap the saffron, which will have darkened slightly and become crisp.

COMBINE THE SAFFRON, garlic, almonds, parsley, and a pinch of salt and either pound together in a mortar or process in a food processor to a coarse paste. Thin with a little of the cooking liquid from the chickpeas, then stir the paste into the chickpeas. Taste and adjust the seasoning.

CHOP THE HARD-COOKED EGGS and sprinkle them over the top when you serve, if you wish.

## COCIDO OR OLLA PODRIDA

*Olla podrida*, or "rotten pot," has always been the great standing dish of the Iberian peninsula. It goes by many other names as well (*escudella*, *puchero*), but it is generally known today as *cocido*, which simply means "cooked." Its roots go back at least into Islamic times and, as *adafina*, it was the Jewish Sabbath dish, prepared on Friday to be consumed on Saturday when it was forbidden to work or to light a fire. We know this because of the quantity of Inquisition records that reveal, in obsessive but fascinating detail, how *conversos*, Jews who had been forcibly converted to Christianity, persisted in their dietary customs. One Inquisition memorandum, calling the stew *ani*, said that the word "means hot food, [and] was usually made with fat meat, chickpeas, faba beans, green beans, hard-boiled eggs, and any other vegetable. . . . And that dish was kept hot on its warming oven until mealtime on Saturday. And thus this *ani* was a principal way of keeping the Sabbath."

Richard Ford ate *olla podrida* too, when he traveled through Spain in the eighteenth century. Ford's *olla*, like the one Don Quixote lusted for, was made in an earthenware pot, or rather two pots, the chickpeas, bacon, and beef or chicken cooking in one, with the vegetables steaming in another, along with chorizo sausages, colored red with an abundance of paprika, and salted pork cheeks for flavor. One cleric Ford met added apples from Ronda and sweet potatoes to the dish and made it on feast days with turkeys instead of chickens. Ford called it a dish into which "the whole culinary genius of Spain is condensed."

# Great Andalucian Stewpot of Chickpeas, Beef, Pork, and Vegetables

## COCIDO ANDALUZ

 Cook the vegetables (except for the potatoes) apart from the meats in order to avoid over-cooking them and making an undistinguished mush.

See page 415 for sources for serrano ham and chorizo.

**Makes 8 to 10 servings**

1 medium onion, coarsely chopped

3 tablespoons extra-virgin olive oil

3 thick slices bacon or pancetta, diced (see Note below)

8 ounces chickpeas, soaked for several hours or overnight

8 ounces stewing beef or veal, cut into bite-sized pieces

1 ham bone (optional) (see Note below)

Water

8 ounces yellow-fleshed potatoes, such as Yukon gold, cubed

3 ounces (3 to 4 slices) serrano ham, diced

3 ounces chorizo, diced, about ⅓ cup

IN A DEEP HEAVY STOCKPOT, combine the onion, 1 tablespoon of the olive oil, and the pancetta or blanched bacon. Set over medium-low heat and cook, stirring occasionally, until the onions are soft and the bacon is giving up some of its fat, 20 to 30 minutes. Do not let the onions brown.

DRAIN THE CHICKPEAS and add them to the stockpot with the beef. Stir to mix, then bury the ham bone in the middle of the pot and add water to cover, about 8 cups. Set over medium-low heat and bring slowly to a simmer. Cover and simmer very gently until the chickpeas are very tender, about 1 to 1½ hours. Add the potatoes and continue cooking another 30 minutes. Remove from the heat and set aside.

IN A SEPARATE SAUCEPAN, gently sauté the ham and chorizo in the remaining 2 tablespoons olive oil for about 5 minutes. Then add the green beans, if you are using them, and the chard and cook just until tender, about 20 minutes. Add a little water if necessary to keep the vegetables from scorching. Add the pumpkin and the zucchini, if you are using it, and cook until tender, another 15 minutes.

WHILE THE VEGETABLES ARE COOKING, crush the garlic in a mortar with the salt. Stir in the red pepper, cumin, black pepper, and tomato paste. Stir this mixture into the chickpea and meat stew and, if necessary, bring it back to a simmer. Then add all the other vegetables, with all their juices, and mix carefully, using a wooden spoon so you don't break up the vegetables. Just before serving, add the parsley.

SERVE IMMEDIATELY. Or set the dish aside in a cool place and serve, warmed in the oven, the following day when the flavors will have melded beautifully.

NOTE: If you can only get smoked bacon and a smoked ham bone or ham hock, they must be blanched first to rid them of an excessively smoky flavor (unsmoked pancetta won't need this treatment). Bring a pan of water sufficient to cover the ham bone to a rolling boil, add the bacon and ham bone and simmer, covered, for 20 minutes. Drain well.

8 ounces green beans, if available, cut in 1½ inch lengths, or 2 to 3 medium zucchini, cubed

8 ounces green chard, slivered

1 pound pumpkin or hard winter squash, cubed

2 garlic cloves, chopped

1 teaspoon sea salt, or more to taste

1 dried Spanish red pepper (ñora), chopped, or 1 tablespoon crushed red pepper flakes or pimentón

Pinch of ground cumin

Pinch of freshly ground black pepper

1 tablespoon tomato paste or concentrate

¼ cup finely minced flat-leaf parsley

# Egyptian Rice and Lentils with a Spicy Tomato Sauce

## KUSHARI

 Made from lentils, pasta, and rice, *kushari* is Egyptian street food par excellence. At lunchtime, wherever you go in the country, from peaceful canalside villages to the bustling main squares of great cities like Cairo and Alexandria, you'll see stalls of vendors scooping out big bowls of *kushari* for hungry workers. Apart from the pasta, it's probably not too different from what the pyramid workers ate. *Kushari* is one of those basic bean-carbohydrate combinations that are the foundation of most culinary cultures, rather stodgy in essence but considerably enlivened by the spicy, tart tomato sauce. In summer, make the sauce from fresh, ripe tomatoes, peeled, seeded, and chopped, and let it cook a little longer to make a puree.

### Makes 4 to 6 servings

1 cup small brown lentils

5 cups light chicken stock

¼ cup extra-virgin olive oil

¾ cup vermicelli or spaghettini or other long, thin pasta, broken into short pieces, no more than 1½ inches long

2 large onions, halved and very thinly sliced

1 cup medium- or long-grain rice

RINSE THE LENTILS carefully under running water. Bring the chicken stock to a rolling boil and add the lentils. Lower the heat and cook until the lentils are soft enough to serve, 20 to 40 minutes, depending on the age and size of the lentils.

WHILE THE LENTILS ARE COOKING, heat the oil in a medium sauté pan over medium heat. Add the broken pasta when the oil is hot and cook, stirring constantly, until the pasta pieces turn golden brown. Be careful not to let them burn. Remove with a slotted spoon and set aside.

ADD THE ONION SLICES to the oil in the pan, lower heat to medium-low, and cook slowly, stirring occasionally, until they are brown. This will take quite a long time, as much as 30 minutes, because the onions must not burn. As they reach the end of their cooking time, they must be watched very carefully and stirred frequently. When they are done, remove with a slotted spoon and transfer to paper towels to drain.

WHEN THE LENTILS ARE DONE, remove them with a slotted spoon and set aside. Add the rice to the stock and boil for about 10 minutes, or until the rice grains have started to soften. Stir in the browned broken pasta and let cook an additional 5 to 7 minutes, or until the rice and the pasta are done. There should be very little liquid left in the pan. Combine the pasta and rice with the lentils, straining away any excess liquid, and set aside.

POUND THE GARLIC in a mortar with the salt. (If you don't have a mortar and pestle, chop the garlic very fine and crush the salt into the garlic with the back of a spoon in a small bowl.) Add enough oil to the pan in which the onions fried to make about 2 tablespoons and heat until very hot. Stir in the crushed garlic paste and cook, stirring, just until the garlic starts to turn golden. (It must not brown.) Immediately add the tomatoes and chili pepper(s) and cook over medium heat, stirring occasionally, until the tomatoes have reduced to a thick sauce. Stir in the vinegar, black pepper, and cumin and continue to cook. When the tomato sauce is thick, remove from the heat and stir in the parsley. Taste and adjust the seasoning.

EGYPTIANS EAT THEIR *KUSHARI* at room temperature or a little warmer, but the tomato sauce should be hot. Serve the lentil-rice mixture in deep plates, topped with a generous dollop of tomato sauce and a healthy sprinkling of browned onions.

6 to 7 garlic cloves, coarsely chopped

1 tablespoon sea salt

2 cups unseasoned tomato sauce or pureed tomatoes

1 or 2 dried hot red chili peppers, crushed

¼ cup red wine vinegar

Freshly ground black pepper

½ teaspoon ground cumin

¼ cup finely minced flat-leaf parsley

# Peppers and Tomatoes

## FROM THE NEW WORLD

WHEN CHRISTOPHER COLUMBUS set sail from the port of Palos off the southwest coast of Spain in early August of the year 1492, few people in that recently reunited country, or elsewhere in Europe for that matter, expected his voyage to amount to anything of great interest. Possibly, if he could find a route to the spice markets of the East, it would give Spain an edge up in that still important trade; possibly a few valuable islands would be discovered in the Ocean Sea of the Atlantic to go along with the Azores and the Canaries, already under the domination of Portugal, on the one hand, and Spain on the other. D. W. Meinig, a historian and geographer who has studied the events leading to the European discovery of the Americas, suggests that the very reason Columbus was awarded so many potential benefits by the Crown of Castile, which sponsored his trip, is because no one, including Ferdinand and Isabella, expected him to find very much at all.

And yet he did. And those who came after him found even more: New worlds to conquer, rich empires of unimaginable—and to the conquerors, quite savage—splendor, the treasures of Montezuma and Atahuallpa, El Dorados of gold, silver, and precious stones in quantities beyond the wildest dreams of Europeans, tropical paradises where sun-ripened fruits seemed to tumble effortlessly into the hands of the natives, and, along with all that, a half dozen simple, humble foods—tomatoes, capsicum peppers, maize corn, potatoes, chocolate, and New World beans—that would change the way the world eats, indeed, the way the world is run.

Not all of these were found by Columbus, and not all of them were found right away. But one of the first products from the New World, brought back by Columbus on that initial voyage, was the piquant, even bitingly hot, red fruits of a plant the natives called *ají*. In the belief, which he carried to his grave, that he had actually found his way to the spice islands of the East Indies, Columbus himself called the fruits "peppers," in Spanish *pimientos* (naming them, to the eternal confusion of students of Spanish, as if they were only a masculine version of the true Indian black pepper—which is feminine, *pimienta* in Spanish). Already in 1493, when Columbus had just returned to offer his first reports to the King and Queen in Barcelona, Peter Martyr, an Italian scholastic in that city, was writing of "the pepper gathered in the islands . . . but it is not pepper, though it has the same strength and the flavor, and it is just as much esteemed. The natives call it axi, . . . When it is used there is no need of Caucasian [*sic*] pepper."

How quickly were capsicum peppers actually adopted in Mediterranean kitchens and gardens? We don't have an exact date, but it seems fair to say that, as with most new products, peppers—and tomatoes, which arrived a little later, after the conquest of Mexico by Cortés in 1521—were cultivated by gardeners as horticultural curiosities for some years before they became adopted as material for the cooking pot by more circumspect and conservative cooks. And since the kind of gardeners who had enough time on their hands to pursue such horticultural curiosities were working either for aristocrats (under royal patronage, botanical gardens were planted in Seville and in Aranjuez, south of Madrid) or for religious orders, and sometimes for both, it's not surprising that monasteries quickly enter the story.

And it's a curious story the Spanish tell, of how Columbus himself brought back the first peppers—actual pepper specimens, not just seeds—and sent them, according to the legend, to the gardeners at a number of Hieronymite monasteries. One was at Ñora in Murcia, which specialized in the long, pointed peppers called *ñoras* with a rich flavor and gentle spice, that are still widely used in Spain, especially as dried peppers, in paellas and many stews and soups. Another group of pepper-cultivating Hieronymites was at Yuste in the westernmost province of Estremadura, along the Portuguese border. Here, in the nearby towns of Jarandilla de la Vera and Jaraíz, red peppers are cultivated to this day and dried over oakwood fires after which they are ground into a fine, brick-colored, silky, smoky paprika (*pimentón de la Vera*), which is the pride of the region.

Why the Hieronymites? Because they were celebrated throughout Spain for their agricultural know-how. But the Yuste monastery was also renowned for the quality of its table—so much so that Emperor Charles V, the gourmet grandson of Ferdinand and Isabella, retired there in 1556, after virtually bankrupting Spain throughout his long reign, despite the American gold and silver that poured through the Casa de Contratación in Seville. The emperor spent his few remaining years at Yuste living up to his reputation as a *comilón*, or big eater. In this parched heartland of Estremadura, far, far from the sea, he dined, it is said, on fresh oysters—and this at a time when the highways of Spain were in ruinous state and barely passable.

It is also said, although there is no real evidence for it, that the retired emperor had the added pleasure of freshly minced red chili peppers and even smoked La Vera *pimentón*, or paprika, with which to spice his oyster sauce. (One La Vera producer assured me, however, that the tradition of smoking peppers to dry them for storage began only in the nineteenth century.) Then, the story goes, Charles in his retirement passed on the secret spice to his sister, who, as it happened, was Queen Marie of Hungary, and the rest, as they say—well, it isn't chicken paprikash, but it isn't really history, either.

APOCRYPHA TO THE CONTRARY notwithstanding, it does seem certain that Capsicum peppers spread with considerable speed not just around the Mediterranean but around the world—already by the late 1500s, they were in China, possibly by way of the Portuguese in Macao. Peppers, in fact, were adopted far more readily and rapidly than were tomatoes, which, in some parts of the Mediterranean, didn't find a place in local cuisines until quite late in the nineteenth century. Even later in some places—in *Voices of the Old Sea*, Norman Lewis's fine documentary portrait of life in a Catalan fishing village in the 1940s, the village nobleman Don Alberto attributes the decadence of modern life at least in part to "the widespread consumption of tomatoes—recently introduced into local agriculture—which reduced fertility and lowered the birthrate."

Why did peppers spread so rapidly and tomatoes so slowly? The answer seems clear: Black pepper was already prized in Mediterranean kitchens, as it had been for centuries, valued for a host of reasons from its presumed medicinal worth to the prestige it conveyed on the table to the not inconsiderable fact that it made bland food taste better. Red peppers, especially hot chili peppers, gave the same kick for a lot less money. A handful of seeds, scattered in the garden and raised under the right conditions of hot sun and enough water, produced in a matter of months a condiment that had the same effect as the precious black pepper brought back from the Malabar coast of India at such great cost. A democratic spice, say the Italians, always alert to the politics of food, a spice of the people. Moreover, as Mexican cooks had shown the conquistadores and as the cooks at Yuste found out, peppers could be dried in the sun or, as at Yuste, over smoky oak fires, and kept throughout the winter. It stands to reason that they would be adopted readily.

Tomatoes, on the other hand, were sour, much more so, apparently, than the tomatoes we know today. Over the centuries, the fruits have been bred for sweetness as well as for market stability so that the familiar flavor of modern tomatoes is very different from what was ordinarily available in earlier centuries. We know they were sour because eighteenth century cookbooks, when they mention tomatoes, often suggest substituting lemon juice, or bitter orange juice, or sour verjuice, made by pressing unripe grapes, in their place: "If you don't have tomatoes, add some unripe grapes," they say.

Mediterranean cooks had plenty of sour ingredients right at hand, from vinegar and verjuice to bitter oranges and lemons, and they cost very little, hence there was no need to substitute. And tomatoes were disdained by most early writers: John Gerarde, in his *Herball* published in England in 1636, claimed tomatoes were "of a rank and stinking savour," and Castore Durante, in the *Herbario Nuovo* (Rome, 1585) said they "give little and bad nourishment." Not only were they unappealing, they were regarded with outright suspicion, like potatoes (also members of the Solanaceae family, along with suspect eggplant and downright dangerous nightshade).

New World beans, on the other hand, were quickly accepted, so quickly indeed that it's hard to set a date for their adoption with any accuracy. Beans, after all, were familiar fare, and the kinds of beans the explorers were bringing back from the New World, with a notable lack of fanfare, could be cooked in exactly the same manner as the fava beans, chickpeas, and lentils known all over the Mediterranean, that is, in an earthenware pot with onions, garlic, a few pot herbs, and a little piece of salted meat. Potatoes, on the other hand, were not only alien to the Mediterranean kitchen—they looked downright scary, unlike any other vegetable known to humankind, which is to say, to Europeans. No wonder they quickly gained a reputation for causing leprosy and various other unappetizing conditions. And tomatoes fell into the same category—weird foods, unlike anything previously known, not something for civilized tables.

What is astonishing, in the face of it, is that all four of these vegetables were eventually adopted, and not only adopted but, along with corn in more restricted regions of the Mediterranean, became staples, so much so that it is almost impossible for us today to imagine the Mediterranean kitchen without peppers, whether hot or sweet, without tomatoes, without potatoes, and without beans. But especially without tomatoes and peppers.

I T   H A S   B E E N   S U G G E S T E D   that peppers arrived in Turkey by way of Portuguese colonies in East Asia, as the result of an encounter in battle or trade. This strains credibility and belies what we know of the Mediterranean in the sixteenth century. Despite ongoing conflicts between Islam and Christianity, between the growing power of Ottoman Turkey, on the one hand, and the West as represented by Spain and the Church of Rome, on the other, trade continued to flourish, scarcely diminished in its vitality except from moment to moment and from place to place. By the time Charles V began his long reign, in 1516, the Spanish ruled most of the western Mediterranean including Castile, Aragon, Navarre, Sardinia, Sicily, the kingdom of Naples, the Roussillon in southern France, and the Spanish colonies in North Africa, not to mention those in the New World. It stands to reason that peppers—and tomatoes—would spread throughout these Spanish domains, and, in fact, Gonzalo Fernandez de Oviedo, the Spanish chronicler of New World discoveries, mentions in the early sixteenth century that peppers had already been taken to Spain, Italy, and other places. Through trade, they arrived in Turkey, whence they spread, as they became fashionable with Turkish cooks and gardeners, into the lands of the Ottoman Empire, which by then stretched from Egypt and Palestine around the eastern Mediterranean, across the Balkans to the eastern shores of the Adriatic and up the Danube to Hungary—a more plausible way for paprika to have arrived in that country than via a recipe exchange among European royal siblings.

We know that peppers reached Germany, whether along this Turkish route or via the Spanish Netherlands, sometime before 1542, because in that year the great Bavarian botanist Leonhard Fuchs published a description of capsicum peppers, complete with illustrations. By 1611, peppers had become common in Germany as well as in Spain, according to Dutch botanist Charles de l'Escluse (also known as Clusius): "This capsicum, or Indian pepper, is painstakingly grown in Castilia [Spain] both by gardeners and by housewives. . . . I remember having seen, in 1585, vast plantations of it in the suburbs of Brunn, this famous town of Moravia; pepper means a considerable income for the gardeners, because *it is commonly used by most people*." [My italics.]

TOMATOES SEEM TO HAVE FOLLOWED a similar course—at least as botanical specimens, if not in the kitchen. In 1554, just 30 years after the conquest of Mexico, the terminus a quo for the discovery of tomatoes, a Dutch scientist, Rembert Dodoens, published his *Cruydt-Boeck* in Antwerp with an entire chapter devoted to the fruit. (Illustrations, however, had to wait for later editions; the *Cruydt-Boeck* in the New York Academy of Medicine Library, dated 1644, has a handsome engraving of a tomato plant, with deeply ridged or lobed fruits similar to the variety modern growers call costoluto.) As culinary specimens, however, tomatoes were deeply resisted, even though the Spanish colonists and conquistadors alike knew exactly how they were used in Mexico. One report, based on documents dated to the 1570s, describes a Mexican recipe that sounds for all the world like modern salsa: "One prepares a delicious dip sauce [*intinctus*] from minced tomatoes, mixed with chili, which complements the flavor of almost all dishes and foods, and wakens a dull appetite."

At Aztec banquets, the Spanish chroniclers wrote, casseroles were flavored with red chilies, tomatoes, and ground squash seeds, and *chilmollis* (moles) of different kinds of peppers (yellow, dwarf, etc.) mixed with tomatoes, were sold as hot dishes in the market. But though the Spanish knew how to prepare them, nonetheless they resisted: "It is said that [tomatoes] are good for sauces," ventured Gregorio de los Rios, a priest who catalogued specimens in the royal gardens of Aranjuez, and by his cautious, circumspect tone it's abundantly clear that you wouldn't catch Padre Gregorio with that kind of a sauce on *his* plate.

The three Spanish cookbooks that we know from the late sixteenth and early seventeenth centuries ignore both peppers and tomatoes, whether because the writers were not familiar with them or because they considered them somehow inappropriate is not clear. But sometime before 1607, Caravaggio painted a still life, now hanging in the Galleria Borghese in Rome, that included in its composition two chili peppers and a tomato, as if they were ingredients for a dish of some sort—which suggests that they were beginning to be used, if somewhat timidly.

The first real recipes, however, were not published until 1692, in Antonio Latini's cooking manual, *Lo scalco alla moderno,* or "the modern steward." Significantly, the book was published in Naples, a city that had been under Spanish rule for several centuries. Latini himself was chef and steward to the Spanish governor of the town. The few recipes that call for chili peppers, tomatoes, or both are always labeled "in the Spanish style" or "*alla spagnuola.*" Modern cooks will immediately recognize Latini's recipe for tomato sauce as a Mexican-style salsa:

### Tomato Sauce, Spanish Style

Take half a dozen tomatoes that are ripe, and put them to roast in the embers, and when they are scorched, remove the skin diligently, and mince them finely with a knife. Add onions, minced finely, to discretion; hot chili peppers, also minced finely; and thyme in a small amount. After mixing everything together, adjust it with a little salt, oil, and vinegar. It is a very tasty sauce, both for boiled dishes or anything else.

GAZPACHO FROM SOUTHERN SPAIN, Neapolitan pizza alla marinara, pasta al pomodoro, North African *chermoula* and harissa, Greek salad and salade niçoise, Catalan romesco sauce and Provençale rouille, caponata, ratatouille, and Tunisian *mechouia,* not to mention all the soups, stews, sauces, ragouts, salads, and even sorbets that require tomatoes, peppers, or both—these New World curiosities have come a very long way, metamorphosed entirely from "rank and stinking savours" to ingredients as highly valued as any precious spice.

Tomatoes, more than peppers, not only supply local markets but are an important export crop in many parts of the Mediterranean, produced in industrial quantities in Israel, Greece, and Turkey, in Sicily, and on the Sorrento peninsula south of Naples, and in Murcia and Almería in southern Spain. Great carloads of these are shipped fresh, but even more are processed into tomato sauce, paste, or concentrate, or as canned whole tomatoes to feed a voracious world market. (The world's leading exporters of fresh tomatoes, however, are the Dutch. Despite their damp and chilly climate, their gray skies, their North Sea outlook, they achieve in energy-intensive heated greenhouses one of the highest yields of tomatoes in the world—four times, for instance, what growers get in hot, sunny southern Spain.)

Spain, however, with a vast acreage of greenhouse production—40,000 hectares (nearly 100,000 acres) in the province of Almería alone—outstrips all the rest of the Mediterranean for industrial production. The plastic greenhouses are laid out in close succession, one after the other across a barren, arid plain that looks like nothing so much as an outcrop of the Sahara, stretching away to the horizon. Coming over the rim of the Alpujarras Mountains and starting down toward the coast, it's a vast inland sea of white plastic glistening in the fierce sun (at first you might mistake it for the sea itself)—miles and miles of plastic, most of it devoted to tomato cultivation, a little bit to peppers. Unfortunately, much of this production comes with a staggeringly high cost in terms of the region's limited underground or fossil water resources (water use is currently at four to five times the annual rainfall) and an indiscriminate distribution of chemical nutrients and biocides—as of this writing, the soil is still fumigated with methyl bromide, although use of the toxic chemical was scheduled to become illegal in 2002.

For a hothouse tomato, those Spanish tomatoes aren't all that bad—if you don't mind the pesticide applications and the environmental consequences. But set them against natural, garden-grown tomatoes, and you begin to understand what real tomato flavor is all about. Try the almost achingly sweet, small, dry, flavor-dense *"anydra"* from the Greek island of Santorini (the name means waterless because the island is just that); or the little cluster tomatoes, about the size of golf balls, grown on Puglia's Salento peninsula, harvested in late autumn and the whole plant hung upside down through the winter while the tomatoes wrinkle slightly and the sugars concentrate; or early Montserrats in Catalonia, big, pale green to pale orange fruits with thick walls of flesh and sweet, meaty flavor—that's real tomato flavor, endlessly varied and yet basically true to type.

Sweetness is only part of the tomato's appeal, although it's a strong part, but sweetness at its best must be balanced by acidity. At certain times in the season, tomatoes from southern Italy or Andalucia can have so much acid in them that you don't need vinegar, just a little olive oil to dress them. On the other hand, if acid tips the balance in a tomato, a good cook often adds a pinch of sugar, especially to cooked sauces, to restore the symmetry. Salt, in the soil or in the irrigation water, has a good effect on tomato sweetness, too, which may be why the best tomatoes always come from gardens near the sea. Sweetness and acidity—it's a flavor combination that appeals tremendously to the Mediterranean palate, and one that goes way back in Mediterranean history, as the few cookery notes and recipes from ancient times tell us. Which only makes it all the stranger that tomatoes took so long to arrive on Mediterranean tables.

For almost as long as they've been using tomatoes, Mediterranean cooks have also been putting them up for the winter store cupboard, initially by cutting them open and setting them on racks to dry, just like figs, in the strong autumnal sun. They could also be reduced to a concentrated paste, as is still done in much of southern Italy. At Regaleali, her family estate in Sicily, Anna Tasca Lanza makes *estratto* or *concentrato* over several days, first preparing a simple tomato puree, cooking it as little as possible in order to preserve the fresh flavors of the tomatoes themselves. The puree is spread on platters or clean boards and set outside in bright sunlight. At night, when it's brought inside, the dried bits of puree around the edges are scraped up and mixed with the rest. After a few days, the sauce starts to thicken and concentrate. Finally, when it's a thick paste, it's transferred to jars and covered with a thin layer of extra-virgin olive oil.

Home-canning of tomatoes (or bottling, which is in fact what it is) spread in Italy after World War II. With an abundance of plum tomatoes from late-summer gardens, my Tuscan neighbors make a simple tomato sauce they call *pomarola* to see their families through until the following summer. And lest you think I'm talking about a minor and rather old-fashioned phenomenon, let me assure you that these country women, many of them young women at that, think nothing of putting up 250 to 300 jars of tomatoes over a series of days. It's often a multigenerational party, if a party that's centered around lots of hard work, as all the bottles and jars that have been saved throughout the year, including rinsed-out beer and Fanta bottles, are brought out of the cantina, given a good wash, and set to dry in sanitizing sunlight. Then the triage begins: Which tomatoes to peel and can whole? Which ones to process into plain tomato *pomarola* by putting them through an ingenious machine that removes seeds and skins, leaving only the pulp? Which ones to elaborate, with onion, garlic, basil, and maybe a little olive oil for richer flavor?

IN RECENT YEARS, interest has grown, in Europe and North America, in heirloom tomato varieties (the British call them heritage tomatoes), varieties that have been around for a while, that are open-pollinated and breed true—meaning that seeds from this year's tomato will produce another similar tomato next year. The opposite of a heritage tomato is a hybrid tomato, with seeds that are unpredictable in their offspring. Popular cluster tomatoes, for instance, big beefsteak tomatoes, and many other familiar types are what gardeners call F1 hybrids; if you plant the second generation of their seeds, you cannot predict what will come up. Heirloom tomatoes are often specific to a region and have folkloric names that tell a story.

Commercially grown tomatoes are almost always from hybrid seeds, which produce predictable, shelf-stable, and by no means entirely boring fruits—but they produce them once, and once only. Heirloom tomatoes have three things these pretenders never have: They are strictly seasonal, almost always strictly local, and most important of all, they have flavor—unique, special, and ranging from sharply acidic to rich and sweet, depending on the variety and the environment in which it has grown.

The *costoluto* tomato—*costola* means rib in Italian—is a good example of these heirlooms. In Spain in the 1960s, all you could find in local markets were *costolutos*. They were on the small side, easily fitting in the cupped palm of the hand, slightly flattened on the top and bottom, and deeply lobed which meant they were hard to peel. But they were delicious, with a depth and intensity of flavor that nothing else I've tasted can match. This old-fashioned tomato is probably more similar to the earliest tomatoes in the Mediterranean than are the smooth, thin-skinned, uniform globes so prevalent everywhere today. With a little diligence, you can still find *costolutos* in Mediterranean markets, but even these heirlooms are hybridized these days: In the Sicilian town of Pachino, famous for the quality of its tomatoes, *costolutos* are grown in open-air greenhouses, yet these *costoluti,* though their ancestors may have been true Sicilians*, are now grown from hybrid F1 seed processed in far-off Dutch laboratories.

PEPPERS CALLED *ñoras,* from the monastery in the town of the same name, are popular all over Spain (and no longer grown only in Ñora). They're almost always available as dried peppers, boxy in shape, deep red in color, and reminiscent of New Mexico or ancho chilies, especially when they hang in long plaits from a wooden beam in an old country kitchen. *Pimientos de Padrón,* on the other

---

*I have been told, but am unable to verify it, that the Pachino tomato is in fact a variety called "Noemi," recently developed in Israel before being brought to Sicily.

hand, from northwestern Galicia, are always served as fresh, green peppers, and always, in my experience, grilled or roasted, a heap of whole little inch-long peppers served as a delightful appetizer, piled high on a plate. Inevitably, someone cautions you: "*Pimientos de Padrón—unos pican, otros non,*" meaning, some burn your mouth, some don't. (In my experience, they're pleasantly spicy but not fiery at all.) Up in the Basque country on the French side of the Pyrenees, there's a long, narrow pepper called *piment d'Espelette,* again named for the town where it's grown, that, when dried and crushed, has a bright orange color and a fine, sweet, penetrating fragrance—I've become addicted to these since finding them in the Bastille market in Paris. And there are Aleppo peppers in Syria and Urfa peppers in Turkey, again named specifically for the place they come from. In Italy, on the other hand, a country that's ordinarily devoted to hair-splitting evaluations of different varieties, a pepper is quite simply a *peperone* if it's sweet, a *peperoncino* if it's a small, hot, red chili—except in Tuscany where, curiously, *peperoncini* are often called *zenzeri,* meaning "gingers," a suggestion of what the spicy flavor was that the *peperoncino* displaced.

Spaniards in general, like most people around the Mediterranean, don't relish the kind of burning hot chilies that North Americans know from Mexico and the Caribbean. Only in North Africa are such fiery sensations appreciated. Even in Tunisia, known for its "hot" cuisine, the heat is more a gentle suffusion of warmth that floods the palate rather than something that sends diners rushing for the water jug. In the eastern Mediterranean, especially in that culturally rich region of southeast Turkey and northwest Syria, around Aleppo and Gaziantep, the use of red peppers—spicy but not fiery ones—turned into pepper sauces, pepper pastes, and preserved peppers, is a true artifact, a distinguishing element in the cuisine. A good cook or a sensitive palate can tell you immediately whether a dried, crumbled pepper used in a sauce comes from Marash or Urfa, Aintab (the old name for Gaziantep) or Aleppo.

In this region, the peppers used as vegetables are fresh green ones, served on their own, stuffed, or as a garnish for many dishes, especially in Turkey. But dried red peppers are the characteristic seasoning, one could say the characterizing seasoning, used in almost every savory dish. In Aleppo in October, the whole town is filled with the seductive fragrance of drying red peppers (distill the essence, please, and I'll rub it behind my ears). These are what they call *flayflee halabiye,* which simply means Aleppo peppers, a gnarled and twisted kind of pepper that's grown in the hidden valleys that surround the ancient city. In the Souk Astar al-Harami, in the northern part of town, the Poladians, an Armenian family living in a ramshackle wooden compound whose various levels are connected by alarmingly dilapidated staircases, make red pepper paste for half the city, it seems.

Rafi Poladian explained to me how the system works, and it couldn't be simpler: Ripe red peppers are harvested, opened, and the core discarded, also the seeds if you want peppers that aren't too hot. These halved peppers are laid out on rooftops and dried in the strong sunlight until they're somewhat less than bone-dry, then brought by the sackful to the neighborhood's market square. There a self-important, well-fed young man with an ancient electric grinding machine that looked like—and might well have been—a 1930s Kitchen-Aid original, once white but stained rusty red by generations of red peppers fed into its maw, ground the peppers in the street in front of his shop, filling the air with pink dust.

After grinding, the peppers were more coral than red, but the color, Rafi assured me, would deepen and darken with the next treatment, which was to mix the ground peppers with a very little olive oil and a judicious quantity of salt and put them back out in the sun to dry again. Then they're brought to the Poladians, who grind the peppers a second time to make *dibbis flayflee* or pepper paste, which Rafi sells by the kilo from the big tins in which he packs the paste to keep it. If it's not dark enough—and a deep red is the most desired color—more oil is added. The whole process is strictly home production, apart from the two milling operations.

Tony Hill, a U.S. importer of Aleppo pepper products, says there are three or four sub-varieties of Aleppo pepper, all related in flavor to New Mexico or Anaheim or ancho chilies. The salt that's mixed in, he pointed out, helps to hold moisture (the moisture content of Aleppo pepper is much, much higher than, for instance, in Italian chili flakes) and encourages fermentation. The slight, pleasant fragrance of fermentation is a plus with Aleppo peppers, which, freshly made, have a bright flavor that starts to fade after two or three months. Made in late October, these pepper pastes are intended to see the family through the winter until the fresh flavors of spring start to come in again. But truth to tell, most Aleppine cooks, like their counterparts to the north in Gaziantep and Marash, use red pepper paste right around the calendar in almost every dish—a constant in this venerable cuisine.

Which leads me straight back to where I always seem to begin: What on earth was Mediterranean cuisine like before these precious New World foods arrived?

## 15 GREAT RECIPES USING TOMATOES AND/OR PEPPERS

Simple Fresh Tomato Sauce and Variations

Four Red-Pepper Sauces:

    Rouille

    Romesco

    Mhammara

    Harissa

Caponata Siciliana

Tunisian Medley of Grilled Summer Vegetables

    *Mechouia*

Balkan Oven-Baked Meat and Vegetable Stew

    *Guvetch*

Tomato Granita

    *Granita di Pomodoro*

North African Salad of Tomatoes and Peppers

    *S'lata Felfel*

Rabbit with Sweet Red Peppers

    *Guisado de Coñejo con Pimientos*

Braised Lamb Shanks with Tomatoes and Peppers

    *Guisado de Cordero con Tomates y Pimientos*

Sweet Green and Red Peppers Stuffed with Lamb and Bulgur

Green Tomato Jam

    *Marmellata di Pomodori Verdi*

Green Tomato Jam Pie

    *Crostata di Marmellata di Pomodori Verdi*

### COOK'S NOTES

The kind of tomatoes you select will depend on what is available in your market, but I urge you not to be satisfied with the run-of-the-mill in most supermarket produce sections. If you don't have access to a farmer's market, during tomato season seek out farms where you might be able to buy a quantity of fresh tomatoes. Or, if you have the space, grow your own—tomatoes fresh from the garden are one of nature's miracles that will forever convince you that January tomatoes from distant places are not really tomatoes at all.

When good-quality fresh tomatoes are not available, follow the lead of cooks all over the Mediterranean and use canned tomatoes, preferably a tasty brand made with organically raised tomatoes—Muir Glen, from California, is very good. Don't assume that the best canned tomatoes are imported from Italy—it ain't necessarily so. If you use a lot of canned tomatoes, you may prefer to have several different brands on hand, to avoid adding the same flavor to soups, stews, and sauces. I favor canned whole tomatoes over purees or crushed tomatoes: It's easier to get whole tomatoes with nothing but salt added, whereas crushed or pureed tomatoes very often have other flavors (basil, sugar, garlic) that change the nature of the dish.

As far as peppers are concerned, we seem in our enthusiasm for this healthy vegetable, to be delivering it the same one-two punch we gave the tomato, breeding peppers for shelf-stability rather than for distinguishing flavor. At a pepper tasting recently, with a dozen varieties of sweet red peppers, all of them field-grown by a conscientious organic grower, it was surprisingly difficult to distinguish among the varieties. All had a uniformly sweet, vaguely pepper flavor, with more or less of a pleasant edge of bitterness. One variety I found recently in a farmer's market was called Apple, and it had sufficient flavor and texture to stand up to long-cooking in a stew.

With one exception, peppers don't take well to canning or any other processing apart from drying. The exception is the beautiful piquillo peppers from Spain, dark red, thick-fleshed, and perfect to use right out of the jar or to stuff with a savory rice mixture and cook further in the oven.

As far as dried peppers are concerned, for the most part I prefer to buy whole dried peppers and crush or powder them as needed for recipes. (If I can't get peppers specific to a Mediterranean region, I substitute New Mexico or ancho chilies, often with a small addition of really hot dried chilies to spice up the mixture.) Some dried peppers, however, are only available in crushed form—all the peppers from the Middle East for instance (Aleppo pepper, Urfa pepper, Marash pepper, *biber kamiz*, which means "hot pepper" in Turkish), as well as the exquisite *piment d'Espelette* from the Basque region of southern France. Ordinary paprika, the kind you find sprinkled over your potato salad at the church picnic, is not worth considering for these recipes, as it has little flavor. Spanish paprika, however, called *pimentón,* can be delicious, whether the smoky-flavored kind called *pimentón de la Vera,* or regular unsmoked *pimentón;* Hungarian paprika, though not a Mediterranean ingredient, makes a good substitute when it's of top quality.

# Simple Fresh Tomato Sauce and Variations

🌿 A simple tomato sauce is part of every Mediterranean cook's repertoire. It forms the basis of dozens of different soups, stews, and more elaborate sauces. Think of it as a master recipe to be added to and changed at will. A cautionary note, however: It *must* be made *only* with fresh, garden-ripened tomatoes, not with hot-house tomatoes, and not with tomatoes that have been imported over great distances. If it's past the season for fresh tomatoes, use the best canned tomatoes you can find.

**Makes 4 cups**

3 to 4 pounds very ripe plum tomatoes

¼ cup extra-virgin olive oil

1 pound yellow onions (3 to 4 medium onions), chopped

6 to 8 garlic cloves, smashed and chopped

1 tablespoon sugar (optional)

1 tablespoon sea salt

Freshly ground black pepper

IF YOU WISH, peel the tomatoes before cooking them by dipping each one in a pan of rapidly boiling water for 12 to 15 seconds, then transferring them immediately to a colander. The peels can be slipped off as soon as the tomatoes are cool enough to handle. (If you don't peel the tomatoes, you'll have to put the sauce through a vegetable mill—see below.) Core the tomatoes and cut away any bruises or bad spots. Roughly chop the tomatoes, saving the juice.

COMBINE THE OLIVE OIL, onions, and garlic in a heavy-duty saucepan and cook over low heat, stirring frequently, until the onions have softened considerably, about 10 minutes. (If the vegetables burn, throw them out and start again; they will give an acrid flavor to the sauce.) Add the chopped tomatoes and, if the tomatoes are acid, the sugar. Add salt and pepper and stir to mix well. Continue cooking over low heat, but when the tomatoes have yielded some juice, raise the heat to medium and cook, stirring frequently, until much of the juice has evaporated and the tomatoes are very soft—20 to 30 minutes.

REMOVE THE TOMATOES from the heat, taste, and adjust the seasoning. If you did not peel the tomatoes, you should put the sauce through the widest holes of a vegetable mill before serving, in order to get rid of the skins. If, after pureeing, the sauce is too liquid, return it to the pan in which you cooked it and simmer until it has reached the desired thickness. The sauce may be served as is, over pasta for instance, or it may be canned or frozen for future use (see below).

IF YOU SERVE THE SAUCE with pasta, top it with freshly grated Parmigiano-Reggiano or Pecorino Toscano. For a Southern Italian touch, top the pasta with bread crumbs fried in a little olive oil and mixed with finely chopped fried or roasted almonds.

## VARIATIONS

IF YOU WANT A SPICIER SAUCE, add a few hot chili peppers, fresh or dried, to the onions while they cook.

FOR DIFFERENT FLAVORS, any of the following may be added with the tomatoes: fresh or dried thyme, bay leaf, or oregano; fresh basil, parsley, or rosemary; dried winter savory. If you add a volatile fresh herb such as basil, set aside a small amount to be stirred in at the last minute, right before serving, to boost the flavor.

FOR A MEATIER SAUCE, dice a couple of ounces of pancetta (Italian unsmoked bacon), prosciutto, or slab bacon. Cook the meat gently in olive oil until it yields some of its fat, then remove the meat and set aside while you continue with the recipe. Stir the meat back into the sauce at the end—after you've pureed it, if you're putting it through the vegetable mill.

OR, CRUMBLE AN ITALIAN-STYLE SAUSAGE into the olive oil and brown it before adding the onions and garlic.

*COULIS DE TOMATES*. Italian tomato sauce can easily be turned into a French *coulis de tomates*, which is really nothing more than a thick puree. Once the sauce is cooked, strain it over a bowl. Set the bowl aside in case you need to use the juice later.

PUT THE TOMATO-ONION MIXTURE through the fine holes of a vegetable mill. You will have a thick puree that you can thin to the consistency you want by adding back some of the strained tomato juice. Any leftover tomato juice that you don't use can be frozen and later added to a soup or stock.

THE TOMATO COULIS can be used immediately, or frozen, or sealed in sterilized jars to keep.

BOTTLED TOMATOES AND TOMATO SAUCE (LA POMAROLA). If you come across a farmer's market with lots of dead-ripe tomatoes (meaning tomatoes that will be over-ripe in another day or two), it's very easy to make tomatoes or tomato sauce to bottle for the winter. Then you'll have an easy resource on hand to turn quickly into a tasty sauce or soup. For ten pounds of tomatoes you will need a half dozen or so clean glass pint-sized canning jars with new lids (once they've been used, lids no longer seal tightly and should be discarded). If you want to be super-safe, you can put the jars through a high-temperature rinse cycle in the dishwasher, or put the jars in a big kettle of water, making sure each one is fully immersed, bring the water to a rolling boil, and boil for 10 to 15 minutes. Plan to use the jars shortly after you've sterilized them.

IF YOU'RE BOTTLING WHOLE TOMATOES, peel them first by dipping each one in a pan of boiling water for 12 to 15 seconds, after which the skin should slip right off. If there are bruises or other undesirable spots, remove them. Push the tomatoes down into the sterilized jars and screw down the lids. There should be sufficient juice released by the tomatoes during processing to cover the fruits.

IF YOU WANT TO MAKE a plain tomato sauce, coarsely chop the whole raw tomatoes (peeling them first is not necessary) and put them through the wide holes of a vegetable mill (better than the food processor because the seeds and bits of skin stay behind). Fill the sterilized jars to within a half inch or so of the tops and screw down the lids.

YOU CAN ALSO BOTTLE the Simple Fresh Tomato Sauce, in the recipe on page 270, but not one with bacon or other meats in it as that requires a different kind of processing.

WHETHER USING WHOLE TOMATOES or tomato sauce, you must process the jars. Once the jars are filled and the lids screwed down, place them in a large stockpot or canning pot and fill with cool water to cover them. (If you wish, use a rack or line the bottom of the pot with old newspapers to keep the jars from banging about.) Set the pot over medium heat and bring to a boil. Boil the jars for about 15 minutes, then turn off the heat and let the water cool somewhat. Then, using tongs, remove the jars and set them on a wooden or plastic surface to continue cooling down. After a while, you'll start to hear the satisfying "ping" as the lids snap shut, signifying a complete seal. Sealed jars of tomatoes or tomato sauce can be kept in a cool (not refrigerated) dark place for several months, until the next tomato season comes around. If any of the jars fail to seal, however, store them in the refrigerator and use the sauce in a week or so.

# Rouille

For today's Provençal cooks, a rouille (*rouio* in Provençal) is really nothing more or less than a mayonnaise flavored with garlic, dried red chili peppers, and sometimes saffron. In times gone by, however, and in more difficult times, it was thickened with bread crumbs rather than the luxury of eggs and olive oil. Rouille is traditionally served as a sauce to accompany a *soupe des pêcheurs* (page 360), but it is awfully good on top of a plain, hot, baked potato, too.

Rouille is best, and most authentic, made with a mortar and pestle, but you may also use a food processor (see variation, below).

### Makes 1½ to 2 cups

3 dried hot red chili peppers, preferably ñoras, or use dried red New Mexico or ancho chilies

1 teaspoon coarse sea salt

4 garlic cloves, coarsely chopped

Large pinch of saffron threads

2 egg yolks

1 to 1½ cups extra-virgin olive oil

1 teaspoon fresh lemon juice

½ teaspoon crushed hot red chili pepper flakes or cayenne (optional)

RINSE THE PEPPERS QUICKLY under running water if they are dusty, then dry them with paper towels. Break them open, discarding the tops, cores, and most of the seeds. Crumble the peppers into a mortar and add the salt. Grind with a pestle to a fine crumb, then add the garlic cloves and continue pounding and stirring until you have a thick paste. Add the saffron threads and work them into the mixture.

ADD THE EGG YOLKS and continue pounding and stirring until they are thoroughly incorporated, then transfer the pounded ingredients to a small bowl.

USING A MEASURING CUP with a pouring lip, gradually pour the olive oil into the egg mixture, beating constantly, exactly as you would for a mayonnaise, adding the olive oil at first almost drop by drop, then, as it grows thicker, in a thin but steady stream, and beating with a small wooden spoon or wire whisk. When you have added half the olive oil, stir in the lemon juice—this will loosen the sauce, so then start adding more olive oil until it has reached the desired thickness of mayonnaise. Taste the sauce and adjust the seasoning, adding a few more drops of lemon juice or the optional hot chilies, if desired.

VARIATION: You can make a lighter sauce in a food processor, using 1 whole egg instead of 2 egg yolks. Make the flavoring ingredients up to the addition of the egg yolks but instead of adding the yolks to the sauce, add the whole egg to the processor. Process briefly, just to break up the egg, then, with the motor running, add the oil in a thin stream, adding the lemon juice halfway through as described above. When the sauce has reached the desired consistency, stir in the flavoring ingredients and process with one or two quick spurts. (I don't do the whole thing in the food processor because in my experience, overprocessing garlic will give this and any other sauce an undesirable bitterness.)

# Romesco

The Catalan version of red-pepper sauce has no egg and is thickened instead with fried bread crumbs and fried pounded hazelnuts or almonds. It is but one in a series of pounded nut and garlic sauces from all over the Mediterranean, the best-known of which is Ligurian pesto (page 166), made with pine nuts, garlic, and basil. But any cook from Tarragona, the old Roman city south of Barcelona where this sauce is said to have originated, will quickly inform you that romesco is not a sauce at all, but a dish—specifically, a dish of seafood, sautéed then stewed in the ingredients of romesco. The sauce, however, is also made on its own, and makes a delicious accompaniment to grilled or sautéed fish or chicken, or stirred into a bean stew.

**Makes 2 cups**

1 small, firm, red-ripe tomato

1 fresh sweet red pepper

3 dried hot red chili peppers, preferably Spanish ñoras, or use dried New Mexico or ancho chilies

Sea salt

¼ cup toasted blanched almonds (see page 412)

¼ cup toasted hazelnuts (see page 412)

½ cup extra-virgin olive oil

1 slice country-style bread, about ½ inch thick

2 garlic cloves, peeled but left whole

1 to 2 tablespoons red wine vinegar

ROAST THE TOMATO and the sweet red pepper over a gas flame or a charcoal grill, or set under the oven broiler, until the surface is completely blackened and cracked (see page 410). Transfer to a paper bag, roll up the bag, and set aside for 15 to 30 minutes to steam.

RINSE ANY DUST OFF the chili peppers and pat dry with paper towels. Break them open and discard the tops, cores, and any excess seeds. Toast the chilies for several minutes in a dry skillet over medium heat, turning them frequently, until they have changed color and become a little crisp. Transfer to a food processor, add a pinch of salt, and pulse to crumble the chilies.

CHOP THE BLANCHED ALMONDS and toasted hazelnuts and add to the food processor. Pulse with the chilies until the nuts are finely ground.

POUR 2 TABLESPOONS of the oil in the skillet and set over medium heat. When the oil is hot, fry the bread until it is crisp and dark gold on both sides. Remove and break the bread into pieces. Add to the food processor and pulse with the nuts and chilies to make a paste.

ADD THE GARLIC CLOVES to the skillet with a little more oil. Roast the garlic in the oil until golden brown. Transfer to the food processor.

PEEL, SEED, AND CHOP the roasted tomato and the roasted red pepper. Add to the food processor and process while you gradually add the remaining oil, a little at a time, and the vinegar—you may not need all the vinegar, so add up to a tablespoon, then taste before adding more, remembering that the flavors will develop as the sauce stands.

LET THE SAUCE STAND for 20 to 30 minutes, then serve to accompany grilled meat, fish, or chicken.

NOTE: Be careful not to overprocess the sauce. It should be bound by the oil and roasted vegetables, but still have a sense of texture from the nuts and chilies.

# Mhammara

Another red pepper and nut sauce, this one from the Eastern Mediterranean. Although the ingredients look quite similar to the Spanish sauce, the flavors are very different. The use of pomegranate syrup, which is made by reducing pomegranate juice and is widely available in Middle Eastern groceries, adds a very different flavor note. If you can't find a source for pomegranate syrup, add a little more lemon juice to taste. You can also substitute a teaspoon of crushed dried New Mexico or ancho chilies, crushing them yourself in a spice grinder or mortar, for the Middle Eastern ones.

*Mhammara* is served as part of a meze table, garnished with toasted pine nuts and accompanied by toasted triangles of Arab bread to dip in the sauce, but you could also serve it with raw vegetables to dip.

For the most authentic texture, make this with a mortar and pestle; for ease in the kitchen, make it in a food processor, but be careful not to overprocess the sauce. It should still have texture from the nuts.

**Makes about 3 cups**

4 fresh sweet red peppers

½ garlic clove, crushed with the flat blade of a knife

Sea salt

1½ cups walnut halves, very finely chopped

½ cup bread crumbs (preferably made from Arab pita bread), toasted

1 teaspoon ground red Middle Eastern pepper (Aleppo pepper, Turkish pepper)

ROAST THE PEPPERS to blacken them, then set aside to steam in a paper bag before peeling, discarding stems, seeds, and membranes (see page 410 for instructions). Coarsely chop the peeled peppers.

IF YOU ARE USING A MORTAR, pound the garlic to a paste with the salt, then pound in the walnuts and bread crumbs. Add the roasted peppers, pounding to a paste. Then stir in the ground pepper, pomegranate syrup, lemon juice, and 1 tablespoon of olive oil. Taste and adjust the seasoning, adding 1 more tablespoon of oil if you wish.

IF YOU ARE USING A FOOD PROCESSOR, after peeling and chopping the peppers, transfer them to the processor bowl and puree until smooth. Add the walnuts, bread crumbs, and ground pepper to the peppers and pulse to a granular mixture. Then add the pomegranate syrup and lemon juice and pulse briefly. Finally add the garlic and salt and, with the motor running, slowly add in about 2 tablespoons of olive oil—although you may not need all the oil to reach the desired consistency. Taste and adjust seasoning.

PILE THE FINISHED SAUCE in a bowl or onto a small platter and garnish with toasted pine nuts. Serve with toasted triangles of pita bread.

VARIATION: Some cooks add ¼ teaspoon ground cumin to the blend.

1 tablespoon plus 1 teaspoon pomegranate syrup

2 teaspoons fresh lemon juice

Extra-virgin olive oil

Toasted pine nuts, for garnish

For serving: triangles of pita bread, toasted

# Harissa

 Every cook, every family, every spice merchant throughout Tunisia seems to have his or her own formula for harissa, the hot chili sauce or paste that is a ubiquitous ingredient in the food of the region. Sometimes harissa is fiery hot; at other times it is just suffused with warmth. Harissa is most often made with dried red chilies, but some cooks make it with fresh peppers; others add a handful of dried mint to the sauce, and I'm told that in Gabes, on the east coast, the locally esteemed salt-preserved onions, which can be kept for up to a year, are pounded into the condiment.

Harissa will keep for a long time in the refrigerator if it is spooned into a clean glass jar and the top covered with olive oil. Use a spoonful any time you want to spark up a sauce or a soup—it's especially good with any kind of legume soups and it's essential with Tunisian couscous (see recipe, page 169).

Harissa is best if made from a selection of three or four different chilies of varying degrees of heat. I have used Anaheims, pasillas, and a small amount of very hot arboles, but you should select from what is available in your market. Just be sure to include at least one very hot variety.

**Makes ¹⁄₂ to ³⁄₄ cup, about 8 servings as a garnish**

15 medium to large dried red chili peppers (see above for suggestions)

2 tablespoons coriander seeds

1 tablespoon cumin seeds

1 teaspoon caraway seeds

Sea salt

4 or 5 garlic cloves, coarsely chopped

About ¼ cup extra-virgin olive oil

RINSE THE CHILIES QUICKLY in running water, then break off the tops and shake out the loose seeds. Set the chilies in a bowl and cover with very hot water. Weight a plate over the chilies to keep them under water. Set aside for 20 to 30 minutes to soften.

MEANWHILE, roast the coriander, cumin, and caraway in a dry skillet over medium heat until the aromas of the spices start to rise. Transfer to a mortar with a pinch of salt and pound to a grainy powder. Add the chopped garlic and pound to a paste.

DRAIN THE CHILIES and discard most of the seeds and membranes. Using a spoon, scrape the softened pulp into the mortar, discarding the tough, papery outside peel of the peppers. Pound with a pestle to a coarse paste. Work in about ¼ cup of oil, 1 tablespoon at a time. Taste and adjust the seasoning. The sauce should be very thick but easy to spread.

IF YOU'RE NOT USING IT RIGHT AWAY, put the harissa in a clean glass jar, smoothing the top, and pour a little more oil over to seal it. It will keep, refrigerated, for 2 to 3 weeks.

# RATATOUILLE, CAPONATA, ESCALIVADA, AND MECHOUIA

The combination of tomatoes and peppers with eggplant and sometimes zucchini, cooked in olive oil with onions and garlic, shows up in one form or another all over the Mediterranean. In southern France, it's called ratatouille or *la bohémienne* (*la boumanio* in Provençal), in Southern Italy it's caponata or *ciambotta*. Related preparations are called *escalivada* in Catalonia and in Tunisia *mechouia*, usually without the eggplant or zucchini. Often olives, black or green, or capers are added at the end, and a Sicilian friend and master cook Gianfranco Becchina serves a caponata that is entirely made up of green peppers and green olives, a handsome presentation. More typically, Sicilian caponata is made with a sweet-and-sour tomato sauce. Sicilian ciambotta is similar, but with grated cheese and/or bread crumbs stirred into the dish while it's still warm—an unnecessary gilding, I feel, of an already handsome lily.

The question with eggplant is always: To salt or not to salt? Although the kind of eggplants available in today's markets lack the bitter juices that once led cooks to salt them as a matter of course before cooking, I still feel that in most situations it's a good idea to cut up the eggplant, salt it, and set it aside to drain for up to 60 minutes before rinsing, drying, and continuing with the recipe. Eggplant is like a sponge for oil, and, since most eggplant is fried as a first step in cooking it, salting it beforehand will cut down on the amount of oil it absorbs.

All of these eggplant-tomato-pepper dishes can be served in several different ways. Warm, they make an excellent vegetable course, served before or to accompany the meat or fish (the combination is especially good with lamb); at room temperature, they can be served with drinks, with crackers or toasted Arab pita bread to use for dipping. They can be the centerpiece of a vegetarian lunch, preceded by a soup and followed by a fruit dessert.

# Caponata Siciliana

If you wish, add some zucchini to this mixture, sautéed like the eggplant (although it does not need preliminary salting) and added to the sauce at the end. Some cooks add a handful of pine nuts, roasted in a frying pan with a teaspoon of olive oil, at the very end.

**Makes 6 to 8 servings**

1 medium or 2 small eggplant

Sea salt

½ pound fresh sweet red and yellow peppers

½ cup plus 2 tablespoons extra-virgin olive oil

2 medium yellow onions, chopped

2 garlic cloves, chopped

1½ pounds red ripe tomatoes, peeled, seeded, and chopped

1 small dried hot red chili pepper (optional)

2 tablespoons red wine vinegar

1 teaspoon sugar

3 celery stalks, sliced

½ cup chopped pitted black olives

½ cup salted capers, rinsed under running water and drained

Handful (about ½ cup) slivered fresh basil leaves

CUT THE EGGPLANT into fingers about 1½ inches long and place in a colander. Scatter a handful of salt over the eggplant, tossing to make sure they are all salted. Set a plate on top, with a weight on it (a can of tomatoes works well for this), and set the colander in the sink to drain for about 1 hour.

WHILE THE EGGPLANT IS DRAINING, pierce the peppers with a long-handled fork and roast them over a gas flame or charcoal embers (or if necessary set them in the oven under an electric broiler) until the thin outside skins are black and blistered. (See page 410.) Peel the peppers and slice lengthwise into ½-inch strips, discarding the seeds, stems, and inner membranes. Set aside.

RINSE THE EGGPLANT well and dry thoroughly with paper towels. Heat the ½ cup oil in a frying pan over medium-high heat and fry the eggplant sticks until they are golden on all sides. Remove them and set them aside to drain on paper towels.

TO MAKE THE TOMATO SAUCE, combine the remaining 2 tablespoons oil, onions, and garlic in a saucepan over medium-low heat, and gently sauté until the onions are very soft, but not brown, 20–30 minutes. Add the tomatoes, the chili pepper, if using, vinegar, and sugar. Continue cooking, stirring, until the sauce is thick and jammy and the tomatoes have broken down, about 20 minutes. Stir in the celery and cook 5 minutes longer, just to soften the celery slightly. Add the olives and capers. Stir in the eggplant and peppers and cook for 2 more minutes just to meld the flavors.

REMOVE THE CAPONATA from the heat, stir in the basil, and set aside to cool to room temperature before serving.

# Tunisian Medley of Grilled Summer Vegetables

## MECHOUIA

 The Tunisian version of the combination omits the eggplant and increases the peppers. Moreover, the vegetables are almost always cooked on a grill, whether charcoal, gas, or electric, before being chopped and mixed together. The flavors are best when the vegetables are charcoal-grilled, but even preparing it under the oven broiler will result in a nice balance.

ROAST THE SWEET AND HOT PEPPERS according to the directions on page 410, using a charcoal grill, if available. When the peppers are roasted and peeled, slice them lengthwise, the sweet ones in ¼-inch or smaller strips, the chilies in slivers. Transfer to a bowl with their juices.

ROAST THE WHOLE TOMATOES on the grill until they are blackened on the outside but still quite firm within. Halve the tomatoes, pull away the skins and squeeze gently to extract the seeds. Cut into strips and add to the peppers.

ROAST THE UNPEELED ONIONS until their skins are thoroughly blackened. Strip away the outside skins and slice the onions in strips. Add to the peppers.

IF YOU DON'T HAVE THE OPTION of roasting the tomatoes and onions on a charcoal grill, turn on the oven broiler. Arrange the tomatoes and onions on a roasting sheet and brush lightly with olive oil. Roast under the broiler, turning several times, keeping an eye on the vegetables and removing them as their skins blister and blacken—the tomatoes will be done before the onions. When they're done, prepare the tomatoes and onions as described above.

ADD THE PARSLEY to the vegetables in the bowl and toss to mix well.

**Makes 6 to 8 servings**

3 to 4 fresh sweet red and green peppers

3 to 4 fresh green chili peppers

3 medium-sized firm ripe tomatoes

2 small to medium onions

½ cup chopped flat-leaf parsley

3 tablespoons extra-virgin olive oil

1 tablespoon fresh lemon juice

Sea salt and freshly ground black pepper

1 tablespoon minced fresh cilantro, for garnish (optional)

1 tablespoon salted capers, rinsed under running water and drained, for garnish (optional)

2 hard-cooked eggs, coarsely chopped, for garnish (optional)

½ small (3½-ounce) can oil-packed tuna, flaked, for garnish (optional)

Chopped peel of 1 salt-preserved lemon (page 44), for garnish (optional)

½ cup coarsely chopped pitted black and green olives, for garnish (optional)

IN A SEPARATE SMALL BOWL, combine the oil and lemon juice with salt and pepper to taste. Beat with a fork, then pour over the vegetables while they're still warm. Toss gently, then taste and adjust the seasoning.

SERVE THE *MECHOUIA* as is, or add any or all of the optional garnishes. Although it may be served immediately, this dish is really better if it can be set aside for several hours to let the flavors meld and develop before it is served.

# Balkan Oven-Baked Meat and Vegetable Stew

### GUVETCH

 The Balkan part of the Mediterranean, stretching from the Adriatic coast to the shores of the Black Sea, adds meat to the basic tomato-pepper-eggplant mixture to create a hearty oven-baked one-dish meal, enriched by a yogurt topping. Feel free to change the vegetables in the dish, depending on what's available. Okra and carrots are often included if they're in season, and some cooks like to add a couple of chopped garlic cloves when sautéing the onions.

TRIM THE EGGPLANT, discarding the top, and cut it into cubes about ¾ inch to a side. Set the cubes in a colander in the sink. Sprinkle with 2 teaspoons salt and toss to mix well. Set the colander in a sink to drain for 30 to 40 minutes.

IN A HEAVY-DUTY SAUCEPAN, combine 2 tablespoons of the oil, the butter, onions, and garlic, if using. Sauté gently over low heat until the onions are very soft, about 30 minutes. Add the meat and raise the heat to medium. Brown the meat, stirring, for 15 minutes or so, until all the pieces have changed color. Add salt and black pepper and cover with water to a depth of about ½ inch. Turn the heat down to low, cover the pan, and just simmer the meat for an hour or so, or until it is very tender.

PREHEAT THE OVEN to 400°F. Lightly oil a baking sheet.

RINSE THE EGGPLANT PIECES well and dry with paper towels. Lay them on the baking sheet and brush them all over with the remaining oil. Roast the eggplant pieces, turning them from time to time, until they are golden on all sides, about 15 minutes. Remove from the oven and turn the oven temperature down to 350°F. (You may also sauté the eggplant pieces in more olive oil, but the oven-baking method cuts down on the total amount of oil used.)

**Makes 6 to 8 servings**

1 medium or 2 small eggplant

Sea salt

6 tablespoons extra-virgin olive oil

1 tablespoon unsalted butter

2 pounds yellow onions, halved and thinly sliced

2 to 3 garlic cloves, chopped (optional)

2 pounds lean lamb or veal, cubed

Freshly ground black pepper

Water

3 medium red-ripe tomatoes, peeled, seeded, and chopped, or 3 canned tomatoes

½ teaspoon sugar (optional)

3 medium potatoes, peeled and sliced

4 ounces green beans, trimmed

2 small zucchini, sliced

2 sweet fresh green peppers, cored and cut into 8 pieces

¾ cup chicken, lamb, or veal stock, heated

¼ cup plain yogurt

2 large eggs

Strained yogurt (page 410), for garnish (optional)

ARRANGE HALF THE EGGPLANT SLICES in the bottom of a large casserole, preferrably of terra-cotta. When the meat has finished cooking, spoon it over the eggplant. Add salt and generous quantities of pepper. Taste the tomatoes and add sugar if you wish. Spread about a third of the tomatoes on the meat, then layer the potatoes and green beans on that; top with half the remaining tomatoes, then the zucchini and peppers, and finally the remaining eggplant slices and tomatoes. Trickle the hot stock over the top and down the sides of the casserole.

BAKE THE CASSEROLE for about 1 hour, or until the vegetables are tender.

MIX TOGETHER THE YOGURT and eggs and spread over the top—the sauce need not cover the entire surface. Raise the oven heat to 425°F. Return the casserole to the oven and bake an additional 30 minutes, or until the top is golden and firm.

REMOVE THE CASSEROLE from the oven and let it sit for about 30 minutes. Serve, if you wish, with strained yogurt (page 410) for a garnish.

# Tomato Granita

## GRANITA DI POMODORO

For best results, the tomatoes should be chilled in the refrigerator overnight, so start this recipe a day ahead of time. It makes an elegant entremet for a dinner party, served between the first and second course, or serve it as a startling but delicious dessert at the end of the meal.

The best tomatoes for this are fleshy plum tomatoes, but in fact any fresh red-ripe tomatoes will do. The important thing is that they should be full of summer flavor. You could also use yellow tomatoes, but again be sure they are very ripe—on the verge of being over-ripe. If you use yellow tomatoes, which are less acid than red ones, cut the corn syrup in half, or add it to taste.

For the chili pepper, I like to use *piment d'Espelette,* a fragrant pepper from the Basque region of southern France but it isn't always easy to find in North America. The point is to provide the flavor of a chili without the mouth-burning sensation you'd get from some Mexican and Caribbean chilies. Ground chili peppers such as Aleppo and Urfa from the Middle East do very well, as do some medium-hot Hungarian paprikas and Spanish *pimentones* (but not *pimentón de La Vera,* unless you want that decidedly smoky flavor).

HALVE THE TOMATOES and gently squeeze out the seeds and excess liquid. Chop the tomatoes coarsely and store them, in a covered bowl, in the refrigerator overnight.

THE NEXT DAY, combine the tomatoes and chili pepper in the bowl of a food processor and process in brief spurts, adding the corn syrup as you do so. You don't want a homogenous puree so much as a thick liquid with little chunks of tomato apparent throughout. (You can also put the mixture through the medium-coarse blade of a food mill.)

IF YOU HAVE AN ICE-CREAM MAKER, proceed according to the manufacturer's directions for sorbets and granitas. Or, turn the tomato mixture into a stainless steel bowl, cover well, and freeze. Every 20 minutes or so, stir the mixture up with a fork. Within an hour or two, depending on the temperature of your

**Makes 8–10 servings as an entremet, 6 servings as a dessert**

1½ pounds very red ripe tomatoes, peeled (see page 411)

1 tablespoon fragrant ground chili pepper (see above)

¼ cup light corn syrup

freezer, the granular ice chunks typical of a granita will have formed; an electric ice cream maker, on the other hand, will make something smoother and closer to a sorbetto.

SERVE AS AN ENTREMET, garnishing each serving with a sprig of basil; as a dessert, serve the granita with buttery shortbread cookies.

# North African Salad of Tomatoes and Peppers

## S'LATA FELFEL

 The recipe for this came from an Algerian friend, but it's the kind of salad that might be found almost anywhere in the Mediterranean during summer or early autumn, when peppers and tomatoes are at their ripest and sweetest. It makes a delicious first course but can also accompany grilled meat or fish.

SLICE THE PEPPERS in ½-inch strips.

SLICE THE TOMATOES in ½-inch strips and combine with the peppers in a bowl or deep serving platter.

MINCE THE GARLIC and transfer to a small bowl with about ½ teaspoon salt. Using the back of a spoon, crush the garlic to a paste. Add the oil, vinegar, and black pepper, beating with a fork. Taste and adjust the seasoning, keeping in mind that the olives and anchovies will add salt to the salad.

ARRANGE THE OLIVES and anchovy fillets over the tomatoes and peppers. Drizzle the vinaigrette over and set the salad aside for at least 30 minutes to let the flavors meld before serving. The salad can be refrigerated, covered with plastic wrap, if necessary, but should be brought to room temperature before serving.

VARIATION: If, like me, you often wonder what Mediterranean cooking was like before 1492, here's a hint: Algerian cooks, I'm told, often substitute thinly sliced oranges for the tomatoes, and thinly sliced red onions for the peppers. Otherwise the recipe stays the same.

**Makes 6 servings**

8 ounces fresh sweet peppers, preferably red and yellow, roasted and peeled (see page 410)

2 large red-ripe tomatoes, peeled and seeded (see page 411)

2 garlic cloves, crushed with the flat blade of a knife

Sea salt

⅓ cup extra-virgin olive oil

2 to 3 tablespoons red wine vinegar

Freshly ground black pepper

½ cup pitted green olives

½ cup pitted black olives

4 salted anchovies, rinsed and filleted (see page 411)

# Rabbit with Sweet Red Peppers

## GUISADO DE COÑEJO CON PIMIENTOS

One of the great country dishes that Richard Ford described during his travels throughout Spain in the middle of the nineteenth century was a stew of hare, partridge, rabbit, pheasant, or chicken, cooked with pimientos, or peppers. This is my own interpretation, based on Ford's notes in *A Handbook for Travellers in Spain,* a wonderful guidebook, even today. It is best made with rabbit, but if necessary, you can substitute chicken. In Ford's time, the guisado was probably served with thick slices of bread fried in olive oil, but it's also very nice served with plain steamed small potatoes, with their skins still on.

When I can get them, I use small sweet red peppers, a variety called "apple" that I get from a farmer in my local market. If you can only get big, fleshy red peppers, four should be enough. In any case, the proportions of ingredients can be varied to taste, but keep in mind that peppers should predominate.

2 ounces lean slab bacon or pancetta, diced

3 tablespoons extra-virgin olive oil, or more as needed

2 medium onions, coarsely chopped

3 garlic cloves, chopped

1 (4-pound) rabbit or chicken, cut in 6 pieces

1 cup dry white wine

Big pinch of saffron, soaked in 1 cup very hot water

Sea salt and freshly ground black pepper

2 or 3 sprigs fresh thyme

6 small fresh sweet red peppers

2 chicken livers (or use the liver from the rabbit), cleaned and cut into pieces

IN A SKILLET over medium-low heat, melt and brown the bacon in the oil. When the bacon is brown and crisp, remove with a slotted spoon and transfer to an earthenware casserole or other suitable dish. Add the onions and garlic to the oil remaining in the skillet and cook, stirring frequently, until the onions are golden but still soft, about 20 minutes. Remove the onions with a slotted spoon and add to the bacon. Set the casserole over very low heat, especially if you are using earthenware—a Flame Tamer will help keep the heat low.

IN THE OIL LEFT in the skillet, brown the pieces of rabbit over medium heat, turning to brown both sides, about 10 minutes to a side, and add to the casserole. Add the wine to the skillet and cook, stirring with a wooden spoon, over medium-high heat, scraping up brown bits. Turn into the casserole. Add the saffron water, with the saffron threads, and salt and pepper to taste. Tuck in the sprigs of thyme. Cover the casserole and let simmer very gently for about 45 minutes.

WHILE THE RABBIT IS COOKING, roast and peel the peppers (see page 410) and cut them into quarters.

WHEN THE MEAT HAS COOKED for 45 minutes, add the livers, stirring them into the other ingredients. Cover again and cook for another 30 minutes.

TASTE THE SAUCE and adjust the seasoning. Discard the thyme and add the peppers, stirring them in. Cook for about 10 minutes more, and as soon as the peppers have heated through, serve the dish.

# Braised Lamb Shanks with Tomatoes and Peppers

## GUISADO DE CORDERO CON TOMATES Y PIMIENTOS

 Another robust Spanish stew cooks lamb shanks in tomato sauce with peppers adding flavor.

**Makes 6 to 8 servings**

¼ cup extra-virgin olive oil

18 small white or yellow onions, peeled but left whole

3 meaty lamb shanks, weighing 4 to 5 pounds total

2 pounds red-ripe tomatoes, peeled and coarsely chopped, or 1 (28-ounce) can whole peeled tomatoes with their juice, chopped

1 whole head of garlic

1 to 2 sprigs thyme, leaves only

¼ teaspoon ground cumin

2 large fresh sweet peppers, preferably red and green, cored and cut into thick strips

Sea salt and freshly ground black pepper

1½ to 2 pounds small new potatoes, scrubbed

IN A HEAVY PAN LARGE enough to hold all the ingredients, combine the oil and onions and gently sauté the onions until they are brown all over. Remove the onions with a slotted spoon and set aside.

ADD THE LAMB to the pan and turn the heat up slightly. Brown thoroughly on all sides. Return the onions to the pan with the tomatoes. Bring to a boil. Brush any loose papery peel off the outside of the head of garlic and as soon as the liquid comes to a boil, nestle the head down in the middle of the stew. Stir in the thyme and cumin.

COVER THE STEW and simmer gently, or cook in a 325°F. oven, for 1 hour. Check from time to time: There should be just enough liquid to keep the meat and vegetables from browning. If necessary, add a little boiling water to the pan. Uncover and add the peppers, pushing them down into the liquid, and salt and pepper. Return the pan, covered, to the heat for another hour. Add the potatoes and cook until tender but not falling apart. If you are cooking on the top of the stove, the stew will be done in another 30 to 40 minutes, or as soon as the potatoes are tender. If you are cooking in the oven, it will need 60 minutes or so.

REMOVE THE STEW from the heat and let cool until you can handle the meat. Strip the meat from the bones and chop into bite-sized pieces. Skim any fat off the top of the sauce and return the meat to the pan. Set aside, refrigerated if necessary, for a day and reheat before serving the next day.

# Sweet Green and Red Peppers Stuffed with Lamb and Bulgur

 This same combination, which is very popular in Lebanon and Syria, could be used to stuff other vegetables as well—tomatoes are delicious, as are zucchini or eggplant hollowed out, then some of the flesh chopped and mixed with the stuffing.

You could also use the lamb-bulgur mixture for grape leaves. If you have a source of fresh tender young grape leaves, rinse them well, nip off the stems, and set the leaves in a colander in the sink. Pour boiling water over them to soften them before you stuff and roll them.

MELT THE BUTTER in 1 tablespoon of the oil in a sauté pan over medium-low heat and add the onion. Cook very gently until the onion is almost melted, 20 to 30 minutes. Raise the heat slightly and add the lamb. Cook the lamb, breaking it up with a fork as you do so, and mixing it thoroughly with the onion. When the lamb has lost its color, stir in the tomato and cook for about 20 minutes, or until the tomato has softened but not melted into the meat sauce.

WHEN THE TOMATO IS SOFT, stir in the green chili, if using, the ground red pepper, salt, and black pepper. Continue cooking for another 5 minutes, then stir in the parsley, allspice, and cinnamon and remove from the heat. Stir in the sumac and pine nuts. Taste and adjust the seasoning.

IN A BOWL, combine the bulgur and enough boiling water to cover to a depth of 1 inch. Set aside for 5 to 10 minutes to soften, then drain well, squeezing the bulgur to rid it of excess water.

TURN THE OVEN ON to 400°F.

LIGHTLY OIL A BAKING DISH large enough to hold the peppers upright comfortably, so they don't topple over nor are they too squeezed. Combine the bulgur with the meat mixture and stuff

**Makes 4 servings
as a main course**

1 tablespoon unsalted butter

1 tablespoon plus 2 teaspoons extra-virgin olive oil

⅔ cup finely minced onion (1 medium-large onion, minced)

8 ounces ground lean lamb

1 large tomato, peeled, seeded, and chopped (see page 411)

1 hot fresh green chili pepper, seeded and chopped (optional)

1 teaspoon ground red Middle Eastern pepper (Aleppo pepper, Turkish pepper)

sea salt and freshly ground black pepper

½ cup minced flat-leaf parsley

½ teaspoon allspice, preferably freshly ground

½ teaspoon cinnamon, preferably freshly ground

2 tablespoons sumac (optional)

¼ cup pine nuts

2/3 cup medium-grain bulgur

Boiling water

4 fresh sweet green or red bell peppers, cored and seeded but left whole

2 tablespoons tomato concentrate or tomato paste

the mixture into 4 large peppers. Set the peppers in the baking dish. Top each pepper with ½ teaspoon of the remaining oil. Mix the tomato concentrate with 1 cup of boiling water and spoon a small amount (no more than a teaspoon) over the top of each pepper. Pour the rest of the tomato water into the baking dish.

BAKE FOR 30 MINUTES. Turn off the heat and leave the peppers in the oven for another 10 minutes. Remove from the oven and let cool slightly before serving.

# Green Tomato Jam

## MARMELLATA DI POMODORI VERDI

 If you have a garden, or shop at a farmer's market, you can plan this ahead of time. The tomatoes to use are ones that are just beginning to ripen, still green but with pale peachy-pink stripes. If you can't get access to green tomatoes, some importers of Italian products offer a green tomato jam that is almost as good as what you can make yourself.

CUT THE TOMATOES IN HALF and gently squeeze out as many of the seeds as you can. Slice the tomatoes as thinly as possible and transfer the slices to a bowl. Sprinkle all the sugar over the tomatoes, stirring gently to distribute it well. Cover the bowl with plastic wrap and set aside overnight.

THE NEXT DAY, collect all the juice that has formed and bring it to a boil in a heavy saucepan. Add the lemon, cloves, and cinnamon, and simmer the liquid, covered, for about 30 minutes. Add the sliced tomatoes and simmer, uncovered, for an additional 30 minutes, or until the tomatoes are tender and slightly falling apart in the syrupy liquid.

HAVE READY 4 to 6 half-pint canning jars or jelly glasses, with lids, that have been sterilized by putting them through the high-temperature rinse cycle on the dishwasher; or put the jars in a big kettle of water, making sure each one is fully immersed, bring the water to a rolling boil, and boil for about 10 to 15 minutes. (Use the jars shortly after you've sterilized them.)

WHEN THE JAM IS READY and very hot, spoon it carefully into the sterilized jars and seal the lids. The seal on the lids should snap shut within the next 30 to 60 minutes, without any further processing. Sealed jars may be kept in a dark store cupboard or pantry for several months. Any jars that don't seal should be refrigerated and used within the next 3 weeks or so.

YOU CAN USE THIS JAM on your breakfast toast or croissant, but it's best, I think, used in a crostata, an old-fashioned Tuscan pie of exquisite simplicity.

**Makes 4 to 6 cups**

2 pounds firm green tomatoes

1 pound (2⅓ cups) sugar

2 lemons, preferably organic, thinly sliced

8 to 10 whole cloves

4 (1- to 2-inch) cinnamon sticks

# Green Tomato Jam Pie

## CROSTATA DI MARMELLATA DI POMODORI VERDI

**Makes 8 to 10 servings**

1 cup unbleached all-purpose flour

¼ cup cake flour

¼ cup sugar

Pinch of sea salt

6 tablespoons unsalted butter, very cold, plus butter to grease a 9-inch tart pan

1 large egg

Zest of ½ lemon, grated

1½ cups Green Tomato Jam (page 295)

1 egg, beaten with 1 teaspoon water

FIRST MAKE THE PIE CRUST, or *pasta frolla*. Mix together the flours, sugar, and salt, tossing with a fork. Add the butter, cut into pieces. Working rapidly, rub the butter into the flour mixture. Make a well in the center and break the egg into the well. Add the lemon zest and, using a fork, mix the egg rapidly into the dough. When it is thoroughly combined, shape the dough into a ball, wrap it in plastic wrap, and refrigerate it for at least 1 hour.

PREHEAT THE OVEN to 350°F. Butter a tart or quiche pan.

ROLL OUT APPROXIMATELY two-thirds of the *pasta frolla* into a 10-inch disk. Because the dough is very buttery, it's easier to do this between two sheets of waxed paper. Line the tart pan with the dough, which should be about ⅛ inch thick. Spread the jam over the dough.

BETWEEN TWO SHEETS OF WAXED PAPER, roll out the remaining third of the *pasta frolla* until it is about ⅛ inch thick and cut into long strips about ½ inch wide. Arrange the strips in a lattice atop the pie. Paint the exposed surfaces of dough with the egg wash.

BAKE FOR ABOUT 20 MINUTES, or until the crust is golden. Remove from the oven, cool, and serve at room temperature.

# The Family Pig

## A PERENNIAL RESOURCE

SPANIARDS WILL TELL YOU—and most non-Spaniards will agree—that without any question the finest ham in the world is the dark red, almost mahogany-colored *jamón iberico* or *jamón de bellota* from southwestern Spain. It's a product that results from a combination of a unique breed of swine, the Iberian black pig, with the methods used to raise the animals, plus a long, slow curing process that converts the hog's hindquarters into these extraordinarily savory hams.

Ask for *jamón iberico* in a good tapas bar anywhere in the country and here is what you will be served: thinly sliced (nearly, but not quite, paper-thin) rashers of ham, carved off the bone by a master of the art, laid in a circle of dark rosy petals curled around a platter, each slice visibly interlayered with fat and lean, studded with tiny white crystals of protein, and surrounded by an unctuous and deeply flavorful rim of creamy ivory fat. Taken as it usually is with a glass of chilled dry fino sherry, *jamón iberico, jamón de bellota, jamón pata negra* (it is called all these) has a taste that is both rich and dry, as nutty as Spanish almonds or Spanish sherry, sweet and salty at the same time, a flavor that is almost indescribably mouth-filling and deeply satisfying.

Possibly the most important element in producing this exquisite ham is the breed of pig itself, for the *cerdo iberico*, or Iberian pig, is an ancient swine, high-legged, narrow-snouted, dark-skinned, an incredibly elegant beast that makes ordinary garden-variety white pigs look like—well, like a bunch of pigs. Spaniards call the breed autochthonous, meaning it's been around on the Iberian Peninsula for as long as anyone can remember, and possibly a good deal longer. But it, or its near relatives, existed in other parts of the pork-eating Mediterranean as well, in southwestern France (the *porc noir gascon*, which is almost extinct) and Italy (also almost extinct except for the related *cinta senese*, now cultivated as a rare breed, and the *nera parmensa*, the black pig that was originally used—but is no longer—for making Parma ham).

At one time, *ibericos* were the standard Spanish breed and occupied the entire Iberian peninsula, but in the nineteenth and twentieth centuries, they were gradually replaced by international breeds like Landrace, York, Large White, and above all Duroc, all of which had a more profitable ratio of meat to fat but not, alas, such flavor. Unlike these inbred parlor pigs, the *iberico* is a tough animal and thrives in a semiwild state in open woodlands where the grazing is rich, and this contributes immeasurably to the flavor of the meat.

By the 1960s, these prize animals were perilously close to extinction. A combination of factors was behind their disappearance. For long decades after the end of the Civil War, Spain was a very, very poor country, the poorest in Europe after Portugal. Quick, cheap, easy pork from international breeds made sense economically. Then, too, impatience with the old ways of doing things and the urge to be "modern," whatever that meant, afflicted many cultures, including our own, in those years.

By the 1970s, the Iberian pig had disappeared from most of its original range, surviving only in environmental niches in the west of the country, in Estremadura and in the northwestern Huelva region of Andalucia and in Salamanca. And it is in these niches that we find the *dehesas*, extensive, often immensely ancient forests of evergreen and cork oaks, majestic trees that limn the hillsides of Estremadura and northern Andalucia, where herds of the distinctive, high-backed, dark-colored native breed still browse. To come across these shy, half-wild beasts, especially in midwinter with the low January sun slanting beneath the guardian oaks, lighting the mist that drifts upward from the bosky undergrowth, is to witness something fundamental, almost prehistoric, that takes us back to the dawn of Celto-Iberian civilization.

Hams from these pigs are notable for the marbling of fat that gives the flesh such a remarkably suave texture, the fat thoroughly penetrating, practically interwoven with the lean. The pigs themselves are not fat so much as big: Mature specimens, ready for slaughter, can weigh 360 to 400 pounds. And they don't look fat, at least in part because their long legs set their bellies well up off the ground. Moreover, these are pigs who know what a good workout means. In the last 3 to 5 months of their lives, Iberian pigs are turned out into the *dehesa* to forage freely on the roots, grubs, and acorns (*bellotas*) of the forest floor. During this time they develop muscle and bulk at the expense of the soft, tender quality that marks a fine prosciutto from Parma, for instance. Each pig augments its weight by 30 to 50 kilos (66 to 110 pounds), all of that coming from a tasty diet that adds deep and complex flavors to the meat. According to the *Denominación de Origen Dehesa de Extremadura,* the Spanish designation for these controlled-name hams, only an Iberian pig that has spent the last months of its life foraging in freedom on the *dehesa* is entitled to become a *jamón iberico,* a guarantee of quality that is supervised by an extensive organization of inspectors at every stage of the pig's career, from birth to finished ham.

The final element in creating one of these exquisite hams is the lengthy care and attention to which it is subjected from the moment of slaughter until the emergence of a well-aged ham 24 to 36 months later. The most ordinary commercial *jamón serrano* (mountain ham) is cured only 3 months, although better serrano hams are kept longer. "A three-month cure?" said Manuel Galan with a dismissive shrug, "That's not *jamón,* that's *carne salada,* salt meat."

Galan is the owner of El Coto de Galan, a commercial ham producer in the town of Castuera in Estremadura. (When I say commercial producer, I mean someone who turns pork into ham by traditional curing methods but on a much larger, commercial scale—Galan told me his factory produces around 40,000 cured hams—*jamónes*—and shoulders—*pelotas*—from acorn-fed Iberian pigs each year.)

Apart from the length of time the hams cure, the process Galan showed me is not so different, up to a point, from that followed by other European producers of dry, salt-cured and aged hams like Parma or San Daniele hams from Italy, or *jamón serrano,* the Spanish ham that's made from ordinary white pigs. At Coto de Galan, *iberico* hams are liberally salted for 8 to 10 days, then washed and left to rest and dry for 15 to 20 days, after which they spend up to 15 months hanging in the *secadero*, or drying shed. Then comes another critical difference: From the *secadero*, the hams are transferred to a *bodega*, an enclosed, rather humid and cellar-like environment, where they spend another 6 to 12 months, depending on the size of the ham. At this stage, a different kind of flavor develops, similar to what happens with the singular Italian ham called *culatello* (see page 310), and this process, I think, is what gives *jamón iberico* its rarified flavor, best described by the Japanese term *umami*, an elusive concept of a kind of meatiness that is a mouth-filling pinnacle of flavor.

ALTHOUGH COMMERCIAL PRODUCERS like Galan make hams all year round, back on the farm, the traditional time for slaughtering the family pig(s) is between St. Martin's Day on November 11 and St. Anthony Abbot's on January 17, which makes sense because it's the coldest time of the Mediterranean year and ideal for preserving meat. (When I first lived in Italy, 30 years ago, pork was so anathema in the heat of summer that you couldn't find it even frozen in the few supermarkets that then existed.)

In January one year I went out to Estremadura with a couple of friends to witness the annual pig slaughter in a village in this westernmost province of Spain. Estremadura pushes hard up against the Portuguese border and is so poor by nature that it's no wonder many of the *conquistadores*, the adventurers who fought for their fortunes in the New World, came from this same land. Our host was Julio Espinoza, a native Estremaduran, though Julio is a good deal milder in temperament than the fierce conquistadors. An expert in raising pigs and curing hams, Julio works for the *Denominación de Origen Dehesa de Extremadura*, the organization that guarantees the quality of hams from this region.

At midwinter the dawn comes late in western Spain, a reminder that we are here close to the very edge of the great European landmass. As we drove up past the dusty yellow walls of the medieval Castillo de Feria heading into the mountains for Julio's home village of Salvaleón, farmers on donkey back, shoulders wrapped in blankets against the morning cold, were trotting out to their fields, while in the higher valleys, the familiar shapes of Holstein cattle stood immobile in the chill, puffs of vapor from their breath the only indication they were still alive. The sun's light was just breaking above the mountains behind us, raking its rays across the climbing terraces of olives and vines, silhouetting dark, somber stands of *cornoques* and *encinas*, cork and evergreen oaks, against the white rime of frost on the ground.

CUNA DEL IBERICO proclaims the sign at the entrance to the village, "cradle of the Iberian pig." Densely settled with low two- and three-story buildings along its narrow streets, Salvaleón is ringed with olive groves, vegetable gardens, orchards, but beyond this belt of cultivation comes the oak forest, the *dehesa*, where the pigs graze. In times past, the village had a *porquero*, or swineherd, who collected all the village pigs each morning and took them to forage along pathways and cart tracks, in common forestlands, and over fallow fields, then returned each one to its proper residence at nightfall. Now, however, the forest land, the *dehesa*, is owned by individuals and families who fence in huge tracts of forest to keep the grazing pigs from straying far.

"Every family in the village slaughters two or three pigs a year," Julio said. Actually, the verb he used in Spanish was *sacrificar*—to sacrifice, a reminder that once upon a time all over the Mediterranean, the only meat consumed was the meat of sacrifice—and most people in fact consumed very little meat at all.

It's a two-day process, slaughtering the pigs one day, making the hams and sausages the next. On the day the animal is killed, they say, the meat is *demasiado caliente*, too hot, to work it. Julio's aunt, Pura Trigo, was sacrificing four pigs that morning. Short, stout but compact, dressed in the rusty black of village tradition, Tia Pura with her hair pulled back in a firm knot looked older than she probably was (I didn't dare ask her age), but she had the energy of a much younger woman. She kissed me on both cheeks by way of welcome, grasping my hand in a calloused grip, then turned immediately back to the serious business of the morning. Recently widowed, Tia Pura has seven adult children, some of them already married off, so the four pigs, two females and two castrated males, were to provide meat for four independent but, by traditional Spanish standards, very small households. And it was a lot of meat—the largest pig weighed 200 kilos (440 pounds), while the smallest was a good 170 (375 pounds).

These pigs were an Iberian-Duroc cross with too much Duroc to qualify for *jamón iberico*, which has to come from a pig that's at least 75 percent Iberian. That was of no concern to Tia Pura because she wasn't planning to sell the hams in any case. Legally, meat from family butchering of this kind must be consumed within the family and sale to outsiders is prohibited. Like most of her neighbors in the village, Tia Pura selects this crossbreed, Julio told me, because she wants more from her pigs than just two fine hams and two meaty shoulders to cure. A well-stocked

Spanish larder requires an enormous range of sausages or *embutidos* (stuffed things, the word means) as well as bacon, cured loins, and, of course, lard rendered from the fat of the pig, the invaluable cooking medium, especially prized for any kind of deep-fat frying. Even the animal's bony ribs are salted, marinated in an adobo of *pimentón* (paprika), water, garlic, and salt, and hung to dry. "Good for *el cocido*," Tia Pura said.

Butchering a pig is hard and exacting work. It took six people, two of them women, plus Pedro, Tia Pura's oldest son—who spent most of his time on his cell phone giving a blow-by-blow (literally) description of the event to various friends—and the butcher's 12-year-old son, who gave up after the first half hour when he cut himself, not badly, with a knife he was using to separate flesh from fat. The *matanchín*, the butcher, had been hired for the job but the rest were family and friends. They were gathered in a courtyard built specifically for this purpose next to the house, with an open space where the pigs are slaughtered and the initial preparation takes place, then a roofed-over section where the women would work on sausage-making next day, with a fire on the hearth at one end and a cauldron of water bubbling over it. Just off the courtyard was the pen for the pigs.

There's a kind of festivity, a frivolity, even a silliness, around the pig slaughter. It's something you see whenever friends and neighbors collaborate on these country tasks, but it serves as well to mask or offset the sense of awe and dread that inevitably accompanies the fact of death. As with the clowns in Shakespearean tragedy, foolishness hides the fact that the gods must be appeased with a life. So the bottle of high-octane *anís* was passed liberally, although those who were really doing the work didn't take much, I noticed, and the jokes and innuendoes flew through the air, especially when sausages were being stuffed.

I can't really tell you how the pigs were killed. I saw the knife, I may even have seen the knife plunge into the pig's throat, but if I saw it (and I would not swear that I did), I brushed it from my memory. For someone who ate nothing but hamburger for the first fifteen years of her life because it was as far from the shape of an animal as you could get, it is not easy to face the bloody nature of death before dining. I love meat, I love pork above all other meats, but I would rather not take any part in the killing.

In Italy (and in most other places too, I believe), pigs are stunned with a bolt shot right into the brain before they're strung up and their throats cut to let the blood run out. In Spain (at least when I was in Estremadura, the laws have changed since), the pigs are simply stuck with a knife, the aorta slit, and the blood gushes forth like water from a hydrant. The noise the pigs make is deeply disturbing, a gasping, high-pitched, unending scream of terror. The rusty iron smell of blood suffuses the courtyard, along with the smell of burnt hair from the pig's bristles when the stiffened carcass is seared with a blowtorch. The pigs, resisting, screeching, are pulled to the slaughter bench. We say animals lack consciousness of self, yet these beasts clearly knew what was in store for them. Once the first had been killed, the next ones fought the encounter with every ounce of strength they could command.

The *matanchín*, the butcher, is always a man. The *tripera*, who works side by side with him, is most often a woman. She drains the precious pig's blood, which will make *morcillas* or blood sausages, into plastic basins, mixing and turning it to keep it from coagulating, and washes and cleans the parts of the slaughtered animal. As he cut and removed each part, the *matanchín* announced it, like a butler announcing arriving guests: *el solomillo, los riñones, el higado, las costilladas, el lomo, la cabeza, el tocino, las pajarillas* (the sirloin, the kidneys, the liver, the spareribs, the loin, the head, the bacon, the spleen). The loin was put in an adobo, a spicy mixture in which *pimentón* and garlic predominate, to marinate overnight. *Las castañetas* (the castanets) are the salivary glands, and they are usually grilled immediately, along with the ears and some of the bonier bits, charred over the wood fire and eaten with lots of salt. "Some people like them, some don't," said Tia Pura, setting her teeth on a chewy bit of *castañeta*.

The hams and shoulders of these pigs would be sent to what they called *el industrial,* an industrial warehouse like El Coto de Galan, where they would be transformed into *jamónes* and *paletas* for the family. She doesn't do the curing herself, Tia Pura said, because it's a delicate process and needs a big attic space to store the meat. But in a brief moment of repose, she recalled for me how her father made hams, immersing them in salt for 15 days, she said, and every few days stamping the joints with his feet to push out the blood. Then, when no more blood issued forth, the ham was rinsed in hot water and hung to dry. That's all. "And they were good hams, too," she said.

With another older woman, she was cleaning the animals' intestines, mainly because no one else would do it or knew how, rinsing and rinsing, inside and out, but taking great care not to tear the membranes which would encase the sausages. "I've seen it done all my life," she said, "but I've never done it myself." Once cleaned, the intestines were put to soak in big plastic basins of cool water with halved oranges and lemons added to perfume the guts. The other woman, her assistant, was the daughter of a famous *tripera* who died without passing on her secrets. Just so the world changes and knowledge of the old ways disappears, not to be retrieved unless someone has taken the care to write it down.

Every pig that is slaughtered in Spain, whether at home or in a factory, is tested by a veterinarian for trichinosis. Parts of the tongue, the diaphragm, and the cheeks of each of Tia Pura's pigs were put aside for the vet who would pass by later in the day to examine them, looking for trichina larvae. There is almost no trichinosis in Europe in general, especially in Spain (one in every 100,000, said Julio) but the government requires this caution nonetheless and no sausages can be made until the vet has approved.

As we left to go out to the *dehesa* to look at pigs in their natural state, Esperanza, one of the butcher's helpers, called after us. "If you want white beans and salt cod, come back," she said. Then, at my look of surprise, she added, "Well, we have to get away from all this meat."

N EXT DAY, Tia Pura was busy cutting up liver for *caldillo de higado*, a liver stew that's always served at the *matanza*, she said, while the other women assembled sausages. Out in the courtyard, a cousin was making *morcón*, a fat sausage with a stuffing that includes chopped onions and parsley, as well as lots of *pimentón* (red paprika made from a pepper called *choricero*, because it's used to make chorizo sausages) and cumin, and is then cooked very gently in just barely shimmering water. Inside the shed, pork fat was slowly melting into lard in a cauldron over the embers on the hearth, while Pura's daughters stuffed sausage casings, making *chorizo rojo*, colored deep red with pimentón; *chorizo blanco*, simply flavored with nutmeg and the pale color of meat and fat; *morcilla negra*, the famed fat Spanish blood sausage, with black pepper and garlic, and *morcilla colorada*, similar but without the blood. As a chain of sausages was finished, it was set with a pole across the beams of the ceiling to dry over the coming weeks, when it would shrivel slightly and darken in the chilly air. The *morcillas* begin with a sort of pinkish gray color, not very appetizing, but gradually they take on a deep, orangey red. By the morning after they were made, they were black and glistening with oozed fat (which is why blood sausage is called black pudding in English and *boudin noir* in French).

The spice combinations in sausages vary from region to region, even from family to family, but somewhere in Spain you can be sure to find a sausage flavored with oregano, or cumin, or cinnamon, or cloves, or nutmeg, or black pepper, or white pepper, or all of the above, and almost always *pimentón*, the all-purpose flavoring and coloring of dried and ground red peppers, full of flavor but not necessarily hot. This southern part of Estremadura is noted for using spices and herbs with considerable abandon. Elsewhere, sausage-makers might rely on a more restrained seasoning, simply garlic, salt, and *pimentón*, often the smoky brick-red pimentón from the valley of La Vera north of here.

Tia Pura's hands were coated with blood from the pork livers she was cutting up. She had started the *caldillo* with a sofrito of onion, garlic, parsley, and chopped fresh red peppers, melting the vegetables in the bottom of a cauldron with fresh *manteca blanca*, plain white lard. All the sausage seasonings went into the *caldillo* pot, too: bay leaves, pimentón, ground cumin and cloves, black pepper, then a little boiling water, and finally the liver, added in small cubes at the last minute so it wouldn't overcook. As she tipped the liver cubes into the cauldron, Tia Pura offered me one to taste, but I excused myself, patting my stomach to show I'd just had breakfast. (Right!) Later we stood around the cauldron of *caldillo*—all of us women, the men having disappeared elsewhere—dipping hunks of bread into the savory stew and slurping it up, the juices running down our forearms. It was a moment of tribal affirmation for sure, fundamental and potent, overseen by the matriarch, the food provider, her hands still red with the blood of sacrifice.

A N ANTHROPOLOGIST WOULD HAVE had a field day with the *matanza* at Salvaleón: The first day, the day for the meat to be slaughtered and cut up, is traditionally the men's day, while the second day, the day for the meat to be transformed into products for long-keeping, is a day for women. What's eaten on the first day, moreover, is grilled meat, cooked plainly and directly over the embers of the fire—and eaten standing up using no utensils, just the hands (what could be more primitive?). What's eaten on the second day is a combination of ingredients that are cooked indirectly, boiled in a container, then eaten from another container using a spoon or a fork, along with hunks of bread (transformation of the primitive into culturally meaningful products). Anthropologists, beginning with the great French savant Claude Lévy-Strauss, speculate endlessly about these kinds of differences.

But anthropologists speculate endlessly, in any case, about the whole subject of the pig. No other animal evokes such strong feelings. For Mediterranean Christians, pork is a fundamental element in cuisine, as well as a vital source of both fat and protein; at the same time, cured pork products provide enormous variety in the diet, far more than any other easily available protein, not an inconsiderable factor in pork's popularity. On the other hand, for observant Muslims and Jews, pork is an abomination, a flesh so thoroughly abhorrent that the thought of touching it (as in pigskin gloves or a pigskin wallet), much less eating it, rouses feelings of uncontrollable revulsion.

Easy explanations for this paradox are also easily dispensed with. Pork was banned, one theory goes, because its association with trichinosis made it dangerous to consume, especially in the hot climate of the Levant. Yet other food animals are also vectors for diseases that are both more immediate and more devastating than trichinosis (anthrax and brucellosis, for instance, which are transmitted by cattle, sheep, and goats).

Or, pork was banned in order to set up cultural boundaries, distinguishing the ancient Hebrew tribes from their neighbors. Yet, it appears that those same neighbors—Phoenicians, Egyptians, Babylonians, as well as pre-Islamic Arabs—also found pork a source of profound distaste, and in any case this becomes a circular argument: Why pork, as the distinguishing factor, and not, for instance, veal?

Or, pork was banned because it was observed that pigs are dirty animals who wallow in filth and eat garbage. Yet pigs are no dirtier than cows who will lie in their own excrement if it isn't cleaned up for them, or chickens who will eat anything that presents itself, no matter how disgusting to humans. In any case, as anthropologist Marvin Harris has pointed out in a wonderfully encompassing essay "The Abominable Pig," the dirtiness of pigs is reflective of the dirtiness of their human keepers rather than vice versa. Harris himself believes a variety of environmental reasons are behind pig aversion, beginning far back in history with the fact that nomadic people—pre-Islamic Arabs, ancient Hebrews—could only care for animals that were easy to herd on the trail, specifically sheep and goats. Later, in Harris's view, environmental degradation, caused by those same sheep and goats, destroyed the original forested landscape along the shores of the Eastern Mediterranean and left a terrain that was only suitable for ruminants.

Whatever the rationale behind it, the fact is that the Mediterranean world is sharply, irrevocably divided between pork lovers and pork haters. Which is all to the advantage of those of us who are indifferent to food taboos, and thus able to enjoy equally the pork sausages of Southern Italy and the lamb sausages of North Africa, the cured-beef pastirma of Turkey and Armenia and the great *jamónes*, *jambons*, and *prosciutti* from the rest of the Mediterranean.

Some historians claim that pigs were introduced into the Mediterranean by Celts when they began moving west of the Rhine and south of the Alps in the middle to late first millennium B.C.E. Unquestionably, pigs are significant in Celtic mythology: The white sow-goddess of Celtic belief was, like Demeter, an important goddess of grain. But there is solid archaeological evidence of pigs in southeastern Europe and southern Anatolia as early as 7,000 years ago. In Homeric times and later, baby pigs were sacrificed to Demeter during the Thesmaphoria, the annual festival in her honor. (Is it possible that the Celtic sow-goddess and Demeter are both descendants of a prehistoric original who has been lost to us?) And the tale of the Gadarene swine, like the parable of the Prodigal Son who left home to find work as a swineherd, are reminders that in Biblical times, the injunction against eating pork was not universally upheld in the Holy Land.

JUST ABOUT EVERY FARMER around the Mediterranean—every Christian farmer, that is—keeps a pig or two or three; farmers who don't actually keep pigs, will buy live pigs at slaughter time and have them killed on the farm to be turned into hams, sausages, bacon, and lard for the year ahead, not to mention fresh meat for immediate consumption. You could argue that sheep are more useful animals, since you get meat, milk, and wool all from the same beast (the milk and the wool, moreover, as renewable resources), but the pig is useful from stem to stern ("everything but the squeal," someone inevitably adds) and, moreover, the meat, which is very tasty when fresh, is made even more delicious by the curing process. Cured pork lasts a long time, often, like those Iberian hams, getting even better with age, and a little goes a long, long way—witness all those sauces and stews, *cocidos* and *ollas* and *pucheros,* ragùs for pasta and ragoûts for the main course, minestrones and risotti, sofritos and *battuti,* all those recipes from Spain, from southern France, from Italy and the islands, that begin with the words: "Take a handful of chopped ham, or pancetta, or tocino and melt it in a little olive oil. . . ."

How many different kinds of cured pork products are there in the Mediterranean world? Possibly as many as there are villages, valleys, and mountain ranges, especially in Spain, southern France, and Italy, where the products of the pig reach their apogee. The Greeks too have an infinity of ways to treat the flesh of swine, although they have not made a high art of ham. Still, when it comes to breadth of scope, no culture can beat the Italians and the Spanish. I once counted 250 different preparations in an Italian book devoted to cured pork. Some of these are well known, like prosciutto di Parma, the fine, salt-cured, air-dried ham from the Langhirano hills above Parma in the Po Valley, and prosciutto di San Daniele, somewhat sweeter and softer, from the northeastern corner of Italy. But what about lightly smoked prosciutto from the Casentino north of Arezzo? Or prosciutto di Pietrarola, from southern Campania, made from the hams of Campanian black pigs and pressed between two heavy stones during the cure? What about coppa or capocollo, the solid muscle from the back of the pig's neck which in Umbria is washed in white wine and wrapped in butcher's paper to age, and in Puglia is smoked over oakwood fires? And what about cotechino, a fat sausage made deliciously sticky from gelatinous bits of pork rind? (In Cremona, vanilla is part of the aromatics added to cured cotechini, a sensational combination of flavors.)

Essential for curing pork of any kind is salt which, sausage lovers say, was sent by God to bring pork to life. But it's the inessentials, the options, that make the difference—spices, especially pepper (black or red or both is de rigueur, as we have seen, in Spain); the traditional *quatre-épices* (cinnamon, clove, mace, and nutmeg) of parts of France; fennel and wild fennel in Umbria and Tuscany; coriander, cumin, garlic, dried orange peel in other regions. Then there's the question of cooking or not. Some sausages, like mortadella from Northern Italy, Spanish morcón, and the many kinds of head cheese (called pihti in Greece), a generic name for a gelatin-rich sausage made with many different parts of the pig's head, benefit from steaming, while others derive their flavor and texture from the fact that the pork, though cured, is essentially raw. Some sausages, like Italian salame and Spanish chorizo, are intended to be eaten raw, while others—all the variety of blood sausages come to mind—can only be consumed after cooking.

To sample most of these, Americans must perforce travel to the Mediterranean. In recent years it has been possible to import *prosciutti*, both Parma and San Daniele, from Italy and *jamón serrano*, but not *jamón iberico*, from Spain. But most of the other range of cured-pork products, including *jamón iberico*, are forbidden by the U.S. Department of Agriculture because of fears of contamination by diseases that might attack pigs in this country. (No one claims that these products are in fact contaminated; the problem is that no meat or meat products can be sold in the United States except those that come from animals slaughtered in the presence of a USDA inspector; the inspectors, or their equivalent, are in place for the hams mentioned, but not for any other meat products.)

So pork-loving travelers to Spain will want to seek out *jamón iberico,* just as those going to Italy will want to look for *culatello* and *lardo di Colonnata,* two nearly legendary products that are often threatened with extinction—not because no one wants them any more, but on the contrary, because the demand for them is such that spurious imitations are claiming the market for each and, following Gresham's Law, driving out good products. The *culatello* producers have responded by organizing themselves into a *denominazione di origine* syndicate to protect their product. The producers of *lardo di Colonnata,* on the other hand, see a protected designation as just one more level of bureaucracy with which to struggle, but with an initiative launched by the powerful Slow Food organization, the product looks as though it may survive, or at least struggle along a few more decades.

*Lardo di Colonnata* is made in the little village of Colonnata up above Carrara in the marble-veined Apuan Alps, where Michelangelo came to select his stone and, it is alleged, to feast on *lardo,* which is essentially nothing more than chunks of cured but unrendered fat from very heavy Italian pigs. Historically, this was the food of the *cavatori,* the men who labored in the marble quarries. Not only was their work demanding, but the *cavatori* walked two or three hours to get to the quarries and then, of course, two or three hours back home again. They needed energy, and they got it, so it's said, from drinking wine and eating *lardo* from morning to evening.

Marino Giannarelli is one of the few remaining makers of *lardo di Colonnata.* Only one in every ninety pigs, he told me, is suitable for *lardo,* and that's the only part of the animal that he buys—the rest goes to other uses, possibly to making prosciutti di Parma, for Parma is not far away over the Appenines. The *lardo* is cured in marble *conche,* or coffins, made from a particular, hard, vitrified marble that is specific to this zone of the marble mountains. He pointed up to a deep white vein of marble, a *canallone* he called it, running up an open scar in the mountain peaks that soared above the high village. "That's precisely where this marble comes from," he said.

The *conche* must be completely filled with lardo with no spaces, no air pockets, Giannarelli told me. The thick strips of white fatback, liberally rubbed with cinnamon, clove, rosemary, whole black peppercorns, ground black pepper and garlic, are set in the *conca,* then smaller pieces are used to fill it up—it's like building a wall, he said. There's a lid on top but it's not hermetically sealed and the contents of the *conca* aren't weighted. They simply sit in their aromatic environment for 6 months and then, when they're ready to use, they are thinly sliced and draped over a piece of hot toasted bread or—most deliciously—over *cecina*, a round unleavened pizza-like flatbread, made of chickpea flour, that is baked in a wood-fired oven (see recipe, page 244).

*Culatello* may be a more easily acquired taste, but it has an equally long history. *Culatello di Zibello* is the correct name for this soft, sweet, aromatic ham, made from a boneless wedge carved out of the upper haunch of the pig—preferably, but not necessarily, a *moro romagnolo*, another in the black pig family. The wedge of *culatello* is rubbed with salt, pepper, sometimes garlic, and white wine, and tied in a tight net of twine that, as the ham loses moisture and decreases in size, loosens and drapes like a thick, graceful spiderweb on the outside of the meat. Traditionally, *culatello* is cured in dank stone basements in the Bassa Parmense, the right bank of the Po between Parma and Piacenza, a region where cotton-thick winter fogs and hot summer humidity add a special sweetness to the meat, according to Massimo Spigaroli, chef, *culatello*-maker, and president of the *culatello di Zibello* consortium.

In the 1990s, the disapproving gaze of sanitary inspectors fell on the dark, damp, mold-encrusted curing cellars, and for a while it looked as though *culatello* would become just another taste memory. Then Spigaroli and his fellow *culatello*-makers organized to defend their beloved ham. Now, with its *denominazione di origine protetta*, *culatello di Zibello* is safeguarded—which does not, of course, mean that it is produced in an unsanitary manner, but rather that unreasonable sanitary regulations that would have entirely changed its nature cannot be foisted on this gastronomic prize of ancient origin.

Over a plate of *culatello* and a glass of the local wine at Spigaroli's riverside restaurant Il Cavallino Bianco one late winter morning, with the sun casting weak rays through dense fog, he explained to me his theory about *culatello*, which he ties firmly to the history of the Bassa Parmense. Roman armies marched through, he pointed out, on their way north over the Alps and into Gaul and Britannia—the ancient Via Emilia still runs south of here, parallel to the modern *autostrada* on its way to the Adriatic. And Roman legions had to be provisioned. Thus, there grew up a market for cured pork, especially hams, that soldiers could carry on the march. And that market grew over time. Strabo the geographer says that Rome in antiquity was fed on Cisalpine pork from this region.

"We have no tradition of eating fresh pork around here," Spigaroli said. "Everything, the whole pig, is cured to provide a year-round meat supply." Back in Roman times, however, when pigs were much smaller than they are today, whole hams, he believes, were cured in the same fashion as *culatelli* are today. Then, with time, pigs got larger, and it took longer for the cure to penetrate the whole leg, so ham-producers switched to smaller pieces cut off the leg.

A person might disagree with Spigaroli's historical thesis, but a person could not argue with the idea that the old French concept of *terroir* plays a role in creating these *culatelli*, possibly even a unique role for this is a unique environment, flat and monotonous, a riverine plain that extends for miles along the banks of the broad Po, interrupted only by wind-bent lines of poplars, with chill winter fogs and hot humid summers that are a bane for inhabitants but soften the meat of a pig, tenderizing it to a velvety, almost silken consistency, like something you might almost rather wear than eat.

But then you eat it, and immediately you understand that that's what it's really intended to be.

## 12 GREAT RECIPES USING PORK, SAUSAGE, HAM, OR PANCETTA

Serving Prosciutto or *Jamón Serrano*

Andalucian Spiced Pork Skewers
 *Pinchitos Morunos*

Neapolitan Christmas Soup of Pork and Greens
 *Minestra Maritata*

Sicilian Stuffed Skewered Pork Rolls
 *Involtini di Maiale*

Tuscan Roasted Pork Loin with Wild Fennel Pollen

Basque Pork Ribs in Adobo with Potatoes and Green Peppers

Cypriote Braised Pork with Coriander
 *Afelia*

Catalan Estouffat

Spanish Saffron-Meatball Soup
 *Sopa de Albóndigas*

Greek Dry-Marinated Pork Chops with Black Olives

Tuscan Sausages with Beans
 *Salsiccie con Fagioli*

Oven-Baked Rice, with Tomatoes, Peppers, and Pork

Much has been written recently about the poor quality of both pork meat and pork husbandry in the United States. The two, of course, are not unrelated. The U.S. pork industry in the last 15 years or so has focused its efforts on producing a low-fat "lite" animal and persuading consumers that this is what they want. (In fact, as wise consumers know, meat with a healthy layer of fat will cook up more tender, succulent, and flavorful than a piece of lean meat.) While breeding out flavor, they have also developed intensive farming methods that are breathtaking in their disregard for the environment.

Without going into a diatribe about pig farming, I do have to stress that if you want a flavorful, well-marbled, healthy, and healthful piece of pork, you most likely will not find it at your local supermarket meat counter, unless it's a market that specializes in products of organic and sustainable agriculture. For the best pork, make an effort to seek out sources for meat that is locally raised by environmentally sustainable methods, without medications or other inappropriate additives to the feed. Farmer's markets are often a good source for this—even if no one is selling pork in the market, as sometimes happens, the farmers themselves often have pork to sell back on the farm or know someone who does. A whole-foods market with a reliable meat section is also a good place to look for the best-quality pork.

One of the most important ingredients in the larder of traditional Mediterranean cooks is the array of cured pork products, from prosciutto, or air-dried hams, to cuts like *guanciale,* the cured cheeks of the pig, and pancetta, cured belly fat streaked with lean. In Spain, which has fully as strong a tradition of *embutidos* as Italy has of *salumi* (meaning, salted and cured pork products), there are marvelous chorizos (sausages cured with strongly flavored paprika and garlic), *lomos* (the loin of the pig, cured like a sausage), and others that are just beginning to be available in North America. While all of these pork products are delightful in their own right, usually served thinly sliced as an antipasto with a glass of chilled wine, their use in the kitchen should not be forgotten. A couple of tablespoonsful of any one of these, added to the first frying of the sofrito or *battuto,* the mixture of aromatics (onion, garlic, parsley, celery, carrot), will lend incomparable flavor to the resulting soup, stew, or sauce. This is what food scholars and nutritionists mean when they speak of the Mediterranean habit of eating meat in small quantities—it might be that this small quantity is consumed every single day, one way or another, but it all adds up, at the end of the week, to not quite half of one typical American beefsteak.

Lard, the rendered fat of the pig, is a traditional cooking medium, as valued as olive oil in pig-raising cultures. It has an undeservedly bad reputation in North America, where most people are totally unaware of the fact, confirmed by the United States Department of Agriculture, that lard is lower in cholesterol than butter. In parts of North America where large numbers of Germans or Central Europeans have settled, you may be able to find a butcher who still makes his own lard by rendering fresh pork fat and preserving it uncontaminated with chemical preservatives. If you can find such a thing, by all means use it wherever indicated in the recipes that follow. Otherwise, I substitute extra-virgin olive oil.

## SERVING PROSCIUTTO OR *JAMÓN SERRANO*

Salted, air-dried raw ham is a great Mediterranean product that has long been available in top North American restaurants but has recently become better-known to home cooks. Don't confuse these with domestic "prosciutto;" most domestic prosciutto has been cooked at some point in its processing, creating an entirely different product. With luck, however, you might come across an enthusiastic butcher or grocer who is taking the trouble to cure ham in the European style. This type of production is usually strictly local, with varying results, but it's the sort of thing that we should encourage.

European raw hams imported into the United States are produced in their country of origin under U.S. Department of Agriculture supervision. It is strictly illegal to bring any other European ham (or any other meat products, for that matter) into the country. Don't even think about trying. Laws such as these have, so far at least, protected our herds from scourges like foot-and-mouth disease, and we should respect them.

Of the imported hams, prosciutto di Parma, cured in the high Langhirano hills south of the city of Parma in Emilia-Romagna, is probably the best known, but prosciutto di San Daniele from the northeastern Italian region of Friuli is also increasingly available and just as high-quality as Parma. Both these Italian hams are usually somewhat sweeter, somewhat less salty, than their Spanish counterpart *jamón serrano,* which is made in airy mountainous regions all over Spain. All three are used in much the same fashion, thinly sliced and served on their own as a first course with very good bread and butter, or often with fresh, sweet, seasonal fruit, such as melons or figs—peaches, too, are excellent with salty ham.

The best ham should come on the bone and be sliced by hand, using a long, thin, flexible knife. This is seldom available, however, so most of us will buy boneless ham from a delicatessen or gourmet products store, where it will be sliced for us on a machine. Only the tough outer rind of the ham should be removed before slicing. Anyone who suggests removing the fat betrays considerable ignorance, since the beautifully clear, white fat is where much of the good flavor of the ham resides. Whether by hand or by machine, ham should be sliced at the very last moment, because it starts to lose flavor as soon as it comes in contact with air. A top-quality ham may be dotted with tiny white crystals that result from the breakdown of proteins. This is a good sign, similar to the crystals of protein in the best, long-aged Parmigiano-Reggiano cheeses.

The message that ham should be sliced thin has created a problem—lots of hams are sliced way too thin, shredded, almost, on the slicing machine. Yes, the slices should be thin, but they should still have sufficient substance that they can be cut with a knife and eaten with a fork.

To serve raw ham as a first course, arrange three or four slices on individual plates, rolling each slice into a loose cone if you wish. Serve it with a good, crusty, country-style bread, sliced thickly, and high-quality sweet (unsalted) butter. Or add fruit to the plate—thin wedges of canteloupe, honeydew, or other melon (watermelon is delicious), with the rind cut away if you wish; or peeled peaches, sliced in wedges; or black figs, sliced open to expose their hearts. In winter, serve raw ham with a salad made from shredded cabbage and root vegetables macerated in a dressing of olive oil and just a little wine vinegar. The point is to contrast the saltiness of the ham with the sweetness of fruit or salad.

# Andalucian Spiced Pork Skewers

**PINCHITOS MORUNOS**

One of my all-time favorite Spanish tapas, these little skewers are very much at home in Andalucia where they are served in tapas bars along with a glass of chilled fino sherry or manzanilla, and where the spice mixture for pinchitos is sold, already mixed, in grocery stores and markets. Your own mixture, made up fresh for the occasion, will of course be superior to anything you can buy. Try the proportions below, but feel free to adjust them to your own taste.

Don't try these with very lean pork as the meat will simply dry out while cooking. Best is a piece, like country-style boneless ribs, with fat mixed in with the lean.

In Andalucia, these are strung on little bamboo skewers no more than 6 inches long, then grilled over a charcoal brazier. You can also cook them under an oven broiler. I find it amusing that these are called "Moorish" skewers, yet they're always, in my experience, made with pork—anathema to any proper Moor.

IF YOU'RE USING BAMBOO SKEWERS, which are best for this, soak them in water for at least 30 minutes.

CRUSH THE GARLIC with the salt in a mortar until you have a paste.

COMBINE THE CORIANDER SEEDS and cumin seeds in a dry skillet. Set over medium-low heat and toast for several minutes, until the aromas start to rise. Transfer the spices to the mortar with the garlic and pound gently to a paste. Mix in the turmeric, paprika, lots of black pepper, the olive oil, and the lemon juice. Transfer the mixture to a shallow plate.

THREAD THE PORK PIECES on the skewers. Turn the skewers in the marinating mixture to coat the meat well on all sides. Set aside to marinate for an hour or so.

WHEN YOU ARE READY TO COOK, prepare a charcoal fire and let the coals burn down until they are white-hot or preheat an oven broiler for at least 20 minutes. Grill or broil the skewers, turning them once, for a total cooking time of 5 to 6 minutes.

SERVE IMMEDIATELY.

**Makes 8 to 10 appetizer servings**

2 garlic cloves, minced

1 teaspoon sea salt

1 teaspoon coriander seeds

1 teaspoon cumin seeds

¼ teaspoon turmeric

2 teaspoons mildly hot Spanish paprika (*pimentón de la Vera* is good)

Freshly ground black pepper

3 tablespoons extra-virgin olive oil

1 tablespoon fresh lemon juice

1¼ pounds pork, cut into small pieces

# Neapolitan Christmas Soup of Pork and Greens

## MINESTRA MARITATA

This great, rich soup is what Neapolitans traditionally serve to open their Christmas Day feast. It's called "*minestra maritata*," married soup, presumably because of the very successful marriage of abundant meats and bitter greens. Among the bitter greens are some that aren't usually available in North American markets, borage and chicory shoots, for example. If you happen to have such stuff in your garden, by all means include them.

Note that you can make the meat stock well ahead of time, refrigerating the skimmed broth and the meats until you are ready to proceed. The greens, however, should be cooked as close to serving time as possible.

**Makes 10 main-course servings or 12 first-course servings**

2 pounds country-style meaty pork ribs

4 ounces pancetta, cut in large dice

1 chicken, preferably a stewing fowl, weighing 3 to 4 pounds (or half a larger bird)

1 to 2 pounds veal shank (osso buco)

Water

Leafy green tops of a bunch of celery

2 medium carrots, coarsely chopped

4 garlic cloves, crushed

1 or 2 small dried hot red chilies

IN A LARGE (10-QUART) STOCKPOT, combine all the meats and cover with water. Bring to a simmer and skim the grayish foam that rises to the top of the pot in the first few minutes of cooking. When all the foam has been skimmed off, add the celery, carrots, garlic, and chilies. Add at least half a bunch of flat-leaf parsley, a small sprig of sage and one of rosemary, as well as a few sprigs of thyme, if available. Add a little more water, if necessary, to just cover everything. Bring it all to a simmer once more over low heat. Add a big pinch of salt and lots of pepper, cover, and simmer gently until the broth is very flavorful, about 3 hours.

WHEN THE BROTH IS DONE, remove the meats, including the pancetta dice, and strain the broth through a fine sieve, discarding the vegetables. Set the broth aside or refrigerate, so that the fat will solidify and be easy to remove. Remove all the meat from the fowl, veal shank, and ribs and cut the meat into bite-size pieces. Combine with the pancetta dice.

BRING A LARGE PAN of lightly salted water to a boil and cook the fresh greens, simmering them for about 10 minutes, then draining very well. (You may have to do this in several batches.) When they're cool enough to handle, squeeze them dry. Chop coarsely.

REMOVE THE FAT from the surface of the broth. Pour the broth into a clean stockpot. Bring to a simmer, taste, and correct the seasoning. Add the meats and greens and return to a simmer. Cook just long enough to heat all the ingredients.

Serve immediately, passing the grated cheese at table.

Fresh herbs: parsley, sage, rosemary (thyme, too, if you wish)

Sea salt and freshly ground black pepper

6 pounds fresh greens, cored, trimmed, and stemmed as necessary, including escarole, chicory, dandelion and turnip greens, broccoli rabe

Freshly grated Parmigiano-Reggiano cheese

# Sicilian Stuffed Skewered Pork Rolls

## INVOLTINI DI MAIALE

I like this recipe not just because it's delicious, which it is, but because it's a nice illustration of how Mediterranean cooks use cured pork to boost flavor. It's adapted from a favorite dish of Sicilian culinary expert Anna Tasca Lanza. At Regaleali, the huge Tasca wine estate in central Sicily, the *involtini* rolls are skewered on a kind of double skewer, like a very long, two-tined fork. I have never seen these for sale in North America, but if I should find them, I'd buy them in a New York minute because they are incredibly useful. If you don't have double skewers, you'll need four normal flat skewers to make these.

Do not, under any circumstances, remove the fat from the prosciutto as it is the most flavorful part and also lends moisture to the *involtini*.

**Makes 4 servings**

1 pound pork loin, very thinly sliced (at least 8 slices)

8 thin slices prosciutto, or 1 slice for each slice of meat

Extra-virgin olive oil

¾ cup fine dry bread crumbs

2 tablespoons finely minced salami, preferably Genovese or Napoletano

2 tablespoons currants, soaked for 15 minutes in warm water to plump

1 tablespoon pine nuts

2 tablespoons grated caciocavallo or Parmigiano-Reggiano cheese

2 medium yellow onions, 1 minced and 1 cut into chunks

Sea salt and freshly ground black pepper

8 bay leaves, preferably fresh

THE PORK LOIN SLICES must be pounded to make them thinner. Place each slice between two sheets of waxed paper or plastic wrap and use a meat mallet, a rolling pin, or an unopened wine bottle to tap gently all over the slice of meat. Don't pound too hard or the meat may shred. The idea is to extend each meat slice by gently pounding and to make it as thin as possible without tearing holes in it. Once all the meat slices are pounded, lay them out on a work surface and set a slice of prosciutto over each one.

IN A SMALL SKILLET, combine 1 tablespoon of the oil and the bread crumbs and gently toast the crumbs over medium-low heat, stirring occasionally and taking care not to burn them. When the crumbs are golden, remove from the heat and stir in the salami. Drain the currants and add to the bread crumb mixture, along with the pine nuts, cheese, minced onion, and salt and pepper to taste.

PREHEAT THE OVEN broiler or light the charcoal grill.

PUT A TABLESPOON or so of filling on one end of a meat slice and roll it over once, then tuck in the sides and continue to roll, so that the filling is concealed inside the rolls and won't spill out while cooking. Using two skewers spaced about 2 inches apart, double-skewer all the rolls—that is, run a skewer through each end of an *involtino*, then push down a bay leaf and/or a piece of onion onto each skewer and continue with the next *involtino*. If your skewers are long enough, you should be able to fit all the involtini on one double set, alternating each involtino with bay leaves and/or a piece of onion, but it may be easier to handle this with two sets of skewers.

BRUSH THE SKEWERED ROLLS with olive oil on both sides and either broil or grill, 7 to 10 minutes to a side, turning once and brushing again with olive oil. The rolls should be spaced a good 6 inches from the heat source so that they cook and brown gently without burning.

WHEN DONE, remove the rolls from the skewers and serve immediately, while still hot.

NOTE: The *involtini* could also be sautéed in a couple of tablespoons of olive oil in a pan set over medium heat.

# Tuscan Roasted Pork Loin with Wild Fennel Pollen

When I first published a recipe for pork roasted with wild fennel pollen a few years ago, I had to suggest crushed fennel seeds as a substitute, since the pollen was unavailable in North America, except to die-hard foodies in California where fennel grows wild along the roadsides. The mustard-colored wild fennel blossoms must be gathered at their moment of maturity, just before they start to fade, and set in a brown paper bag to dry and release their pollen. Now, however, enterprising importers like Zingerman's Deli in Ann Arbor and Formaggio Kitchen in Cambridge, Massachusetts, are bringing in Tuscan pollen with which to give a pork roast that authentic Tuscan flavor (see Where to Find It, page 415).

P.S. If you go to Tuscany in the late summer or autumn, ask for *polline di finocchio* (POH-lee-nay dee fi-NOH-kyo) in country markets. It's perfectly legal to bring some back with you.

A good butcher, if informed ahead of time, should be able to provide a pork loin with the rind or crackling attached.

**Makes 8 to 10 servings**

1 (4-pound) center-cut boneless pork loin, preferably with the rind still attached

3 garlic cloves, chopped

1 tablespoon sea salt

Freshly ground black pepper

1 tablespoon wild fennel pollen, or 1½ tablespoons fennel seeds, ground in a spice mill to make 1 tablespoon

4 to 5 bay leaves, coarsely chopped

2 (4-inch) sprigs fresh rosemary

1 cup dry white wine

LAY THE PORK LOIN out on a work surface, fat side down. Combine the garlic, salt, pepper, pollen, bay leaves, and rosemary and chop to a fine mince. Moisten the mince with a tablespoon or two of the wine to make a coarse paste and rub the exposed pork meat with most of the paste, reserving a few tablespoons to rub on the outside. Roll the meat so that the flesh part is tucked inside and tie with butcher's twine every inch or so. Rub the outside surface with the remaining aromatic paste. Set the roast aside to absorb the flavors while you preheat the oven. (The roast may be prepared ahead of time and left for several hours or, refrigerated, overnight before cooking.)

WHEN YOU ARE READY TO COOK, preheat the oven to 450°F.

SET THE PORK ON A RACK in a roasting pan. Roast for 15 minutes, then baste with half the wine. Baste again after another 15 minutes. Turn the heat down to 350°F. Continue basting every 15 to 20 minutes, using the pan juices and adding a little water to the pan if necessary, until the pork is done. After the first hour, lower the oven heat to 300°F. The pork should be done in 2 hours, or when it has reached an internal temperature of 145°F.

REMOVE THE ROAST from the oven and set aside to rest for about 20 minutes. Cut off the butcher's twine and, if you have a roast with a good brown crackling, score the crackling with diagonal lines before serving.

MEANWHILE, transfer the pan juices to a small saucepan and let rest, then skim the fat off the top. Boil down the remaining juices, if necessary, to make about ½ cup of thick sauce.

THE PORK MAY BE SERVED, thinly sliced, with the sauce as a garnish, but it is even better left to cool down to room temperature or slightly warmer, when it is easier to slice thinly. It is also absolutely delicious cold.

# Basque Pork Ribs in Adobo with Potatoes and Green Peppers

Anthropologist Susan Freeman has spent much of her career observing and writing about the foodways of country people in northern Spain. I have adapted this recipe from one she brought back from a *matanza,* or pig slaughter, in the mountainous regions south of Bilbao. The garlic-and-pepper rub is the initial step in preparing a confit of pork, to be dried, roasted, and covered with lard for the winter. But it makes a fragrant stew when prepared simply with fresh pork, as in the recipe below.

If you wish to use regular pork ribs, rather than the meaty ones called country-style, you will require 4 pounds; ask the butcher to chine the bones so they will be easy to separate one from the other. If using country-style ribs, have the butcher chop them into smaller pieces—three pieces from each rib.

I prefer yellow-fleshed potatoes, such as Yukon gold, which hold up well to long cooking, but one or two russet potatoes, included in the total, will dissolve and nicely thicken the stew.

Pure pork lard, untreated with stabilizing chemicals, is the most authentic fat in which to sauté the meat, but it is very hard to find. You can substitute extra-virgin olive oil.

DRY THE MEAT well with paper towels. Crush the garlic cloves to a paste with the salt in a mortar. (You may also do this in a large bowl, using the back of a spoon to crush the garlic cloves into the salt.) Add the black pepper and oregano and continue working in the mortar or with a spoon until you have a smooth paste. Work in the wine. Rub this mixture all over the surface of the meat pieces and set aside to marinate overnight in the refrigerator.

REMOVE THE MEAT PIECES from the bowl and gently pat dry with paper towels. Heat the lard in a heavy saucepan over medium-high heat and brown the ribs on all sides. When the ribs are thoroughly brown, add boiling water just to cover them. When the water has returned to a simmer, lower heat to medium low, cover the pan, and simmer gently for 15 minutes. Then add the potatoes, onions, green peppers, and bay leaves. Bring the stew back to a simmer, lower heat to low, cover again, and simmer gently for 30 to 45 minutes, until the potatoes are very tender.

SERVE THE STEW IMMEDIATELY, or set it aside and reheat for later service. If the stew is too liquid for your taste (it should be rather soupy), remove the lid and boil rapidly until it has reached the right consistency.

**Makes 8 servings**

3 pounds partially boned country-style pork ribs, each cut into three pieces

1 head of garlic, the cloves peeled and crushed with the flat blade of a knife

4 tablespoons sea salt

1 teaspoon freshly ground black pepper

1 tablespoon crumbled dried oregano, preferably Sicilian or Greek oregano (*rígani* is best)

¼ cup dry white wine

2 tablespoons pure pork lard or extra-virgin olive oil

Boiling water

1½ pounds potatoes (see headnote), peeled and thickly sliced or cut into chunks

1 large or 2 medium yellow onions, coarsely chopped

2 large sweet green peppers, stemmed, cored, and coarsely chopped

2 bay leaves

# Cypriote Braised Pork with Coriander

**AFELIA**

A particularly fragrant variety of coriander is grown on the island of Cyprus and used widely in local cooking. Local red wines tend to be big, full-flavored, and on the sweet side, so keep that in mind when selecting a wine for this dish.

**Makes 6 servings**

2 pounds boneless lean pork, cut into stewing pieces

2 cups dry red wine

2 tablespoons coriander seeds

1 (3-inch) cinnamon stick, snapped in two

¼ cup extra-virgin olive oil

24 small white onions

3 bay leaves

Sea salt and freshly ground black pepper

COMBINE THE PORK PIECES with the wine in a bowl. Crush the coriander seeds in a mortar to release their flavor (don't use already ground coriander) and add them to the pork, along with the cinnamon pieces. Mix the meat with the spices, cover the bowl, and set aside to marinate for several hours in a cool place or the refrigerator.

WHEN YOU ARE READY TO COOK, remove the pork pieces from the marinade and dry them well with paper towels. Reserve the marinade. In a heavy pot or saucepan large enough to hold all the pork with the onions, heat the olive oil over medium-high heat. Add a single layer of pork pieces and brown on all sides, removing the pieces as they brown. When all the pork is well-browned, add the onions. Continue to brown the onions, stirring to make sure they brown evenly on all sides.

RETURN THE PIECES OF MEAT to the pot with the onions. Pour the reserved marinade over the meat and bring to a simmer. Add the bay leaves, along with a little salt and a lot of black pepper. Turn the heat to low, cover the pan, and simmer very gently for 2 hours or more, until the meat is fork-tender and the sauce is thick and syrupy. If the sauce is still too liquid when the pork is done, remove the meat and onions and rapidly boil down the sauce over high heat until it reaches the desired consistency.

# Catalan Estouffat

 Similar to the Cypriote pork stew in the previous recipe, this one, from Spain's Catalan region, has very different flavors that, to me at least, seem to hark back to a dish that might have been popular when Roman swineherds were driving pigs to market up and down the via Augustea along the Catalan coast.

If you have a source of pure pork lard, uncontaminated by preservatives, by all means use it in place of the olive oil in the recipe.

DRY THE MEAT WELL with paper towels. In a heavy saucepan or casserole, heat the lard over medium-high heat. When it is hot, add the pork and brown well on all sides. When the meat is well-browned, stir in the onions, garlic, carrots, and celery, and continue cooking for another 15 minutes, or until the vegetables start to soften.

ADD THE WINE and vinegar, along with the salt and pepper, the bay leaves, cinnamon, and the thyme. Stir to mix everything together well. Add enough stock to just cover the meat and vegetables. Lower the heat to a bare simmer, cover the pan, and simmer gently for 2 to 3 hours, until the meat is fork tender.

WHEN THE MEAT IS TENDER, remove it and set it aside. Cut the figs into quarters, discarding the tough stems, and cover them with boiling water.

TASTE THE SAUCE and adjust the seasoning. If you wish to make a slightly thicker sauce, remove about a cup and puree in a vegetable mill or food processor. Return to the pot along with the meat. Drain the fig quarters and add them to the sauce with the parsley, stirring carefully to mix everything well without breaking up the figs. Simmer for another 10 minutes. Remove the bay leaves, transfer the stew to a serving dish, and serve immediately.

**Makes 6 servings**

2 pounds boneless lean pork, cut into stewing pieces

2 tablespoons pure pork lard or extra-virgin olive oil

2 medium onions, coarsely chopped

2 whole heads of garlic, cloves peeled but left whole

2 medium carrots, coarsely chopped

1 celery stalk, coarsely chopped

1 cup dry red wine, preferably a Spanish Priorato or Rioja

2 tablespoons aged sherry vinegar

Sea salt and freshly ground black pepper

2 bay leaves

1 (3-inch) cinnamon stick

1 teaspoon chopped fresh thyme, or 1/2 teaspoon dried

About 1 cup light chicken or beef stock

8 dried figs

Boiling water

1/2 cup finely minced flat-leaf parsley

# Spanish Saffron-Meatball Soup

## SOPA DE ALBÓNDIGAS

Saffron is a characteristic seasoning in Spain so it's not surprising if it shows up in meatballs. These are often served in a plain but tasty chicken broth as a first course at dinner. If you wish, add a few saffron threads to the broth, to color it golden.

**Makes 8 servings**

1 cup torn pieces of stale bread, crusts removed

¼ cup whole milk, or more as needed

½ cup coarsely chopped onion

½ cup chopped flat-leaf parsley

1 garlic clove, smashed with the flat blade of a knife

1 pound lean ground pork

2½ grams (half a small package) saffron, crumbled (see page 413)

1 large egg

Sea salt and freshly ground black pepper

¼ cup fine dry bread crumbs (optional)

¼ cup extra-virgin olive oil

8 cups light but flavorful chicken or meat broth

1 large leek, trimmed and thinly sliced

COMBINE THE TORN BREAD and the milk in a bowl, mixing to ensure that all the bread is moistened. Set aside for 10 to 15 minutes.

MINCE TOGETHER, or process in a food processor, the onion, parsley, and garlic. Squeeze the bread dry and mix with the vegetables. Add in the meat, saffron, egg, and salt and pepper. Combine well, using your hands to knead the mixture. When shaped into a small ball, the mixture should hold together. If it is too wet, add the bread crumbs. (If, on the other hand, it's too dry, add ½ teaspoon or more of milk.) Shape the mixture into small balls no bigger than a large olive. You should have about thirty meatballs.

OVER MEDIUM HEAT, sauté the meatballs in the olive oil, browning them on all sides. Bring the chicken broth to a simmer and add the leek slices. As each meatball browns, add it to the simmering broth. When all the meatballs are done, cover the broth and let the meatballs cook at a very low simmer for another 30 minutes. Serve immediately.

**VARIATION:** Omit the milk-soaked bread. Add pinchito seasonings (see recipe, page 315) to the meat. You may need to add more bread crumbs so the mixture will hold together. Sauté the meatballs and add to the broth, as described above.

# Greek Dry-Marinated Pork Chops with Black Olives

USING A MORTAR, pound the garlic cloves with the sea salt to make a paste. Break up the bay leaves and add them to the mortar, along with the coriander seeds. Continue pounding until you have a coarse paste. Stir in the oregano and plenty of black pepper. Add 2 tablespoons of the olive oil and stir to make a thick paste.

SMEAR SOME OF THE PASTE on both sides of each pork chop and set the chops on a platter, covered with plastic wrap, to marinate for 2 to 3 hours, refrigerating the platter in warm weather.

WHEN YOU ARE READY TO COOK, preheat the oven to 325°F.

HEAT THE LARD or the remaining 2 tablespoons of olive oil in a heavy skillet over medium-high heat and brown the pork chops on both sides. As the chops finish browning, transfer them to a baking dish large enough to hold all the chops in one layer.

WHEN THE CHOPS ARE ALL BROWNED, add the wine to the skillet and bring to a boil over medium-high heat. Pour the wine over the chops in the baking dish, scatter the olives all around the sides. Bake for 20 to 30 minutes, until the chops are cooked through.

SERVE IMMEDIATELY.

VARIATION: You can also grill the chops on a charcoal grill, set about 5 inches from the source of the heat. Do not brown first in the sauté pan. The chops should be turned frequently to keep them from burning or drying out. Baste them occasionally, as they cook, with the remaining 2 tablespoons of olive oil. You will not need the white wine for the sauce, but you could scatter the black olives over the chops as a garnish before serving.

**Makes 4 servings**

2 garlic cloves, crushed with the flat blade of a knife

½ teaspoon sea salt, plus more to taste

2 bay leaves

1 teaspoon coriander seeds

½ teaspoon dried Greek oregano (*rígani*) or thyme

Freshly ground black pepper

2 tablespoons extra-virgin olive oil and 2 tablespoons pure pork lard, or ¼ cup extra-virgin olive oil

4 pork loin chops, at least ½ inch thick

½ cup dry white wine

¼ cup dry-cured black olives, pitted and coarsely chopped

# Tuscan Sausages with Beans

## SALSICCIE CON FAGIOLI

I have not included many sausage recipes in this section simply because of the difficulty of finding good fresh sausages in North American butcher shops. Even in Italian neighborhoods, the selection seems restricted to "hot" or "sweet" sausages. The hot are all too often fiery with chilies, while the sweet are bland and flavorless. This is probably because our pork is so lacking in flavor. Every now and then you find a sausage-maker who knows the subtlety of good seasoning, whether it's the fennel and light touch of garlic that goes into a Tuscan pork sausage or the nutmeg and allspice that flavors one from farther north. When you find such a creature, stock up on as many sausages as you can afford. They freeze well, and, properly wrapped, will keep for months in the freezer, affording a valuable resource. One sausage, crumbled into the sofrito of onion, garlic, and parsley, makes a robust start to a vegetable soup or tomato sauce for pasta. Several more sausages—two per serving—will make an easy and comforting meal on a cold winter night.

The most authentic beans to use in this recipe are white cannellini beans, but any kind of light-colored beans will do, including speckled borlotti beans, Maine soldier beans, and small white navy beans. I would not use red kidney beans or black beans simply because the dark color seems inappropriate to the dish.

**Makes 6 servings**

1½ cups dried beans, soaked for several hours or overnight

Water

3 tablespoons extra-virgin olive oil

3 sprigs fresh sage

2 bay leaves

3 garlic cloves, coarsely chopped

1 small dried hot red chili pepper (optional)

Sea salt

IF YOU WISH TO COOK THE BEANS in the oven, preheat it to 300°F.

DRAIN THE BEANS and transfer to a terra-cotta beanpot, if you're baking in the oven, or to a heavy saucepan, if you are cooking on top of the stove. Add enough fresh water to cover the beans by 1 inch. Set over medium-low heat (if you are using a terra cotta pot, set a Flame Tamer beneath the pot) and let the water come to a simmer while you add the oil, sage, bay leaves, garlic, and chili, if using. When the water is just beginning to simmer, cover the pot and either place in the preheated oven or let it continue to simmer, very gently, on top of the stove until the beans are done. Check from time to time and add more *boiling* water as necessary to keep the beans just covered with water. When the beans are tender (this could take as little as 40 minutes on top of the stove, or as long as 2 to 3 hours in the oven), and napped in the velvety cooking liquid, remove them from the heat and add a little salt, keeping in mind that the sausages may be quite salty, and black pepper. If you can, remove and discard the bay leaves and sprigs of sage.

MEANWHILE, either grill the sausages over charcoal, turning frequently until they are done all the way through, or put the sausages in a heavy frying pan in which they will all fit in one layer (or do this in two batches) and add water to the pan to a depth of about ½ inch. Set over medium-high heat and cook the sausages, turning occasionally, until the water has evaporated away. If the sausages have not released enough fat to continue cooking them, add 2 tablespoons of extra-virgin olive oil to the pan, lower the heat to low, and sauté the sausages until they are brown on all sides. Test for doneness by cutting open a sausage in the middle. There should be no pink rawness in the center.

TRANSFER THE BEANS to a deep serving platter, sprinkle with chopped parsley, and line the platter with the sausages. Serve immediately.

Freshly ground black pepper

12 small fresh pork sausages

Chopped flat-leaf parsley, for garnish

# Oven-Baked Rice, with Tomatoes, Peppers, and Pork

A dish of baked rice with pork comes, in slightly different forms, from both ends of the Mediterranean, the Spanish end where pork with rice and peppers is a favorite of the Basques, and the Black Sea end where Bulgarian cooks make something very similar. In both, lard is the cooking medium, as it often is with people for whom the pig is almost a sacred animal, and dried red chili pepper is the flavoring of choice. If you can find lard, by all means use it. Otherwise, substitute extra-virgin olive oil. For the peppers, use Basque *piment d'Espelette* or Middle Eastern dried red peppers from Aleppo or eastern Turkey.

**Makes 6 servings**

2 pounds boneless lean pork, cut into stewing pieces

2 tablespoons pure pork lard or extra-virgin olive oil, plus a little more to oil the top of the casserole

2 medium yellow onions, coarsely chopped

1 tablespoon ground red Middle Eastern pepper (Aleppo pepper, Turkish pepper) or *piment d'Espelette*

Water

2 fresh sweet red peppers

1½ cups long-grain rice

3 to 4 ounces chorizo sausage, coarsely chopped

4 medium firm, ripe tomatoes, peeled, seeded, and sliced

¼ cup minced fresh flat-leaf parsley

PAT THE MEAT DRY with paper towels. In a heavy casserole, one that can go in the oven later, brown the meat in lard or oil over medium heat, turning to make sure the meat is well-browned on all sides. Add the onion and continue cooking, stirring frequently, until the onion begins to brown, about 15 minutes.

AWAY FROM THE HEAT, stir in the ground pepper along with enough water to cover all the pieces of meat. Cover and simmer gently until the meat is tender, about 1 hour. While the meat cooks, cut up the fresh peppers, discarding the seeds, tops, and inner membranes. Chop the peppers very coarsely, in large pieces.

PREHEAT THE OVEN to 350°F.

WHEN THE MEAT IS TENDER, stir in the peppers, rice, and chorizo, adding boiling water if the liquid in the pan has boiled away (there should always be enough liquid to cover the pieces of meat). Cover and cook for about 10 minutes on top of the stove over medium heat, again adding a little boiling water if it seems necessary. Cover the rice with slices of tomato, dribble a few spoonsful of olive oil over the top, and transfer the casserole, uncovered, to the oven. Let bake for 30 minutes.

WHEN DONE, the rice will be tender and most of the liquid will have been absorbed. Remove from the oven, sprinkle with parsley, and let sit, covered, for 10 minutes before serving.

# The Sea

## A LIMITED RESOURCE

AT THE EXTREME southwestern tip of the island of Sardegna, Portoscuso is as picturesque a little village as any photographer in search of postcard views could imagine. The name of the town means something like "hidden port" or "enclosed port" or even, being a little more fanciful with the local dialect, "safe harbor." It is that indeed, as evidenced by the multitude of boats, both sailing yachts and motor launches, that line the docks and marinas within the harbor mole. Not too long ago, it was also a locally important fishing port, but today just eight fishing boats call Portoscuso home, all that remain of what was once a much larger fleet.

Larger in numbers of boats, that is, but not in the size of the vessels. Fabrizio Cherchi, a stout and pleasantly thoughtful young man dressed in bright yellow rubber overalls, is one of the last Portoscuso fishermen. His open wooden boat, painted blue and spanking white, with a long wooden steering shaft connected to the rudder and a small engine house amidships into which he can duck in rough weather, is typical of what the Portoscuso fishing fleet was (and is) made up of. Not built for stormy seas or long-distance journeys, boats like these are the archetypal Mediterranean fishing vessel, the kind that romantic writers like me like to think go back to Homeric times, if not even earlier. And, in a sense, they probably do.

I had been sent to Fabrizio by the owner of a tiny hotel and restaurant right on the beach in Portoscuso, a man who sympathized with my interest in traditional ways of harvesting the sea. Like almost every other Sardinian I met on the island, the owner had said to me, "*Più pastori che pescatori*" (We Sardinians are more shepherds than we are fishermen, and our cuisine shows it.) As he said this, he set before me a handsome plate of arselle con fregola, the local couscous-like pasta in a soupy sauce of deliciously meaty, sweet, and salty clams that reminded me more than anything else of miniature cherrystones (see recipe, page 350). "I have some beautiful little *triglie da scoglio* for your next course," he added. "Grilled red mullet from right off the coast." Shepherds, indeed!

Actually, when they say that, Sardinians are only reflecting the reality of the Mediterranean. This sea, so beloved of poets, painters, and myth-makers, so color-drenched, so intensely saturated with a heart-stopping clarity of light, so elemental to any understanding of Mediterranean culture or history, this sea has never been kind to those who live around it. Treacherous by its very nature, the Mediterranean batters coastlines in winter, while in summer the blackest of storms often seem to brew up suddenly out of the most pristine afternoon skies. Moreover, the sea has always been the route most favored by pirates, robbers, marauders, armies, and invading hordes. Christian coastal towns feared Turks and Saracens, while Turks and Arabs feared Christian crusaders, Albanians fear Serbs, Sicilians fear Tunisian pirates, Lebanese fear Israelis, and vice versa down the ages. Back in the twelfth century B.C.E., Trojans trembled at the threat of the Greeks whose boats were drawn up on the shores of the Dardanelles very near where British and Anzac troops, little but marauders in the eyes of their Turkish enemies, were annihilated at Gallipoli in 1914.

Of course, throughout history the sea has not been entirely the carrier of bad news, danger, enemies. For millennia, it was also a well-traveled highway that brought goods, people, and new ideas from one end of the Mediterranean to the other. Still, circumnavigating the Inner Sea, a traveler quickly recognizes that the old towns are the ones set back from the shore, usually on a hilltop surrounded by stout walls from which the community can be defended. Down at the water's edge is where you find the fishing ports—picturesque, yes, but strictly utilitarian until the most recent, and some would say most insidious, invasion, that of the tourists whose numbers, beginning in force after World War II, have expanded geometrically with each passing season since.

So it's no wonder if Sardinians for the most part turned their backs to the sea and followed their flocks up into the mountains. Still, the sea provides sustenance, and on an island where food has not always been abundant, every resource must be tapped. Like similar communities all around the Mediterranean, Portoscuso sends out its little fleet of boats each morning, and if the size of the fleet has diminished over the years, the fact is that fishermen like Fabrizio Cherchi still represent something important in their communities, not just a source of things to eat but an identity around which the community itself has coalesced.

Fabrizio works closely with his *marinaio,* a word that translates as "sailor" but that I take to mean his sternman, a lean and mustachioed factory worker named Giancarlo. With Fabrizio at the helm, it takes them about 40 minutes to get out to the position in the broad, shallow channel between the mainland of Sardinia and the small island of San Pietro where they stretch their gill nets. They spend an hour or more, hauling nets that were set the day before and carefully removing anything that seems to promise a profit, rejecting a number of fish that are too small, too bony, too nasty, or otherwise undesirable. Then they stretch their nets again, sometimes adjusting the position a little, but basically maintaining their own well-established turf. Together with the return trip to port, their expedition lasts no more than three or four hours a day, after which Fabrizio spends a few more hours cleaning his fish for sale and tidying the boat, while Gianfranco goes off to his shift at the chemical plant whose bulk looms over the sunny little port like a cloud of doom on the horizon.

It was a brilliant morning late in June when I went out fishing with Fabrizio and Giancarlo, the sun warm, the air crisp and clear with a thin, cool edge that countered the sun's strength. Beyond the last marina at the rim of the harbor, they pointed out to me an abandoned *tonnara,* a factory at the water's edge where in the old days giant bluefin tuna were brought in for processing, salting, and canning. You come across these derelict *tonnare,* solidly built of brick or local stone, in many parts of the Mediterranean, but especially here in the western basin of the Inner Sea. I've seen several along the west coast of Sicily (at least one of them converted into a time-share condominium), and I've been told of others along the east coast of Spain and in Tunisia.

Very few *tonnare* are still functional largely because the nature of the fishery has changed, with smaller catches of ever smaller and younger fish. The prized tuna were once harvested by means of a long series of net traps, called an *almadraba* in Spanish. In an *almadraba* (the word, like many associated with this kind of fishing, is Arabic in origin), the fish are moved gradually through a succession of traps that decrease in size. Finally, when enough tuna have accumulated, the last trap is hauled like a purse seine, constricting the fish even further, and in a bloody ritual called in Italian *la mattanza* (the slaughter), the panicking fish either kill each other in their fright or are harpooned by gangs of fishermen working together.

On the island of Favignana off the west coast of Sicily, a *tonnara* still functions, but mostly as a spectacle for tourists and French television cameramen, and there's another off the Sardinian island of San Pietro, right across the channel from where we were motoring out. (In the 1999 season, I was told, the *tonnara* off San Pietro caught more than two thousand fish, most of them weighing a good deal less than 200 pounds. A mature bluefin ought to weigh up to 1,500 pounds.) I've been told that tuna are still harvested in the traditional manner at Zahara de los Atunes (appropriate name) near Barbate on the Spanish coast just outside the Straits of Gibraltar, but I was also told that Barbate is dead as far as fishing is concerned. It turns out both statements are correct—Barbate has been dying since Morocco banned Spanish fishing vessels from the rich resource in the Moroccan Atlantic, but tuna fishing still takes place off Zahara, the teams of fishermen coming in from nearby communities during the season for the harvest.

The Mediterranean tuna harvest is ancient, going back at least to the Phoenicians who headed west out of Lebanon at the beginning of the first millennium B.C.E., looking for tuna and salt. For as long as the bluefin tuna have coursed the North Atlantic, they have come into the warmer, more saline waters of the Mediterranean (and of the Gulf of Mexico on the other side) each year to spawn. The Phoenicians must have known that—or they knew the Mediterranean part at least—although subsequent generations forgot. As late as 1972, when Alan Davidson published his encyclopedic *Mediterranean Seafood*, still the most useful book on the subject, many authorities, Davidson among them, believed on the evidence that there was a more or less static population of Mediterranean bluefin tuna, that is, fish that never left the Inner Sea. More recent investigation has shown that to be incorrect.

When Davidson's book was published, there were, he says, about a hundred tuna fisheries left in the Mediterranean, most of them in Sicily and Spain, but also in other parts of Italy, Yugoslavia, Greece, Turkey, Libya, Tunisia, Algeria, and Morocco. Today, 30 years later, there are very few left.

But if the *tonnare* are declining, so are the fish—by some 80 percent over the last two decades, according to sources like the Worldwide Fund for Nature and the National Marine Fisheries Service. To put that figure in perspective, imagine this: You are the mayor of a smallish, Midwestern city with a population of 100,000. You do such a good job that you stay in office for twenty years. At the end of that time, your city has a population of 20,000.

Wouldn't you begin to wonder what was going on?

In fairness, the blame for this decline cannot be laid to the fishermen of San Pietro, Favignana, Barbate, or any other place where traditional fishing methods continue. They are merely continuing age-old practices that, even in the days when the fish were huge and their populations high, sustained rather than destroyed the resource. No, the blame for the decline goes to the long-liners and factory ships that patrol the North Atlantic with ruthless intent, eager to harvest, cut, ice, and dispatch tuna by air to feed a voracious Japanese market where, I was told, fresh bluefin tuna of the finest sushi grade commands $80,000 or more a fish—the figures vary from one season to the next, but the impact has been spectacular.

Tuna is not what Fabrizio and Giancarlo were after, however, and they lacked the equipment to harvest one even if it should happen to bump into their nets. The morning I went out with them, their catch was unimpressive—a few *daurades,* some small red mullet (but smaller is better as far as mullet are concerned), and a greater number of unidentifiable fish that would go into *sa cassòla,* the splendid seafood stew characteristic of Sardinian kitchens (see recipe, page 358). They also caught a couple of Mediterranean lobster, the spiny kind with no claws and all its meat in the tail. That, they said, was because of the good luck I had brought, and they insisted on dividing the lobster catch with me.

It's hard to see how Fabrizio can make a living doing this. The cost of gas alone for the motor is about four times what it is in North America, and, although fish are pricey in Italian markets, Portoscuso is a long way from where consumers can and will pay the kind of money that would make it worthwhile. The other Portoscuso fishermen are people who inherited the job, often the boat and nets too, from their fathers, but Fabrizio doesn't even come from a fishing family. Still, he says, he has always loved the sea. It's enough for him to pursue this slow and deliberate craft, and when the yield from the sea is insufficient, he can always pick up work at the chemical plant.

The MEDITERRANEAN, although it always surprises people to hear this, is not and never has been a rich sea, especially when compared with an ocean as prodigal of fishy wealth as the North Atlantic once was. Of the 1,255 species recorded for the Northeast Atlantic and the Mediterranean, fewer than half are actually present in the Mediterranean. The reasons for this dearth have to do primarily with geography and climate, although in the last half-century the human hand has weighed heavily on the sea's fragile ecosystem. Despite its poverty of resources, though, the Mediterranean has always carried a great, at times almost a sacred, significance for the people around its shores. You can go way back in history, even to prehistory, and find images of dolphins, octopus, tuna, running borders of curling waves—drawn on the walls of caves, painted on pottery, pressed into metal coins, carved into sculptures, and molded above the peristyles of temples. And that significance continues, a tightly braided cord that marries past and present. I love the story I've been told of Greek fishermen who, to this day, are prepared for a mermaid rising from the waves who demands, "*Zi o Megalexandros?*" (Does Alexander the Great still live?) To which the wise fisherman replies, "*O Megalexandros ʒi ke vasilevi*" (Great Alexander not only lives, he still reigns!) Poor in resources, the sea is rich in cultural significance, the very emblem of Mediterranean civilization.

The reasons for the poverty of the sea are simple. This nearly enclosed body of water has what oceanographers call a negative hydrological balance, meaning that more water is lost through evaporation than is added through runoff and precipitation. Very little in the way of fresh water feeds into the Mediterranean, and the saltwater that pours in from the Atlantic over the high sill at Gibraltar is nutrient-poor surface water, not deeper Atlantic water filled with living matter. On top of that, the Mediterranean climate is dry, with not much rainfall and most of that concentrated during the winter months, while for almost two-thirds of the year, a combination of dry winds and sunshine produces evaporation. Mediterranean water is noticeably saltier than the Atlantic, and the deeper you go, the saltier it gets. Major rivers flowing into the inner sea can be counted on the fingers of one hand, from the Ebro around the northern shores to the Nile—and even the Nile, since the construction of the High Dam at Aswan in the 1960s, no longer floods the eastern Mediterranean with its annual spate of muck and silt, phosphates and silicates, on which feed the phytoplankton that provide nutrients for the bottom link in the food chain. Moreover, the Black Sea, the only other major source of fresh water in the eastern Mediterranean, has suffered a sudden, recent, and catastrophic degradation, its entire ecosystem in a state of collapse, with unknown implications for the future of the Mediterranean.

The lack of fresh water is what makes the Mediterranean so poor in nutrients. This was brought home to me several years ago when I was diving from the deck of a Turkish *gulet,* a beamy old Eastern Mediterranean transport vessel retrofitted for the tourist trade, off the southern Turkish coast—called the Turquoise Coast because of the transparent aquamarine color of the sea. The clarity of the waters was stunning, redefining the word *crystalline,* like looking through one of those lenses that sharpens outlines and accentuates details. When I stopped to rest and tread water, I could see, far below my paddling feet, sunlight dappling the smoothly rounded white and grey stones of the bottom, with a few—a very few—sea grasses waving their fronds. It was in these waters of the Eastern Basin that a world record for a Secchi disk was set at 53 meters.* Water this clear and clean is as devoid of nutrients as a vast bathtub—beautiful for swimming, but for fishing not so great.

But at least the water off the Turquoise Coast is clean, which cannot be said for many other parts of the Mediterranean. The Adriatic, the long, narrow channel that trends northwest along the Italian peninsula, is a sorry example of the environmental degradation to which the Mediterranean is subject. Heavy industrial pollution around Venice, factory effluent and agricultural run-off from the Po Valley, overdevelopment of tourist infrastructure all down the Italian coastline, and over-exploitation of the resource, with ever more sophisticated and rapacious fishing gear going after an ever-diminishing population of fish, are all part of the problem. And because the Mediterranean is not subject to the strong tides of a big sea like the Atlantic, what goes into the water tends to stay there, whether it's factory waste or plastic water bottles, and not get washed out. (A complete change of Mediterranean water takes more than 100 years.) Sadly, the northern Adriatic, once proud bastion of the Venetian Republic, has been declared a "lost zone" by the Worldwide Fund for Nature/World Wildlife Fund, meaning it is so degraded that there is almost no hope of recovery.

The biggest problem for the Mediterranean as a region, as much as for the sea itself, is tourism, which is also in most of the region a major source of income. The

---

*A Secchi disk is a white plastic disk used to measure water clarity; the disk is lowered in the water and the depth at which it disappears is noted. Fifty-three meters is about 159 feet.

Mediterranean is the Number One tourist destination in the world. In some especially popular coastal environments, like much of Mediterranean Spain, along with Aegean Turkey and many of the Greek islands, local populations quadruple during July and August. Tourism brings with it rapid urbanization and population growth, as service infrastructures—hotels, roads, airports, marinas—move in to take advantage of the tourists. The Catch-22 of tourism, of course, in the Mediterranean as elsewhere in the world, is that once this infrastructure takes over, it undermines all the aesthetic reasons why tourists came in the first place.

Another major impact with a long-range effect has been almost invisible to all except marine biologists who know where to look. All over the Mediterranean, at the edge of the shoreline, sometimes in a narrow fringe and sometimes extending out for miles, are underwater meadows of seagrasses, called *Posidonia*, after the Greek god who was the protector of the sea. These meadows constitute the most important and the most characteristic marine ecosystem of the Mediterranean, the nursery for an astounding 80 percent of the annual yield of fish in the Inner Sea. They play a vital role in stabilizing the shore itself and in maintaining water quality. And when the heavy earth-moving equipment comes in to build up the runways and the marinas and the seaside swimming pools and the hotels and apartment blocks and nightclubs and restaurants and postcard and T-shirt shops (*"Maman s'est allée a San Tropez et m'a porté seulement cette misérable T!"*)—the first to go are the seagrass meadows.

F OR ALL THE PAUCITY OF FISH in the Mediterranean, seafood in some form is very often part of a Mediterranean feast, whether a humble salt cod at the center of a Provençale *grand aïoli*, or the splendor of lobster and prawns on the banquet table at an aristocratic wedding. It has not always been thus. Fish, especially among Christians, was linked to Lent and fasting, a food of deprivation. Salt fish, especially, was despised as the food of the poor. How many legends exist in how many communities, from Syria to Spain (even to Ireland!) of the family salt fish (herring, sardine, anchovy, cod) that hung from a string over the family table. You took a spoonful of polenta or porridge, passed it beneath the hanging salted protein to absorb what it could of the flavor, then consumed it. Or, in another version, the fish was immersed in the family cauldron just long enough to flavor it, then removed, rinsed, and dried, and put aside for the next meal. Whole generations are said to have been nurtured thus.

Today, however, seafood—even salt cod—is as fashionable, as much in demand, as ever it was in Athens in the fifth century B.C.E. In a witty study of food and banquets in classical times, James Davidson shows how, in a society where the only meat consumed was what had first been sacrificed on a temple altar, eating seafood had a kind of rebellious, countercultural chic. When fish is in short supply, as it is nowadays, it becomes all the more fashionable—supply goes down, cost goes up, and seafood becomes precious. The perfect food for post-modern sensibilities, it's light, white, and expensive, its simplicity of presentation belying the skill required to prepare it well.

The Spanish are widely reputed to be the best seafood cooks in the entire Mediterranean. The Spanish passion for fish goes back a long way: In medieval times, Madrid chef Norberto Jorge told me, there were *pozos de nieve*, ice-filled wells, some ten meters across and very deep, positioned across the land, so that, as fish was transported from the coast to the interior of the country, ice could be bought to keep it fresh along the way. The Spanish still insist on that quality and freshness. Once when I was dining in Córdoba on an impeccable *lubina*, a sea bass, I reached for a lemon wedge only to have my host slap my hand: "No!" he commanded, "*never* lemon on fresh fish—lemon is for *old* fish!"

Turks and Greeks are also champion fish cooks, though they have to be reined in from overcooking it. But everywhere, throughout the Mediterranean, there are dishes and techniques that are common to the whole. Just look at the ubiquitous Mediterranean seafood stew, found along every coastline from Málaga to Marseilles, from Genova to Istanbul to Beirut and back again along the North African littoral. It could be *kakavia*, made with copious amounts of olive oil and a generous squeeze of lemon juice on a Greek island, a Sardinian *cassola* with tomatoes and hot peppers, or a zarzuela from Spain's Mediterranean coast, thickened with a *picada* or romesco sauce of pounded almonds and hazelnuts. No matter its name, the stew will be based on a host of small bony fish, eels, crabs, and mollusks too little to bother with, leftovers from the catch of the day, boiled together in a cauldron with olive oil, plenty of garlic, and all the resinous aromatics of the Mediterranean maquis, the scrubland that hovers over these rocky fishing ports.

As it happens, the best seafood cook I know is Sicilian. Gianfranco Becchina spends part of his life as a Basel-based dealer in the rarest of antiquities for some of the world's most important museums and collectors; for the other part, the more interesting part for me, he raises olives and makes a lush green oil called Olio Verde in his home town of Castelvetrano in the Bellice Valley near the south coast of

Sicily, where he also entertains a steady stream of visitors with his own incomparable cooking. Villa Becchina, painted a deep Pompeian rose, sits amid groves of nocellara olives and fragrant lemons; the deep portico along the house front, where we dine in summer, faces the twin pools of an Egyptian water garden with waving fronds of papyrus, yellow lotus blossoms, and the frogs and waterfowl that Ancient Egyptians loved. "We'll have fish for dinner," Gianfranco announces and off we go in the early morning to the fish market in Mazara del Vallo, just along the coast from Castelvetrano.

Italy's largest fishing port, Mazara del Vallo, is actually much closer to Tunis than it is to either Rome or Naples. And the town feels like North Africa, with its flat-roofed houses, narrow, winding streets as in a medina, palm trees that clack their branches in the hot sirocco that blows up from the Saraha. According to a recent survey, 340 vessels (and some 1,600 regular fishermen) call this port home. Only 40 of them go beyond 40 miles to fish (and 15 of those leave the Mediterranean entirely and go down the Atlantic coast of West Africa); a little more than half the vessels fish between 20 and 40 miles out, while 133 are strictly coastal. The coastal fishing boats practice what more and more is being referred to approvingly as artisanal fishing, meaning fishing that has less environmental impact and concentrates more on feeding local consumers, including tourists, and less on feeding the residents of downtown Tokyo.

Mazara's fish market, right across from the principal dock where the fishing boats tie up, is a big white-tiled space lined with vendors overseeing their stalls, a spectacle of briny splendor. "Smell!" Gianfranco commands, stopping at the door and inhaling deeply. "Nothing nasty here—it's all fresh-fresh-fresh!"

And he's right—the air is clean, brackish but not fishy, and the cement floor is hosed down with a constant flow of water. Gianfranco is a familiar of this place. Vendors call out to him, "*Aaoo, Gianfranco, vieni qua!*" and hold up a section of pearlescent monkfish or a huge grouper with its pink scales like an armor of giant sequins. They open oysters and clams for us to sample on the spot, dandle a plump red mullet under our noses, invite us to smell, taste, poke at the flesh, examine the scarlet gills and the prawns still throbbing with life.

Gianfranco, generous to a fault, always buys way too much food. Once I wanted a chunk of bottarga, the wildly expensive salted tuna roe that's a great delicacy in this part of the world, and he insisted on buying me an entire block of the stuff. If I admire the tiny pink shrimp, he buys a kilo—no, two—in addition to everything else we have in the market basket. The day we bought the shrimp, we also went home with tiny clams called *vongole verace,* fresh tuna roe, a magnificent wild sea bass (*spigola* in Italian), a styrofoam case full of fat portugaise oysters, and several dozen tiny red mullet (*triglie*) not more than six inches long. That night we had bowls of *vongole verace* steamed with a little white wine, garlic, and parsley as an appetizer, followed by a salad of the shrimp, just barely poached and tossed in Gianfranco's olive oil with crisp, spicy *rughetta* (arugula), then linguine with a sauce made from the fresh tuna roe, and finally that magnificent wild sea bass, roasted whole in the oven (page 352).

The next morning when I came downstairs, I found Gianfranco in the kitchen, opening oysters at the kitchen sink. We started all over again, at a table under the jasmine vines on the verandah with a breakfast feast (I couldn't call it brunch) of fresh raw oysters and the tiny *triglie* we had not had room for the night before, plainly roasted with a dribble of olive oil in a hot, hot oven. Everything was pure, almost austere, but delicious—this, I thought, was exactly the way those old Athenians feasted in their countercultural bliss.

## 14 GREAT RECIPES USING SEAFOOD

Seafood Salad with a Green Sauce
    *Insalata di Mare con Salsa Verde*

Tuna or Swordfish Carpaccio
    *Carpaccio di Tonno o di Pesce Spada*

Provençale Mussel-Saffron Soup
    *Soupe aux Moules*

Sardinian Clam Soup with Fregola Pasta
    *Zuppa di Arselle con Fregola*

Oven-Roasted Sea Bass or Snapper

Oven-Braised Bluefin Tuna
    *Tonno Arrosto*

Tuna with Tomatoes and Black Olives
    *Tonno in Umido*

Spiced Herb Marinade for Fish
    *Chermoula*

Franco Crivello's Tuna Fishballs with Fresh Herbs and Tomato Sauce
    *Polpettine di Tonno*

Sardinian Seafood Stew
*Sa Cassòla*

Provençale Seafood Stew
*Soupe des Pêcheurs*

Stuffed Squid
*Seppie Ripiene*

Baked Swordfish Rolls with an Orange Sauce
*Involtini di Pesce Spada*

Fried Fish in a Sweet-Sour Marinade
*Escabeche*


## COOK'S NOTES

Many otherwise fine cooks resist fish because it's rumored to be difficult. Actually nothing could be further from the truth. It is a fact that any seafood must be watched carefully to make sure it's not overcooked, but since most of it cooks in a matter of minutes rather than hours, it commands the cook's devoted attention for a short period of time.

North American cooks seldom have the luxury of choice available in the Mazara del Vallo market. In many parts of the country, it's almost impossible to find a whole fish, with its head and tail on—which any fish cook will tell you is the best way to prepare it to retain the flavor—unless it's a farmed salmon. Old-fashioned cookbooks always tell you to "cultivate your fishmonger" and that's still good advice, even in these days when most of us are lucky if the local supermarket carries fresh fish at all. Fortunately, when it exists, the supermarket seafood section is one of the last places in the supermarket where individuals are still in charge, still serve customers themselves, and still know something about what they're offering, even if it's just the answer to whether or not the seafood is fresh or in that enigmatic state called "fresh-frozen" (believe me, if the fish ain't fresh when it's frozen, I don't want to know about it!). So the wise consumer can indeed "cultivate the fishmonger" by buying frequently, asking intelligent questions, and being very firm about the quality one is seeking.

The first tool necessary for selecting fish is a good nose. If it doesn't smell right, it *isn't* right and no amount of saucing will *make* it right. The eyes, the books say, should be bright, not cloudy, and the gills should be rosy—not useful advice when you're confronting a swordfish steak. Flesh that looks yellowed or dry, flesh that is parting along the flakes, flesh that lacks the pearly moistness of fresh fish—all should be rejected.

Actually, the situation is much better than it was even ten years ago: As more consumers have heard the message that fish is good for you, as high-speed transportation has become cheaper and more efficient, as sustainable methods of raising farmed species (salmon, sea bass, Arctic char) have been adopted, fish has become more plentiful and in greater variety than ever. One thing the cook should always keep in mind is the acceptability, even the advisability, of substitutions. There is no hard and fast rule about this except that in general, oily fish should be substituted for oily fish, and lean white-meat fish for the same. I have tried to suggest substitutions in the recipes that follow, but cooks should use their own good sense in proceeding. I wouldn't, for instance, substitute chunks of cod for chunks of swordfish to be skewered and grilled—the cod would simply fall off the skewers as it cooks. But substituting tuna or thick steaks of halibut for the swordfish is perfectly acceptable and makes an interesting variation on the recipe.

In general, it seems to me, the greatest mistake we make as fish cooks is overcooking. Unfortunately, it's very easy to do. Years ago we were taught to observe the "Canadian rule," which called for cooking a fish for 10 minutes per inch of thickness, measured at the thickest part. But even at the thickest part, that is often way too much. To be on the safe side, measure the fish at the thickest part and cook it for *five* minutes per inch. Remove the fish from the heat and test it for doneness—you can do this easily by gently parting the flesh to see if it's just barely opaque all the way through. If necessary, it can be cooked a little longer.

# Seafood Salad with a Green Sauce

### INSALATA DI MARE CON SALSA VERDE

A seafood salad (*salade des fruits de mer* in French) should include a variety of different fish and shellfish, although it's quite possible of course to make a salad of, say, shrimp or lobster alone.

In choosing fish, select ones with firm white flesh—snapper and halibut are both good choices; swordfish, cut in small chunks, is also good, while the pink flesh of salmon makes a nice color contrast with paler white-meat fish. Tuna? For my taste it's too assertive in flavor to be successful in a salad unless it's on its own. A *salade des fruits de mer* will have only shellfish, since that's what *fruits des mer* means—a combination might include steamed lobster and shrimp, poached scallops, and perhaps some small mussels. A few rings of squid are not out of place in a *salade des fruits de mer*.

For a main-course *insalata di mare* for six to eight people you will need a total of 3 pounds of mixed seafood, whether fish and shellfish, or either of these alone. But if you are using lobster, where so much of the carcass must be discarded, you will need 2 pounds of whole live lobster for a pound of picked-out meat.

In any case, the fish and shellfish should be gently poached or steamed, individually, since they all have slightly different cooking times. Be careful not to overcook—texture is an important consideration and you want to be sure the salad will hold up to the sauce.

As soon as each of the seafoods is done, drain it and dress it while still warm with a very small amount of extra-virgin olive oil and lemon juice. Then set it aside, covered, until you're ready to assemble the finished dish.

In selecting the ingredients to accompany the seafood, use your imagination to choose those that will complement each other in terms of flavor and add color and definition to the plate. Instead of the Green Sauce, if you wish, you can simply dress the salad with a simple vinaigrette or the Salmoriglio on page 69. Be sure to make extra in order to have sauce to pass with the salad.

GENTLY POACH OR STEAM the seafood; cook each type individually in order not to overcook any element of the salad. As each type of seafood finishes cooking, drain it and dress it while still warm with a little of the olive oil and lemon juice blended together. Set aside.

ARRANGE THE LETTUCE LEAVES on a serving platter. When all the seafood is cooked, combine it in a bowl with a selection of the other ingredients. If you are using the roasted chopped nuts or the chopped herbs, set aside a few tablespoons of each to garnish the finished dish.

SPOON A FEW TABLESPOONS of the Green Sauce over the salad in the bowl and toss gently to mix. Mound the salad on the greens, then spoon more of the sauce over the top. Garnish with the roasted nuts and/or chopped herbs, if using. Pass the rest of the sauce in a small bowl so that guests can help themselves to more.

**Makes 6 to 8 main course servings**

3 pounds (boneless, shell-less weight) mixed cooked seafood, cut in bite-sized chunks, to make 6 to 8 cups in all (see headnote)

3 to 4 tablespoons extra-virgin olive oil

1 tablespoon fresh lemon juice

1 head romaine or curly-leaf lettuce, leaves separated, rinsed, and dried

About 1¼ cups Green Sauce (recipe follows)

A selection of at least 4 and no more than 6 or 7 of the following:

  Little fresh spring onions or scallions, green and white parts, slivered

  Celery and/or bulb (Florentine) fennel cut in julienne strips

  Artichoke hearts, cut in wedges and lightly steamed

  Fresh raw sweet red or yellow peppers, or roasted peppers (see page 410), sliced in thin strips

  Green or black olives, pitted and coarsely chopped

  Rind of North African salt-preserved lemons (page 44), slivered

  Salted capers or caper berries, rinsed and added whole

  Almonds or hazelnuts, roasted (see page 412) and coarsely chopped

  Fresh green herbs in season, basil, dill, or that good soldier, flat-leaf parsley.

# Green Sauce

### SALSA VERDE

 This green sauce, by the way, is also very good with a cold roast chicken or capon.

**Makes about 1¼ cups sauce, or enough for 6 to 8 servings of salad**

6 anchovy fillets, preferably salted

¼ cup salted capers, rinsed under running water and drained

1 packed cup coarsely chopped flat-leaf parsley and basil combined (or use flat-leaf parsley alone)

2 to 3 thick slices country-style bread, crusts removed

1 tablespoon white wine vinegar

Water

Yolks of 2 hard-cooked eggs

½ cup extra-virgin olive oil, preferably Ligurian

1 clove garlic, coarsely chopped

Sea salt

PREPARE THE ANCHOVIES (see page 411).

CHOP THE ANCHOVY FILLETS into several pieces and transfer to a food processor along with the capers and herbs. Process briefly, just to mix everything together.

TEAR THE BREAD SLICES into rough crumbs—you should have enough to make 1 loose cup of torn crumbs. Add the vinegar, along with 1 to 2 tablespoons of water. Turn the crumb to dampen it thoroughly and then squeeze to get rid of any excess liquid. (If the bread is very dry, you may need to add another tablespoon of water.)

ADD TO THE FOOD PROCESSOR, along with the hard-cooked egg yolks. Process briefly. With the motor running, add the olive oil in a slow but steady stream until it has been thoroughly incorporated and the sauce is a thick green mayonnaise.

IN A SMALL BOWL, crush the garlic clove to a paste with a little sea salt, using the back of a spoon to mash the garlic into the salt. Remove the green sauce from the food processor and stir in the garlic paste, mixing well. If you're not serving the sauce right away, transfer it to a bowl, pour a little coating of oil over the top to keep the sauce from darkening, and refrigerate. When you are ready to serve, simply stir the oil into the sauce. The sauce is best when freshly made but may be refrigerated up to 3 or 4 days, if necessary.

# Tuna or Swordfish Carpaccio

## CARPACCIO DI TONNO O DI PESCE SPADA

 A fresh and refreshing summer starter, this is often served at dinner parties in southern Italy. It goes without saying (but I'll say it anyway), the fish must be impeccable—as must all the other ingredients, too.

You will need two to three very thin slices for each serving. The slices should be no more than $\frac{1}{16}$ inch thick. This is best done by freezing the fish slightly in order to firm it up before slicing—but do not freeze it into a hard block. You will do well to persuade the fishmonger to put a beautiful piece of tuna or swordfish in the freezer for just 30 minutes and then slice it with an electric slicer. If your powers of persuasion are ineffectual, freeze it yourself in the home freezer, then slice with a very sharp knife.

AN HOUR OR SO before serving, put the plates you'll be using in the refrigerator to chill thoroughly. If the tuna is a little bloody, rinse it quickly under cool running water and pat dry with paper towels.

JUST BEFORE SERVING, again pat the slices of fish dry with paper towels and arrange them on the chilled plates. Combine the lemon juice, olive oil, capers, parsley, and mint and beat well with a fork or a wire whisk to amalgamate. Taste and add a little salt and pepper if you wish. Spoon the sauce generously over the fish slices and serve immediately, passing more sauce at the table.

**Makes 8 servings**

16 to 24 thin slices very fresh sushi-grade bluefin tuna or swordfish

3 tablespoons fresh lemon juice

$\frac{1}{2}$ cup extra-virgin olive oil

1 to 2 tablespoons coarsely chopped capers—preferably salted capers that have been rinsed and drained

1 to 2 tablespoons finely minced flat-leaf parsley

1 to 2 tablespoons finely minced fresh mint

Sea salt and freshly ground black pepper

# Provençale Mussel-Saffron Soup

## SOUPE AUX MOULES

 Cultivated mussels, the kind you buy at most fishmongers', won't need the careful cleaning that makes wild mussels such a tedious chore to prepare (although, according to true mussel-lovers, the intense flavor of wild mussels makes them worth all the tedium). A quick and simple rinse under cold running water should be all that's necessary. Any beards, the tufts of blackish hairs sprouting from the shells, should be pulled off, using a small sharp paring knife, but don't do this until you're ready to cook them; once the beards have been removed, the mussels start to decline and die. Discard any dead mussels—the ones with wide gaping shells—or any that feel suspiciously heavy, as if they were full of mud, which they probably are. How to tell if a mussel is truly dead? If the shells are somewhat open and don't close up quickly in response to a rap on the side of the sink, they should be discarded.

**Makes 8 servings as a first course, 5 to 6 servings as a main dish**

About 5 pounds fresh mussels in their shells

Sea salt

1 cup dry white wine, plus more as needed

3 cups water, plus more as needed

1 medium yellow onion, finely chopped

2 bay leaves

3 sprigs fresh thyme, or ½ teaspoon crumbled dried

1 (2-inch) strip orange zest

RINSE THE MUSSELS well under running water, rubbing the shells with a little salt to rid them of any grit. Rinse all the salt off and set the mussels in a large heavy-duty soup kettle. Add the wine, water, onion, bay leaves, thyme, and orange zest. Cover the kettle and bring the liquid to a simmer over medium heat; cook, stirring occasionally, just long enough for the shells to open wide, 5 to 10 minutes. (Discard any mussels that don't open at the end of this time.)

WHILE THE MUSSELS ARE COOKING, line a colander with a double layer of cheesecloth and set it in a bowl large enough to hold all the mussel liquid. Turn the cooked mussels into the colander and set aside to drain. Once the mussels are drained, remove and discard the shells but reserve the mussels and their cooking liquid.

RINSE OUT THE SOUP KETTLE and return to the stove over medium-low heat. Add 2 tablespoons of the olive oil and the leek, garlic, and tomato and cook gently, stirring, until the vegetables have softened, about 20 minutes. Measure the cooking liquid from the mussels. You will need 6 to 8 cups. Top up the measuring cup with a mix of half white wine and half water, enough to make the necessary quantity. Add this to the vegetables in the pan and bring to a gentle simmer. Stir in the rice and saffron and cook, partially covered, until the rice is very soft and bursting open—*à crever*, it's called in French—20 to 30 minutes.

MEANWHILE, set a freshly toasted slice of bread in the bottom of each soup plate. Dribble the remaining 2 tablespoons oil over the bread slices. When you are ready to serve, stir the mussels into the soup. As soon as the mussels are hot, spoon the soup over the bread slices. Sprinkle with black pepper and parsley and serve, accompanied by aïoli or rouille.

4 tablespoons extra-virgin olive oil

1 large leek, white part only, cleaned and finely chopped

2 small garlic cloves, finely chopped

1 large red-ripe tomato, peeled, seeded, and finely chopped

¼ cup round-grain rice, such as Italian arborio

Big pinch of saffron

Freshly ground black pepper

6 to 8 slices country-style bread (1 per serving), toasted

Freshly ground black pepper

¼ cup minced flat-leaf parsley

Aïoli (page 64) or Rouille (page 274), for garnish

# Sardinian Clam Soup with Fregola Pasta

## ZUPPA DE ARSELLE CON FREGOLA

*Fregola* is Sardinian and best described as halfway between pasta and couscous. It is available by mail order from Todaro Brothers and some other suppliers (see Where to Find It, page 415). If you don't have *fregola,* try this with the large-grain couscous called *maghrabiye* in Lebanon and Israeli couscous in Israel.

The clams are excellent on their own, minus the tomatoes and fregola.

**Makes 6 first-course servings**

48 small Manila or mahogany clams or cockles

Sea salt

¼ cup extra-virgin olive oil

1 garlic clove, finely chopped

2 sun-dried tomatoes, rehydrated and finely chopped

¼ cup finely chopped flat-leaf parsley, plus 2 tablespoons for garnish

1 cup dry white wine, preferably a Sardinian wine, such as Nuragus

Freshly ground black pepper

Pinch of hot red pepper flakes

4 cups light chicken stock

8 ounces (1½ cups) Sardinian *fregola*

PLACE THE CLAMS in a large colander and scrub them together under running water to rid them of any surface grit. Put about ½ cup of salt in a large basin and fill with cool water. When the salt has dissolved, add the clams and leave for an hour to purge them further. When you are ready to cook, rinse them again and drain.

COMBINE THE OLIVE OIL, garlic, tomatoes, and 2 tablespoons of the parsley in a saucepan large enough to hold all the ingredients. Gently sweat the aromatics in the oil over low heat until the garlic is softened but not brown. Add the clams, cover the pan, raise the heat, and cook over medium-high heat, shaking the pan occasionally, for about 5 minutes. Uncover and turn the heat back to medium as you add the wine, the remaining 2 tablespoons parsley, black pepper, and red pepper. Stir with a wooden spoon to mix well and continue cooking until all the clams have opened, a total of 8 to 10 minutes. (Any clams that have not opened after 10 minutes should be discarded.) As the clams open, remove them from the pan with tongs and set aside. When all the clams are done, strain the liquid in the pan through a double layer of cheesecloth and set aside.

HAVE READY a pan with the stock heated to a rolling boil. Drop in the fregola, a little at a time so that the stock never ceases boiling, and cook for about 8 minutes, or until the fregola is tender. Drain, reserving the cooking liquid.

MEASURE 2 CUPS OF *FREGOLA* cooking liquid and return to the pan along with all the liquid from the clams and bring to a boil. While the broth is coming to a boil, arrange the clams in six deep pasta bowls. As soon as the broth boils, add the *fregola* and immediately spoon the broth and *fregola* over the clams. Garnish with the remaining 2 tablespoons parsley and serve immediately.

VARIATION: If you wish to make a clam sauce for *spaghetti con vongole*, prepare the clams as described above. As soon as the clams are done, set them aside, in their sauce, and do not strain the sauce. Cook the spaghetti or linguine in the usual manner, draining the pasta when it's not quite done. Turn the drained pasta into the clams with their sauce and cook for about 1½ minutes more, garnishing the pasta with more chopped parsley and garlic.

# Oven-Roasted Sea Bass or Snapper

This recipe can be adapted for fillets or steaks, but it is at its finest when made with a whole fish. If you can't find sea bass or snapper, you may be able to get a whole small salmon. While salmon is not a Mediterranean fish, in recent years Mediterranean cooks, like their colleagues around the world, have developed an appreciation for farmed Atlantic salmon, which is cheap, accessible, and can be, if properly handled, of good quality.

Small black Gaeta or niçoise olives are best for this dish. If you can find it, Greek or Sicilian oregano, with a pungent, lemony aroma, is a far cry from the usual dusty dried oregano in most supermarkets; if you can't find it, substitute a good pinch of fragrant dried thyme.

**Makes 4 to 6 servings**

1 (2½- to 3-pound) whole sea bass, snapper, or salmon, or 2 pounds halibut, swordfish, or other firm-textured fish steaks or fillets

Juice of ½ lemon

Sea salt and freshly ground black pepper

About ¼ cup extra-virgin olive oil

2 medium onions, halved and thinly sliced

2 celery stalks, coarsely chopped

2 garlic cloves, finely chopped

½ cup finely minced flat-leaf parsley

2 teaspoons dried Sicilian or Greek oregano (*rígani*), or large pinch of dried thyme

½ cup dry white wine

4 medium, red-ripe tomatoes, peeled, juiced, and coarsely chopped, or 5 or 6 canned tomatoes, well-drained and coarsely chopped

12 small black olives, preferably Greek, or more to taste

½ cup dried bread crumbs

RINSE THE FISH and pat dry with paper towels. Set on a rack and sprinkle both sides, or inside and out, with lemon juice, salt, and pepper. Set aside for an hour or so.

MEANWHILE, in 2 tablespoons of the olive oil over medium-low heat, gently sauté the onion and celery until they are very soft and almost melting, about 20 minutes. Stir in half the garlic and ¼ cup of the parsley. Remove the pan from the heat and set aside to cool slightly. Stir in the oregano and white wine.

PREHEAT THE OVEN to 350°F.

SMEAR A LITTLE OLIVE OIL over the bottom of a baking dish large enough to hold all the fish in one layer. Set the fish in the dish and spoon the onion-celery mixture over and around it, covering the top. Distribute the tomatoes over that, adding the olives and a little more black pepper. Combine the remaining garlic and ¼ cup parsley with the bread crumbs and sprinkle over the tomatoes. Dribble the remaining 2 tablespoons olive oil over the top.

BAKE 20 MINUTES, until fish is tender and cooked through. (Fish steaks or fillets take less time than whole fish.)

SERVE IMMEDIATELY; or, to be truly Mediterranean, let it cool to almost room temperature before serving.

# Oven-Braised Bluefin Tuna

## TONNO ARROSTO

 Studded with fragments of garlic and sprigs of thyme, this roasted tuna will remind you of pork or lamb roasts done in a similar fashion. If you wish, serve the tuna on a bed of steamed vegetables—zucchini sliced the long way, little new onions, fingerling potatoes, small chunks of carrot, all steamed and tossed in a flavorful olive oil make a nice presentation. Or let the roast cool to room temperature and serve it sliced with an herbal vinaigrette and a simple tomato salad.

PREHEAT THE OVEN to 400°F.

USING THE SHARP POINT of a knife make little cuts about ½ inch deep in a pattern all over the tuna and insert a slice of garlic or a sprig of thyme in each one. Sprinkle salt and pepper all over the tuna, then wrap the slices of prosciutto around it so that the tuna is covered except for the two ends. If necessary, tie the tuna with kitchen twine. Use your hands to smear the olive oil all over the outside. Set the roast on a rack in a roasting pan.

PLACE IN THE OVEN, turn the heat down to 350°F, and roast for about 25 minutes, or until the ham is crispy around the edges. The tuna should still be quite pink in the middle.

REMOVE THE TUNA from the oven and set aside for about 10 minutes before serving. Or let it cool to room temperature as described in the headnote.

REMOVE THE STRING before serving the tuna, and slice the fish with a very sharp knife.

**Makes 4 to 6 servings**

1½ pounds fresh tuna, in 1 piece

3 to 4 garlic cloves, sliced

3 or 4 sprigs fresh thyme

Sea salt and freshly ground black pepper

4 thin slices prosciutto di Parma or, if you can find it, Spanish *jamón serrano*

¼ cup extra-virgin olive oil

# Tuna with Tomatoes and Black Olives

## TONNO IN UMIDO

This recipe comes from the restaurant Al Tonno di Corsa in the town of Carloforte on the island of San Pietro, off the big island of Sardinia. Secondo Borghero, the engaging chef-owner, is an enthusiast for the local culture and cuisine, especially for dishes involving tuna harvested in a traditional *mattanza*. *Tonno di corsa* is the name for the tuna as it's coming into the Mediterranean in the late spring; *tonno di turno*, or *tonno di ritorno*, is the same fish on its return, now considerably slimmed down after the rigors of spawning. *Tonno di corsa* is obviously the more prestigious fish.

The sweet-and-sour sauce would also work well for thick salmon steaks.

**Makes 4 servings**

1 pound fresh tuna steaks, about ¾ inch thick

2 tablespoons extra-virgin olive oil

1 cup peeled, seeded, juiced, and chopped fresh, very ripe tomatoes, or 1 cup drained canned plum tomatoes

¼ cup red or white wine vinegar

2 Turkish bay leaves

3 tablespoons coarsely chopped pitted small black olives, preferably Gaeta or niçoise

½ cup dry red wine

Sea salt and freshly ground black pepper

USING A SHARP KNIFE, trim the skin off the tuna. Rinse under cool running water to get rid of any excess blood, then pat dry with paper towels.

OVER MEDIUM-HIGH HEAT, heat the oil in a frying pan large enough to hold all the fish in one layer. When the oil is almost at the smoking point, drop in the tuna and sauté until brown on both sides, turning only once—about 5 minutes to a side.

BRING THE TOMATOES TO A BOIL with the vinegar and bay leaves in a small saucepan. Boil rapidly to concentrate the vinegar and make a thick sauce; fresh tomatoes will take longer to reduce than canned ones. Stir in the olives and remove from the heat.

WHEN THE TUNA IS WELL BROWNED, add the wine to the pan and boil rapidly to reduce by about one-third to one-half. Stir in the tomato sauce, lower the heat to low, cover the pan, and simmer gently for about 20 minutes, checking from time to time to make sure the sauce is not burning. If the sauce reduces too much, add a little boiling water to thin it. Remove the pan lid and continue cooking an additional 10 minutes or so. In the end, the sauce should be very thick. Taste the sauce and add salt and pepper if you wish.

THE TUNA CAN BE SERVED IMMEDIATELY, with its sauce, or left to cool to room temperature before serving.

# Spiced Herb Marinade for Fish

## CHERMOULA

 *Chermoula* is a traditional North African marinade for fish, especially in Morocco where, surprisingly, it's often used with shad. It has become very popular recently with North American restaurant chefs as a quick and easy (and cheap!) way to add lots of flavor to bland fish. Many old-fashioned recipes don't call for cilantro and parsley at all, but the fresh flavor of the green herbs adds a great deal to the preparation.

Instead of shad, which is hard to find even when it's in season, and very difficult to bone, I use salmon steaks or fillets. You could substitute many other kinds of fish, including swordfish, halibut, haddock, and even fresh-water fish, such as catfish and perch.

CHOP THE CILANTRO and parsley leaves together to a very fine mince. You should have 1 cup of minced herbs. Transfer to a saucepan.

CRUSH THE GARLIC with the sea salt in a mortar, or using the back of a spoon in a small bowl, to make a paste. Stir in the cumin, dried pepper, paprika, olive oil, and lemon juice. Add to the saucepan with the herbs and mix well.

HAVE THE FISH STEAKS READY in a baking dish large enough to hold them all in one layer.

SET THE HERB MIXTURE over medium-low heat and warm until it is very hot, but not boiling. Taste and adjust the seasoning. When it is the way you want it, pour the warm marinade over the fish steaks. Cover with plastic and set aside for an hour or so.

WHEN YOU ARE READY TO COOK, preheat the oven to 350°F.

REMOVE THE PLASTIC WRAP and transfer the fish with their marinade to the oven. Bake for 20 to 30 minutes, or until the fish is done, basting every 5 minutes or so with the marinade.

SERVE IMMEDIATELY, spooning a little of the marinade over each serving.

**Makes 6 servings**

1 large bunch fresh cilantro

1 large bunch flat-leaf parsley

8 garlic cloves, crushed with the flat blade of a knife

1 teaspoon sea salt, or more to taste

1 tablespoon freshly ground cumin, or more to taste

1 tablespoon very fragrant crushed dried red pepper, or more to taste

1 tablespoon ground sweet red pepper paprika, or more to taste

½ cup extra-virgin olive oil

¼ cup fresh lemon juice or white wine vinegar (lemon is better, I think)

6 to 8 small salmon steaks, each weighing about 6 ounces

# Franco Crivello's Tuna Fishballs with Fresh Herbs and Tomato Sauce

## POLPETTINE DI TONNO

 At his restaurant in the little Sicilian fishing port of Porticello, Franco Crivello serves these tuna "meatballs," no bigger than marbles, as an appetizer or antipasto. At that size, I could easily imagine them also making a tuna sauce or ragù to dress spaghetti or linguine. Slightly larger, the size of pingpong balls, with their sweet-and-sour sauce, they make an excellent main course.

**Makes 4 servings as a main course, 8 servings as an antipasto**

2 tablespoons dried black currants

2 tablespoons pine nuts

¼ cup extra-virgin olive oil

1 pound fresh tuna

1 large egg

⅓ cup fine dry bread crumbs

¼ cup freshly grated Pecorino Sardo or PecorinoToscano cheese

¼ cup minced flat-leaf parsley

2 tablespoons fresh mint, leaves only, minced, plus whole fresh mint leaves for garnish

Sea salt and freshly ground black pepper

1 medium yellow onion, finely chopped

1 garlic clove, finely chopped

¼ cup dry white wine

½ cup crushed canned tomatoes

½ teaspoon sugar

IN A SMALL BOWL, cover the currants with very warm water. Set aside to soak for at least 15 minutes.

COMBINE THE PINE NUTS in a small skillet with about ½ teaspoon of the olive oil and toast over medium heat, stirring constantly, until the pine nuts are golden. Set aside.

USING A SHARP CHEF'S KNIFE, chop the tuna by hand until it is very finely chopped. (You can do this in a food processor, first cutting the tuna into small bits, then pulsing with brief spurts, but you must be very careful not to reduce the tender fish to a pulp.) Transfer the tuna to a bowl and add the egg, bread crumbs, cheese, parsley, and minced mint. Mix in the toasted pine nuts. Drain the currants well, patting dry with paper towels, and add to the mixture. Add a pinch of salt and black pepper. Use your hands to mix everything together very well. The mixture should hold together when shaped into a small ball. If the mixture seems too wet, add more bread crumbs. If, on the other hand, the mixture seems too dry, break another egg in a bowl, beat it lightly with a fork, and add a few teaspoonsful to the tuna mix. Taste and adjust the seasoning.

WET YOUR HANDS to keep the tuna from sticking to them and shape the mix into balls, either small ones for an antipasto, or larger ones for a main course. As you make them, set them aside.

WHEN ALL THE BALLS ARE SHAPED, warm 2 tablespoons of the oil in a sauté pan over medium heat and brown the tuna balls in the hot oil, turning to brown all sides, about 15 minutes in all. Remove and set aside as the balls finish cooking.

DISCARD THE OIL and wipe out the sauté pan. Add 2 tablespoons of fresh oil and the onion and garlic and very gently cook over low heat until the onion has almost melted into the oil. Turn the heat up to medium and add the wine. Cook, bubbling, until the liquid has reduced slightly. Add the tomatoes and the sugar and continue cooking for about 15 minutes, or until the tomatoes are soft and have thickened to a sauce. Stir in the tuna balls and cook another 10 minutes, or until the balls are heated through.

SERVE IMMEDIATELY.

# Sardinian Seafood Stew

## SA CASSÒLA

 *Sa cassòla* is similar to many different seafood stews made all over the Mediterranean. What makes it Sardinian is the use of fish found in the island's waters: sea bass, gurnard, sea robin, eel, skate, bream, and mullet, as well as tiny squid, chunks of octopus, sometimes small crabs or baby clams called *arselle,* and, when it's available, Mediterranean spiny lobster. This version is my take on the *cassòla* served at the delightful La Ghinghetta, in the little fishing port of Portoscuso, using fish native to my local fishmonger—fish such as haddock, halibut, monkfish, snapper, squid, small clams (mahogany or Manila clams, or cockles), and the tails and claws of Maine lobster or fresh shrimp, large enough to provide at least two per serving. The fish should be cut in 1-inch-thick slices or chunks; the squid should be cleaned and sliced, unless they are very small; the clams should be left whole but scrubbed to rid them of sand; and the lobster should be steamed, then the meat extracted and coarsely chopped.

**Makes 10 to 12 servings**

About 3 pounds fish (haddock, halibut, monkfish, snapper, or similar firm-textured fish are all good choices)

2 pounds mahogany or Manila clams, cockles, or mussels

½ cup extra-virgin olive oil, plus more for the toasted bread garnish

1 medium onion, coarsely chopped

2 garlic cloves, coarsely chopped

About ¼ cup chopped flat-leaf parsley, plus more for garnish

3 pounds very ripe plum tomatoes, peeled, seeded, chopped

HAVE THE FISH CLEANED, sliced, cut into serving-sized chunks, and ready to cook. Prepare the clams, cockles, or mussels by purging and/or trimming. To avoid getting sand in the *cassòla*, steam each variety separately in about an inch of boiling water. As soon as the shells open, remove the shellfish from the water and set aside. When all the shellfish are done, strain their liquid through several layers of cheesecloth and reserve it.

SA CASSÒLA IS TRADITIONALLY COOKED in a terra-cotta pot but a heavy saucepan will be easier to handle. It must be large enough to hold all the ingredients. In the cooking pot, combine the olive oil with the onion, garlic, and parsley. Set over low heat and cook gently until the vegetables are softened, about 20 minutes. Add the tomatoes and cook, uncovered, stirring occasionally, until the tomatoes are reduced and thickened to a sauce. Stir in the squid or octopus, if using, the wine, and the strained broth from cooking the clams or mussels. (The stew can be made ahead to this point, then the tomato mixture reheated when you are ready to continue.)

BRING THE TOMATO-WINE BROTH to a gentle simmer. Add the fish, stirring gently to mix the fish into the sauce. If the sauce still seems too thick, add a little boiling water to thin it. Taste and add salt and red pepper flakes. Cover and cook steadily for about 15 minutes, then add the shrimp, cover again, and cook for another 5 minutes. Finally, add the precooked clams, in their shells, and the lobster, if using, and cook just long enough to heat them through.

TO PREPARE THE BREAD for each serving, either toast the bread and drizzle with olive oil or fry the bread in olive oil until golden on both sides (the latter is more traditional).

TO SERVE, place a bread slice in the bottom of each deep dish and pile the *cassòla* on top, making sure that each serving includes some of each variety of fish. Sprinkle with a little more parsley and serve immediately, providing your guests with plenty of paper napkins and finger bowls for eating this rather messy but delicious dish.

8 ounces small squid or octopus, cut into rings (optional)

½ cup dry white wine

Boiling water (optional)

Sea salt

Pinch of red pepper flakes, or to taste

1 pound medium (20-count) shrimp, peeled, or 1 pound cooked lobster meat, chopped

10 to 12 slices of bread

# Provençale Seafood Stew

## SOUPE DES PECHEURS

🌿 Another in the great series of Mediterranean seafood stews, made with a variety of fish and shellfish, along with plenty of olive oil, tomatoes, and garlic. (The term "dry scallops" refers to scallops that have not been plumped in a sulfite solution.) The addition of orange zest and saffron to the basic stew marks this as a Provençal preparation.

**Makes 6 to 8 servings**

2 cups coarsely chopped yellow onion

2 garlic cloves

About ¾ cup extra-virgin olive oil

2 (2-inch) pieces orange zest

2 bay leaves

1 celery stalk, coarsely chopped

½ cup coarsely chopped flat-leaf parsley

1 teaspoon fresh thyme, leaves only; or ½ teaspoon crumbled dried

¼ teaspoon crumbled saffron threads

1 (14-ounce) can imported tomatoes with their juice

2 cups fish stock (page 408) or light chicken or veal stock, hot

1 pound mahogany or Manila clams or mussels, scrubbed

½ cup dry white wine

1 pound medium (20-count) shrimps, peeled

½ to 1 cup instant flour

8 ounces dry scallops

12 ounces firm, white-fleshed fish fillet, such as haddock or snapper

COMBINE THE ONION, garlic, and ¼ cup of the oil in a heavy saucepan large enough to accommodate all the ingredients. Set over low heat and cook very gently, just sweating the vegetables, until they are very soft.

RAISE THE HEAT SLIGHTLY and add the orange zest, bay leaves, celery, parsley, and thyme. Cook for 2 to 3 minutes, or just long enough to bring out the flavors. Stir in the saffron, then add the tomatoes and their juice, breaking up the tomatoes with the side of a wooden spoon. When the tomato juice is simmering, stir in the fish stock. Cover the pan and simmer for about 30 minutes.

MEANWHILE, combine the scrubbed clams or mussels in another saucepan with the white wine. Set over high heat and steam the shellfish, giving the pan a shake every now and then, until they start to open. As they open, remove the shellfish from the pan and set aside. When all the clams or mussels are open (discard any that do not open after 10 minutes), strain the liquid through two or three layers of cheesecloth to remove all the grit, and add to the pan with the tomatoes. Discard the shells and set the meats aside. (The recipe can be made ahead to this point and reheated when ready to continue.)

HEAT 2 TABLESPOONS OF THE OIL in a sauté pan over medium heat. While it is warming, dip the shrimp in the instant flour, shaking off any excess. As soon as the oil is hot, sauté the shrimp quickly, 30 seconds on each side, remove from the pan, and set aside. Proceed with the scallops and the pieces of fish, dipping them in flour and browning quickly, no more than 1 or 2 minutes to a side, adding more oil to the pan as necessary.

WHEN YOU ARE READY TO SERVE, toast the bread, drizzle a little olive oil on each slice, and arrange in the bottom of a tureen or in individual soup plates. Add the clams, shrimps, scallops, and fish to the tomato stew, mixing carefully to distribute them well. Bring to a simmer and cook for just about a minute, or long enough to warm the seafood through. Spoon over the toasts, then top with a dollop of rouille or aïoli (rouille is more traditional but aïoli is awfully good, too). Serve immediately.

6 to 8 slices Classic Mediterranean-Style bread (page 106) or similar bread, cut 1¼ inches thick, toasted, and drizzled with a little olive oil, for serving

Rouille (page 274) or Aïoli (page 64), for garnish

2 tablespoons grated Parmigiano-Reggiano cheese, for garnish

# Stuffed Squid

**SEPPIE RIPIENE**

If you can find whole squid, with their tentacles attached, that's what you'll want for this dish. Clean the squid, being careful not to split the bodies, by pulling out and discarding their insides, including the "bone" that feels like cellulose. Cut off the tentacles and, if they are large, chop them coarsely. Rinse the bodies inside and out and dry them.

**Makes 6 servings**

6 to 12 fresh whole squid (quantity depends on the size of the squid)

3 or 4 leaves chard, preferably white and green

½ cup dried bread crumbs

4 tablespoons extra-virgin olive oil

½ cup finely minced yellow onion

½ cup minced flat-leaf parsley

2 garlic cloves, chopped

2 tablespoons salted capers, rinsed under running water and dried

2 tablespoons pine nuts

2 tablespoons golden sultanas or black currants, softened in warm water

4 salted anchovy fillets, cleaned and chopped (see page 411)

1 tablespoon Sicilian or Greek oregano (*rìgani*) (optional)

Sea salt

2 bay leaves

Freshly ground black pepper

¼ cup dry white wine

CLEAN THE SQUID, cutting off the tentacles and setting aside and pulling away and discarding the innards. Rinse the squid bodies inside and out and pat dry with paper towels. Chop the tentacles coarsely.

TO MAKE THE STUFFING, strip the chard leaves from the center stalks, which are too firm for this dish. (Reserve the stalks for another use.) Set the leaves in a colander over a pan of boiling water to steam until they are tender, 10 to 15 minutes. Remove and coarsely chop the chard.

TOAST THE BREAD CRUMBS by stirring in a dry skillet over medium-high heat until they have turned golden.

IN 2 TABLESPOONS OF THE OIL sauté the onion, parsley, and garlic over medium low heat until soft, then stir in the tentacles and cook, stirring, just until they have changed color. Add the chard and stir to mix well. Cook for about 5 minutes, or just long enough to heat the chard thoroughly. Remove the pan from the heat and stir in the capers, pine nuts, raisins, and anchovies. Add oregano, if you wish, and the bread crumbs, mixing well. Taste and add salt.

PREHEAT THE OVEN to 350°F. Use 1 teaspoon of the oil to grease an oval or rectangular baking dish large enough to hold all the squid in one layer.

LOOSELY STUFF THE SQUID with the chard–bread crumb mixture. Each squid should take 2 to 3 tablespoons, depending on its size. Don't overstuff—the stuffing will expand as it cooks. Close the end of the squid with a toothpick to prevent the stuffing from escaping and arrange the squid in the baking dish. Tuck the bay leaves around the squid, then sprinkle with salt, pepper, and the remaining oil.

IN A SMALL SAUCEPAN, bring the wine just to the boiling point and pour over the squid.

BAKE FOR ABOUT 30 MINUTES, or until the squid are tender and lightly golden on top.

SERVE IMMEDIATELY.

# Baked Swordfish Rolls with an Orange Sauce

## INVOLTINI DI PESCE SPADA

 Thin slices of swordfish can be rolled around a stuffing similar to the one used for squid. Have your fishmonger slice the swordfish very thinly—¼ inch or less. Otherwise, the rolls will be too bulky.

**Makes 6 servings**

12 thin slices fresh swordfish

4 tablespoons extra-virgin olive oil

3 to 4 chard leaves, preferably white and green

½ cup dry bread crumbs

½ cup finely minced yellow onion

½ cup minced flat-leaf parsley

2 garlic cloves, chopped

2 tablespoons capers, preferably salted capers, well rinsed under running water and drained

2 tablespoons pine nuts

2 tablespoons golden sultanas or black currants, softened in warm water

4 salted anchovy fillets, cleaned and chopped (see page 411)

1 tablespoon Sicilian or Greek oregano (*rìgani*) (optional)

1 tablespoon freshly grated orange zest

Sea salt

2 tablespoons fresh orange juice

¼ cup dry white wine

PAT DRY THE SWORDFISH SLICES with paper towels and set aside. Use a little of the olive oil to grease an oval or rectangular baking dish that is large enough to hold all the swordfish rolls in one layer.

TO MAKE THE STUFFING, strip the chard leaves from the center stalks, which are too firm for this dish. (Reserve the stalks for another use.) Set the leaves in a colander over a pan of boiling water to steam until they are tender, 10 to 15 minutes. Remove and coarsely chop the chard.

TOAST THE BREAD CRUMBS by stirring in a dry skillet over medium-high heat until they have turned golden.

IN 2 TABLESPOONS OF OLIVE OIL, sauté the onion, parsley, and garlic over medium-low heat until soft. Add the chopped chard and stir to mix well. Cook for about 5 minutes, or just long enough to heat the chard thoroughly. Remove the pan from the heat and stir in the capers, pine nuts, raisins, and anchovies. Add the oregano, if you wish, the bread crumbs, and the orange zest, mixing well. Taste and add salt.

PREHEAT THE OVEN to 425°F.

SPREAD 2 TABLESPOONS of the stuffing at one edge of a swordfish slice, leaving a good margin at each end, and roll the slice as tightly as you can, securing it with a toothpick. Set the slices, toothpick side down, in the prepared baking dish.

COMBINE THE ORANGE JUICE and white wine and heat to just below boiling. Pour over the swordfish rolls, then dribble the remaining oil over the top.

BAKE FOR 20 MINUTES, or until the fish rolls are cooked through and the tops are starting to brown.

SERVE IMMEDIATELY, spooning the pan juices over each serving.

# Fried Fish in a Sweet-Sour Marinade

## ESCABECHE

 Like many other fish dishes, this treatment can be found almost everywhere in the Mediterranean and often with a name, like *escabeche* (Spanish) and *scapece* (Italian) that recalls a common heritage. It is sometimes said to be a fisherman's dish, but I think that's one of those bits of folklore that people like to claim on no basis except that it sounds good. When you examine the dish, there's precious little, apart from the fish itself, to interest a fisherman, or a fisherman's wife. It seems much more likely this was a dish invented by thrifty landlubbers looking for a way to preserve the catch.

Depending on where you go in the Mediterranean, this may be made with whole small fish, fresh anchovies or sardines, or slices or fillets of fish. It works as well with oily fish as it does with white-meat fish, and is brilliant with salmon. The most important consideration is that the fish should be quite firm-textured.

**Makes 8 appetizer or first-course servings**

8 small fish steaks or fillets, each one about ½ inch thick (about 1½ pounds, total)

¾ cup unbleached all-purpose flour

2 large eggs, lightly beaten

1 cup unseasoned dry bread crumbs

¾ cup extra-virgin olive oil

2 medium onions, halved and very thinly sliced

2 cloves garlic, finely chopped

2 bay leaves

¼ teaspoon black peppercorns

½ cup white wine vinegar

¼ cup golden sultana raisins

¼ cup pine nuts

½ teaspoon sugar (optional)

RINSE THE FISH and dry well with paper towels. Arrange the flour, eggs, and bread crumbs in three separate shallow soup plates. (The flour dries the fish so that the egg will adhere, and the egg acts as the glue to hold the bread crumbs.) Dip the pieces of fish first in the flour, then the egg, and finally in the bread crumbs, patting off the excess but making sure the entire fish is covered.

WHEN ALL THE FISH HAS BEEN BREADED, heat ¼ cup of the oil in a skillet over medium heat and fry the fish in the hot oil, turning each piece once, until it is golden on all sides—about 2 minutes to a side. As the fish pieces finish cooking, remove them and set them aside in a shallow bowl.

WHEN ALL THE FISH ARE DONE, discard the oil in the pan and rinse it out. Add ½ cup of fresh oil and set the pan over medium-low heat. Add the onions and garlic and cook very gently, stirring occasionally, until the onions have softened almost to a golden puree; this can take as long as 30 minutes and must not be hurried as the onions must be truly golden and melting, not brown and crisp. After 15 minutes, add the bay leaves and peppercorns and continue gently frying the onions until they are golden.

STIR IN THE WINE VINEGAR, raisins, and pine nuts and raise the heat to medium. Cook for about 5 minutes, or just long enough to meld the flavors. Taste the sauce and, if you wish, add sugar—there may be sufficient sweetness from the onions, in which case the sugar may be omitted.

POUR THE HOT ONIONY SAUCE over the fish in the bowl, making sure that all the pieces are thoroughly covered. Let cool slightly, then cover the bowl and set it aside in a cool place (but not refrigerated) overnight. Serve the next day at room temperature.

NOTE: It is often said that this dish will keep for 7 to 10 days, because of the vinegar. I think it's wise, if you wish to keep it for several days, to refrigerate it, but it should be brought back to room temperature before serving.

# From the Pasture

CHEESE AND YOGURT

O N A SMALL FARM NESTLED SNUGLY into a cleft in the hills of the Var *département* of eastern Provence, Yves van Weddingen produces goats' milk cheeses of a singular quality. His herd is small, just thirty-five friendly, curious Alpine goats, and he makes his cheeses entirely by hand, selling them from a stall he operates by himself at weekly markets in nearby towns, at Draguignan on Saturdays and Tourtour on Wednesdays. In this still deeply rural part of France, he is not yet an anachronism, but that time is coming, probably within Yves' lifetime, too, and he knows it.

Yves' farm is down a long, unpaved country lane that winds back and forth across the wooded hillsides and past a couple of similar places that were once small farms and are now *maisons secondaires* for people who live in distant cities and come for Christmas and Easter and the formulaic four weeks summer holiday. This is a growing phenomenon in southern France—as well as in Spain, Italy, and parts of Greece—as great swathes of countryside are turned from more or less productive agriculture to sporadic, seasonal occupation by people who have a romantic interest in maintaining the picturesque nature of the landscape, but no productive economic interaction with the land itself. There's an unreality in this situation that does not escape people such as Yves, himself by no means a typical local Provençal farmer, but rather an import from Belgium who escaped here a quarter-century ago to pursue a countercultural sort of lifestyle.

This place is what's called locally a *bastide,* meaning it was once a miniature fortified farm, but any fortifications disappeared a long time ago. Instead there's a low but airy and spacious barn, open at both ends, with the goats on this hot summer afternoon milling about in the shade inside; next to the barn is a tidy little creamery where the cheeses are made and aged in their *cave,* and on a hill above the barn is the house Yves built some years ago for his family, which includes his wife, Michelle, and their two children. The verdant little valley, protected on either side by low mountains, has a lush feel to it. And like a high Alpine pastureland, the terrain is scattered with meadows where the goats can browse on a wide assortment of fragrant herbs and grasses.

All good cheese-makers know that if you want a high-quality cheese, whether from cows', goats', or ewes' milk, the milking animals must feed as much as possible on a complex mixture of flavorful herbs that add both aromas and structure to the milk. French cheese experts have counted between two and three hundred different kinds of pasture grasses and herbs that goats select while they are grazing. Lack of this kind of feed at commercial, nontraditional dairies, where animals are fed a simple diet based primarily on grain, is one important reason why modern, industrially produced cheese is so bland and unsatisfying—one reason why cheese-lovers seek out individual farmers like Yves van Weddingen who continue to practice the old-fashioned ways of doing things.

But Yves' goats on this midsummer afternoon are not grazing. The cicadas are shrilling in the tops of the stone pines, and it's too hot for goats to be out in the sun. They're ruminating, Yves said, "ruminating and making milk." From the time the kids are born in the spring, the goats produce milk, peaking three months later between April and June. The kids suckle their mothers for a maximum of 10 days only. "I don't think there's a farm anywhere in France," Yves told me, "where kids are still raised on mother's milk." It's simply too expensive to give them anything but powdered milk when goats' milk can make such elegant cheese. By late July, milk production will start to decline, and by late August, another season of cheese production will be over until the following year.

Like other dairy animals, the goats are milked twice a day, but cheese is made once only, after the morning milking. Temperature is critical in cheese-making. The evening milk is kept at 12°C (53.6°F) overnight. "Anything less than that and you destroy the taste," Yves explained. "Above that, it gets a little bit dangerous." The morning milk, naturally, is at the animal's body temperature and, when mixed with the cooler evening milk, comes out at 20° to 22°C (68° to 72°F), just the right temperature, he said, for making cheese. "You could get the cheese out faster with higher temperatures," he told me, "but it wouldn't be a better cheese."

More important even than the temperature of the milk is its acidity. Yves saves the whey from the previous day's cheese-making and sets it aside to ferment a little. He adds this starter culture to the milk to give it, and eventually to give the cheese, a slightly more acid flavor, as well as to help set the curd. As in bread-making, this slowly fermented starter is called a *levain,* and as with bread, it's important in producing more complex and interesting flavors in the finished product. "I make my own *levain,*" Yves explained. "I take the whey from the morning cheese and add it to the evening milk to increase its acidity—that's the only secret to my cheese-making. If the acidity isn't high enough, the milk curd will spoil instead of turning into cheese."

Two hours after the morning milking, Yves and his assistant Nicole, a retired restaurant chef who has become almost as engrossed in the business as Yves himself, add a natural animal rennet to the mixed and fermented milk and set it aside to curdle. Nicole is as emphatic as Yves: "What's important to make a good curd," she said, "is to use good, clean milk, raw milk. Raw milk, that is," she said again, "not cooked, not pasteurized."

Once the day's milk has been curdled, the curd from the previous day must be dipped into the little perforated molds that shape the small traditional fresh goats' cheeses, while the curd that was molded the day before must be unmolded and salted. It's a continuous process: Curdle the milk, fill the molds, turn out the molds from the day before, while the fresh curd in each mold must be turned over and salted after 10 or 12 hours so it will ripen evenly. (Some cheeses are not turned out after 24 hours, but instead left in the molds for 2 full days to make a moister, creamier cheese.) Finally, the cheeses are put to *affiner,* to age and "fine" themselves, laid out one by one on wooden boards in the cheese room where the temperature is a constant 14°C (57°F) and the humidity is kept at 85 to 90 percent. They are delicious in the fresh state, but develop more flavor as they age. Many people prefer them at just two days; after ten days, they will develop a fine, bluish mold; and after two months, they will become very dry, waxy, and firm, and the cheese will flake when cut with a knife. But most of what Yves sells, more than two-thirds he says, is in the medium stage, neither fresh and creamy nor firm and dry.

Like many French cheese-makers, Yves works only with raw, unpasteurized milk, and like all French dairies, his is inspected three times a year, with both milk and cheese analyzed in government laboratories as a safety control. Agents from the Ministry of Agriculture can come onto a farm whenever they choose to do so, without any prior warning, to take their samples. Beyond that, there's also the government's *contrôle laîtier,* that checks each individual goat for quality and quantity of production. "It used to be brucellosis was a major problem, but it hasn't been seen for twenty years," Yves said. The Direction de Service Veterinaire also checks for staphylococcus germs, E. coli, listeria, and salmonella, and periodically the purity of the water on the farm also is checked by the government.

Making cheese from raw milk requires a great deal more skill on the part of the individual artisan than does making pasteurized-milk cheese, not so much to insure safety as to guarantee the quality that French consumers demand. In other Mediterranean countries, while small-scale dairies may still work with raw milk, moderate-sized enterprises, with more employees and broader markets—for instance, most Tuscan Pecorino cheese producers—use pasteurized milk simply because it's the easiest way to be certain of a consistent product.

As is usual in the world of food and wine, however, consistency comes at the considerable expense of quality. Although there is less risk of accidental spoiling with pasteurization, which helps to ensure that the cheeses produced will be alike and like every other similar cheese made by that dairy, pasteurizing the milk also destroys the complex culture and rich flavor of the resultant cheese. You may not get bad cheese using pasteurized milk, but you will never get very good cheese. "We can afford to have an accident with our cheese," Yves says, "because we produce on such a small scale that if we have to throw out a day's production, it's not such a big deal. But the big companies, Dannon, Gervais, Nestlé, Parmalat, they can't afford an accident—so they have to work with pasteurized milk."

The issue of pasteurization is a hot one in Europe these days, particularly in France, Spain, and Italy, countries that have long recognized the deleterious effects the process has on fine cheeses. Many cheese-makers and *affineurs* (specialist merchants who take finished cheeses and ripen them in temperature- and humidity-controlled *caves*) are quick to blame the United States for a movement calling for the pasteurization of all commercially available cheeses. U.S. law currently requires pasteurization of all cheeses except those aged 60 days or more, by the end of which period any contaminants are naturally destroyed. This requirement applies both to cheeses made in this country and to ones made elsewhere but imported for sale here. But the federal Food & Drug Administration, which is in charge of enforcing the law, sometimes honors it in the breach as far as imported cheeses are concerned, and alert consumers may be able to find raw-milk French cheeses, for instance, in fine cheese shops. There is also a healthy commerce in raw-milk cheeses through the Internet, with several French sites providing such cheeses—at a cost—within 24 hours, so they claim, of placing an order.

The French consider raw milk indispensable for the production of fine cheeses. Indeed, French cheese-makers say, it's the very richness of the milk's biological life that produces complex and varied flavors in the cheese made from it. In its raw state, milk contains natural lactic acid bacteria that play a vital role in cheese production and cheese ripening, encouraging the development of rich and recognizable flavors that vary according to the milk's origin—not just what animal it came from, but where that animal grazed and how she was treated. And those natural bacteria are destroyed by pasteurization.

When cheese is produced industrially on a mass scale, on the other hand, milk must be pasteurized. That's because it usually comes from many very different, and very distant, sources, and is frequently three or four days old by the time it's transformed into cheese. Moreover, the dairy animals that produce the milk are intensively bred and raised to be high-yielding milkers, meaning they're much more susceptible to sanitation problems. During long-distance transport and storage, bacteria in the milk, good and bad alike, will multiply. If the milk has not been pasteurized, contamination can make the milk unsuitable for consumption, whether as milk or as cheese. And since pasteurization destroys all bacteria, including those necessary for cheese-making, in order to produce cheese, the processor then has to introduce a selection of lactic-acid bacteria, themselves industrial creations lacking the richness and diversity of more natural starter cultures—yet another reason why raw-milk cheeses have so much greater flavor than ones made from pasteurized milk.

Tasty though they may be, however, aren't raw milk cheeses dangerous? No, says Steve Jenkins, a leading expert on cheese in America, not nearly so dangerous as cheeses made from pasteurized milk. Almost every instance of contaminated cheese found in the United States in the last dozen or so years, Jenkins told me, was traced to milk that had been improperly or incompletely pasteurized. Pasteurization creates a sort of tabula rasa, he said, a clean slate, so there is no longer any competition among the bacteria, both good and bad, that are present in raw milk. Then, if it becomes contaminated, the milk has no defense against the contamination.

Pasteurization won't necessarily combat listeria, for instance, one of the most dangerous food-borne bacteria, which flourishes at low temperatures (that is, between 3°C and 5°C—about 37°F to 41°F—the lower range of normal refrigerator temperatures). Leo Bertozzi, the articulate and knowledgeable spokesman for the Parmigiano-Reggiano Consortium in Italy, told me that listeria actually seems to get into the milk in the *post*-pasteurization stage. "So pasteurization doesn't affect it," Bertozzi said, "but, in fact, actually sets up an environment in which the listeria bacteria can flourish. It is very rare as a disease but very, very dangerous for the very young, the very old, or people with compromised immune systems."

The worry over "bad" milk seems especially misplaced to Daphne Zepos, a Greek-American cheese-maker and head of Cheese of Choice, a coalition to educate the U.S. public about raw milk cheeses. "If you make cheese with bad milk," she said, "99 percent of the time, theatrical things will begin to happen with the cheese very quickly"—meaning, the cheese will fill up with nasty gases and explode before anyone could even want to eat it.

Nonetheless, the United States government has angered cheese-lovers everywhere and made them apprehensive with a proposal before the World Trade Organization, supported by Australia, New Zealand, and some developing nations, that *all* cheeses in international trade, whether fresh, aged a few weeks, or matured, like Parmigiano-Reggiano, for as much as two years, should be made only from pasteurized milk. The proposal, which is still on the table as of this writing, threatens the existence of almost all the world's great cheeses, including Parmigiano-Reggiano and Roquefort, as well as many lesser-known cheeses of the Mediterranean.

I T  H A S  B E E N  S A I D  O V E R  A N D  A G A I N that the process of making cheese is nothing more than the controlled spoiling of milk. Once upon a time, all cheeses were made with raw milk, either right at the farm where the milk is collected, often by the shepherd in charge of the herd or by a family member, as it still is at Yves van Weddingen's,* or at a dairy close enough to the farm for milk to be delivered twice daily. When milk quality is good, it is not difficult to produce sound and delicious cheeses, given sufficient expertise and ability on the part of the cheese-maker.

Most cheese-makers feel that some kind of starter, whether natural like Yves' or commercial, is necessary. Otherwise, they say, the milk proteins won't coagulate when rennet is added. A starter culture also contributes to the cheese's eventual flavors during the ripening process. But not every cheese-maker uses starter, and the lack of it often indicates a very old, one might even say, primitive or at least prehistoric, cheese tradition. The French divide the world into lactic curd (*caillé lactique*) cheeses, in which a starter is added to acidify the curd, and the much rarer sweet curd (*caillé doux*) cheeses (not to be confused with sweet-cream cheeses) in which no starter is used. Many people, among them France's premier chef, Alain Ducasse, trace the latter practice back to the original cheese-makers of the Mediterranean basin and claim a southern, olive-growing, *langue d'oc* heritage for it, while the *caillé lactique* style of cheese-making is more associated with the north—and with butterfat and the *langue d'oïl*. To compensate for the lack of starter, those who choose to work with nonacidified curds must add three times as much rennet to curdle the cheese, resulting in a firmer curd. At sites in southern France and elsewhere, especially in the Eastern Mediterranean, archaeologists have turned up pottery cheese-drainers with large holes, indicating that the sweet-curd cheeses, with their larger, firmer curds, were probably what was being drained by Neolithic cheese-makers.

Whether starter is added to culture the milk or not, the next step is adding rennet, to curd or curdle the milk, coagulate the protein casein, and allow it to be separated from the whey. Traditionally rennet came either from the lining of an animal's stomach (lamb, calf, even in some regions pig, said to make a particularly digestible cheese) or from certain plants. In Homeric times, the rennet used came from the milky sap of the fig tree, while another useful, traditional source was dried wild artichokes or cardoons (*Cynara cardunculus*)—still much used in Portugal to make the fine artisanal cheeses for which that country is renowned. Animal rennet is still required for many traditional cheeses, but modern artisanal cheese-makers are more apt to use a plant-derived rennet.

---

* In France (and in England), only cheese made on the farm from the milk of animals raised on the farm is entitled to the designation *fromage fermier* (farmstead cheese, in the UK).

Once the rennet has been added, the curd is left to set up. The curds may be heated or "cooked"—low temperatures at this stage produce softer cheeses, higher temperatures firmer cheeses. Before or after that, the still-soft curd may be cut—a more frequent practice with cows' or ewes' milk cheeses than with goats' milk—into grains as small as lentils or seeds of wheat or as large as walnuts. All of these practices produce different flavors and, especially, different textures in the cheese.

The curds are then gathered together by the cheese-maker and placed in perforated forms whose size depends on what kind of cheese is being made, to drain the whey. (The whey, rich with its own proteins, is valuable. It makes wonderful food for pigs—Parma pigs, they say, get a lot of their flavor from the whey of Parmigiano-Reggiano—but whey can also be turned into ricotta, as it most often is in Greece and Italy, literally "re-cooked" to re-coagulate the remaining proteins, and marketed as a fresh cheese.) Then the cheese—for by now we can call it a cheese—is salted, with salt either mixed into the curd, or rubbed or sprinkled over the surface of the cheese; or the cheese may be washed with a brine-soaked cloth or actually submerged in brine for a period of time. After salting, the cheese is aged or cured, usually in a cool, somewhat humid environment where it will remain anywhere from a few days to many months.

Some cheeses get further treatments to add to their flavor and potential for long-keeping. *Morchia,* which is the antiseptic black yuck deposited at the bottom of olive oil storage tanks, is often rubbed over ewes' milk Pecorino cheeses in Tuscany to preserve them, while in Spain and on some Greek islands, cheeses are submerged in olive oil to keep them soft and give them flavor. The lees of red wine make another favorite "rub" for the outsides of cheeses, as does tomato paste, which gives the cheese an appetizing color, if it doesn't add much to the taste. Some cheeses are wrapped in chestnut or walnut or grape leaves, others are encased in resinous bark, and in Sogliano al Rubicone, a small town in Romagna on the eastenmost border with Tuscany, Pecorino cheeses are buried in pits in the ground for a period of three months, after which they have the gnarled appearance of prehistoric survivals and an extraordinarily high flavor.

As with bread-making and winemaking, slow is the operative adjective for quality throughout the process. Slow coagulation of the milk, slow raising of the temperature in which the curd cooks—which must never be too hot—slow aging in a well-ordered cellar. Good shepherds will even admit that slowness and gentleness in the pasture and while milking the animals can effect a positive outcome for the cheese.

THE GOAT, THEY SAY IN THE MEDITERRANEAN, is the cow of the poor. And it's true that goats seem ubiquitous, especially in places where the soil is poor, thin, and stony, or where the terrain is desert for much of the year, as in much of the Middle East and North Africa. Cows, to be happiest, to produce at their best, need grassy meadows and a gentle, easy landscape—think of those big plodding hooves compared to a goat's agile limbs and you'll immediately understand why. Cows aren't much used in the Mediterranean, but where they do fit in, their milk makes extraordinary cheeses—I think of Parmigiano-Reggiano from the south side of Italy's Po Valley, or caciocavallo, especially that produced around Ragusa in southeastern Sicily. Caciocavallo ragusano, a cheese with a very old tradition, is made from the milk of Modicana cows, a gorgeous breed with dark mahogany to reddish-black coats. Then there are the water buffalo from Caserta and Battipaglia, near Naples, with their gracefully sweeping racks of horns, whose milk makes the rich and prized *mozzarella di bufala.* (In the Nile valley, another Mediterranean home of these beasts, buffalo don't seem to be valued as milkers, or at least I've never encountered buffalo milk cheese in Egypt; in Turkey, on the other hand, a delicious clotted cream called *kaymak* is made from buffalo milk, especially in the region around Afyon, where the buffalo are fed on the residues from opium poppies cultivated for the government-supervised production of morphine.)

But all over the Mediterranean, sheep are without question the most important dairy animal, as they have been since Homeric times, providing not just milk but other benefits as well: their meat, which is at the center of the festive board for all three of the great Mediterranean religions, and their wool, less important now that synthetics have replaced it, but for centuries the most valuable commodity in international trade throughout the region. Ewes' milk, on its own or mixed with goats' milk, provides both cheese and yogurt, valuable protein on the tables of rich and poor alike. Wool and milk, moreover, are replenishable resources—not an inconsiderable benefit in itself.

One-eyed Polyphemus the Cyclops, in his dung-raddled island cave, is the first shepherd known to literature, and Odysseus' account of how he slew the monster, in Book IX of *The Odyssey,* is a good description of a Bronze Age cheese-maker in his admittedly dirty dairy: "Here crates were standing, loaded down with cheese," Odysseus says, "and here pens thronged with lambs and kids. In separate pens each sort was folded: by themselves the older, by themselves the later born, and by themselves the younglings. Swimming with whey were all the vessels, the well-wrought pails and bowls in which he milked. . . . Into the wide-mouthed cave he drove his sturdy flock, all that he milked; the males, both rams and goats, he left outside in the high yard. . . . Then sitting down, he milked the ewes and bleating goats, all in due order, and underneath put each one's young. Straightway he curdled half of the white milk, and gathering it in wicker baskets, set it by; half he left standing in the pails, ready for him to take and drink, and for his supper also."

What breeds of sheep Polyphemus milked we don't know, but it's possible they were the same fat-tailed sheep found to this day all over the Middle East, especially in Lebanon and Syria. (The tail fat, rendered like lard, is prized for use in cooking and preserving.) Here farming families make a peculiar local cheese called *anbaris*, accumulating sheeps' milk and goats' milk, from the family herd, over the spring months. The milk is added, a little at a time as the animals are milked, to unglazed terra-cotta jars in which a live culture develops and with time produces, over many months, a soft, sour, rather salty cheese that is highly prized. This, archaeologists tell us, is pure Neolithic cheese-making technology.

Among Mediterranean ewes' milk cheeses, one of the best-known outside its Italian home is Pecorino (the name comes from *peccora* for sheep). Made all over Central and Southern Italy, mostly from the milk of a Sardinian breed, Pecorino can be eaten at many different stages, from fresh, young, soft, and almost curdy in texture, to a hard, dry, well-aged cheese with a characteristic nutty sharpness and waxy firmness. An entirely different style of sheeps' milk cheese comes from western Spain where, in the province of Estremadura, merino sheep, prized for their wool, are milked to make two deliciously rich and runny cheeses, La Serena and Torta del Casar—a good example of how historic breeds, many with low yields of high-quality milk, are being restored to productivity after decades of decline.

In Greece, the sheeps' milk cheese of choice is feta (the name means "slice"), the kind of soft, tart, white cheese that seems to have been known in the Balkans forever. Greek feta is made from at least 70 percent ewes' milk with up to 30 percent goats' milk, while Bulgarian feta is traditionally half goat and half sheep. The more goats' milk in the mix, the firmer the cheese, I was told in Greece. In that part of the world, even butter is made from ewes' and goats' milk. On the island of Crete, the butter is called *staka*, and in southern Turkey and Syria, clarified ewes' milk butter is the key ingredient in the fine, crisply layered pastries of the region.

And then there's yogurt, made from ewes' milk most of the time, but also from goats' milk and, less frequently, from cows' milk. Until some time after World War

II, yogurt was almost unknown outside the Eastern Mediterranean; now, of course, it's available around the world in all flavors and colors, but never so good as the plain white, unflavored, creamy ewes' milk yogurt available in Greece, Turkey, and Lebanon. Yogurt may have been brought into the region by the Turks, long before the Ottoman conquest of Istanbul in the fifteenth century, although there is some evidence for yogurt in classical times. Nonetheless, wherever they went, the Turks took yogurt with them.

Over on the Asian side of the Bosphoros in Istanbul, across from the mosque in the little waterside village of Kanlicar, is a sort of dairy bar that serves what is reputed to be the best yogurt in the world. Nothing but yogurt is served here, and plain yogurt at that. But what yogurt! Thick and almost chewy, yet refreshing to the palate, with a characteristic sweet tang and just a hint of the barnyard in its aftertaste, this is the kind of lightly strained yogurt that Turks and Bulgarians, Greeks and Arabs, consume at every meal—it's a quintessential part of breakfast, often accompanied with olives, possibly a few crisp scallions or radishes depending on what's in season, and a dollop of olive oil; at lunchtime, perhaps with garlic and chopped herbs added, it makes a sauce for grilled meat or for rice or bulgur pilaf; in the evening, it's a base for hot or cold soup for supper, and, thickened to a cream by straining the whey, it makes an exquisite dessert, like the most refreshing pudding imaginable, served with a dribble of mountain honey or, as it's sometimes presented on the island of Crete, with a dollop of deep red rose-petal jam.

Yves van weddingen has had a stand in the Saturday market in Draguignan for as many years as he has been making cheese. It's a simple, hand-built affair, a sort of two-tiered glass case or vitrine, sitting on a small oak table in which he displays an array of small, round cheeses in varying stages of *affinage,* from a few days to several weeks old. The last time I was in Draguignan at the market, Yves had a bit more gray in his temples. He had shaved his moustache, he said, in order to look younger, but he still had the handsome, tanned face of a man who spends most of his working days out-of-doors among his goats.

The U.S. demand for pasteurized milk cheeses doesn't worry Yves so much any more, since his market is right here in these hills, in the triangle formed by Draguignan, Lorgues, and Tourtour. As long as he doesn't export his cheese, and he has no plans to do that, he figures he's safe from the draconian sanitary regulations that he knows would spell the end of his high-quality chèvre.

Lately, however, there's been a new worry for Yves, and for his fellow market vendors of cheeses, meats, and seafood. Proposed new French regulations, going way beyond anything determined by the European Union in Brussels, are setting temperature controls on these products with the requirement that they be kept under a minimum temperature of 6°C (about 43°F) from the moment they leave the production site to the moment they arrive in the customer's care. "I can't do that," Yves said. "If I go below 10°C (about 50°F), it's not the same cheese. It changes its nature completely. And if I take it down to 6°C and then you, the consumer, bring it back up to 14°C (about 57°F), it will ruin the cheese entirely." What Yves didn't mention, but what I know from talking with other producers, is that the cost of refrigeration is also prohibitive. At $50,000 and up for a refrigerated van, it's enough to drive a small-scale producer right out of business. Which may be what was intended.

Yves' life, which has been simple by choice since he opted to become a goatherd and cheese-maker in the hills of the Eastern Var, suddenly looks to become a good deal more complicated. And more expensive. Which is what many critics say is precisely the goal of the new legislation, to make the lives of small artisanal producers so complex and so expensive that they will gradually be driven out of business, leaving a clear playing field for the big guys.

"But even if the law changes, of course, I wouldn't pasteurize. It destroys the culture and the flavor of the milk—and the cheese. Look," Yves said to me, "I've changed my business many times, and I can do it again. But it doesn't make sense. You can drink Cognac and drive a car—and that's truly dangerous. How many people die from eating bad cheese?"

## 12 GREAT RECIPES USING DAIRY PRODUCTS

Yogurt "Cheese" Balls with Za'atar and Sumac

Focaccia di Recco

Tarte au Chèvre

Green Salad with Toasted Goat Cheese

Tagliatelle ai Quattro Formaggi

Turkish Yogurt Soup with Tiny Meatballs

Spinach Baked with Feta

Knafe

Sweet Cheese Ravioli with Bitter Honey
   *Sebadas*

Eastern Mediterranean Yogurt Cake with Almonds or Pistachios

Torta di Ricotta

Ricotta Fritters


## COOK'S NOTES

The quality of cheeses in the United States has improved to an astonishing degree in recent years. (Canada, on the other hand, has almost always had a steady supply of excellent French cheeses, especially since Canadians don't share the raw-milk phobia that infects their cousins to the south.) Both imported cheeses and our own domestic production have made great strides in the last decade or so, the latter under the aegis of the American Cheese Society, an association of small-scale, often farmhouse cheese–producers. There are still more strides to be made, particularly with sheeps' milk cheeses, but when I think back to just a few years ago, I have to remind myself that for most of the country the choice for consumers was between processed American cheese and cheddar. In the recipes that follow, I have almost always given the type of cheese that is used where the recipe originated, but you should feel free to experiment—within reason, of course, as there's no way a hard grating cheese could ever substitute for a ricotta, or vice versa.

Another area where North Americans are making great improvements is in the concept of serving cheese, sometimes even a selection of two or three cheeses, at the end of a meal, surely a more welcome and healthful finish than a big lump of chocolate cake with icing on it. (Chocolate cake has its place in the universe, for sure, but not, I've always believed, at the end of a substantial meal.) Many restaurants now offer a cheese course, and many also try to feature locally made cheeses as part of that, which is all to the good. The more local cheese production is encouraged, the better it is for all us cheese-lovers.

Cheese is wonderful on its own, served with bread or crackers, perhaps a few olives, and a glass of wine—red or white, it doesn't matter, although the latest food fad is for white wine with cheese, contrary to what we all learned in our youth, that only red wine should be served with cheese. Turns out, as with so many things, it all depends, it depends on the cheese, it depends on the wine.

Cooking with cheese, as you will see in the recipes that follow, is an altogether different experience. Even though every culture around the Mediterranean makes several different kinds of cheese, not every one finds cheese an essential ingredient in the kitchen. Italian cooks are way ahead of everyone else in this department, since cheese goes on almost every pasta and pizza with the exception of a few that are made with fish or lots of garlic, and on or in dozens of other dishes as well. Italians have developed a whole range of cheeses made for grating into or on top of other dishes—from caciocavallo in the south to Pecorino in the center to Parmigiano-Reggiano and grana in the north. (But don't forget that Parmigiano-Reggiano is also one of the world's greatest eating cheeses, often served as a dessert in Italy, with a few drops of precious *aceto balsamico tradizionale* sprinkled on top.) Softer cheeses also enter into the Italian kitchen, like *mozzarella di bufola* or *fior di latte* (the proper name for mozzarella made from cow's milk), or softest of all, ricotta—which is actually a secondary product, made by reheating the whey left over from the first stage of cheese-making.

Whether you buy cheese for the kitchen or the table, it is best stored at a cool but not refrigerated temperature. In modern American homes, unfortunately, this is not often possible. If you must chill your cheeses, bring them out of the refrigerator several hours before serving them in order to let their flavors expand and their textures soften before the meal. (This, obviously, is not a requirement if you're simply cooking with cheese.) How to wrap cheeses for storage at home is one of those questions that causes the drawing of metaphoric daggers. I follow the lead of Steve Jenkins, dean of American cheese-lovers, who says plastic wrap is fine for firm and semi-soft cheeses, but little fresh goat's milk cheeses that are still developing flavors are much better wrapped in waxed paper, aluminum foil, or a glass or plastic refrigerator container with a tightly fitting lid.

# Yogurt "Cheese" Balls with Za'atar and Sumac

A Lebanese favorite, these are often served on toasted crisps of bread as part of a meze or with wine before dinner, but they're also good at breakfast with a round of freshly baked pita bread, a handful of black and green olives, and a few radishes or scallions. The yogurt is not really cheese, of course, but thick, strained yogurt, put to drain in a fine-meshed sieve for 24 hours or more until it is very thick and creamy.

The term *za'atar* is a source of confusion as it refers both to a dried herb, wild thyme or oregano, that grows on the slopes of Mt. Lebanon (very similar in flavor to Greek wild oregano), as well as to a spice mixture in which the wild herb features. *Za'atar* the mixture is what's called for here. It's made with dried wild thyme (the herb *za'atar*) and sumac, in a ratio of 2 to 1, then the mix is measured and a quarter of that is added in toasted sesame seeds. So, for instance, if you had 2 cups of dried thyme and 1 cup of sumac, you would add ¾ cup of toasted sesame (this would be an awful lot of *za'atar*, but Lebanese cooks tend to use it a lot). Some cooks add roasted chickpeas or roasted melon seeds, ground to a powder. You can buy the already mixed spices (see page 415 for sources), or you can mix your own.

The spice mixture is often sprinkled on bread, especially Arab bread pulled warm from the oven, spread with olive oil, and dashed with *za'atar* for a great breakfast bread called *man-aqish*. And a pinch of *za'atar* is also terrific on a plain boiled egg in the morning, especially if a teaspoon of olive oil is added along with it.

PUT THE YOGURT TO DRAIN in a fine-mesh sieve or a special yogurt strainer for at least 24 hours. When the yogurt is very thick and has reduced to about half the original quantity, remove from the strainer, discarding the whey. Transfer the yogurt to a bowl and add the salt, mixing it in very well.

HAVE READY A TRAY or baking sheet spread with clean dish towels. Dip your hands in water, then take a small amount of yogurt and shape it into a ball the size of a walnut. Set the ball on the tray and continue with the rest of the yogurt. When all the yogurt is shaped, set another dish towel lightly on top of them and put them aside to dry for at least 24 hours.

IN A SMALL BOWL, mix together the *za'atar* and sumac, with the red pepper if you wish. Take a ball and roll it gently in the mixture to coat it lightly. Continue with the other yogurt balls. When all the balls are coated, set them in a single layer on a tray or refrigerator dish. Refrigerate them until you are ready to serve.

VARIATION: Instead of rolling the yogurt balls in the herb mixture, transfer them to a clean glass jar and fill the jar with extra-virgin olive oil, to which you could add a couple of whole dried red chili peppers and a few bay leaves. Submerged in the oil, they will keep for a week to 10 days. If refrigerated, however, they must be brought back to room temperature before serving.

**Makes 35 to 40 small yogurt balls**

4 cups whole milk yogurt

1 teaspoon sea salt

2 tablespoons za'atar (the spice mixture)

1 tablespoon sumac

1 teaspoon ground red Middle Eastern pepper (Aleppo pepper, Turkish pepper) (optional)

# Focaccia di Recco

I was introduced to this delectable confection by American food writer Fred Plotkin, who has a boundless enthusiasm for and delight in the foods of his adopted Italian home in Liguria. *Focacce* are made all over Liguria (all over Italy!), but this one from the little seaside town of Recco is very special, with a thin, unleavened dough to encase the melting cheese. Most often you'll find it baked in a wood-fired oven, but one woman I met along the Italian Riviera said, no, no, no, it was most authentic when fried in a frying pan. I've tried both, and while the frying pan method is delicious, the oven-baked version is somewhat more digestible.

A problem is the cheese to be used. It is always a particular Ligurian runny rindless cheese with a decided tang, that's called *crescenza* or *stracchino* (and is *not* the same as *stracchino* from Lombardy, which is what's mostly available in North America). When Fred told me that the old-fashioned Recchesi used to make their focaccia with goats' milk cheese, I decided to try the following mixture.

You will need a 14-inch pizza pan, the cheaper the better—thin metal will more quickly transmit the heat of the oven.

**Makes 2 focacce, enough for 6 to 8 abundant servings**

**For the dough:**

2½ cups unbleached all-purpose flour

½ teaspoon sea salt, or to taste

3 tablespoons extra-virgin olive oil, plus more as needed

¾ to 1 cup warm water

**For the cheese:**

8 ounces taleggio

8 ounces fresh young goat's milk cheese

¼ cup sour cream

FIRST MAKE THE DOUGH. Combine the flour and salt in a food processor and process continuously while you slowly add the olive oil, a tablespoonful at a time. When all the oil has been added, start to add the water, in increments of ¼ cup. You will probably need at least ¾ cup, but you may not need the entire amount—a lot depends on the ambient humidity in the kitchen.

WHEN THE DOUGH FORMS a soft ball, remove from the food processor and knead a half dozen strokes on a dry unfloured board. Then roll the dough into a ball, cover with plastic wrap, and set aside to rest for at least 1 hour.

WHEN YOU ARE READY TO PROCEED with the preparation, preheat the oven to 450°F, preferably with a pizza stone or baking tiles in place. Use a little oil to grease the pizza pan lightly.

DIVIDE THE DOUGH IN TWO, with one half a little greater than the other. Roll the greater half out on a board to a very, very thin circle about 16 inches in diameter. Transfer the circle to the oiled pan, fitting the edges and draping the dough over the sides.

MIX TOGETHER the two cheeses and the sour cream, using a hand mixer to blend them. They don't have to be a homogeneous cream, just well mixed. Drop generous, tablespoon-sized blobs of the cheese mixture all over the surface of the dough.

ROLL OUT THE REMAINING DOUGH to make a very, very, very thin circle, even thinner than the first one, about 14 inches in diameter. Stretch this over the cheese and use the edges of your hands to press the dough around the cheese blobs, but be careful not to tear or make holes in the dough. Smear a little oil on your fingers and roll the edges of the two dough sheets together to seal them. Take another teaspoon or so of olive oil and dribble it over the top.

AS SOON AS THE FOCACCIA IS READY, slide it into the oven and bake it for 20 to 30 minutes, or until the dough is golden and starting to crisp around the edges.

SERVE IMMEDIATELY, cutting the focaccia into pie wedges and being careful not to drop the melting cheese.

# Tarte au Chèvre

Michelle van Weddingen, Yves' wife, makes this goat-cheese tart, using her husband's hand-made cheeses, and serves it for tea at the couple's home on their goat-farm *bastide* near Ampus.

The tart shells, tomato sauce, and cheese cream may all be made well ahead, then combined at the last moment before the final baking.

**Makes 8 servings**

**For the dough:**

1 teaspoon active dry yeast

1 cup very warm water

2 cups unbleached all-purpose flour

½ cup cornmeal

Pinch of sea salt

2 tablespoons extra-virgin olive oil

**For the tomato sauce:**

6 to 8 shallots, finely minced

5 garlic cloves, finely minced

3 tablespoons extra-virgin olive oil

1 (28-ounce) can whole tomatoes, drained and chopped, the juice reserved

1 sprig fresh rosemary, chopped

3 to 4 sprigs fresh thyme, chopped

1 bay leaf

1 teaspoon sugar

½ teaspoon coarse sea salt

2 tablespoons fresh orange juice

Grated or julienned zest of 1 orange

FIRST, MAKE THE DOUGH. In a mixing bowl, combine the yeast and warm water and set aside until the yeast is thoroughly dissolved. Add 1 cup of the flour and mix well. Cover with plastic wrap and set the bowl aside in a warm place for about 1 hour, or until the sponge rises slightly and bubbles.

ADD THE REMAINING 1 CUP FLOUR and the cornmeal, along with the salt and olive oil. Use a wooden spoon at first, and then your hands to mix it. When the ingredients are combined, but still raggedy in texture, turn them out on a lightly floured board and knead with your hands until the dough is soft and elastic. Transfer the dough to a lightly oiled bowl, cover the bowl with plastic wrap, and set aside in a warm place to rise for 1 hour.

WHILE THE DOUGH IS RISING, make the tomato sauce. Over medium-low heat, gently sweat the shallots and garlic in the oil until the vegetables are soft, about 10 minutes. Do not let them brown. Add the tomatoes, herbs, and the bay leaf. Stir in the sugar and salt. Raise the heat slightly and continue cooking the sauce, adding a little of the reserved juice from the can if necessary to keep the tomatoes from burning. Break up the tomatoes with the edge of a spoon as they cook down. After about 20 minutes, you should have a thick, coarse-textured sauce. Remove the pan from the heat and stir in the orange juice and orange zest.

IN A MIXING BOWL, mash the goat cheese with a table fork. Stir in the eggs. Add the parsley, shallots, milk, and oil. Beat with a wire whisk to make a thick cream.

PREHEAT THE OVEN to 400°F.

PUNCH DOWN THE RISEN DOUGH and divide it into two equal portions. Roll each one out into a disk about ⅛ inch thick to fit the bottom and sides of a 9-inch tart pan, preferably the kind with fluted sides and a removable bottom. Set each disk into a tart pan, pressing the bottom edges into the corners and fluting the top edge. Prick the bottom all over with a fork. Bake the tart shells for about 10 minutes, or until they are golden and firm. Remove from the oven and set aside to cool.

IF YOU WISH, the tart shells can be removed from the tart pans at this point and set on a baking sheet.

REDUCE THE OVEN temperature to 375°F.

SPOON HALF THE TOMATO SAUCE over the bottom of each tart shell. Top the tomato sauce with the cheese cream. Dot the cream with black olives and sprinkle each tart with 2 tablespoons of the Parmigiano and a few grinds of black pepper.

BAKE FOR ABOUT 20 MINUTES, or until the tarts are firm. Remove from the oven and let cool slightly before serving.

**For the cheese cream:**

12 ounces creamy, fresh, young goat cheese

4 large eggs

½ cup finely minced flat-leaf parsley

¼ cup finely minced shallots

½ cup skim milk

⅓ cup extra-virgin olive oil

**To finish the tart:**

½ cup pitted black olives, preferably oil-cured

4 tablespoons freshly grated Parmigiano-Reggiano cheese

Freshly ground black pepper

# Green Salad with Toasted Goat Cheese

 The combination of crisp salad with a melting warm goat cheese is another Provençal favorite that has become increasingly popular in North America in recent years.

**Makes 4 to 8 servings**

½ cup walnut halves

4 to 6 cups salad greens, rinsed and dried

1 (10- to 12-ounce) log goat cheese, about 2 to 3 inches in diameter

4 to 5 slices plain white country-style bread, crusts removed

2 tablespoons finely minced green herbs, including flat-leaf parsley and basil, chervil, or sorrel, if available

1 large egg

About 6 tablespoons extra-virgin olive oil

½ garlic clove, finely chopped

Pinch of sea salt

½ teaspoon French-style mustard (optional)

1 tablespoon red wine vinegar or juice of ½ lemon

PREHEAT THE OVEN to 350°F.

SPREAD OUT THE WALNUTS on a baking sheet and toast in the oven for 10 to 15 minutes, or until they are brown and aromatic, but don't let them burn. Set aside to cool slightly.

ARRANGE THE SALAD GREENS on a serving platter. Slice the log of goat cheese into eight equal disks. Chop the walnuts very finely with a knife or use a food processor to reduce them to crumbs—but be careful not to turn them into a paste. Transfer the crumbed walnuts to a shallow soup plate.

IN THE SAME FOOD PROCESSOR, whizz the bread slices to make fine crumbs. Mix the crumbs with the walnuts and add the minced herbs. Toss with a fork to mix well.

IN A SEPARATE SHALLOW SOUP PLATE, beat the egg with a fork until the yolk and white are thoroughly combined.

SET A SAUTÉ PAN over medium heat and add 2 tablespoons of the oil. Dip each goat-cheese disk in the egg, then coat it thoroughly with the crumb mixture. Sauté the disks in the oil until golden brown on each side and creamy in the middle, 2 to 3 minutes to a side. As each disk finishes browning, remove it and drain it on absorbent paper. Add more oil to the pan if you need to.

WHILE THE DISKS ARE BROWNING, make the salad dressing. Place the garlic and salt in a small bowl and, using the back of a spoon, crush the garlic into the salt to make a smooth paste. Stir in the mustard, if desired, then 3 tablespoons of oil and the vinegar.

SPOON THE DRESSING over the salad. Arrange the browned disks on top and serve immediately.

# Tagliatelle ai Quattro Formaggi

 This famous Italian delicacy calls for four different cheeses, not just as an extravagance, but also to provide the kind of contrasts in flavors and textures that would otherwise brand *Tagliatelle ai Quattro Formaggi* as plain-old, same-old macaroni and cheese. I have suggested cheeses from four different parts of the Mediterranean, just as a challenge, but if you can't find one or more of these don't worry—either substitute something else, or increase the quantity of one of the other cheeses, making it thus *Tagliatelle ai Tre Formaggi,* or even *ai Due.*

IN A LARGE STOCKPOT over medium-high heat, bring 6 quarts of water to a rolling boil.

WHILE THE WATER IS HEATING, combine the cream and all the cheeses except the Parmigiano in a small saucepan. Bring to a gentle simmer over low heat, whisking occasionally to blend the cheeses. When the sauce just begins to bubble, stir in about ⅔ cup of the Parmigiano. Taste the sauce and add salt, if necessary, and lots of black pepper, and a few gratings of nutmeg.

ADD 2 TABLESPOONS of salt to the boiling water and plunge in the pasta, stirring to immerse it all at once and bring the water quickly back to the boil. Boil the pasta, uncovered, for 7 to 8 minutes, or follow the package instructions.

WARM A PASTA BOWL with some of the boiling pasta water. When the pasta is just al dente, turn the water out of the pasta bowl, drain the pasta, and turn it immediately into the warmed bowl. Pour the cheese sauce over the pasta and toss to mix the sauce into the pasta very well.

SERVE IMMEDIATELY, passing the remaining ⅓ cup Parmigiano to sprinkle on top.

**Makes 4 to 6 servings**

Water

⅔ cup light cream or half-and-half

⅔ cup (about 4 ounces) freshly grated Pecorino Toscano or Pecorino Sardo (do not use Pecorino Romano as it is too strong for this dish)

⅔ cup (about 7 ounces) fresh young goat cheese, preferably imported from France, although a good domestic goat cheese will do very well

⅔ cup (about 4 ounces) freshly grated Garrotxa (goat cheese from northeast Spain)

1 cup freshly grated Parmigiano-Reggiano cheese

Sea salt and freshly ground black pepper

Freshly grated nutmeg

1 pound tagliatelle, linguine, or other long, thin pasta

# Turkish Yogurt Soup with Tiny Meatballs

Yogurt soup is one of the most soothing dishes imaginable, carrying that great comfort-food chicken soup to yet another level of consolation. The meatballs are not necessary, but lend added richness—this could even be served as a main course for a light supper.

You will need a very flavorful chicken stock for this soup, preferably one you have made yourself (see page 406 for recipe).

If you can find goat's milk yogurt, you will not need to stabilize it before cooking it. Because of the fat structure, it doesn't separate on boiling, the way cow's milk yogurt does; moreover, it gives richer flavor and texture to the soup.

Make the meatballs ahead of time, if you wish.

**Makes 8 servings**

½ to ¾ cup finely chopped onions (2 medium onions)

4 tablespoons extra-virgin olive oil

¼ cup long-grain rice

Boiling water

Sea salt

½ pound lean ground lamb

2 tablespoons finely minced flat-leaf parsley

¼ cup finely minced fresh dill

2 tablespoons finely minced fresh mint

Freshly ground black pepper

½ teaspoon ground red pepper, preferably Middle Eastern (Aleppo pepper, Turkish pepper)

1 large egg, lightly beaten

MIX THE ONIONS with 2 tablespoons of the oil and set over medium-low heat. Cook gently, stirring, until the onions have softened, about 20 minutes. Add the rice and 1 cup of boiling water with salt to taste. Continue cooking for about 10 minutes, or until the rice has softened somewhat and absorbed most of the liquid. Remove from the heat and set aside to cool.

IN A BOWL combine the lamb, parsley, dill, and mint. Mix well, using your hands, then add lots of black pepper and the red pepper. Mix again and taste for seasoning. Stir in the rice-onion mixture, which will have cooled somewhat, and mix. Add the egg and enough bread crumbs to make a mixture that is moist but will hold together well. Form into small meatballs, about the size of marbles.

COMBINE THE CHICKEN BROTH with 1 cup water and bring to a simmer. Add the meatballs and let simmer very gently until the meatballs rise to the top of the liquid, indicating they are done. Remove them with a slotted spoon and set aside.

IF YOU ARE USING COW'S MILK YOGURT, beat the egg yolk in a bowl with a wire whisk, then gradually beat in the yogurt. Whisk in 1 cup of cold water. Measure out 1 cup of the soup and whisk it into the yogurt, then pour the yogurt into the soup pot and stir it in. Bring to a simmer. Cover and simmer very, very gently, watching carefully so that the soup does not come above a very gentle simmer, for 10 minutes. Then taste and add salt if needed.

IF YOU ARE USING GOAT'S MILK YOGURT, combine the yogurt in a bowl with 1 cup of simmering soup stock. Stir to temper the yogurt, then pour it into the soup and bring to a simmer. Taste and add salt if needed.

RETURN THE MEATBALLS to the soup and simmer just long enough to heat them through.

WHEN YOU ARE READY TO SERVE, melt the butter in a small saucepan. Crumble in the dried mint, then use this to dribble over the top and garnish the soup. Serve immediately.

2 to 3 tablespoons fine dry bread crumbs

5 cups flavorful chicken broth

1 egg yolk (optional)

4 cups whole-milk yogurt, preferably goat's milk yogurt

2 tablespoons unsalted butter

2 tablespoons dried mint

# Spinach Baked with Feta

A favorite way to treat spinach in Greece, this is a great dish for dedicated vegetarians, at least for those who allow dairy products in their diet, and makes a good first course for confirmed carnivores.

If the feta is very salty, put the whole cheese in a small bowl and cover with cool water. Set aside for an hour or so until the cheese has lost much of its salt.

**Makes 4 servings**

2 pounds fresh spinach

5 tablespoons extra-virgin olive oil

1 small yellow onion, finely chopped

Nutmeg for grating

Sea salt and freshly ground black pepper

¾ cup grated feta

¾ cup ricotta, drained for at least 1 hour

½ cup coarsely chopped flat-leaf parsley

PICK OVER THE SPINACH carefully, discarding any wilted, yellow, or otherwise faded leaves. Wash in several basins of water, until the water is clear without any sand at the bottom.

TRANSFER THE SPINACH, with the water clinging to its leaves, into a heavy-duty saucepan, cover the pan, and set it over medium heat until the spinach starts to cook. Lower the heat to medium-low and cook for about 20 minutes, or until the spinach is thoroughly tender. Drain in a colander and chop the spinach while it's still in the colander (using a curved chopping blade), to further drain excess liquid.

PREHEAT THE OVEN to 350°F.

IN A SKILLET, combine 3 tablespoons of oil with the onion. Set over low heat and cook, very gently, until the onion is soft and melting, about 15 to 20 minutes. Stir in the spinach. Grate in nutmeg to taste and add sea salt and black pepper. Continue cooking for about 5 minutes more. Remove from the heat and once more drain away any liquid released by the spinach.

STIR THE GRATED FETA, the ricotta, and the parsley into the spinach. Taste and adjust the seasoning.

USE A SMALL AMOUNT of the remaining olive oil to generously oil the bottom and sides of a small oval gratin or other type of baking dish. Spoon the spinach into the baking dish and dribble the remaining olive oil over the top. Bake for about 20 minutes.

SERVE IMMEDIATELY or, following Greek custom, let the spinach cool to just above room temperature before serving.

VARIATION: To make a nice lunch dish, remove the spinach from the oven after 10 minutes. With a spoon, make four indentations in the top of the spinach and drop an egg in each indentation. Sprinkle a few drops of olive oil over each egg and return to the oven for the final 10 minutes of cooking.

# Knafe

Arab pastries, crisp with buttery, crunchy layers and drenched in sugar syrup, are the province of professional cooks all over the Eastern Mediterranean and seldom, if ever, made at home. The best, they say, are made with ewes' milk butter, and while that may sound strange, even a little off-putting, it's true that the finest pastries I've had always turn out to have butter made from ewe's milk as their prime ingredient. The other important ingredient is the hard durum-wheat flour from which the pastry dough is made.

Certain towns are famous, sometimes for a particular pastry, sometimes just for pastry in general. Saida (Sidon) and Trablus (Tripoli) in Lebanon, and Gaziantep in Turkey are celebrated for a whole range of pastries, while Aleppo in Syria is renowned for *ghorayeb*, a crumbly shortbread, and Nablus in Palestine for this peculiar pastry called *knafe* (KNAH-fay), or *konafe*, or *kinafeh*, or, in Turkish, *kadayif*. Like *ghorayeb*, however, *knafe* is made all over the Middle East, from the Egyptian desert oases all the way up into the Balkans, wherever Ottoman cooks took this tricky preparation. Tricky only so far as the dough is concerned, however, and once you've found a source for fresh or frozen dough (I get it by mail order from Adriana's Caravan in New York, see page 415 for details), the rest is mainly a question of assembling ingredients and combining them.

It was in an oasis town in Egypt's Western Desert that I first saw *knafe* dough, which is called *kataifi* and looks like shredded wheat, being made. It was evening and the window of the shop, which sold nothing but *kataifi*, was brightly lit. Just inside, a large, flat metal disk was revolving above a low gas ring. The disk, I was told, was rubbed with wax or oil from time to time to keep the cooked pastry from sticking. The dough, which was more like a batter than a proper dough, dropped through the holes of a perforated funnel that floated above the disk, which gradually, as it turned, accumulated more and more threads of dough. Indeed, it was very much like a Pennsylvania Dutch funnel cake. "It doesn't really cook so much," the pastry-maker explained to Sari Abul-Jubein, the friend who was with me, "it just dries out."

Usually, *knafe* is made either with walnuts or with cheese in the middle. I wondered about combining them and worried that I would never be allowed back in the Middle East if I did so. Then I found an old Palestinian cookbook with a recipe that did exactly that, so I took it as carte blanche for a walnut-cheese combination.

*Kataifi* comes in a long twist, like a skein of yarn or, more aptly, a skein of rice noodles. It has to be thawed before working it, so, if you have frozen dough, take it out of the freezer the day before you intend to make the *knafe*. You can get all the ingredients ready the day before and then assemble them the next day.

With its combination of cheese, clotted cream, and clarified butter, this recipe is a good example of the refinement and attention to detail that marks good pastry chefs in the Eastern Mediterranean world.

Believe me, it's a lot easier than it looks and the result is delicious.

LEAVE THE *KNAFE* DOUGH in the refrigerator to thaw if necessary, but keep it well covered at all times until you are ready to use it, to prevent it from drying. Put the feta cheese in a bowl and cover with cool water. Set aside to desalinate, changing the water periodically, for a couple of hours. When the feta tastes sweet rather than salty, drain it and crumble into a bowl.

COMBINE THE MILK and cream in a wide saucepan, in order to expose as much of the liquid to the heat as possible. Set over the lowest possible temperature and bring slowly to a simmer. The milk should never be in danger of boiling over—in fact, it should just simmer throughout the cooking time, which will take 2 to 3 hours. During this time, much of the water that is naturally present in the milk will evaporate, leaving a concentrate similar to clotted cream. After the milk has cooked for 2 hours, stir in 2 tablespoons of the sugar. When the milk has finished cooking and a thick scum of cream has formed on the top, sprinkle the rosewater over it and set aside to cool for 2 to 3 hours.

WHEN THE MILK IS COOL, lift the cream off the top with a slotted spoon or spatula and set aside, refrigerating if you are keeping it overnight. (The liquid remaining in the saucepan can be discarded.)

**For the dough:**

8 ounces freshly made or thawed frozen *knafe* dough, called *kataifi*

8 ounces feta cheese

4 cups whole milk, preferably not homogenized, if you can find it

1 cup heavy cream

5 tablespoons sugar

2 teaspoons rosewater

1 cup unsalted butter

1⅓ cups walnut pieces lightly toasted in the oven

1 teaspoon ground cinnamon

½ pound real mozzarella, either cow's milk or buffalo milk

**For the sugar syrup:**

1¼ cups sugar

¼ cup water

1 tablespoon fresh lemon juice

1 teaspoon rosewater

WHILE THE MILK IS COOKING, clarify the butter. Melt it in a saucepan, but don't let it cook. Skim off and discard the solids that rise to the top, then pour off the melted butter into a small bowl or pitcher, leaving behind any milky residue in the bottom. Set aside, covered, until you are ready to use it.

RUB THE TOASTED WALNUTS TOGETHER in a kitchen towel, then pick them over, using the pointed end of a paring knife to remove, as far as possible, the flaky skin on the outsides. You won't be able to get rid of it all, but it has a tannic quality that you don't want in your *knafe*. Put the nuts in a food processor with the remaining 3 tablespoons of sugar and the cinnamon and process to a fine crumb. Don't overprocess—you want crumbs, not walnut paste.

GRATE THE MOZZARELLA on the large holes of a cheese grater and combine with the feta.

ALL OF THIS MAY BE DONE AHEAD, if you wish, and left until the next day, but refrigerate the dairy products if you do so. The clarified butter must be brought to room temperature before you can use it so it will have the proper soft texture for working it into the dough.

WHEN YOU'RE READY to put the *knafe* together, preheat the oven to 375°F.

OPEN THE PACKAGE OF *KATAIFI* and twist the skein apart. (Most *kataifi* comes in 1-pound packages. You'll only need half of this, so pull about half the *kataifi* away and return the rest, tightly wrapped in plastic, to the refrigerator. If you're not going to use it right away, it may be refrozen.)

NOW, WORKING WITH THE CLARIFIED BUTTER, pull and tease the strands of *kataifi* apart, dribbling a little clarified butter over them and working it in. The strands will crumble a little while you're doing this but that's okay, that's what they're meant to do. Keep adding clarified butter and pulling and rubbing the strands. It sounds much more complicated than it is and you will quickly develop a rhythm for doing this. Use all the clarified butter. There will be some places with lumps of butter, but that's okay, too, just so long as most of the strands of kataifi are coated with butter.

TAKE ABOUT HALF the prepared strands of dough, which by now are rather short, noodley-looking things, and use it to line the bottom of a 9-inch, straight-sided tart pan. It should make a layer about ½ to ¾ inch thick.

MIX THE CLOTTED cream in with the two cheeses and add the ground walnuts. Stir with a spatula to mix it all well, then spread it over the layer of *kataifi*. Use the rest of the *kataifi* to make a layer over the top of the cheese layer, making sure that it is completely covered. Press gently all over the top with the flat of your hand to firm up the cake.

BAKE 30 MINUTES. Invert the pan onto a flat plate and slide the *knafe* back into the pan so the other side will turn crisp and golden. Return it to the oven and bake for 20 minutes. If, after 10 minutes, the knafe still looks a little pale, raise the heat to 400°F or 450°F. for the last 10 minutes.

WHILE THE *KNAFE* IS BAKING, make the sugar syrup. Combine the sugar and water in a small saucepan and bring to a slow boil. Continue boiling for about 5 minutes, or until the syrup is fairly thick. Remove from the heat and let it cool slightly, then stir in the lemon juice and rosewater. Set aside to cool to room temperature while the *knafe* finishes baking.

WHEN THE *KNAFE* IS DONE, remove it from the oven and immediately pour the syrup all over the top. Set it aside for 20 minutes or longer, until you can handle the pan without burning yourself, then transfer it to a cake plate for serving.

# Sweet Cheese Ravioli with Bitter Honey

### SEBADAS

These lightly sweetened cheese tarts are made on the island of Sardinia and served with the island's famous *miele amaro,* bitter honey. If you can't find *miele amaro,* use a richly flavored honey—chestnut honey, for instance, would be good. Fresh sheep's milk cheese (not ricotta), a creamy cheese with a pleasantly acid tang, is not easy to find, but the folks at Old Chatham Sheepherding Company in New York's Hudson Valley will happily ship it for overnight or second-day delivery. (See page 415 for ordering information for the cheese and the honey.) Although no other type of cheese will do as well, you could substitute a creamy fresh goat cheese in a pinch.

**Makes 16 to 20 sebadas, 5 to 6 servings**

**For the dough:**

1½ cups semolina

½ cup unbleached all-purpose flour

1 whole large egg

3½ tablespoons pure pork lard, if available; otherwise use solid white vegetable shortening

Big pinch of sea salt dissolved in ½ cup very warm water

**For the filling:**

2 abundant cups fresh sheeps' milk cheese

½ cup hot water

2 to 3 tablespoons semolina

1 teaspoon sugar, or more or less to taste

Grated zests of 1 medium lemon and 1 small orange, preferably organically raised

2 cups extra-virgin olive oil, for frying

FIRST MAKE THE DOUGH. Toss together the semolina and unbleached flour in a bowl. Make a well in the middle. Add the egg and lard to the center and mix with your hands, rubbing the lard into the flour until the dough is quite sandy in texture and the lard is evenly distributed throughout. Add the salty water by the tablespoon—5 to 6 tablespoons should be the right amount, but you may need more or less depending on relative humidity. The dough should be quite soft and malleable but not sticky. Knead the dough a few strokes on a very lightly floured board, just to incorporate everything very well. Shape it into a ball, cover with a damp towel or a piece of plastic wrap, and set it aside to rest while you make the filling.

IN A SMALL PAN over medium-low heat, combine the cheese with the hot water. As soon as the mixture starts to bubble around the edges, stir in 2 tablespoons of semolina and continue to cook very gently, stirring with a wooden spoon, until the cheese thickens. You may add all or part of the remaining 1 tablespoon semolina. The cheese mixture should be thick but not solid—about the consistency of commercial soured cream. Remove from the heat and stir in the sugar and citrus zests. Taste and add a little more sugar if the cheese is still very acid, but keep in mind that the cheese should not be noticeably sweet.

DIVIDE THE DOUGH into four equal portions. Roll one portion out on a very lightly floured board until it is very thin—less than ¹⁄₁₆ of an inch. (Italian cooks say you should be able to read a newspaper through the dough—but whatever you do, do *not* roll the dough out on a newspaper as it will pick up a nasty taste and possibly other nasty things as well from the newsprint.)

USE A CIRCULAR BISCUIT-CUTTER about 3¼ to 3½ inches in diameter to cut circles from the dough. Drop about a teaspoon of the filling into the center of half the circles. Dip your finger in warm water and run it around the edge of each circle, then cover with the remaining circles and press the two together with the tines of a fork. Set the completed *sebadas* on a rack while you continue assembling the remaining pasta dough and filling.

WHEN ALL THE *SEBADAS* have been shaped, bring the olive oil to frying temperature (350° to 360°F). Use a thermometer to make sure the oil is hot enough before you start frying. Have another rack ready with paper towels underneath to drain the fried *sebadas*. Drop 3 or 4 *sebadas* into the hot oil and let them fry, turning them once after they have risen to the surface of the oil. Fry until they are lightly golden rather than brown in color. As soon as they are ready, remove with a slotted spoon and set on the draining rack. Then continue with the remaining *sebadas*.

MEANWHILE, warm the honey in a small saucepan, adding a few tablespoons of water or of orange juice from the grated orange, until it is liquid and quite warm. Serve the sebadas, 2 or 3 to a serving, with honey liquid drizzled over the top.

¾ cup Sardinian bitter honey (*miele amaro*)

Fresh orange juice or water

# Eastern Mediterranean Yogurt Cake with Almonds or Pistachios

Yogurt gives this rich, dense cake an extraordinarily buttery flavor. You won't believe it's not butter, especially if you can find goat's milk yogurt to use. I serve this with a sprinkle of confectioners' sugar over the top. If you wish, you could ice the cake, but it almost seems unnecessary.

Note that it's important to have the yogurt, butter, and eggs at room temperature.

**Makes 8 to 10 servings**

1½ cups whole milk yogurt, preferably made from goat's milk, at room temperature

Butter and flour for the pan

1 cup whole blanched almonds or shelled pistachios

2½ cups unbleached all-purpose flour

1½ teaspoons baking powder

¼ teaspoon sea salt

1 cup butter, at room temperature

1 cup plus 2 tablespoons sugar

5 eggs, separated, at room temperature

3 tablespoons grated lemon zest, preferably from organic lemons

Confectioners' sugar for the cake top (optional)

SET THE YOGURT in a strainer or in a colander with a triple layer of cheesecloth and strain for 30 or 40 minutes. Measure out 1 cup of strained yogurt.

PREHEAT THE OVEN to 350°F. Butter and flour a 9- or 10-inch cake pan.

IF THE NUTS HAVE NOT BEEN PREVIOUSLY TOASTED, spread the nuts out on a baking sheet and set in the oven for about 15 minutes, or until they are lightly toasted, but not a rich brown. Remove and set aside to cool. Then chop the nuts very fine or process them with brief pulsing spurts in a food processor. The nuts should be fine but not at all pasty or buttery. Measure out 1 cup of chopped nuts.

COMBINE THE FLOUR, baking powder, and salt, and sift into a small bowl. Mix the nuts into the flour mixture, tossing to combine well.

BLEND THE BUTTER and 1 cup of sugar, beating well until the butter is very pale and creamy. Add the strained yogurt and beat again until smooth. One after the other, beat in the yolks of the eggs. Fold in the lemon zest.

IN A SEPARATE BOWL, using clean beaters, beat the egg whites to soft peaks. Add the remaining 2 tablespoons sugar and continue beating to stiff peaks. Now fold a third of the flour mixture into the yogurt, followed by a third of the egg whites. Continue folding in the dry ingredients and the egg whites by thirds until everything has been combined thoroughly. Pour into the prepared pan. Bake for 50 to 60 minutes, until the cake pulls away from the sides of the pan and the center springs back when pressed lightly with your finger.

REMOVE FROM THE OVEN and invert on a rack to cool. After removing the pan, lightly dust the top of the cake, if you wish, with confectioners' sugar.

# Torta di Ricotta

Southern Italian pastry cooks are adept at producing these light, refreshing, delicately perfumed cheesecakes, a revelation to anyone accustomed to the stodgy, overly sweet versions available in New York City and points west. Much of the character comes from the ricotta itself, naturally, since that's a principal ingredient. If you can find (and it isn't easy) goats' milk or sheep's milk ricotta, that's the one to use. Otherwise, taste, taste, taste, until you find a ricotta made from cows' milk that is not bland and characterless.

This is made with a sweet *pasta frolla* dough, enriched with egg yolks, or with a sweetened yeast dough. I prefer the former because it's easier to roll out.

If you have small individual tart pans, you can make little ricotta pies called *cassatine,* and serve them one to a customer. Then there's the renowned Neapolitan Easter pie, *pastiera di grano,* which is nothing but a *torta di ricotta* to which has been added lots of candied peel and pine nuts, as well as a good cup of peeled (hulled) wheat berries that have been cooked in 1 cup milk, 1 cup sugar, and 1 tablespoon unsalted butter for as long as it takes to soften them—which could be anywhere from 30 minutes to 2 hours. If you want to make this magnificent Easter sweet, prepare the wheat several days in advance. It can be refrigerated without any problems.

A lovely flavoring called *fiori di Sicilia* (Sicilian flowers), made from citrus oils, is available from *The Baker's Catalogue* (see page 415). It gives a most authentic flavor to this and to the ricotta fritters that follow. If you have *fiori di Sicilia,* use it instead of the orange-flower water in this recipe.

**Makes 10 to 12 servings**

**For the *pasta frolla*:**

2 cups unbleached all-purpose flour

½ cup cake flour

⅓ cup sugar

Pinch of sea salt

¾ cup unsalted butter, at room temperature

2 large eggs

FIRST MAKE THE PIE CRUST. Mix together the flours, ⅓ cup sugar, and the salt. Cut the butter into pieces and work rapidly into the dry mixture. Make a well in the center. Separate one of the eggs and reserve the yolk. Add the white to the pie dough along with the second egg in its entirety. Add the lemon zest and, using a fork, gradually work all the elements of the dough together, working in the wine or water. When everything is well mixed, shape into a ball, cover with plastic wrap, and refrigerate for at least 1 hour. Note that this dough is fragile and crumbly. It is easiest to roll out between two sheets of waxed paper, working quickly because the more it's handled, the crumblier it gets.

WHILE THE DOUGH IS RESTING, drain the ricotta in a fine-mesh sieve, to get rid of excess liquid. When you are ready to make the filling, turn the drained ricotta into a bowl and add the citrus zests, ⅓ cup sugar, vanilla, and orange flavoring, beating with a wire whisk until the ricotta is light and fluffy. (Don't use an electric beater as it's easy to overbeat.) Beat in the egg yolks, one at a time, beating well to incorporate the yolk after each addition. Beat in the milk. The filling mix should be like a loose custard, not too firm to pour, yet not at all soupy. If it's too firm, beat in a bit more milk. If it seems too loose, on the other hand, beat in another egg yolk.

PREHEAT THE OVEN to 375°F. Lightly butter and flour a 10-inch springform pan.

ROLL THE PASTRY DOUGH out between two sheets of waxed paper to make a disk large enough to fill the tart pan, with a little excess to flute around the top.

USING CLEAN BEATERS, beat the egg whites in a separate bowl to soft peaks. Sprinkle on the remaining 2 tablespoons sugar and beat to stiff peaks. Gently fold the egg whites into the filling mixture, then turn the filling into the pastry case. Use the reserved egg yolk from the pie dough, mixed with a little water, to paint the exposed surface of the pastry.

BAKE FOR 45 TO 60 MINUTES, or until the filling is set and the crust is golden brown. Remove to a rack and let cool to room temperature, but do not chill, before serving.

VARIATION: You don't need to wait for Easter to add things to the filling. If you wish, stir a handful of pine nuts into the mixture before you fold in the egg whites; ¼ cup of finely slivered candied peel also makes a nice addition, but the peel should be tossed with a tablespoon or so of flour to keep it from clumping together in the filling.

Grated zest of 1 lemon

2 tablespoons dry white wine or water

**For the filling:**

12 ounces whole-milk ricotta (¾ cup)

Grated zest of 2 lemons, preferably organic

Grated zest of 1 orange, preferably organic

⅓ cup plus 2 tablespoons sugar

1 teaspoon pure vanilla extract

1 tablespoon orange-flower water, or 1 teaspoon *fiori di Sicilia*

3 large eggs, separated

2 tablespoons whole milk, or more as needed

Butter and flour for the pan

½ cup confectioners' sugar, to sprinkle on top

# Ricotta Fritters

These exquisitely light little puffs of sweetened ricotta are a southern Italian specialty, most often served with coffee in the late afternoon. They're also good as a dessert served piping hot with ice cream—a nice contrast in temperatures. (Definitely not a do-ahead item, these fritters, like most deep-fried foods, are spectacular when hot and quite indifferent a few hours later.)

If you don't have anise- or orange-flavored liqueur, use rum. In the absence of other choices, I've also made them successfully with a sweet muscat after-dinner wine. Or, if you have *fiori di Sicilia* (see headnote, page 402), substitute 2 teaspoons for the 2 tablespoons of liqueur.

**Makes about 50 small fritters**

1 pound fresh whole-milk ricotta

3 large eggs

2 tablespoons sugar

2 tablespoons anise- or orange-flavored liqueur

1 cup unbleached all-purpose flour

1 tablespoon baking powder

¼ teaspoon salt

Extra-virgin olive oil, for deep-frying

¼ cup confectioners' sugar, or more as needed

DRAIN THE RICOTTA in a fine-mesh sieve or a double cheesecloth bag for about 1 hour. Transfer the ricotta to a large bowl and add the eggs, sugar, and liqueur. Beat with a wire whisk or an old-fashioned rotary beater until the mixture is thick and smooth—about 5 minutes with a rotary beater. (An electric beater will homogenize the mixture.)

SIFT TOGETHER THE FLOUR, baking powder, and salt. Fold into the ricotta mixture gently but thoroughly. Cover the bowl and set aside, refrigerated, to rest for about 1 hour.

OVER MEDIUM HIGH HEAT, bring the oil to a frying temperature, 350° to 360°F. If you don't have a thermometer, test the heat by tossing in a cube of white bread; if it sizzles and browns quickly, the oil is ready.

DROP THE RICOTTA MIXTURE by teaspoons into the hot oil. Turn once to brown both sides. After a minute or so, when they puff up and are well browned, remove with a slotted spoon and drain on a rack covered with paper towel. Once drained and just slightly cooled, the puffs should be sprinkled with confectioners' sugar. Serve them immediately, while the outsides are still crisp.

# HOW TO DO IT

## BASIC RECIPES AND PROCEDURES

### BASIC STOCKS

In an ideal world, I would have time enough, and room enough in my refrigerator, to keep a good supply of basic stocks—chicken, vegetable, and fish—always on hand, the way most chefs do in good restaurants. While waiting for the ideal to materialize, however, I do find that life in the kitchen is much easier with, at least, a quart or so of chicken stock in the freezer. I use big (2-pound) empty yogurt cartons but I also try to keep a few 1-cup containers of chicken stock on hand for the odd moment when I need just a small amount to add to a sauce or stew.

# Basic Chicken Stock

**Makes 10 to 12 cups**

4 to 5 pounds chicken parts, including wings and backs, preferably from a free-range bird, rinsed and dried

2 tablespoons extra-virgin olive oil (optional)

2 medium yellow onions, quartered

1 big pinch saffron threads (optional)

¼ cup warm water (optional)

2 garlic cloves, crushed with the flat blade of a knife

1 medium to large carrot, cut into chunks

½ cup flat-leaf parsley leaves

2 bay leaves

1 teaspoon dried thyme, crumbled

1 (3-inch) cinnamon stick (optional)

10 to 12 cups cold water

Sea salt and freshly ground black pepper

IF YOU WISH to make a richly colored golden-brown stock, make sure the chicken pieces are very dry. Put them in a stockpot with the olive oil and the onions and set over medium heat. Brown slowly, turning frequently, until all the chicken and the onions are golden, 20 to 30 minutes. Meanwhile, put the saffron threads to soak in ¼ cup warm water.

IF, ON THE OTHER HAND, you want a clear, light chicken stock, omit this first step and simply put the chicken pieces in a stockpot.

ADD THE GARLIC, carrot, parsley, bay leaves, thyme, cinnamon, water, and salt and pepper. Set over medium-low heat and slowly bring to a simmer. For the clearest stock, carefully skim the foam as it rises to the top. When the foam has ceased rising, cover the pot and simmer very slowly for at least 1½ hours, or longer if necessary—the chicken should be so thoroughly cooked that it is falling apart.

AT THE END OF THE COOKING TIME, strain the stock through a double layer of cheesecloth or a fine-meshed sieve. Discard the solids, which will have given up all their savor, in any case. Taste the stock and add more salt and pepper if you wish, but keep in mind that if the stock is to be reduced later on, it will concentrate the salt.

TRANSFER THE STOCK to the refrigerator to let the fat rise and solidify, after which it can be removed easily with a slotted spoon. Once the fat has been removed, the stock can be frozen for long keeping.

# Vegetable Stock

If you have to feed lots of vegetarians on a regular basis, this is probably a more essential stock to have on hand even than chicken stock. Although it's rarely used in Mediterranean cooking, it's perfectly acceptable to substitute for chicken stock in any dish that would otherwise be considered vegetarian.

PREHEAT THE OVEN to 425°F.

COMBINE THE ONIONS, carrots, celery, and garlic in a glass or metal roasting pan with the olive oil, turning the vegetables in the oil to coat them thoroughly. Roast for 15 minutes. Add the mushrooms, stirring them in. Roast for another 15 minutes. At the end of this time, the vegetables should be starting to crisp on the edges and giving off a delicious aroma.

REMOVE THE VEGETABLES from the oven and scrape them into a stockpot. Add the wine to the roasting pan and set over medium heat, scraping up as much of the brown bits in the pan as you can; add this to the vegetables and put the stockpot over medium heat. As soon as the wine starts to simmer, add the water to the stockpot along with the leek, fennel, bay leaves, thyme, parsley, and cinnamon. Bring to a simmer and cook gently for about 1 hour.

WHEN THE STOCK IS DONE, strain it through a double layer of cheesecloth or a fine-mesh sieve, discarding all the vegetables and the aromatics. Taste the broth and adjust the seasoning, keeping in mind that if the stock is to be reduced later on, it will concentrate the salt. Transfer the broth to refrigerator or freezer containers and refrigerate or freeze until you are ready to use it.

**Makes 8 to 10 cups**

2 medium yellow onions, quartered

3 carrots, cut into chunks

3 dark green outer celery ribs, cut into chunks

3 garlic cloves, crushed with the flat blade of a knife

2 tablespoons extra-virgin olive oil

6 fat brown shiitake or cremini mushrooms, thickly sliced

1 cup dry white wine

9 cups hot water

1 large leek, trimmed to white part and cut into chunks

1 bulb (Florentine) fennel including leafy tops, trimmed and cut into chunks

2 bay leaves

1 teaspoon dried thyme, crumbled

½ cup flat-leaf parsley leaves

1 (3-inch) cinnamon stick

Sea salt and freshly ground black pepper

# Fish Stock

In many regions it may be next to impossible to get the most essential ingredient in a good fish stock—the heads and bones of large, meaty, white-fleshed fish, such as haddock or cod. In that case, you will have to use a commercially prepared fish stock or a dried mix (but not bottled clam juice as it's way too salty), adding wine and aromatics to the stock to give it individuality and flavor.

**Makes 6 to 8 cups**

Head and bones of 1 (4- to 6-pound) fish, preferably cod or haddock

2 bay leaves

1 carrot, halved lengthwise

1 medium onion, halved

½ teaspoon black peppercorns

¼ cup coarsely chopped flat-leaf parsley

1 cup dry white wine

6 cups cold water

Sea salt and freshly ground black pepper

COMBINE ALL THE INGREDIENTS in a large, heavy stockpot, cover the pot, and bring to the boil slowly over medium-low heat. Simmer for about 45 minutes, no longer. Strain the broth when done and discard the solids. Taste, adding sea salt and pepper if desired, keeping in mind that if the stock is reduced later, it will concentrate the salt.

# Basic Short-Crust Pastry

 There are many recipes for short-crust pastries, some of which call for other ingredients, such as sugar, white wine, eggs. This is one of the simplest and easiest, equally useful for savory and sweet dishes.

TOSS THE FLOUR AND SALT TOGETHER with a fork. Cut the butter into small pieces and toss with the flour. Then rub the butter and flour together with your fingers to make a crumbly mixture. Add a tablespoon of icy water and stir it in. If necessary add 1 to 2 more tablespoons.

GATHER ALL THE PASTRY mixture together in a ball and knead it 4 or 5 strokes on a marble or wooden surface. Gather into a ball again, cover with plastic wrap, and refrigerate for at least an hour before rolling out.

THIS PASTRY IS EASIEST TO ROLL OUT if it's placed between two sheets of waxed paper.

**Makes enough for
two pie crusts**

1½ cups unbleached,
all-purpose flour

Pinch of sea salt

½ cup unsalted butter, chilled

2 to 3 tablespoons icy cold water

## STRAINING YOGURT

Many recipes call for strained yogurt, drained yogurt, or yogurt cheese (although it isn't really cheese at all). They all refer to yogurt that has been thickened by draining away some or all of the whey that is a natural occurrence. Special plastic strainers are available in some specialty kitchenware shops or from mail-order sources like Williams-Sonoma and Chefshop (see Where to Find It, page 415), but you can also make your own, with a colander and cheesecloth. Set the colander in the sink or over a bowl to collect the whey. Drape at least three layers of cheesecloth over the colander, and turn the yogurt into it. Leave it to drain—the longer it drains, obviously, the firmer the texture will be in the end. In general, 2 cups of plain yogurt, whether full-fat, low-fat, or nonfat, should yield 1 cup of very firm-textured strained yogurt, which will look like a soft, creamy cheese. In fact, this is a delicious spread on breakfast toast, and it can be combined with other flavors (salt, garlic, parsley, chili peppers) to make a spread for crackers with before-dinner cocktails.

## ROASTING PEPPERS

All kinds of peppers can be roasted—green ones, red ones, fiercely hot chilies, sweet bell peppers. Roasting brings out the pepper flavor at the same time that blackening the thin pepper skin allows you easily to peel it away—left on, it adds a touch of bitterness that is not always desirable. The object of this procedure is not to cook the peppers but to prepare them to be eaten raw or further cooked.

For the best flavor, peppers should be roasted over the embers of a charcoal or wood fire, although this is obviously not always possible. Set the peppers on a grid over the embers, turning them frequently with tongs, charring the peppers on all sides until the skin is blackened and blistered and the peppers have lost their stiffness. When they're thoroughly blackened, transfer to a brown-paper shopping bag, roll it up, and set aside for 15 to 20 minutes while the peppers continue to soften and their skins continue to loosen. Then, using a paring knife, carefully scrape the blackened skin away. Cut the peppers open, discard the seeds and internal white membrane, and slice or dice the peppers as required for the recipe.

The second best way is to use a gas flame from stovetop burners, following the procedure above.

If you have neither a charcoal grill nor a fireplace nor a gas burner on top of your stove, you will have to use an electric oven, set on broil; this requires a lot more care and attention than the other two procedures, because, as I noted above, you don't want to actually cook them. The idea is to have only the skin blackened and ready to be lifted off. Keep checking the peppers and turning them so that the skins blacken but the insides don't cook. Then transfer to the paper bag as above and skin and trim them.

### PEELING TOMATOES

It's not always necessary to peel tomatoes but, as with peppers, the skins add a certain bitter tang to a dish that isn't always desirable. To peel them, bring a large pot of water to a rolling boil. Drop a few tomatoes in and count to 13 seconds, then remove them with a slotted spoon. (If you do more than two or three tomatoes at once, you may find them difficult to handle; plus, too many tomatoes will drop the temperature of the water below boiling, wreaking havoc with your counting.) Use a sharp paring knife to pull the skins away and discard them. If the skins aren't sufficiently loose, drop the tomatoes back in the boiling water. But do remember, again, as with the peppers, the point is not to cook the tomatoes but to loosen the skins.

Once skinned, you may wish to cut them in half and gently squeeze out the excess juice and seeds, before chopping or slicing the tomatoes.

### SALTING EGGPLANTS

In older times eggplants were often unbearably bitter and had to be salted liberally and set aside to draw out the bitter juices before cooking. Modern eggplants don't need that treatment, but there's another eggplant problem: They are like sponges for any kind of fat, and drawing the juices out helps to mitigate that somewhat. If a recipe calls for baking or (rarely) simmering eggplant, I don't bother with the salting, even if the recipe calls for it. If, as is most typical, the eggplant is to be fried, I almost always salt the slices or cubes quite liberally and set them in a colander in the sink to drain for 45 to 60 minutes. Then they must be rinsed to rid them of excess salt and firmly patted dry with paper towels before continuing to cook.

### PREPARING ANCHOVIES

Anchovies come packed in oil, brine, or salt. The best quality are the ones packed in salt, though good-quality oil-packed ones are not too far behind. (The brine-cured ones are fine to put out for cocktails, but I don't find many uses for them in the kitchen.) A good source for salt-packed anchovies is a Greek or Italian neighborhood deli, where very often the fish can be purchased, as they are in the

Mediterranean, from a big open tin. Buy in quantity, if you like anchovies and use them a lot; they will keep well in the refrigerator in a lidded glass or plastic refrigerator dish.

To prepare salted anchovies for use, simply rinse them off in cool running water, rubbing the surface to remove excess grains of salt. Pull away the fins and break off the heads, discarding both. Open the fish up down the belly into two fillets and pull out the backbone. Usually the tail will come along with the backbone. Don't worry if you don't get all the tiny bones out—they're very soft and easy to chew. If you prepare a lot of anchovies and don't use them all, put them in a glass or plastic container and cover them with extra-virgin olive oil. They'll keep a long time in the refrigerator.

### BLANCHING AND TOASTING ALMONDS

The best way to buy almonds is whole, with the skin on, but you will need to blanch them for most recipes, and often you'll need to toast them as well. Here's how: For, let's say, a pound of almonds, bring 3 cups of water to a rolling boil, add the almonds, bring the water back to a simmer, and let simmer for about 5 minutes, no more. Turn the almonds into a sieve and immediately start to press the skins off. In most cases, you can just squeeze the almonds gently and they'll pop right out of their skins. Once all the almonds have been skinned, if you must then toast them, set the oven at 325°F. Spread the almonds in a thin layer on a sheet pan and set in the preheated oven until they are golden brown, about 15 minutes. Stir them every 5 minutes or so to expose as much of them as possible to the heat. Be careful not to overtoast them. Once they're done, simply remove from the oven. When they're cool, they can be stored in a covered tin until you are ready to use them.

Incidentally, if you first toss the blanched almonds with about a teaspoon of fine sea salt and a tablespoon of extra-virgin olive oil, then toast them, they will make a magnificent treat to serve with drinks in the evening.

### TOASTING HAZELNUTS

Hazelnuts, too, must frequently be toasted before using in Mediterranean recipes. Simply spread the hazelnuts in a thin layer on a sheet pan and set in a preheated 325°F oven, stirring frequently, for about 15 minutes, or until the hazelnuts give off a pleasant aroma and start to turn golden. Spread a clean dish towel out on a counter and turn the hazelnuts into the dish towel. Gather the ends together and rub the hazelnuts vigorously. This will get rid of as much of the skins as possible.

## PREPARING SAFFRON

Do not buy powdered saffron. It most likely is not the genuine article since saffron is the most expensive aromatic in the world and is easy to falsify. It is best to buy it in long, thin threads so that you can actually see the stigmae of the crocus, which is what saffron is. In Spain I learned that saffron should be crisped before using so that it's easier to crumble it into a stew or paella. To do this, take a clean white sheet of paper (typing paper, for instance). Drop the saffron you will use—usually a big pinch of threads—in the middle and fold the paper over the saffron to make an envelope. Set the envelope in a dry frying pan over medium-low heat and turn the envelope, using tongs, until it starts to turn a little brown around the edges. Remove from the pan and when the paper is cool, open it up, being careful not to spill the saffron threads. You will then be able to crumble the crisp saffron into whatever dish you are preparing.

# WHERE TO FIND IT

## SOURCES FOR INGREDIENTS

ADRIANA'S CARAVAN, Grand Central Market, Grand Central Station, 43rd Street and Lexington Avenue, New York, New York 10016. Tel. 800-316-0820; www.adrianascaravan.com. Good source for spices, peppers (including Middle Eastern red peppers, Spanish pimentón, piment d'Espelette), and spice blends; also frozen Middle Eastern pastry doughs (kataifi, phyllo, etc.).

THE BAKER'S CATALOGUE (King Arthur Flour Company), P.O. Box 876, Norwich, Vermont 05055. Tel. 800-827-6836. An excellent mail-order source for baking supplies, grains and flours, seasonings, and many other ingredients and equipment, not just for baking. Also a great resource for help with questions and problems that come up in baking.

BROWNE TRADING, 260 Commercial Street, Portland, Maine 04101. Tel. 800-944-7848; www.browne-trading.com. Excellent salt cod (*bacalao*), as well as imported and domestic fresh seafood and caviar.

CHEFSHOP.COM: tel. 877-337-2491; fax: 206-282-5607; www.chefshop.com. Good online service primarily (there's a small retail shop in Seattle) for a variety of interesting food products, many from the Mediterranean.

LA ESPAÑOLA MEATS, 25020 Doble Avenue, Harbor City, California 90710. Tel. 310-539-0455; www.spaincuisine.com. Imported Spanish ham (*jamón serrano*) and Spanish-style sausages (made in USA), also various Spanish peppers and pepper products.

A.G. FERRARI FOODS, 14234 Catalina Street, San Leandro, California 94577. Tel: 877-878-2783; fax: 510-351-2672; www.agferrari.com. Imported Italian food products, with a small chain of retail specialty shops in the Bay Area, plus mail order.

FORMAGGIO KITCHEN, 244 Huron Avenue, Cambridge, Massachusetts 02138. Tel. 888-212-3224; www.formaggiokitchen.com. Fine imported and domestic cheeses, olive oils, pastas, honeys, and other products. Retail shop with mail-order service, catalog available.

KALUSTYAN'S, 123 Lexington Avenue, New York, New York 10016. Tel: 212-685-3451; www.kalustyans.com. Retail shop with wholesale and mail order service, specializing in food products from all over the Mediterranean, but especially focused on Eastern Mediterranean cuisines.

OLD CHATHAM SHEEPHERDING COMPANY, 155 Shaker Museum Road, Old Chatham, New York 12136, tel. 1-888-SHEEP-60 (743-3760); fax 518-794-7641; www.blacksheepcheese.com. A good source for many sorts of ewe's milk cheeses, including, especially, fresh cheese curd.

THE SPANISH TABLE, 1427 Western Avenue, Seattle, Washington 98101. Tel: 206-682-2827; 1814 San Pablo Avenue, Berkeley, California 94702. Tel: 510-548-1383; www.tablespan.com. Specialty Spanish food products.

THE SPICE HOUSE, 1031 North Old World Third Street, Milwaukee, Wisconsin 53203 (with branches in Evanston and Chicago, Illinois). Tel: 414-272-0977; fax: 414-272-1271; www.thespicehouse.com. Exotic and common spices and spice mixtures from all over the world.

SUR LA TABLE, many retail outlets around the United States. Tel: 800-243-0852 or 866-328-5412; www.surlatable.com. Specialty cookware, couscoussières, etc.

LA TIENDA, INC., 4514 John Tyler Highway, Williamsburg, Virginia 23188. Tel. 888-472-1022 or 757–220–1143; fax: 757–564–0779; contact@tienda.com. Specializes in Spanish food products.

TODARO BROTHERS, 555 Second Avenue, New York, New York 10016. Tel: 877-472-2767; www.todarobros.com. First-rate Italian and other imported food products; retail and mail order.

ZINGERMAN'S DELI, 422 Detroit Street, Ann Arbor, Michigan 48104. Tel: 888-636-8162; www.zingermans.com. Fine imported and domestic cheeses, olive oils, pastas, honeys, and other products; retail shop with mail-order distribution, catalog available.

# BIBLIOGRAPHY

## MEDITERRANEAN HISTORY, FOOD HISTORY, GEOGRAPHY, CULTURE, AND RELATED SUBJECTS

Anderson, Jean. *Peppers: The Domesticated Capsicums.* University of Texas Press: Austin, Texas, 1984.

Benporat, Claudio. *Cucina italiana del Quattrocento,* Firenze: Olsch, 1996.

Betri, Maria Luisa. "L'alimentazione popolare nell'Italia dell'Ottocento." In *Storia d'Italia: Annali 13: L'alimentazione,* a cura di Alberto Capatti, Alberto De Bernardi, e Angelo Varni. Torino: Giulio Einaudi Ed., 1998.

Bisio, Angela, and Luigi Minuto. "The Prebuggiun." In *Erbi boni, erbi degli streghi,* edited by Andrea Pieroni, pp. 34–46. Cologne: Experiences Verlag, 1998.

Bloch, Marc. *French Rural History.* Berkeley and Los Angeles: University of California Press: 1966.

Bober, Phyllis Pray. *Art, Culture and Cuisine.* Chicago and London: University of Chicago Press, 1999.

Braudel, Fernand. *The Mediterranean and the Mediterranean World in the Age of Philip II.* New York: HarperCollins, 1992.

Buttitta, Antonino, and Antonino Cusumano. *Pane e festa: Tradizioni in Sicilia.* Palermo: Ed. Guida, 1991.

Camporesi, Piero. *Le Vie del latte, dalla Padania alla steppa.* Milano: Garzanti, 1993.

Corbier, Mireille. "The Ambiguous Status of Meat in Ancient Rome," in *Food & Foodways* 3, no. 3 (1989), pp. 223–64.

Dalby, Andrew. *Siren Feasts: A History of Food and Gastronomy in Greece.* New York: Routledge, 1996.

Davidson, James. *Courtesans and Fishcakes: The Consuming Passions of Classical Athens*. London: Dunne Books, 1997; paperback, New York: HarperCollins, 1999.

Ducasse, Alain. *Rencontres Savoureuses: Petit traité de l'excellence française*. Paris: Plon, 1999.

El-Sayed, Sayed, and Gert L. van Dijken. "The southeastern Mediterranean ecosystem revisited: Thirty years after the construction of the Aswan High Dam." On line at <<http://www-ocean.tamu.edu/Quarterdeck/QD3.1/Elsayed/elsayed.html>> Updated July 24, 1995.

Filatenko, A. A., A. Diederichsen, and K. Hammer, "Vavilov's Theories of Crop Domestication in the Ancient Mediterranean Area," in *The Origins of Agriculture and Crop Domestication: The Harlan Symposium, 1997*, edited by A. B. Damania, J. Valkoun, G. Willcox, and C. O. Qualset, Aleppo: ICARDA, 1998.

Fletcher, Richard. *Moorish Spain*. Berkeley: University of California Press: 1992.

Fois, B. "Annotazioni sull'alimentazione nella Sardegna del trecento: i prodotti, le vivande, pressi e salari." In *Manger et Boire au Moyen Age*, *Actes du Colloque de Nice* (15–17 octobre 1982), pp. 183–97. Centre d'Etudes Medievales de Nice, 1984.

Ford, Richard. *Gatherings from Spain*. London: Pallas Athene Publishing, 2000.

Fox, Robert. *The Inner Sea: The Mediterranean and Its People*. New York: Knopf, 1991, 1993.

Frayn, Joan M. *Markets and Fairs in Roman Italy*. Oxford, England: Clarendon Press, 1993.

Freeman, Susan Tax. "Mining the Pig Slaughter," *Petits Propos culinaires* 48 (November 1994), pp. 47–50.

———. "The Spanish Pig Preserved: the Olla and the Ham." In *The Anthropologists' Cookbook*, Jessica Kuper, ed., pp. 37–44. London: Kegan Paul, 1998.

Garnsey, Peter. *Famine and Food Supply in the Graeco-Roman World*. Cambridge, England: Cambridge University Press, 1989.

———. *Food and Society in Classical Antiquity*. Cambridge, England: Cambridge University Press, 1999.

Goethe, J. W., *Italian Journey* [1786–1788], translated W. H. Auden and Elizabeth Mayer. London: 1962.

Goitein, S. D. *A Mediterranean Society*, revised and edited by Jacob Lassner. Berkeley and Los Angeles: University of California Press, 1999.

Grewe, Rudolf. "The Arrival of the Tomato in Spain and Italy." *Journal of Gastronomy* 3, no. 2 (summer 1987).

Haddadou, Mohand Akli. *Le Guide de la culture berbère* Paris et Alger: (Ed. Paris-Méditeranée, 2000.)

Harris, Marvin. "The Abominable Pig." In *Good to Eat: Riddles of Food and Culture*. New York: Waveland, 1998.

Kanafani-Zahar, Aïda. *Mune: La conservation alimentaire traditionnelle au Liban*. Paris: Musée des Sciences de l'Homme, 1994.

Kondoleon, Christine, ed. *Antioch: The Lost Ancient City* (catalog of an exhibit organized by the Worcester Art Museum). Worcester, Mass., and Princeton, N.J.: Princeton University Press, 2000.

Lewis, Bernard. *The Jews of Islam*. Princeton, N.J.: Princeton Univ. Press, 1984.

Lewis, Norman. *Voices of the Old Sea*. London: Penguin, 1985.

Maggio, Theresa. *Mattanza: Love & Death in the Sea of Sicily*. Cambridge, Mass.: Perseus, 2000.

McArdle, Frank. *Altopascio: A Study in Tuscan Rural Society, 1587–1784*. Cambridge, England and New York: Cambridge University Press: 1978.

Meinig, D. W. *The Shaping of America*, vol 1. *Atlantic America, 1492–1800*. New Haven and London: Yale University Press, 1986.

Montanari, Massimo, *The Culture of Food*. Oxford, England, and Cambridge, Mass.: Blackwell, 1994.

Parker, Robert M., Jr., *Wines of the Rhone Valley*. Rev. ed. New York: Simon & Schuster, 1997.

Parsons, Russ. "The Long History of the Mysterious Fava Bean," *Los Angeles Times*, June 22, 2001.

Robinson, Jancis. *Vines, Grapes and Wines*. New York: Random House, 1986.

Rodinson, Maxime, A. J. Arberry, and Charles Perry. *Medieval Arab Cookery*. Totnes, Devon, England: Portland Publishing, 2001.

Sereni, Emilio. *History of the Italian Agricultural Landscape*. Princeton, N.J.: Princeton Univ. Press, 1997.

Simeti, Mary Taylor. *On Persephone's Island: A Sicilian Journal*. New York: Knopf, 1986.

Spencer, Colin. *The Heretic's Feast: A History of Vegetarianism*. London: Fourth Estate, 1993.

Terron, Eloy. *España, Encrucijada de culturas alimentarias*. Madrid: n.d. (probably 1992).

Teti, Vito. "Le culture alimentare nel Mezzogiorno continentale in età contemporanea." In *Storia d'Italia: Annali 13; L'alimentazione,* a cura di A. Capatti, A. De Bernardi, A. Varni, p. 79, Torino: Giulio Einaudi, Ed., 1998.

Weiss, Walter M., and Kurt-Michael Westermann. *The Bazaar: Markets and Merchants of the Islamic World*. London: Thames & Hudson, 1998.

## COOKBOOKS

Algar, Ayla. *Classical Turkish Cooking: Traditional Turkish Food for the American Kitchen*. New York: HarperCollins, 1991.

Andrews, Colman. *Catalan Cuisine*. New York: Atheneum, 1988.

Artusi, Pellegrino. *La scienza in cucina e l'arte di mangiar bene*. Many editions, but first published in Firenze, 1897.

———. *Science in the Kitchen and the Art of Eating Well*. translated by Murtha Baca and Stephen Sartarelli. New York: Marsilio, 1997.

Barron, Rosemary. *Flavors of Greece*. New York: Morrow, 1991.

Boubezari, Karimène. *Ma cuisine algérienne*. Aix-en-Provence: Éditions du sud, 2000.

Brennan, Georgeanne. *The Food and Flavors of Haute Provence*. San Francisco: Chronicle Books, 1997.

Chatto, James, and W. L. Martin. *A Kitchen in Corfu*. London: Weidenfeld & Nicolson, 1987; paperback edition, 1993.

David, Elizabeth. *French Provincial Cooking*. New York: Harper & Row, 1962.

Davidson, Alan. *Mediterranean Seafood*, 2nd ed. London: Penguin, 1981.

Domingo, Xavier. *El Sabor de España*. Madrid: Tusquets Editores, 1992.

Ducasse, Alain. *Méditerannées: Cuisine de l'essentiel*. Paris: Hachette Pratique, 1996.

Duplessy, Bernard. *Cuisine traditionnelle en pays niçois*. Aix-en-Provence: Edisud Broché, 1996.

Fàbrega, Jaume. *La Cucina de l'Emporda y la Costa Brava*, Barcelona: 1990.

———. *Traditional Catalan Cooking*. Barcelona: (Edicions de la Magrana, 1997).

Field, Carol. *The Italian Baker*. New York: HarperCollins, 1985.

Gedda, Guy. *La table d'un provençal*. Paris: 1989.

Gitlitz, David M., and Linda Kay Davidson. *A Drizzle of Honey: The Lives and Recipes of Spain's Secret Jews*. New York: St. Martin's Press, 1999.

Gosetti della Salda, Anna. *Le ricette regionali italiane*, 4th ed. Milano: 1976.

Halici, Nevin. *Nevin Halici's Turkish Cookbook*. London: Darling Kindersley Ltd. 1989.

Hamady, Mary Laird. *Lebanese Mountain Cookery*. Boston: David Godine, 1987.

Helou, Anissa. *Lebanese Cuisine*. New York: St. Martin's Press, 1998.

Jenkins, Nancy Harmon. *The Mediterranean Diet Cook Book*. New York: Bantam, 1994.

———. *Flavors of Puglia*. New York: Broadway Books, 1997.

———. *Flavors of Tuscany*. New York: Broadway Books, 1998.

Kochilas, Diane. *The Glorious Foods of Greece*. New York: Morrow, 2001.

Kouki, Mohamed. *Cuisine et patisserie tunisienne*. Tunis-Carthage: 1991.

Kremezi, Aglaia. *The Foods of the Greek Islands*. Boston, New York: Houghton Mifflin: 2000.

Lanza, Anna Tasca. *The Flavors of Sicily*. New York: Clarkson N. Potter, 1996.

———. *The Heart of Sicily*. New York, Clarkson N. Potter, 1993.

Louis, Diana Farr, and June Marinos. *Prospero's Kitchen: Mediterranean Cooking of the Ionian Islands from Corfu to Kythera*. New York: M. Evans, 1995.

Luard, Elisabeth. *The Flavours of Andalucia*. London: Collins and Brown: 1991.

Médecin, Jacques. *Cuisine Niçoise*, translated by Peter Graham. London: Penguin, 1983.

Morsy, Magali. *Recettes de Couscous*. Aix en Provence: Éditions du sud, 1996.

Olney, Richard. *Simple French Food*. New York: Atheneum, 1975.

Plotkin, Fred. *Recipes from Paradise: Life and Food on the Italian Riviera*. New York: Little, Brown, 1997.

Psilakis, Maria, and Nikos Psilakis. *Cretan Cooking*. Chania, Crete: Karmanor, 2000.

Reboul, J.-B. *La Cuisinière Provençale*. Marseille: P. Tacussel Éd., 1997.

Roden, Claudia. *A Book of Middle Eastern Food*. New York: Knopf, 1974.

Saleh, Nada. *Fragrance of the Earth: Lebanese Home Cooking*. London: Saqi Books, 1996.

Sammut, Reine. *La cuisine de Reine: Heures et saveurs méditerranéennes*. Paris: Hachette Pratique, 1997.

Santamaría, Juan. *Arroces, experiencias y recetas varias* Madrid: Incipit Ed., 1997.

Sevilla, Maria Jose. *Spain on a Plate*. London: BBC Consumer Pub., 1992.

Shehab, Aziz. *A Taste of Palestine*. San Antonio, Tex.: Corona, 1993.

Simeti, Mary Taylor. *Pomp and Sustenance: Twenty-five Centuries of Sicilian Food*. New York: Knopf: 1991.

Uvezian, Sonia. *Recipes and Remembrances from an Eastern Mediterranean Kitchen*. Austin: University of Texas Press, 1999.

Weiss-Armush, Anne Marie. *The Arabian Delights Cookbook*. Los Angeles and Chicago: Lowell House, 1994.

Wolfert, Paula. *Couscous and Other Good Food from Morocco*. New York: Harper & Row, 1974.

———. *Mediterranean Grains and Greens*. New York: HarperCollins, 1998.

Zana-Murat, Andrée. *De mère en fille: La cuisine juive tunisienne*. Paris: Albin Michel, 1998.

# INDEX